First published by:

   Miango Books,
   Miango
   Trewirgie Road
   Redruth, Cornwall TR15 2SX.

Git Up and Go © Arthur Langford 2002

The right of Arthur Langford to be identified as the
author of this work has been asserted in accordance with
Copyright, Designs and Patents Act 1988.

ISBN: 0 9542535 0 7

British Library Cataloguing in Publications Data. A cat-
alogue record for this book is available from the British
Library.

Jacket design by:
   DP&D Design Consultants
   www.serva.com/dpddesign

Typesetting and project management by:
   Richard Joseph Publishers Ltd
   PO Box 6123
   Basingstoke
   Hampshire RG25 2WE.

Text set in Bembo.

Origination by:
   Tradespools Ltd
   Robins Lane
   Frome
   Somerset BA11 3EG

Printed in Great Britain by:
   Antony Rowe Limited
   Bumper's Farm Industrial Estate
   Chippenham
   Wiltshire SN14 6LH.

To my mother Edith (Harris) Langford
who earnestly endeavoured during my formative years to encourage and develop in me
a penchant for history but who passed away long before my interest was kindled.

And to my wife Glencoe
for her forbearance and indulgence over the several
years of my preoccupation with research and writing.

Jessie (Jones) Harris
1896 – 1990

Jay A. Harris
1941 –

CONTENTS

Introduction

At Olivet in South Dakota, Jessie (Jones) Harris, the wife of John Matthew Harris, felt very strongly that she wanted to know more of the Cornish origins of her husband's family and to ascertain if there were relatives on the other side of the Atlantic.

John Mathew was a second-generation American and grandson of Matthew Harris, who had first gone out to America in 1850.

Jessie could not understand the reluctance of the family in South Dakota to make any endeavour in the matter. She persistently expressed her feelings at their tardiness with the question, 'What sort of family are you Harrises who make no attempt to trace your relatives in Cornwall?'

As the story unfolds it will be seen that the credit for starting it must go to Jessie, for her persistence raised a desire in her nephew, Jay Harris, to do something about it, and so she passed to Jay a copy of a precis which recorded the wanderings of her husband's grandfather. To Jay here was a mystery, and he was always intrigued by mysteries - but where and how to start?

Due to a singular coincidence Jay, then residing at Wayne, Michigan, was browsing around a library in downtown Detroit in April 1981 and came across D.M. Thomas' *Songs from the Earth - Selected Poems of John Harris Cornish Miner 1820–1884*. At this time Jay had no real knowledge of his relationship to the Poet, but he decided to purchase the book. Noting the acknowledgement on the flyleaf to Leslie Harris of Troon, Camborne, and also to myself, both great-nephews of the Poet, he wrote to enquire if John Harris could possibly be a mutual relative. In order to reply to the letter from Jay, I commenced research on the Harris family of Bolenowe. The unfolding story proved to be so remarkable that it seemed important to place it on record.

Other than the Miner Poet, John Harris, very little information was previously known, especially of those of his brothers who left home and went out to the New World to seek for better opportunities and new prospects. The brothers who emigrated were copper miners at the famous Dolcoath Mine at Camborne, excepting the younger ones who became tin miners when the mine changed in depth to tin. They had all been following occupations which were hard and oft-times financially unrewarding. That they were of independent spirit is beyond doubt. Nurtured by their method of employment as 'tributers', where they were paid for a percentage of the value of ore which they sent to surface, and coupled with the ever-present dangers of their calling, where the miner's life was, and still is, largely in his own hands, they nevertheless continued initially as miners overseas, which was the field in which their expertise lay.

But why did the Harrises and other Cornish folk from the area decide to emigrate during the third and fourth decades of the nineteenth century? There was the uncertainty of continuing employment in Cornish mines as the copper orebodies were becoming exhausted and in the fourth decade the dire hardship of the Hungry Forties. But the Harrises had their small farm and livestock, like many others, so were unlikely to starve. These people had been schooled in hardship and knew poverty, so the question arises, bearing in mind that it would not have been possible for them to anticipate the social, economic and climatic conditions obtaining in the New World, whether there was another reason for their decision to emigrate other than those enumerated above and which have been historically perpetuated? It seems highly probable that they possessed, poorly educated though the majority may have been, a spirit of adventure which prevailed and influenced their ultimate decision.

Almost all the Harris brothers from very humble beginnings, with little or no formal education, by persistence, native ability and a deep desire for self-improvement, all of which required strenuous effort and tenacity, variously left their marks in literature, business, mining and farming and inevitably in Methodism, the latter whether in Cornwall, Michigan, Missouri, Iowa, Georgia or South Dakota. The influence on their children and succeeding generations can still be seen today. They created opportunities for their children, who in turn demonstrated by diligence in their chosen professions that these opportunities made possible by the faith and pioneering spirit of their parents were not thrown away.

This family with roots deep in their Christian upbringing, nurtured in the then discipline of Methodism together with respect for home and family and love and appreciation of nature, were spiritually and mentally equipped for whatever lay ahead.

Their humble home on Bolenowe Carn was situated above the hamlet of Bolenowe and stood 700 feet above sea level. It was some two miles south-east of the town of Camborne. Geologically forming part of Carnmenellis granite mass, Bolenowe stands on the mid-southern edge of the great central mining district but situated above the disfigured and desolate area with its widespread paraphernalia of machinery, buildings and huge heaps of debris, with red waters flowing from the mineral processing floors into the steams, all of which were so much a part of the scene in the Brea and Red River Valley when the Harrises lived on Bolenowe Carn. Compared to these desolate scenes, Bolenowe Carn must have seemed a real haven, a place apart, as indeed it still is, with views of Carnmenellis Hill, Carn Brea, St Ives Bay and the Atlantic Ocean. This contrasting scenery embedded itself in the minds of the poet and his brothers.

Essentially it is of the children of John and Christian Harris around whom the story evolves. It is, however, first necessary to take a look at their forebears and parents and to glimpse at their way of life, because the influence of these folk and the environment in which the family grew up had such a marked effect on John and Christian's descendants.

Arthur Langford
Redruth, Cornwall
2000

Bolenowe Hill

How pleasant 'tis to ramble
On this my native hill;
And linger 'mong the heath and rocks
The place how quiet, how still.

The July sun is setting
In the distant west,
The labourer has left his toil
With thoughts of home and rest.

Before me is Bolenowe
Sheltered 'mong the trees,
Like an infant sleeping
Fanned by summer breeze.

Looking round about me
From this heathy height,
Pleased with its surroundings
Charmed to see the sight.

Adown the sloping hillside
Which we called Croft and Green,
We played in childhood's morning,
Until evening shadows gleamed.

The old moor in the valley
With its feather beds and moss,
The bubbling well, the running stream
Which we have often crossed.

A few steps in the distance
Is the place where I was born,
Where parents lived and children played,
Now from each other torn.

The old home lies in ruins,
The inmates all are fled,
Away in distant lands are some
And some are with the dead.

And while I sit and ponder
Strange visions seem to rise,
My early home, my childhood days
They pass before my eyes.

I hear sweet voices ringing
From days long past and gone,
From parents, brothers, sisters
As I journey on and on.

They come from fields and hedges,
From lanes and shady walks,
From heath and furze, from croft and downs
While lingering 'mong the rocks.

O sacred spot Bolenowe Hill
I love thy walks and bowers,
The larks sweet song, the summer breeze,
The fragrance of thy flowers.

While looking at thy ruins
And the changes which are past,
May onward, homeward, upward
Be our motto 'till the last.

Mark Smith Harris, c.1890

Arthur Langford (1918 – 2000)

Arthur Langford was born on 16 July 1918 at Lanner, near Redruth in Cornwall, the eleventh and youngest child of Walter and Edith Langford. He attended Lanner School, though he missed three years of formal education (from age five to eight) when he was ill with Brights Disease, a kidney condition. On his return to school he read every book in the school library by the time he was eleven. Books and reading remained an abiding interest for the rest of his life.

On leaving school, Arthur worked for his father, Walter Langford, who was in business, largely involved at that time with installing plant and machinery on various mines in the area. After a hard days work, Arthur attended evening classes at Redruth in engineering and related subjects.

The Second World War found Arthur in the army. He had, in fact, reported for duty, as one of the first Militia conscripts, to 220 Searchlight Regiment, Royal Artillery, at Houndstone Camp, Yeovil, Somerset on 15 July 1939. He spent the next day, his 21st birthday, peeling potatoes. On declaration of war on 3rd September 1939, Arthur immediately applied for a transfer to the Corps of Royal Engineers.

From 8th January to 31st May 1940, he served with the 48th Division Royal Engineers in France and Belgium. At the time the order to fall back was received, he was six miles south of Brussels. Arthur was to come out over the beach at Dunkirk. During this time Arthur had been despatch rider, motor mechanic and batman.

In September 1940, Arthur embarked at Liverpool for Gibraltar with the 180 Tunnelling Company of the Royal Engineers. Engaged as a surveyor on the labyrinth of tunnels created in The Rock, he was promoted to the rank of Sergeant on 12th March 1942. Five days later he was granted an emergency Commission (with the rank of 2nd Lieutenant) on the recommendation of Lord Gort, Commander-in-Chief, Gibraltar. Arthur was responsible for the Technical Services Section. A few months later he was promoted to Lieutenant and instructed to form, and take charge of, the first Diamond Drilling Section in the army. Arthur left Gibraltar in February 1944 and in October of that year was promoted to Captain.

Arthur embarked at Glasgow for India on 13th December 1944. On arrival, he crossed the sub-continent by train from Bombay to Madras. Stationed at Avadi, sixteen miles outside of Madras, he was subsequently employed managing and operating pumping stations, water purification plants and generating plants in South India. This was to ensure continuity of supplies prior to the impending handover of political power to India. In October 1945 Arthur was promoted to the rank of Major. On 30th January 1946 he left India and the army on Class A Release to return to civilian life.

Arthur immediately joined Holman Brothers, Camborne, where he worked for two years in the Research & Development department. He then set up and ran the 'Holbit' department.

After seven years with Holmans, Arthur entered the construction industry. His first project was to drive a tunnel through the cliffs at Swanpool, near Falmouth in Cornwall, something for which his experience in Gibraltar stood him in good stead. Among the many other projects he was involved in were the construction of Porth Dam, near Newquay, and the anchorages for the Tamar Road Bridge. Arthur worked for a number of companies in various management roles, finally becoming an executive director of a company operating in the south of England. He was responsible for their work in Devon and Cornwall and had input into projects in other areas.

Arthur did not slow down a great deal in retirement. He continued his interest in family history, resulting in numerous files on his family, and also on the family of his wife, Glencoe. Over a twenty-year period he also wrote and researched this book, completing it shortly before his death. Partly to research the book, Arthur and Glencoe undertook a 4000 mile trip in the Midwest of the United States of America in 1985.

A lifelong Methodist, his faith was evident during his final days as he faced death without fear and at peace. His interests ranged wide and included the history of Cornish mining, on which he had considerable knowledge. Arthur also wrote a number of articles on the history of Cornish Methodism, and enjoyed gardening. Above all, Arthur was a family man—he married Glencoe Dunstan on 13 July 1943 at Redruth Fore Street Methodist Church, and they had two sons, Tony and Roger – delighting in big family occasions.

Since Arthur's death certain facts, largely concerning changes to family situations, have come to light. Such information has been placed within square brackets. Our grateful thanks to Jay and Sue Harris for their continued support for the project.

Tony Langford

1. The Forebears

As a starting point we go back to the year 1743 when a certain Benjamin Harris married Elizabeth Vine at Camborne Parish Church and went to live at Bolenowe.

For simplicity and due to perpetuation with the family of first or Christian names, alike names are numbered in date order of birth.

Benjamin (1) and Elizabeth had two sons and two daughters. The elder son Benjamin (2) was baptized at Camborne Church on 16 March 1745 and was married there to Joan Bennatts, also of Bolenowe, on 5 June 1774. Benjamin (1) died in 1754 and was buried at Camborne on 22 December. Elizabeth lived on until 1797.

At the time of his marriage Benjamin (2) was described as a tinner, implying that he worked the local eluvial/alluvial deposits of tin, either singly or as a member of a syndicate. His name is recorded on the Stannary List of Miners and Working Tinners of Camborne Parish for the year 1798. It was also noted that in case of National Emergency he was willing to be engaged either gratuitously or for hire as a pioneer or labourer in defence of the realm, and that he would present himself for duty complete with a pickaxe! John (3), the poet, tells us that Benjamin (2) was a tall person who wore a wide-brimmed hat and a Quaker-cut coat with shining buttons together with polished buckles on his shoes. The utterances of Benjamin (2) were few, but when chided for some act of supposed indifference he would gaze into his accuser's eyes and deliberately reply 'Thee show me a man without a fault and I will show thee a man without a head!'

In 1779 Benjamin (2) obtained a lease[1] from John Stackhouse of Pendarves Estate for a smallholding of approximately twelve and a half acres on Bolenowe Carn, at a rent of two pounds five shillings per year. The lease was on three lives: himself, his wife Joan and their then only son Benjamin (3), at that time five years of age. The period of the lease was limited to ninety-nine years and included the east end dwelling of a row of cottages known locally as Six Chimneys.

The dwellings were built of moorstone, namely the granite stones and boulders which were to be found in great abundance scattered over the hilltop. According to John (3) the cottages had reedy (thatch) roofs, bare rafters and clay ground floors. These cottages closely resembled in mode of construction a Scottish crofter's cottage except that they were two storied. As the occupants of the other cottages left they fell into disrepair and by the 1850s the Harris cottage was also in ruins, and undoubtedly there were two reasons for this. Firstly, a foolish act by Matthew (1), second son of Benjamin (2), who decided to dry some blackpowder in front of the open kitchen fire! Not surprisingly the powder exploded, extensively damaging the eastern end of the dwelling, and although the wall was crudely rebuilt it was never again structurally sound. Fortunately and surprisingly there were no human casualties. The second reason for the dwelling falling into ruin was due to the inability of John (2), third son of Benjamin (2) and father of the poet, to carry out annual maintenance in the latter years of his life.

The lease excluded mineral rights, trees and saplings and all water and water courses. The rental was required to be paid on the four usual feast days of the year and should the rent at any time be thirty days in arrears, the landlord retained the right to repossess. All property maintenance including structural repairs was required to be carried out by the tenant. In addition, all corn grown by the tenant had to be ground at the landlord's Manor of Treslothan Mill. The manorial system was not without benefit to the local communities because in reality the Lord of the Manor was the only person with sufficient finance and resources to carry out works for the benefit of the community, and to insist that his tenants were to grind their corn at his mill was the quickest way to get a return on his capital.

A fair amount of land which Benjamin (2) leased was boulder-strewn croft and he must have worked extremely hard to bring it to a state of cultivation; especially so because this work would have been additional to his daily labour as a tinner and the normal requirements of farming a smallholding. Benjamin (2) was apparently unable to write his full name but appended a well-formed capital B as his mark on the lease. He died in February 1827 aged eighty-two and was buried in Camborne churchyard.

Joan Bennatts, eldest child of Henry Bennatts and his wife Elizabeth Lemon, undoubtedly exerted a considerable influence on her children and grandchildren. She possessed a wealth of common sense, a methodical and tidy mind coupled with a simple and deep faith. She made a great impression on her grandson John (3) who, in his twenty-one-verse poem *My Granny Joan*, extols her virtues which are simply portrayed in the following few verses:

Her living room

And sure a cosy room it was;
Let's paint it, if we can,
The mantle-piece so dazzled me,
Shining with cup and can.
Small scripture pictures on the wall,
King David's sling and stone,
Our Saviour in his Manger-crib,
How loved my Granny Joan!

How orderly all things appear'd,
Arranged with cottage grace!
She had a place for everything,
Gave everything its place.
With earnest hands her work was done:
'It saves us many a moan
To do the thing in proper time',
Oft said my Granny Joan.

Her strongest beer was water clear
Brought from the meadow well,
With which she made her cup of tea,
As toll'd the curfew bell.
Poor Benny tippled now and then,
Till quiet was o'erthrown.
'Tis best I think without the drink',
So preached my Granny Joan.

If trial came, or pinching want,
She utter'd no complaint,
She ate her crust with simple trust,
As thankful as a saint.

With patient hope, her load she bore
In silence and unknown.
'A better day, though far away,
Will come', said Granny Joan.

In person she was somewhat short,
With face as clear as day.
Her eyes were black and bright, her hair
Had fallen into grey;
Her gait was slow, her voice was low
As any brooklet's tone;
And 'everything was for the best',
So said my Granny Joan.

When'er she walk'd abroad, she wore
A coat of burning red,
Whose dimpled hood would nearly hide
The bonnet on her head;
And how the little ones would run,
When forth she walk'd alone,
And cluster lovingly around
The path of Granny Joan.

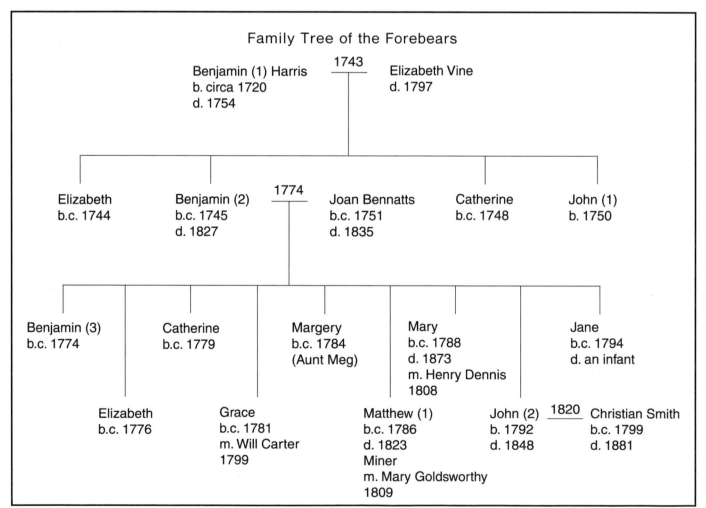

Family Tree of the Forebears

Benjamin (1) Harris
b. circa 1720
d. 1754

— 1743 —

Elizabeth Vine
d. 1797

Elizabeth
b.c. 1744

Benjamin (2)
b.c. 1745
d. 1827

— 1774 —

Joan Bennatts
b.c. 1751
d. 1835

Catherine
b.c. 1748

John (1)
b. 1750

Benjamin (3)
b.c. 1774

Catherine
b.c. 1779

Margery
b.c. 1784
(Aunt Meg)

Mary
b.c. 1788
d. 1873
m. Henry Dennis
1808

Jane
b.c. 1794
d. an infant

Elizabeth
b.c. 1776

Grace
b.c. 1781
m. Will Carter
1799

Matthew (1)
b.c. 1786
d. 1823
Miner
m. Mary Goldsworthy
1809

John (2)
b. 1792
d. 1848

— 1820 —

Christian Smith
b.c. 1799
d. 1881

The poet in his autobiography also provides a glimpse of Joan as a widow in her later years. 'She kept a goat or two, which she often milked at her door under the great elder tree; and I cannot forget the rich flavour of the cream the milk produced! I often watched them feeding from her hand, when in a very gentle voice, which I still seem to hear, she taught me the lesson of kindness. Her garden contained beds of choice herbs, which she used to dry and preserve in paper bags, hanging them in the great chimney. She kept the walls of her room whitewashed and the clay floor well sanded; and the shining pewter plates on the dresser had a great attraction for me. On her return from market or shop I was sure to steal into her room, our house being next door, to receive my accustomed packet of sweets and a piece of hot heavy potato-cake baked in the ashes. As I ate the crisp cake and listened to the music of the crackling furze and heath under the pot, the click of her needles as she sat by the hot embers, and her enchanting story as wild as our own hills, I felt sure that I had the dearest, kindest grandmother in the world.'

Joan died of a paralytic seizure 17 April 1835 aged eight-four and was buried in Camborne churchyard along with her husband.

To the Constable of the *Parish of Camborne*

to wit. {BY Virtue of an Order from Sir *John Morshead*, Baronet, Lord Warden of the STANNARIES in and for the said County, unto me directed, you are hereby required to make out a fair and true List, in Writing, of all the Miners and Working Tinners usually, and at this Time dwelling within your Constablewick, between the Ages of *Fifteen* and *Sixty* Years, distinguishing therein which of them are willing to engage themselves to be armed, arrayed, trained and exercised, for the Defence of the Realm, and which of them are willing to engage, in Cases of Emergency, either gratuitously, or for Hire, as Pioneers or Labourers, and such of them as by Reason of Infirmity are incapable of active Service, according to the Form hereunto annexed: which List, so fairly made as aforesaid, you are hereby required to return to ~~the Deputy-Lieutenants and Justices of the Peace for the said County; at their Meeting for that Purpose to be held, on the~~

Given under my Hand this *24* Day of *April* 1798.

John Hichens **High Constable.**

The Stannary List

The name of Benjamin (2) Harris is to be seen at the top of this page of the Stannary List

THE Names of all MINERS and WORKING TINNERS, between the Ages of 15 and 60 Years, living within the Parish of *Camborn* distinguishing which of them are willing to engage themselves to be *armed, arrayed, trained* and *exercised*, for the Defence of the Realm; and which of them are willing to engage in Cases of Emergency, either gratuitously or for Hire, as PIONEERS or LABOURERS, and which of them by reason of Infirmity are incapable of actual Service.

PERSONS NAMES.	Ages	Willing to be armed, arrayed, trained and exercised, either with Firelocks, or Pikes.		Willing to engage either gratuitously, or for Hire, as Pioneers or Labourers, and what Implements they can bring.				Incapable of active Service by reason of Infirmity.
		Firelocks.	Pikes.	Falling Axes.	Pick Axes	Spades.	Shovels	Bill Hooks.	
Benj. Harris		"	"	"	do	"	.	"	"
Thomas Trythall	32	"	"	.	do	"	.	"	"
Wm Thomas	37	"	"	"	do	.	.	"	"

2. The Parents

Benjamin (2) and Joan Harris had six daughters and three sons all born at Bolenowe Carn. Their eighth child, John (2), was born 28 March 1792; in 1820 he married Christian (Kitty) Smith at Camborne Church.

John (2) was a copper miner at Dolcoath mine, which was situated about three miles down the valley from their home. Astonishingly there is a very commonly-held idea that tin is the only economic mineral to have been found in Cornwall, whereas, in fact, the boom mineral was copper. It is, however, true to say that tin has been worked in Cornwall for possibly 2,500 years, but the conception that tin mining has been carried on since the ancient trade with the Phoenicians is an absolute fallacy.[1] It was the deep-level mining resulting from the pursuit of copper lodes that led to the introduction of steam power for pumping and hoisting and also for the development of the Cornish mining ports. Great as the Cornish copper industry had been, the new sources from Chile, Upper Michigan and South Australia brought about the rapid demise of this extraordinary but short-lived industry. Not surprisingly, it was this sudden demise that initiated the great emigration of Cornish folk to various parts of the world during the second half of the nineteenth century,[2] including four of John's sons, who found employment on the southern shores of Lake Superior.

John (2) worked as a tributer (a miner paid according to the amount he produced), having to provide his own tools, black powder, candles and so on and was required to transport the broken ore to the shaft ready for hauling to surface. Although paid only a percentage of the value of the ore sent to surface, a tributer was the very best quality of miner, skilled at recognising the signs, characteristics and complexities of the orebody. John's earnings were on occasions so little or non-existent that it was only with difficulty that he could obtain food for his growing family. The poet tells us that on these occasions he never heard his father or his mother complain. Christian would often cheer John (2) with some word of encouragement, saying it would be better next week or next month. He adds that 'Though I remained with my parents for twenty-five years, I never heard them speak disrespectfully or even look angry at one another. They humbly walked in the fear of the Lord, and their gentle influence was sensibly felt by their household.' He goes on to say that John (2) 'Was diligent in his work and a humble Christian. It may well be said of him that he studied one book and that book was the Bible. He expressed himself in few words, made no parade of his religion before his fellows, rarely engaged in any public duty, except occasionally offering prayer in cottage meetings and teaching a small class of boys in Troon Wesleyan Sunday School.'

In addition to his shift work at Dolcoath and attending to the small farm he also carried out all shoe repairs for his growing family. The shoe-mending scene is described for us by the poet: 'Here he sat on a low stool in the old hall, cobbling away as patiently as the angler by the brookside. This he did repeatedly evening after evening, so that he rarely had time to look into a book. Six wild boys racing over the highlands brought him no small task for leather and nail. A cobbler was never hired, he sitting at his labour from January to June, and from June until January came again.'

In 1817, three years prior to his marriage, John (2) and his brother Matthew (1) of blackpowder fame, arranged a new lease[3] for the smallholding and dwelling at Bolenowe Carn, and one assumes took over running the smallholding. Presumably this was because their parents, Benjamin (2) and Joan, were now seventy and sixty-five years old respectively, and their eldest brother Benjamin (3), who had been one of the three lives on the original lease, had either left the area or had died. Unfortunately it has not been possible to verify either of these two possibilities. The new lease was made with E.W.W. Pendarves[4] of Pendarves and was generally similar to the former. Although also for a period of ninety-nine years, this period of time was only to commence on the death of the older surviving parent.

The rent was to increase considerably more than the two pounds five shillings which Benjamin (2) had paid. It was now to be six pounds fifteen shillings until the death of the older surviving parent and nine pounds thereafter, despite the improvements to the land which Benjamin (2) had effected.

John (2) was obliged under conditions of the lease to act as Reeve (or steward) for the Manor of Treslothan as often as elected. This entailed being the spokesman for the tenants in negotiations with the landlord and possibly receiving payments from other tenants on behalf of the landlord.

Also included was a clause to the effect that a good and sufficient certificate should be made available following three months notice or within a reasonable time if John (2) was in foreign parts, proving that John (2) was still alive! This is an interesting clause because it was included some time before the general exodus of Cornish miners to mining camps overseas; one wonders why John's brother Matthew was not included in this particular clause, but be that as it may, it must be assumed that Pendarves Estate had earlier found it difficult to prove either the death or the whereabouts of signatories who had gone overseas for one reason or another or had simply disappeared. Is it possible that Benjamin (3) had disappeared in this way? John's full signature was ascribed on the lease but Matthew could only make his mark.

Christian was the eighth child and third daughter of William Smith, a tinner and farmer of Beacon near Camborne, who had married Ann Hocking at Camborne Church in 1799. Their farmhouse still stands on the north side of the Camborne to Troon road at the junction of the road leading to Condurrow.

The poet has left us a picture of the Smith family at Beacon, although his maternal grandfather William Smith had died prior to the poet's birth. He says, 'For a long time we visited the farmhouse at Beacon annually at the Parish Feast, when we generally dined off roast goose; and it was a wonderful luxury for me to turn the spit in the old parlour. At such times my uncles would tell stories as we clustered around the November log. One of those whose name was Bill, and who had been in the French Wars, much amused me with his accounts of sieges and shipwrecks. Another, Uncle George, used to entertain us on his flute. We continued to go to the farmhouse on the annual feast day until my brothers and sisters became too numerous for my grandmother's table. We were also welcome visitors at the farmhouse at Christmas, when the great log smouldered on the chimney hearth and carol singers came into the court. There was always plenty of good cheer and tales told till the fire seemed to crackle with delight, and I caught whisperings which issued not from the ashes of the birch. How we loved to sleep in uncle's bed on Christmas Eve! That night our shoes were cleaned and brightly blackened, taken upstairs with us and placed just behind the bedcurtains where old Father Christmas could not miss seeing them. We lay awake with bated breath and beating ears listening for his soft footsteps up the stairs or down the rafters, until at last we fell asleep; and in the morning we were sure to find them stuffed with sugar-candy and other sweets.'

John (2) died on Sunday, 23 April 1848, aged fifty-six. It appears that he had been in poor health for some time and unable to work. His poor health was not surprising considering the rigours and demands of his working life. Working underground in high temperatures, dust, foul air produced by the sulphurous fumes of blackpowder,[5] inadequate ventilation and the long daily climbs over a variety of ladders taking up to an hour at the start and end of each shift, make it seem remarkable that he had been able to endure these conditions for such a long period. Indeed, it has been said that a working miner over the age of fifty was almost a rarity, and as late as 1892 it was recorded that three and a half times as many Cornish miners than coal miners died of lung disease and phthisis.[6] There was little attention paid

to welfare in Cornish mines at this time: the changing house was quite often the blacksmith shop, usually some distance from the shafthead, which was where the miners would change their clothes after climbing out of the mine. According to the poet this was the case at Dolcoath until after 1847, although it is recorded that improvements such as warm changing houses and hot soup were available at Dolcoath at least as early as 1845,[7] but whether these benefits were available at all of the several Dolcoath shafts is not stated. Little wonder that John (2) was unwell and when he eventually suffered a fall underground it hastened his death.

With John (2) unwell and without income because of his sickness, it is small wonder that the family were hard pressed and their dwelling fell into disrepair. It is also significant that whereas John (2) had leased twelve and a half acres from Pendarves Estate in 1817, by 1840 this had been reduced to seven and a half acres, either given up on John's brother Matthew's death in 1823 or repossessed by Pendarves Estate.

Christian was left with the six youngest children. James aged seventeen, Samuel aged fourteen, Kitty aged twelve, Benjamin aged ten, Mark aged seven and Jacob (1) aged five. It seems that Matthew (2), Christian's third son, had already left the family home, possibly working in some other part of Cornwall and living in lodgings with little opportunity to make any effective financial contribution to his mother. By this time the three children had left home: Ann (2) and William had gone to America and John (3) was married. Although James and Samuel were working by this time, their earnings were so small that when the next rent was due at Michaelmas 1848, immediately after John's death, Christian was in arrears and continued so. On Lady Day 1849 she paid a portion of the arrears with four pounds sterling worth of oats, but thereafter was unable to pay any more. In view of this and the state of the cottage, at the following Michaelmas, Pendarves Estate wrote off the debt on the basis of 'tenant poor and house down'.[8] In consequence Christian and her six children left Six Chimneys and moved into a small cottage at Laity, Troon, about a mile away. The poignancy of the situation in which the family found themselves was later partly recorded in a verse by the poet taken from *Who Tills My Father's Farm*.

I ask, because when Spring was young,
And larks were on the down,
And father in the silent grave
Was sleeping in the town,
We left with tears, and children clung
To mother's lonely arm;
And so I ask, with backward glance,
'Who tills my father's farm?'

John (2) and Christian had eleven children, but their third child died as an infant. The remaining ten all became members of the Christian Church. Five sons became Methodist local preachers (laymen), one of whom was later ordained into the Methodist Episcopal Church in Missouri. A daughter became the wife of a miner who was also ordained into the Methodist Episcopal Church in Wisconsin and shared with him the labours of the Pastorate.

A picture of John and Christian's close-knit family is depicted by the poet in *The Burial*. It appears that a ferret had been left in the younger brothers' and sisters' care when the older brother William emigrated to the lead mines of southwest Wisconsin in 1845, hence the great concern and sadness felt by the youngsters when the ferret died.

Will's ferret was buried this morn:
When Samuel came down from his bed,
He whisper'd with aspect forlorn,
'O Kitty, Will's ferret is dead.'

And Kitty soon told it to Mark,
And Mark to the rest of his clan.
We sorrow'd with visages dark,
As if we were mourning a man.

'Come, Ann, let us lay her to rest,
And you must prepare us a bier;
We will heap the cold earth on her breast,'
And we wiped from our eyelids a tear.

So Ann made a coffin so small,
Of cast-off brown paper and thread;
This served for a shroud and a pall
False trappings, unknown to the dead.

And Samuel was sexton and Clerk,
And Benjamin bearer so brave,
While Kitty and Jacob and Mark,
Soon bore her away to the grave.

My mother was curious enow,
And so she came softly behind,
Well pleased with her children, I trow,
Who to the poor brute was so kind.

'Neath the hawthorn its grave was dug deep,
With sharp-pointed pickaxe and spade,
Lie down, little ferret, and sleep
On the couch that affection has made.

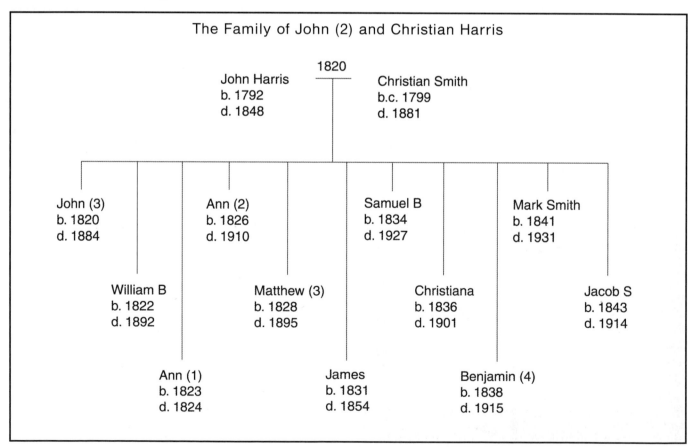

The Family of John (2) and Christian Harris

1820

John Harris
b. 1792
d. 1848

Christian Smith
b.c. 1799
d. 1881

John (3)
b. 1820
d. 1884

Ann (2)
b. 1826
d. 1910

Samuel B
b. 1834
d. 1927

Mark Smith
b. 1841
d. 1931

William B
b. 1822
d. 1892

Matthew (3)
b. 1828
d. 1895

Christiana
b. 1836
d. 1901

Jacob S
b. 1843
d. 1914

Ann (1)
b. 1823
d. 1824

James
b. 1831
d. 1854

Benjamin (4)
b. 1838
d. 1915

John (2) was buried in Camborne Churchyard on 25 April 1848 in the area where only poor people were buried and which was liable to be subsequently buried over, a practice which precluded the possibility of future intimate burial of relatives or future location of a particular grave. In his poem Monro the poet sums up the situation:

> His nameless grave was made among the hills,
> Where rows of miners in their white shrouds lay,
> And rank grass battened 'neath the old church cills,
> Which weirdly waved beneath the moon's pale ray,
> Not to be noticed now in garish day,
> Lost mid the myriads that around him sleep;
> And Monro knows not where to mark his clay,
> Or plant a floweret on the hallowed heap,
> Where Loneliness and Death their endless vigils keep.

The poet's tribute to his father is quoted in the following verse from his poem *The Death of My Father* and movingly sums up the character of John (2):

> He left no wealth behind,
> No riches but his name;
> No honour but his honesty:
> He was unknown to fame.
> His grave is with the poor,
> That rude, unlettered clan;
> But from the tomb a voice breaks forth,
> 'He was an honest man!'

Christian died at 48 Laity Row, Troon, on Saturday, 17 September 1881 at the age of eighty-two. John (3) in his autobiography says, 'She died in great peace. To her daughter Kitty, who was with her in her last moments, she expressed herself as having no fear, none at all. She anticipated great joy in meeting her long-lost friends in heaven, and in seeing Jesus her Redeemer and Saviour. For more than fifty years she was a consistent member of a religious community, serving God in humbleness and fear, without any pretence or show.' She was buried at Treslothan churchyard, presumably because of the impracticability of locating her husband's grave at Camborne.'

> Sleep on dear Mother, death can do no more,
> From earthly ills set free.
> Thou art a watcher on the quiet shore,
> Where God's own angels be.

from *My Autobiography*

The poet in composing these lines said that he lost the gentlest mother the world ever saw.

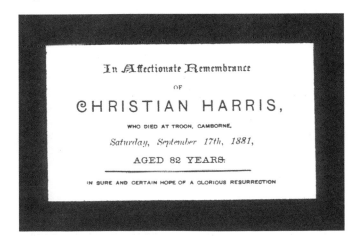

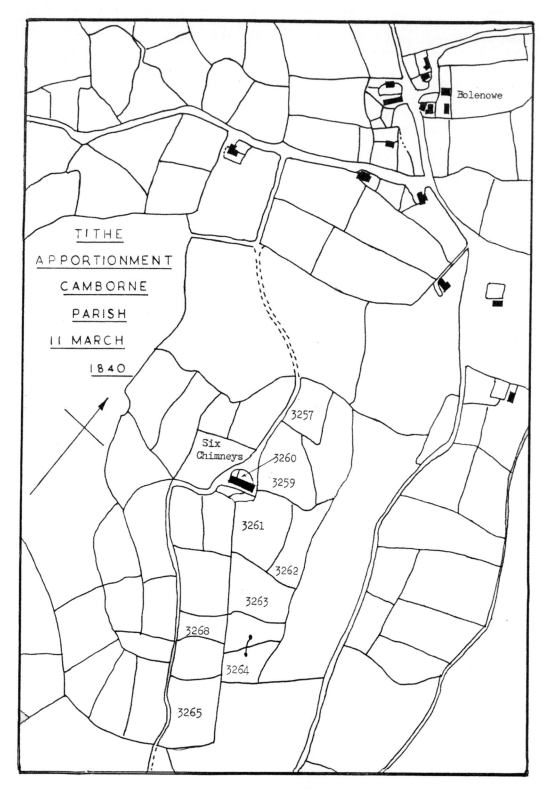

Camborne Parish 1840 Tithe Map. Cornwall Record Office ref. TM.
The numbers denote the fields and so on of the small farm of John (2) Harris.
The Harrises lived in the east end of the row of cottages, none of which is extant.

CRO Ref. TA/27

Tithe Apportionment 1840.
Land for which John (2) Harris was liable for tithe payments to the Anglican Church.

Owner: E.W.W. Pendarves.   Location: Bolenowe.   Charge: 17 shillings and 10 pence per annum.

Occupier	Ref. No.	Field name	Description	Acres	Roods	Perches
John Harris	3257	Croft	Arable	–	2	18
	3259	Field behind house	”	1	0	25
	3261	Field fore door	”	1	0	22
	3262	Long field	”	–	2	32
	3263	Water field	”	–	3	33
	3264	Downs field	”	–	3	38
	3268	Croft	”	1	0	14
	3260	House and garden	”	–	–	31
	3265	Farther croft	Arable	1	0	5
			Total acreage	7	3	18

Permission to reproduce County Record Office References TM, TA/27 and PD58/14 has been obtained from County Record Office but copyright and publication rights are retained by them.

CRO Ref. PD58/14

Extract from Manor of Treslothan Rentals
Bolenowe.   Lease No. 39.   Tenements: House and land.

Tenants	Lives or Years	High and Conventional Rent	Arrears	Due	Received
Kitty Harris	At will	£2/12/6	£6/0/0	Lady Day 1849 £2/12/6	Allow for oats supplied to Mr Pendarves £4. remains due £4/12/6
Kitty Harris	At will	£2/12/6	£4/12/6	Michaelmas 1849 £7/5/-	Allowance £7/5/- lost in consequence of tenant poor and house down
Kitty Harris	Now Unoccupied			Michaelmas 1850	

Extracts from Census Returns of Camborne Parish

Name	Relationship	Status	Age	Occupation	Place of Birth
7 June 1841	*Location: Bolenowe Carne*				
John Harris			40	Copper miner	
Kitty Harris			40		
John Harris			20	Copper miner	
William Harris			18	Copper miner	
Ann Harris			15	Mine girl	
Matthew Harris			12	Copper miner	
James Harris			9		
Samuel Harris			7		
Kitty Harris			5		
Benjamin Harris			3		
Mark Harris			4m		
Eleanor Pascoe			2		
30 March 1851	*Location: Troon*				
Kitty Harris	Head	Widow	50	Home with family	Camborne
James Harris	Son	Unmarried	19	Copper miner	”
Samuel Harris	Son	Unmarried	17	Copper miner	”
Kitty Harris	Daughter		15	Scholar	”
Benjamin Harris	Son		12	Copper miner	”
Mark Harris	Son		10	Scholar	”
Jacob Harris	Son		7	Scholar	”
7 April 1861	*Location: Troon*				
Christian Harris	Head	Widow	60		”
Christian Harris	Daughter	Unmarried	24	Work to mine	”
Benjamin Harris	Son		22	Tin Miner	”
Mark Harris	Son		20	Engine Man	”
Jacob Harris	Son		17	Tin Miner	”
2 April 1871	*Location: Troon*				
Kitty Harris	Head	Widow	70		”
Kitty Harris	Daughter	Unmarried	33	Milliner	”
Mark Harris	Son	Married	30	Engine Man	”
Jane Harris	Daughter-in-Law	Married	35	Engine Man's Wife	”

3. John (3) Harris F R Hist S

John (3) Harris - The Miner/Poet
Line drawing per courtesy of the Langford
private collection.

A large photograph of John Harris hangs in The Methodist
Sunday School at Troon. It carries the following inscription:

> John Harris the Cornish Poet.
> Born Bolennow Hill 1820.
> A Troon Sunday School Teacher,
> Librarian and Local Preacher.
> Buried at Treslothan 1884.

Early Life

John (3), the eldest child of John (2) and Christian,
was born at Six Chimneys on Bolenowe Carn on 14
October 1820 and was baptized at Camborne Church
on 4 November the same year.

John (3) describes his humble natal home and that of
his brothers and sisters as a rough-built house, without
any rear entrance door or any windows on that elevation excepting a small one about a foot square which
gave light to the pantry. The front elevation, facing
south, had four windows and an entrance door sur-
mounted by a crude granite porch. At the end of the
row of cottages on the south-facing wall was a sort of
archway, probably the door lintel of a cottage that had
collapsed prior to the birth of John (3). The lintel was
covered with turf on which young John (3) spent many

happy hours of his childhood sitting and daydreaming
while watching the quiet pastoral scene. Inside the house
there were no partitions upstairs and no ceiling. All the
roof timbers were visible and the poet records that on
occasions when lying in bed at night he could sometimes
see the stars through the thatch. Below stairs was the
small pantry off the kitchen, the former being separate
from the kitchen or living room, or as the poet called it
'The old hall'.

The simplicity of his early life on the hilltop, watching and observing the wild flowers in their season, the
distant views, the modes of the weather and the wind
from gentle breeze to south-westerly gale, all left their
imprint on John's mind, which later on numerous occasions found such gentle expression in his poetry. His affection for the environment in which he grew up and
for his early life is recorded in one of the last poems he
wrote prior to his death:

The Old Deal Form

How old I was I cannot tell,
Perhaps from three to four,
When roses gem the path of life,
And songs fill up the hour;
When in a cottage crowned with thatch,
And wrenched with many a storm,
Aunt Meg first knelt in prayer with me[1]
Beside the old deal form.

The door was halved, the floor was rough[2]
The chimney low and wide,
No paper hung upon the screen,
Or graced the dwellings side.
One little window in the north,
With panes not uniform,
Threw light upon aunt Meg and me
Beside the old deal form.

Oft robin from the elder tree
Would drop upon the hatch,
And turn his bright eyes on us there,
A few feet from the thatch,
And sometimes sing his sweetest song,
Not heeding fly or worm,
While with aunt Meg I knelt in prayer
Beside the old deal form.

As duly as the time came round,
Let it be foul or fair,
At noon of day she knelt to pray,
And took me with her there.
This gentle vision of the past
I see in calm and storm,
When my aunt Meg knelt down with me
Beside the old deal form.

Farewell, aunt Meg! The rich can leave
Their favoured kindred gold,
And honours which to wealth belong,
Stamped deeds and castles old,
Estates surrounded by the sea,
Sublime in calm and storm,
But thou did'st give me more than these
Beside the old deal form.

18 December 1882

Another of John's earliest memories, which greatly affected him, was when almost four years of age he witnessed the tiny white coffin of his little sister, the first Ann, being carried out of the cottage; she was just twelve months old.

Almost as soon as John was able to walk his father took him on Sundays, when the weather was fine, to the simple Wesleyan Methodist Chapel in the village of Troon. The original Wesleyan Society at Troon had been formed circa 1795, and the first chapel built circa 1798. In *Early Days of Methodism in Troon*, which was compiled from the diary of Capt. James (Jimmy) Thomas and edited by James Howard Harris, son of the poet, it states, 'We now began to think of having a chapel of our own, and we prayed very much about it. After waiting some time we had the grant of a piece of land, on which we built a small house, covered with thatch; it had one door but no glass in the windows, and a cart lent by a kind neighbour, was used as a pulpit.' From the same source it also states: 'About this time our little chapel became too small for the congregation, and we one and all set to work and soon had a larger one.' This was circa 1808 and would have been the chapel to which John (3) was taken by his father. The present chapel is an enlargement of the second chapel, and was constructed 1863-64 together with a Sunday School.[3] Of the walks to chapel John records, 'Our path lay chiefly through the meadows, and it was very pleasant to me to watch the birds and butterflies and to listen to the hum of the bees among the flowers. The solemn silence of the sabbath rested on my child-spirit and I would fain believe that God and angels came nearer to earth on that holy day.' John's feelings and gratitude for these Sunday walks to worship are contained in the following verses:

The Gothic window where I sit
Looks out upon the moor,
And Autumn's hand has thickly strown
The dry leaves at our door.
But o'er the hills I dimly see
Another golden morn,
When father led me by the hand
Through fields of waving corn.

The path was narrow which we walked,
With daisies in the sod,
And cheerfully we travelled on
Towards the house of God.
I hear the larks again today
Above the flowering thorn,
When father led me by the hand
Through fields of waving corn.

The hedges showed unnumbered gems,
Which Flora scattered there,
And every breeze that murmured by
Was wooing us to prayer.
The blooms are here which then I saw
My native meads adorn,
When father led me by the hand
Through fields of waving corn.

The bench was lowly where we sat
To hear the preacher pray.
Unbacked, uncushioned, roughly planed,
Yet tears were wiped away.
And thankful was my childish heart,
Not then with sorrow torn,
That father led me by the hand
Through fields of waving corn.

from *My Autobiography*

In this environment and amid these surroundings it is small wonder that John (3) grew up loving God in nature.

Education

John's schooldays, if such they can be called, commenced when he was about six or seven years of age and lasted until he was nine. The availability of places of learning for youngsters of his social level was very limited at the time when John (3) started his 'education'. Mrs Percival's Endowed School at Penponds had actually been in existence since 1761, but the number of pupils was limited to twenty who were enrolled free and ten fee paying.[4] The school was more than three miles from John's home, over poor roads and rough tracks and much too far for a youngster of his age to travel alone on foot, and John (2) would probably not have been able to pay fees and most likely never even considered it.

It is recorded that a joint Anglican/Methodist school existed on Methodist premises in Camborne from circa 1805. Additionally a nucleus National School was held in the gallery of Camborne Parish Church from about 1820,[5] but these would have posed the same distance problems to John (3) as the school at Penponds. School Boards were not established until 1870 and compulsory attendance until 1876 and the latter was not enforced until 1882, just two years prior to the death of John (3). However, the Act did bring schooling within the reach of every child. The Board School at Troon was first opened in 1875, only five years after passage of the Act. And so initially John (3) was sent to a dame school (a school for young children, usually run by a woman) in the hamlet of Bolenowe, just below his hilltop home of Six Chimneys. There were about a dozen pupils and the curriculum was limited to learning the alphabet. John made rapid progress at this school of Dame Trezona and was soon able to read. In his Monro John (3) has given a brief and somewhat humorous account of the manner in which Dame Trezona dressed:

> Clad in a bedgown with the quaintest sleeves,
> Its pattern was the wain and harvest sheaves,
> She on head a cap of muslin wore,
> Which she lay by when dusky twilight leaves.

Apparently she also took snuff! His father was very pleased with John's reading ability at this time and rewarded him with a one-penny copy of *Robinson Crusoe*. This, together with his school primer, was the first book which he could call his own. This little action and display of appreciation on the part of his father shows how, despite the lack of books in his home and the general ignorance of things scholastic amongst the majority of working-class folk of those days, John (2) had a desire for his son to progress; more so because later on he seemingly felt that John was devoting too much time to books and study and stated that he doubted if John would ever earn a living! This statement should, however, be taken in context with the great need in those days for children to be put to work as early as possible in order for the family to benefit from their earnings, however small.

Leaving Dame Trezona's school John was sent to Dame Penpraze, whose school was held at Troon Wesleyan Methodist Chapel. Very little has been told about this establishment or of John's experience there. We only know that in due course he was transferred to a boys' school presided over by a very harsh person by the name of Reed. This person's form of correction for boisterous and slow-to-grasp pupils was to cane them with a flat piece of wood studded with sharp nails so that blood flowed at every administration! In later years John likened Reed to Wackford Squeers in *Nicholas Nickleby* by Charles Dickens. After witnessing the blood issuing from a friend's lacerated hand following castigation by Reed, John implored his parents to send him to some other, as he termed it, 'academy'.

His request was acceded to by his parents, and so he joined a fourth establishment run by a disabled miner by the name of John Roberts in a cottage at Forest Gate.

Although the place name has long since disappeared, its location was on the present B3297 road from Redruth to Helston some 250 yards south-south-west of Forest Methodist Chapel, and according to tradition was in one of the row of cottages which still occupy the site. John's memories of Forest Gate are described in his poem of that name, written during his final illness in April 1883:

> A few roods only from a carn,
> 'Mid Druid rocks sedate,
> In sun and shower, in calm and storm,
> Lay sleepy Forest Gate.
> And here it was my school days passed,
> 'Mid flowers and humming bees,
> Like winds that lead the summer hours,
> Or brooks among the trees.
>
> O Forest Gate, O Forest Gate,
> Beside the lone highway!
> There is a fragrance in thy name
> Which never will decay.
> Around thee lie the granite tors,
> On hill and mystic moor,
> And all thy rushy hollows teem
> With legendary lore.
>
> What games we played when lessons closed,
> And out we rushed with glee,
> Like sheep through some down-trodden fence,
> Or wire-caged birds set free!
> And how we told our simple tales
> Within the hawthorn bower,
> Till eve had called the glow-worms forth,
> And folded every flower!
>
> The low house with its roof of thatch,
> Beside the highway pool,
> Has passed away, as well as he
> Who kept the country school.
> But ever pleasant are my thoughts,
> Even at this distant date,
> When memory leads my spirit back
> To dreamy Forest Gate.
>
> O Forest Gate, O Forest Gate,
> A spell is on thee yet,
> Although thy dim scholastic sun
> In clouds and storms has set.
> No Greek or Latin could atone,
> Or bring so rich a meed ,
> For what I learnt in simple phrase
> Beneath thy roof of reed.

A portion of John's poem *The Country Schoolmaster*, which he also wrote in 1883, best describes this particular teacher and his method of instruction:

> The master of the country school,
> Had lost his leg below,
> Where shadows hide the cavern-roof,
> And miners come and go;
> And so he wore a wooden stump,
> On which we oft did gaze,
> As he came thumping down the road
> With many a curious phrase.
>
> He knew no more of sciences
> Than Maggie of the mill
> Could just add up a simple sum,
> And use his stumpy quill,
> And teach his pupils how to read
> Out of the book of Psalms,
> And bring the dreaded ruler down
> Upon their smarting palms.
>
> In person he was somewhat short,
> And he wore rustic clothes,
> And he had metal spectacles,
> Which rested on his nose.
> This long appendage seemed to be
> Distinctly understood,
> For he could scent the wicked boys
> From where his rostrum stood.

John's first attempts at rhyme were made while at this cottage school, and these he wrote in the blank spaces of his cipher book because he had no other paper on which to write. He says that 'Having discovered the secret of rhyme and the mystery of inventing couplets, I found it impossible to stop'. His desire for reading material also increased so he decided to search his sparsely-furnished home where he was surprised to find on an old shelf a ragged copy of *Cottars Saturday Night* by Robbie Burns; this was John's first taste of poetry. He was so enthralled that he read it over and over again.

He was grateful to Christian, his mother, who had also helped him to read from the Bible while he sat on her knees; but the instruction he later received in Troon Wesleyan Sunday School was without doubt the most consistent, although limited to Sundays, in this period of developing interest. It extended over a period of twelve years from the age of four. What is perhaps most surprising is that the Sunday School had a library! At sixteen he became a teacher in the school and eventually and not surprisingly the librarian. A portrait of John (3) in his later years is to be seen hanging in the present upper schoolroom.

The Start of His Working Life

Soon after his ninth birthday John (3) started work as a ploughboy with, as he described him, Uncle George Harris of Bolenowe. Actually George was not his uncle, although possibly was a distant relative. John's usage of the term 'uncle' was probably due to the then custom of children calling older and distant relatives or family friends uncle or aunt as a term of affection and respect. This George was born circa 1766 according to the 1841 Camborne parish census, the birth date being twelve years after Benjamin (1) died and eight years before Benjamin (2) was married.

Whether John received monetary payment for his labours is not known, but it is more probable that he was paid solely by his midday meal, thus easing the responsibility of his parents in the provision of food. George was unmarried but employed a housekeeper - Rose Williams - who John remembered as being somewhat rotund in stature but was an excellent cook of simple dishes.

John's employment by George only lasted for a few months. He was then put to work for a tin-streamer or tinner who operated in Forest Moor. For three pence a day John worked day after day with bare feet in cold running water shovelling sand. John recorded that whilst at work he ate his dinner in a peat-built rush-covered hut. This form of construction for their working place dinner hut had been used by the tinners for centuries. Thomas Beare in *Bailiff of Blackmore* - 1586 described such a hut as 'A little lodge made up with turfes and covered with straw'.[6] This employment continued until John's tenth birthday when his father took him to Dolcoath Mine where John was employed in 'dressing'[7] the copper ore. Here as well, the work was mostly carried out in the open, with the incessant din in the background of Cornish stamps crushing the ore. John relates: 'Sometimes I had to wheel the mineral in a barrow until the skin came off my hands, and my arms were deadened with the burden'. A standard barrow contained three hundredweight of copper ore.[8] The barrow itself was of stout construction, probably much more robust than the person using it! John also relates: 'Sometimes I was scorched with the sun until I almost fainted; and then I was wet with the rains of heaven so that I could scarcely put one foot before the other. I left home at six in the morning and returned to it again at six in the evening'. His comrades would have been boys of similar age and young women, 'bal-maidens' as they were described. It is recorded that at about this time there were 30,000 persons employed in Cornish mines; 18,000 men, 7,000 children and 5,000 women, but the latter were all employed on surface.

His Life as a Miner

John (3) continued in the foregoing occupation until he was thirteen. At this point his father made the ultimate decision to take him underground to train him in the art of extracting ore; and doubtless in the hope that John's earnings would increase together with his contribution to family finances.

John's first descent into the mine must have been a very frightening experience at this young age, but he may not have fully realised just how hazardous it really was. His father went first with a rope fastened to his waist with the other end being fastened to, as John said, 'my trembling self'. If either had slipped it is doubtful that they would have survived, because over certain lengths the ladder-run was not enclosed and only poorly supported, thereby warping and shaking at every step. The descent was over sixty or seventy ladders to a depth of almost 200 fathoms or 1,200 feet.

John's description of the daily climb out of the mine for the next twenty-two years or so speaks for itself. He says, 'But the climbing up evening after evening, that was the task of tasks! Ladder after ladder, ladder after ladder until they seemed interminable and the top would never be reached. Panting and perspiring after stopping again and again we reached the top at last where the pure air of heaven fanned our foreheads and filled our lungs with new life, though our flannel dress could not have been wetter if immersed in a river.' The climb took place carrying the blunt drill steels and after working a whole shift underground, drilling by hand labour, mucking and wheeling the broken ore to the shaft ready for hoisting, all these operations being carried out in high temperatures, poor ventilation and a dust-laden atmosphere. Also their only means of illumination being from tallow candles stuck with a ball of clay onto their underground hats, or when in their workplace, attached by the same means to the sides of the level or stope. Following their climb to surface and changing their clothes they then walked back home in all weathers, and John said 'I was often so weary I could scarcely drag myself along.' It is therefore not surprising that death from pulmonary complaints was an all too common event amongst the miners.[9]

Sabine Baring-Gould[10] writing in his *Cornish Characters and Strange Events* in 1908 says of John (3) Harris, 'I have known many a man who has worked underground as a common miner without whining and breaking into extravagance such as this.' Baring-Gould in writing this shows in his impulsive and presumptuous manner, his complete misunderstanding of deep-level mining and the working conditions of those days. Additionally, Baring-Gould seems to have missed the point that very few miners of the period would have been sufficiently articulate to express a view of their working conditions in writing! It can only be inferred that Baring-Gould had never been underground and was unaware of the comparison which could be made between this horrific climb out of a deep mine and that instrument of excessive severity from prison discipline, the treadmill. For many years after John (3) first descended into Dolcoath mine a climb on the treadmill of 1,200 feet per day was the maximum permitted to be inflicted on criminals undergoing hard labour; and remember, the treadmill was eventually phased out because of its severity.[11]

But out of this hardship and mining environment and the contrasting beauty around his home on the hill-top, a seemingly inexhaustible flow of poetry and prose resulted and this extraordinary mixture is epitomised in John's lines from Monro:

> The heat the cold, the sulphur and the slime,
> The grinding masses of the loosened rock,
> The scaling ladders, the incessant grime,
> From the dark timbers and the dripping block,
> The pain of thirst when water was so near,
> The aching joints, the blasted hole's rude shock,
> Could not dash out the music from his ear,
> Or stay the sound of song, which ever
>   murmured clear.

The contrast is also expressed in lines from his poem *To My Lyre*:

> But when digging in the ground,
> Oft thy tunes are tingling round;
> Oft I hear thy simple strain
> Floating over hill and plain.

And in *My Own Beloved Hills*:

> My own beloved hills!
> My thoughts fly up to you,
> When chain'd in Plutus' copper-caves
> With the hard-toiling crew.
> My own beloved hills!
> The dwelling place of rest,
> The summer home of solitude!
> Of hills, all hills, the best.

John remained an underground miner until the latter end of 1857, a period of twenty-four years, and saw this famous mine pass from copper to tin, and by this time, prior to the introduction of the man-engine, he was climbing at the end of his shift 240 fathoms or 1,400 feet! John (3) had become a tributer, as his father had been, experiencing the same problems of uncertainty in respect of his earnings. He said, 'Sometimes I had wages to receive at the end of the month and sometimes I had none.' The pathos of the latter situation is very evident in his poem *Lines for My Little Ones*:

Come to me, my smiling little ones,
And prattle in my ear,
Don't let it fright you from your sire,
This big, round, falling tear.
It comes into your father's eye,
When coming home to you,
Although the earth was beautiful,
The far-off sky was blue.

I'll tell you why the tear appeared,
When travelling o'er the mead;
Tis pay-day, and my hard-earned hire
Was very small indeed:
No! not enough to purchase food,
In this dark day of dearth,
For you my shining olive leaves,
That gem my household hearth.

I plucked those berries from the bush,
In coming o'er the lea;
And here they are, my little loves,
As ripe as ripe can be.
Ye eat them up so heartily.
And seemed so pleased and gay,
I'll smile again, my babes, with you,
And dash the tear away.

Despite the unremitting struggle against poverty, the mental picture of and his joy in his wife and children spurred John (3) on and increased his determination to continue with his occupation against all odds. This scenario is portrayed in his poem *The Bright Image*.

All day I breathed the burning smoke,
Within my poison-hole;
All day I sicken'd in the mine,
Which dimm'd my clouded soul.
All day I dug for daily bread,
In penury's vestments clad:
Returning weary as could be,
I felt exceeding sad.

The fields, the fruitful farms around,
The gorse, the waving trees,
The orchard, and the clustering vine,
The corn that kiss'd the breeze,
The berries on the bending bush,
The peaceful grazing kine,
Houses and lands had other lords,
And none of them were mine.

My hands were sadly labour-scarr'd,
My joints were almost dead;
My frame writhed 'neath toil's mangle-wheel,
My soul sank down like lead.
And as I lonely trudged along,
My spirit oft would sigh;
And tears fell down upon the road
In streamlets from mine eye.

But rising on my eager gaze
Sweet bursting on my sight,
Smiling beyond this sea of grief,
A cheering image bright;
My wife and lovely little ones
Awaiting in my cot!
I dash'd the burning tear away,
And bended to my lot.

John (3) does, however, record that 'It was pleasant on one occasion to be called into the Account House at Dolcoath, and to be presented by the Agents with a half sovereign for my sobriety and good conduct.'

The problem of climbing the ladders was to some extent solved when a man-engine was installed in the mine in 1854/55, but this was only two years or so prior to John (3) leaving the industry, and in any case the man-engine only extended to 1,440 feet whereas the bottom of the mine at that time was down to 2,172 feet.[12] During his final two years underground John (3) was involved in an accident whilst riding the man-engine when a section of rod broke, hurling twenty miners downwards, but he thankfully records that 'A few scars and bruises were my only injuries.'

Towards the end of his period underground, when the mine was working primarily for tin, John (3) wrote a poem for his brother William in Wisconsin which sums up his desire to find work on surface and in fresh air:

It Blows a Full Furious March Wind

I ask not wealth or title deeds,
Or self-indulgent ease,
But what the strong yeoman enjoys,
The pure air of the leas.

Today I've thrashed an old tin-rib
Till I could thrash no more;
While streams of perspiration ran
Unchecked from every pore.
A fire-cloud drank my spirits up:
How longed I for the breeze
The hoary-headed woodman quaffs
Among the forest trees!

Who would not leave the smoky mine,
And his unhealthy trade,
To carol on the shepherd's crook,
And wear the shepherd's plaid?
Ay, brother, I have often thought
With lassitude oppressed,
When gasping in its cloudy cells,
A rag-man's lot the best.

Self-Improvement

On 2 August 1842 some two and a half months before his twenty-second birthday, John (3) wrote in an old account book of his father's: 'I resolve this day to devote Mondays and Wednesdays to grammar, Tuesdays to history or such books as I may have from the (Sunday School) library, Thursdays to poetry reading, Fridays to composition, Saturdays to miscellaneous works and Sundays to theology,... and may my literary acquirements be devoted to the honour and glory of God.' This obviously referred to his leisure time after completing his shift as a miner, attending to duties in the home and on the small farm, and those on Sundays in Church and Sunday School.

We have already learned of his desire for reading material while at Forest Gate school and his searches for books in his parents' home, where eventually it seems a copy of Bunyan's *Pilgrim's Progress* also turned up. In addition, his younger brother James loaned him an eighteen-penny copy of Robert Burns' poems. The search also extended to Granny Joan's home, but he records: 'In all my boyhood searches over my grandmother's dwelling I do not remember discovering any books.' He selected from the Sunday School library such books as *Campbell's Gertrude of Wyoming*, and Pollick's *Course of Time* which he said 'I carried with me wherever I went when I was not in the mine,... by brooks and streams it was my choice companion. Capt. Jimmy Thomas[13] threw open his library door to me, and the Rev. Hugh Rogers,[14] the Rector of Camborne, lent me Southey's *Remains of Henry Kirke White* which I pondered with great avidity and delight.' He also bought himself a dictionary from a blacksmith at Dolcoath mine. Later the Rev. G.T. Bull, first incumbent of Treslothan, seeing that John (3) was fond of poetry loaned him a copy of Shakespeare. John (3) said, 'The first play I read was *Romeo and Juliet* which I greedily devoured travelling over a wide downs near my father's house. The delight I experienced is beyond words to describe... a new world burst upon my view. Admitted into the palace of enchantment I passed the gateway again and again, and heard music and saw visions of ethereal loveliness which filled me with a fuller existence.' Additionally the Rev. Bull had formed a little select group to read and discuss poetry. John (3) says, 'In the home of the Misses Thomas (at Treslothan) I first heard Mr Bull read some choice extracts from Byron's *Childe Harold*. The masterly might of this powerful magician held me entranced. For weeks and months I could hear or think of nothing else. To borrow the book and read it myself, what a treat! But nobody would think of lending it to me.'

John also recorded that he paid great attention to any speakers he could depend upon, and thus learnt to pronounce many difficult words, and also to improve his grammar. Later still he notes from his Troon Moor home the extent of his library, 'A few worn books are piled up in a corner on some narrow shelves, three of the most conspicuous being Walker's Dictionary, sweet Burns and Shakespeare. Nor must I forget my Bible, the gift of my sainted father.'

Despite all his problems John (3) did progress, and his attainments were later voiced by the *Ladies' Edinburgh Magazine* of April 1876 which said, 'The strange thing about this man's writings is that with his limited education and more limited society, his language as well as his thought should be so refined, so free from provincialisms, so grammatically correct.' Indeed several other critics remarked on his absolutely correct use of grammar for one who had had no formal education. Perusal of the seventeen books which he published has proven that his use of colloquialism was the exception rather than the rule, excepting in the connotation of mining terms where it is perfectly admissible.

Marriage and First Homes

John (3) was married at Camborne Church 11 September 1845 to Christiana Jane Rule of Troon. Jane was a milliner and only daughter of James Rule, a miner, and his first wife Jane Penprase; this Jane had died in 1824 when only twenty-six years old, leaving Jane aged four years and her brother Francis just two years old. Francis died when only twelve years old. James was a brother to John Rule who married Anne Mayne and who were the parents of Capt. Francisco (Frank) Rule who amassed a considerable fortune in Mexico,[15] and therefore Jane was a first cousin to Francisco. Both Jane's and John's fathers signed the marriage register as witnesses, and they were the only other persons present.[16]

Thirty-seven years later John wrote:

No bells proclaimed our marriage-rite,
No herald rode before,
No buds were offered to the bride,
Yet love a garland wore.
And though much trial has been ours,
Much hardship have we seen,
Amid the sunshine and the showers
That wreath is ever green.

from *The Watcher*

Their first home was a two-roomed house in Troon. At that time Troon consisted of only about thirteen sets of buildings, possibly inhabited by twenty-five families or so. All thirteen buildings were contained in a radius of about one hundred and twenty-five yards, centred more or less on the present Troon Methodist Church. Their cottage stood on the northern edge of the hamlet, almost surrounded by the devastation and spoil tips resulting from the operation of Wheal Gine or Polgine Mine, the forerunner of the Grenville mines. In consequence of the discovery of the Great Flat Lode in the 1850s, the Grenville mines entered a period of expansion and success,[17] and as more employment was provided by the mines the small hamlet of Troon developed into a sizeable village. In fact, the population reached 400 by 1860 and 1,000 by 1864.[18]

Up to two years prior to his marriage, John (3) had given all his earnings to his mother and for the greater part of the first year of his married life his earnings averaged only ten pence per day. John said, 'How we contrived to exist on this small pittance without going into debt, I cannot tell; yet so it was.' Small wonder that he was depressed when he wrote the following lines in a poem on Dolcoath Mine:

The last eleven months thou'st been too hard -
Ten pence a day is all I've had of thee,
And this has caused the silent tear to flow;
My wife and I have sat beside the hearth,
And told our sorrowing tale, with none to hear
But Him who listens to the raven's cry.
My silent lyre has rusted in my cot,
Or, if 'twas strung, 'twas strung to notes of woe.
But I forgive thee for the cruel past;
Years of my fleet existence are lopped off
By thy unwieldy hatchet, and I go
The silent way, whence there is no return.

It seems probable that at this time John (3) considered that, of necessity, he might have to go overseas in order to earn a living, for in his poem *My Mountain Home* he postulates:

Should fate command me o'er the seas,
I'll think upon thy healthy breeze;
To barbarous climes where blackness lowers,
I'll muse upon thy dear wild flowers;
To barren isles mid pagan men,
I'll turn and gaze upon thee then.
Where'er my weary footsteps roam,
I can't forget my mountain home.

Eventually the fortune of John (3) changed when a fairly rich bunch of ore was revealed by his labours and that of the little band of miners with whom he worked. In a short space of time he was richer by £200! He goes on to say that 'With a portion of this sum I built a house at Troon Moor by the river, where we lived happily for many years. In the erection of this dwelling I worked laboriously. Following my stated duties in the mine, I gave up every hour of leisure, for two summers and two winters, in procuring material for its walls. Evenings and mornings I was in the quarry and sometimes by moonlight, raising and conveying stone to the site of the building.... My brother William assisted me in cutting the granite in our croft on Bolenowe Carn, where we used drills and iron wedges.[19] These heavy pieces of stone were all carted from the downs, at a distance of more than a mile, I always driving the horse myself. Thus with an incredible labour I accomplished all, raising and carrying every stone and every shovelful of clay in the building and also in the walls of the garden.' This latter sentence is undoubtedly a correct statement in respect of the house at Troon Moor, in that John (3) raised and carted all the stone and clay for construction, the actual building work, together with dressing and shaping the rough-hewn stone being carried out by tradesmen employed by him.

John (3) arranged a lease[20] with Pendarves Estate, Manor of Treslothan, for the ground and house which was to be built. The lease was on three lives; himself, his wife Jane and daughter Jane who had been born in the two-roomed cottage at Polgine. The first annual rent of five shillings and sixpence was due on Lady Day 1848 when the house was completed, which implies that John

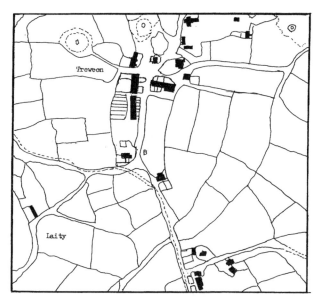

Traced from the 1840 Camborne Parish Tithe Map. CRO Ref. TM

Note: No building existed at that time in the lower section of Plot 3152. Trewoon is an early spelling of Troon.

had paid the usual capital sum deposits for the site at least by Lady Day 1847.

The location of the house is shown on the 1850 Symons map of Camborne and Illogan Mining District. It was situated on the north side and eastern end of the present Pendarves Street.[21]

John (3) and his family lived in the house at Troon Moor for just over nine years until they moved to Falmouth in the autumn of 1857. It was in this house that his second child and daughter Lucretia was born on 10 August 1849 and where she died on 23 December 1855. Here also his elder son James Howard was born on 15 January 1857. There was one disappointment in respect of this house in that John (3) had been unable to afford, at the time of building, an additional room for himself where he could study and write. In fact, he was not to have this facility for another twenty-six years or so, and then after only three and a half years he gave it up in 1877 so that his younger son John Alfred, an invalid, could use it as a photographic studio.

It is interesting to note that after the family moved to Falmouth John (3) retained the lease of the Troon Moor property for at least another twelve years.

Jane Rule proved to be a very supporting and loving wife to John (3) and also a critic of his poetry. Twenty years after their marriage in his poem *My Little Wife and I* he says:

> Oft when my rhyme-scrap is complete,
> What'er that scrap may be,
> I read it to my gentle Jane;
> A faithful critic she,
> She stops her needle for a while,
> The thread hangs from the eye,
> As we con o'er the written sheet,
> My little wife and I.

From the account of John (3) in his autobiography, it seems probable that Jane encouraged him to write the *Shakespeare Commemorative Poem* following the suggestion from William Catcott and to enter it in the competition. There is no evidence that Jane herself ever discovered the secret of rhyme.

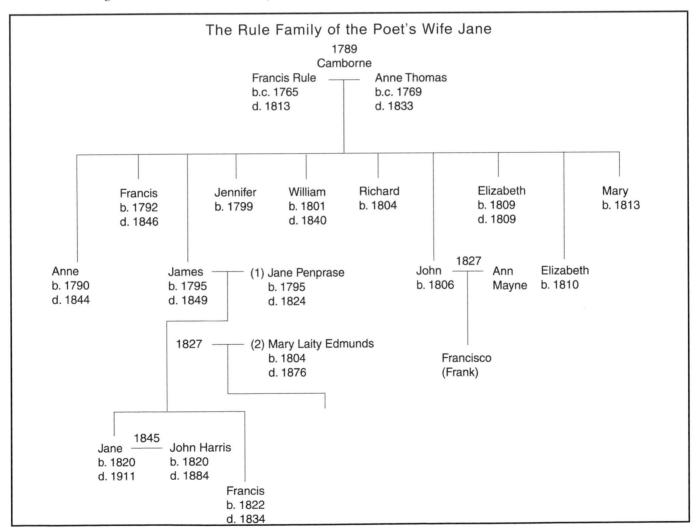

The Rule Family of the Poet's Wife Jane

1789
Camborne

Francis Rule — Anne Thomas
b.c. 1765   b.c. 1769
d. 1813   d. 1833

Francis   Jennifer   William   Richard   Elizabeth   Mary
b. 1792   b. 1799   b. 1801   b. 1804   b. 1809   b. 1813
d. 1846   d. 1840   d. 1809

Anne   James — (1) Jane Penprase   1827
b. 1790   b. 1795   b. 1795   John — Ann   Elizabeth
d. 1844   d. 1849   d. 1824   b. 1806 Mayne b. 1810

                    1827 — (2) Mary Laity Edmunds
                                   b. 1804   Francisco
                                   d. 1876   (Frank)

            1845
Jane — John Harris
b. 1820   b. 1820
d. 1911   d. 1884
      Francis
      b. 1822
      d. 1834

Poetry Making

It will be remembered that the first attempts at rhyme by John (3) were when he was about eight years old during his schooldays at Forest Gate under the one-legged miner-cum-schoolmaster. He goes on to say, 'Whether I sat by the kitchen fire with the usual household duties enacting around me; whether I drove the horse in the plough to my father, or wheeled the sod of the meadows into heaps; whether I collected sheep from the down or drove the cow to watering, my mind was ever active with my verse-making as the one object of my life.... Thus I travelled on through the vale of boyhood, labouring with my hands, and singing with my soul, as solitary as a stranger among my own people, without a single friend to direct me.... Wherever I went my harp was with me. The love of song grew with my physical growth and was dearer to me than the smile of friendship. I wrote in the dear old chimney by the winter firelight while my buxom brothers were shouting around me. And this was my only study save the barn or cow-house.... I often sat in my bedroom with my feet wrapped in mother's cloak, with a pair of small bellows as my writing desk.... I sometimes made ink to write my idyls with the juice of blackberries. Paper too was a scarce commodity; so I used the clean side of cast-off labelled tea wrappers, which my mother would bring from the shop.'

Underground in Dolcoath in his teens he scratched couplets on the iron wedges used for splitting the rock, undoubtedly giving vent to his love of nature and his longing for the pure air above ground. These couplets were as ships in the night, in that soon after writing them he would have inserted the wedge into the rock face and the writing would be lost forever. This latter aspect would not have been disregarded by John (3) and would seem to demonstrate his belief in his ability to write poetry against the odds of hardship, lack of formal education and academic advice. Likewise his writings on the inside of his miners' helmet and on his thumb nails would vanish as quickly as he had written them.

> And so he raised aloft his ponderous sledge,
> At every blow he chimed some ringing stave
> And wiped his forehead on his flannel's edge,
> Or pencilled down his psalm upon the iron wedge.

from *Monro*

On the walk back to Bolenowe Carn from Dolcoath after completing his shift John (3) was composing verse. He says, 'After labouring underground we had to return to our home on the hill, which was about three miles off. Father walked before and I followed at a short distance behind him; and often the whole journey was traversed without scarcely a word having passed between us. But all the time I was at my rhyming, quietly putting my thoughts together, and writing them in some shady corner of the kitchen on my return.' He remembered these walks in 1882 when he wrote the following poem:

The Silent Walk

> Up from under, up from under,
> Where 'tis ever dark,
> And my thoughts would wander, wander,
> To the soaring lark.
>
> I a lad of thirteen summers,
> Father full and strong,
> Stained with ore, and dust, and sulphur,
> Plutos's caves among.
>
> Homeward three miles through all weathers,
> He a trifle bent
> With the weight of tribulation,
> I on song intent.
>
> On before me walked my father,
> Silent as a shade,
> And I followed musing, musing,
> With the rhyming Maid.
>
> Caught I visions which the rower
> In the sunset sees,
> Waters falling down the mosses,
> Song-birds in the trees.
>
> Then my rhyme-mill worked the fastest,
> Where the firelight streamed,
> As my mother with her needle
> Some old garment seamed.
>
> Thank I now my pious father,
> Careful thus of talks,
> In the land where trouble ceases,
> For these silent walks.

From twelve years old until he was thirty John (3) carried a piece of slate in his waistcoat pocket together with a sharp pointed nail to scratch down verses as they occurred to him. He said, 'Poetry was everything, and in all things - the great inspirer, ay, the upholder of my life.' He continues in his autobiography, 'From first to last the majority of my poems have been written in the open air, in lanes and leas, by old stiles and farm gates, rocks and rivers and mossy moors.' The following verses portray his enjoyment of, and the inspiration gained, out of doors:

O, sweet from man to fly,
And mid your flowers lie,
Winding my simple fancies into rhyme!
And sweet your halcyon calm,
And sweet your breezy balm,
Like fragrance wafted from some holier clime.

And when eve's purple vest
Hangs round the sleepy west,
And twilight's dusky gates wide open stand,
I ask no higher bliss,
No fuller cup than this,
To rove in rhyme-dreams o'er the meadow land.

from *Green Fields*

Again in his poem to William Catcott - the Baker Poet - who corresponded[22] with John (3) and the person who sent him the advertisement from a London journal containing the invitation to enter for the Shakespeare Tercentenary Poem, John emphasizes the inspiration to be obtained by the observation of nature in the open air:

What has the bard to do with schools,
Or tedious academic rules?
He finds his idyls where the breeze
Walks like a prophet through the trees.
The bud, the flower, the last leaf sere,
All teach the true-born bardie dear.

John (3) had a favourite spot which he called his bower. Here he retreated alone either to read or to write. It was on his father's land and had been formed by excavation of a ditch to supply material to fill a gap in a Cornish hedge between a meadow and croft land. At the foot of the hedge a bank of about two feet high had been left and this grassy ledge formed a seat which was surrounded with heather. He said of his bower, 'Not a sound disturbed the solitude, save the clear river in the valley, or the last lay of the lark among the crimson clouds. It was the undisturbed realm of contemplation... the golden bells of the heather, gently touched by the fingers of the wind, made music to my ears.' His pleasure in his bower is depicted in the following extracts from two of his poems:

I've not much leisure. When I get an hour,
How sweet it seems
To hie me to the muses' breezy bower
In rhyming dreams!
Then inspiration takes up Fancy's wand,
And turns these heath-nooks into fairy land.

from *Spring*

From the bustle of life how delicious to steal
To this grotto of quiet, my sadness to heal!
'Tis like balm to my spirit, like rest to my frame,
When I gaze on the height whence my
    forefathers came.
How familiar each rock in its ivy-clad throne!
How each hedge to my eye-ball distinctly is known!
How I love the fresh breeze! How I prize the
    young flower
That smiles forth at spring in my
    heath-covered bower!

from *To My Bower*

A claypit on Bolenowe Carn from which he later dug clay to build his cottage at Troon Moor was also another spot where John (3) sought inspiration:

In a clay-pit on the common
I have written rhymes,
When the heath was full of echoes,
And the air of chimes.

In the distance shone our cottage,
Overhead the sky,
Where the larks in ringing numbers
With each other vie.

Close at hand the mere was gleaming
By the mossy bank,
Over which the swallows floated,
Out of which they drank.

Druid relics spoke distinctly
On the rocky moor,
And the small fays by the crosses
Danced when day was o'er.

With my pencil, book, and paper,
And the moorland chimes,
I was joyous in the clay-pit
Trilling forth my rhymes.

One of the earliest efforts of John (3), written when in his teens after returning from a night shift underground, illustrates his feeling for the coming spring, in three poems entitled *March*, *April* and *May*. The first is quoted below:

Hail, early spring! when buds and blossoms shine,
And new-born flowerets make the earth Divine,
Almighty Ruler, who hast all things made,
The snow-clad height, the grass upon the glade,
The roaring torrent, the low-murmuring rill,

The stately oak, the heather of the hill,
The unletter'd hind, and learning's sacred sire,
O, tune the Muse, that with true poet-fire
I may breathe forth the dear delights of Spring,
That to my soul with sweetest fragrance cling,
Winter, adieu! I'll off to yonder plain,
To list with rapture to the lark's sweet strain,
Pore with deep pleasure o'er the rippling rill,
Or gather daisies from our own dear hill;
Linger to watch still Eve's approaching car,
While through the tree-tops shines the lovers' star,
And up the valleys steals the year's fair queen,
To clothe all nature with a living green.

Beyond doubt the heat, the cold, the sulphur and the slime served to increase John's (3) love for all the beauty and mystery of nature. Eventually he decided to collect together and retain his compositions. He said, 'I sewed some leaves together and began to copy my effusions.' And again in his autobiography, 'The first essay of mine ever steeped in printer's ink was a dirge on the death of some miners who were accidentally killed in Carn Brea Mine. These verses were given to a poor blind man; and I remember with what intense joy I listened in the crowd as he sang them up and down the market at Camborne.'

John (3) attempted two satirical poems, one about a young schoolmaster and the other about a dentist who had given him a rough time when he attended for treatment. The former took offence so John (3) tore it up in front of him. He read the second to a friend at Camborne who advised him to burn it! He did exactly that and recorded: 'Thus suddenly and wisely ended my composition of satire.'

As a devout Christian and Wesleyan Methodist and ultimately a member of the Society of Friends, a proportion of the poems by John (3) and especially his prose dealt with moral themes. This latter was very much in line with the perspective of local Methodist Leaders and relative to the social conditions of the time. He believed that it was God's will that he should endure hardship, and that he was obeying the call of his master to make and write poetry. He wrote about death and the grave but these expressions and outpourings should not be viewed in a morbid sense but rather in their contemporary context. Death was never far away from the miner in these and even later times; sometimes sudden, sometimes long and lingering. To a person who longed deeply and consistently for a change to a more healthy working environment, but to whom it seemed the opportunity would never present itself, death could be viewed as an escape. But John (3) was not obsessed with these aspects; he believed in the Providence of God and he was possessed of a sense of humour which can be found in a number of his poems. He wrote of real life situations, of poverty, human suffering, and later of intemperance and the horrors of war. In respect of the latter he declared quite rightly that disputes should be settled by arbitration rather than war, and extolled the benefits of peace. During his lifetime, England had been involved in over thirty wars, mostly colonial, but including the Crimean War, and this latter war was probably the catalyst that inspired his long blank verse poem The War Fiend. His *Peace Pages for the People*, a series of four-page tracts, were written at the request of John Gill[23] of Penryn, his friend and member of the London Peace Society which had been formed in 1818. Accordingly John Gill influenced John (3) to publish *The Cruise of the Cutter*, a small volume extolling the benefits of peace. This was ostensibly to provide John Gill with a series of poems which he could read to children in his work among them in Sunday Schools. John Gill was an unrepentant pacifist and it is recorded[24] that he considered the Duke of Wellington an enemy of peace. When the Mayor of Penryn requested all the shops in the town to close as a mark of respect on the occasion of the Duke's funeral in 1852, John Gill kept his shop open! It must be said that John (3) never wrote about the great Duke, but he did venture a poem on Napoleon, which not surprisingly deprecates Napoleon's commitment to war and conquest.[25] Some people have described John (3) as a pacifist, but his own struggle through life against poverty and his endeavours to educate himself shows him to have been a fighter in this respect; it is difficult to conceive that he would not, if occasion demanded it, defend his wife, family, and the land he loved so well. He hoped and prayed for peace, as any thinking person would, but one doubts that he was so naive as to assume that keeping the peace and settling international disputes could come about by refusing to take up arms in the face of an aggressor, and this is borne out in his long poem *Luda: A Lay of the Druids* where he endorsed the defence of Carn Brea by the 'British' and the total rout of the attacking Vikings. Also he was a Royalist which is demonstrated in several poems.[26]

Of real-life situations John (3) records in *A Story of Carn Brea*:

My own old county is my copy-book,
From which I cull my pictures; and its leaves
Are like her mines, exhaustless in their worth.
My hero-miner is no gilt ideal,
Pull'd in to make a poem, but a man
Who really lived, and acted, and expired;
A noble man, a man to imitate.

It was understandable and characteristic of John (3) that he should write about the Giant Drink as alcoholism grew to gigantic proportions in the nineteenth century.

The working class was poor by any standards, and it is obvious that outside of the not infrequent physical mistreatment by the inebriates of their wives and children, and the resulting anguish and terror of the recipients, the money spent on drink only increased their poverty and misery. John (3) would have understood how easy it was for these folk to give over to drink in order to assuage their drudgery, and would feel it his Christian duty and moral obligation to endeavour to turn them away from intemperance and to point them to a better way of life. Here again John Gill was requiring material for his Sunday School work and so John (3) compiled *The Two Giants* (war and drink) which became the first book that John Gill printed and published for John (3).

It does appear that war, peace and intemperance became something of an obsession with John (3) and this obsession overshadowed his poetry making and dimmed the flame. Beyond this he was now writing under influences which he had not previously experienced. These influences hung over him like the Sword of Damocles. His subject matter was now decided for him and he was led to express the opinions and outlook of his employers. In order to obtain his remuneration he was subjected to a time scale and therefore was unable to alter and polish at will. In short, his normal form of expression and his inspiration was being sacrificed to the treadmill of a form of mass production. It is almost tragic that John (3) could not appreciate what was happening. One supposes that with his limited social mixing he tended to assume that those who were better educated than himself were all-knowing and never thought to sometimes question their views. Equally, while he took and enjoyed frequent walks along the seashore and coastline at Falmouth, the change from his work here as a scripture reader was far less dramatic and inspiring than coming up from underground and being able to refresh himself and recharge his batteries with walks over his beloved Carn and to rest in the solitude of his bower. He describes in a verse in *Monro* how underground in the mine among 'caverns grim with greedy gloom' he was provided with inspiration:

The cavern's side, the vagues of shining spar,
The roof of rock where scarce the candle gleams,
The hollow levels strangely stretching far
Beneath the mountains, full of mineral seams,
Were evermore to him befitting themes,
For meditation and his rustic lay;
While in the darkness his pale visage gleams,
To read rich sonnets on the furrowed clay,
And craggy slabs that jut the ladder's way.

But above all John (3) wrote about subjects in which he believed and loved or abhorred. It is also apparent that while working as a miner and to a lesser extent as a scrip-

ture reader, composing poetry became a form of escapism so that he took walks in the contrasting environment of the countryside to be able to fine-tune his poems into their final tasteful form.

John (3) wrote over a thousand pieces of poetry including over a hundred hymns. His publications also included over fifty items of prose together with several sermons and in these his descriptive powers are very evident. He wrote fifteen major poems, mostly in blank verse, which varied from one to as many as five parts each. Several of these major poems were dramatized.

Finally, the influence of his parents, John (2) and Christian, and also Granny Joan, should not be overlooked. While their influence upon him by their mode of living, their simple expressions of faith and their voiced wonder of God in nature would have been intended to guide him through the path of life, unsuspectingly to themselves their actions and words influenced his poetry. One pictures the occasion when John (2) took his young son for a walk to the highest point of Bolenowe Carn. It was a beautiful autumn starry night. The scene and his father's few but profound words stirred John (3) to write in later years:

Ye shining, solemn, silver stars,
I stretch my hands to you,
Because His throne I worship now
Is fixed beyond the blue.
No walk was like this autumn one,
Nor brings such lasting joy,
When father whispered on the hill,
'God made the stars, my boy.'

from *Under the Stars*

Appointment as Scripture Reader at Falmouth

By 1857, having spent twenty-four years underground at Dolcoath, John (3) had long been aware that the prospect of his living to the allotted span of three-score years and ten was very remote. He longed for a change to a more healthy form of employment where hopefully his life would stand some better prospect of being prolonged. This desire was known to those who closely followed his endeavours at poetry making. One of these interested persons, a certain Edward Bastin[27] of Redruth and later of Camborne, who had corresponded with John (3) over a long period, arranged a post for him with Falmouth Scripture Readers' Society. This society had been established in 1852 together with Falmouth Town Mission Society. Both societies were unsectarian but having more or less the same organising committees. Rev. C.R. Gardener of the Congregational Church was very active in both organisations; he was also secretary of the Religious

Tract Society in Falmouth, a society for whom John (3) later wrote many tracts. The societies were supported by voluntary contributions and had been established to promote and extend a knowledge of the Gospels by domiciliary visits, irrespective of a person's tenets.

John (3) was appointed in August 1857 at a wage of £30 a year.[28] His wage never varied during his term of office except when he was taken ill in 1878 when it was reduced to £15. Of this circumstance he said, 'My yearly earnings snapped in two like a thread.' It is apparent from his poem *Thirty Pounds a Year* that he had anticipated or hoped that his wage was to have been progressive, but it was not to be. Verse four of the poem demonstrates his determination to carry on despite his disappointment in this respect:

I've toiled along my humble way
Without the least regret,
And knew 'twas better far to work
Than idly fume and fret.
And still I mean to walk upright,
And keep my conscience clear,
Though thou hast nought to offer me
Save thirty pounds a year!

It is interesting to note that despite the small scale of remuneration to John (3), his Christian charity and that of his wife Jane extended to taking into their home a destitute ten-year-old boy, John Ley. This information is contained in the 1871 census for Falmouth and shows that the lad had been born at Cubert. It is possible, but not proven, that the story of the boy's arrival and his absorption into the family is told in the poem *Little Joseph*:

The day was done, the supper past,
The Bible brought once more;
But ere the good man read a line,
A knock was on the door.
And there a boy of ten years old
Stood underneath the vine,
An O how very pale he looked,
And how his eyes did shine!

'What do you here, my little lad?
Why are you not in bed?'
He touched his cap respectfully
'I seek for work,' he said.
'Last Sunday night our bread was done,
And mother did so weep!
So we went supperless to bed,
And cried ourselves to sleep.'

'And when the morning light appeared,
I left my mother there,
And on the door-step of our home
I made my little prayer, -
That God would tell me where to go,
And guide my wandering feet,
That dearest mother might not starve,
But have enough to eat.'

'I slowly oped the garden gate,
That mother might not hear,
And, looking back to see our home,
I brushed away the tear;
Then hurried on, I know not where,
So hungry and alone,
And said my prayer when night was come,
And slept upon a stone.'

'Then I got up and ran for heat;
And thus a week passed by,
My bed the ground, my covering grass,
My roof the starry sky.
I think the Lord has sent me here,
And you will let me stay:
I came straight onward to your door,
And never missed the way.'

'Come in, come in,' the wife exclaimed,
And he was washed and fed,
And very soon lay fast asleep
Upon the softest bed.
There little Joseph laboured long,
Through many a changeful year.
A faithful servant to his trust,
Following the Lord with fear.

John (3) and his family took up residence at Falmouth in the autumn of 1857. Originally they lived at 7 Wellington Terrace and it was in this house where their second son, John Alfred (1), was born in 1859. At or about 1862 they moved to 6 Killigrew Street, and by the 1871 census they had moved yet again, further down the same street to what would be their final Falmouth home No. 85 Killigrew Street. The move from number 6 probably took place in the second half of 1866 when the building was taken over by West Cornwall Bank. Barclays' Bank now occupy the site.

It was at number 85 in October 1874 that John (3) was to realise an ambition to have a study of his own which he arranged to be constructed over the kitchen. Finance for this project was made possible by an award of £50 from the Royal Literary Fund. But alas, as previously mentioned, he gave up the study three and a half years later during his period of illness so that his younger son,

John Alfred (1), could use it as a studio. John (3) wrote a poem, *On Leaving My Little Room*. The first and last verses describe the happiness and enjoyment that had been his in the study, coupled with the sorrow he felt when giving it up:

And must I part from thee so soon,
Mine for so brief a span?
Thy very walls were steeped in song,
When first thy reign began.
And idyls cluster by thy hearth,
And round thy lattice bloom:
The happiest hours of all the year
Were in my little room.

I go, I go with many a tear,
And lift my thoughts above;
The sacrifice is less severe
When made for those we love.
He who has led me year by year,
Will guide me through the gloom;
And, if 'tis well, will give me here
Another little room.

Of the work of John (3) in his duties as a scripture reader his elder son Howard recorded: 'In the homes of the poor his influence was good and lasting. He was universally beloved as a Scripture Reader at the bedsides of the sick and dying. Ready at all times to heed a request to attend the poor in their homes, his services were deservedly esteemed. He was peculiarly suited to the position he occupied. Combining a simplicity of speech with spiritual teaching his visits were valued by all.'

The Town Mission Library was operated by the Scripture Reader from 1871 onwards, and the library received financial support from the Religious Tract Society. An indication of the extent of work carried out by John (3) is contained in the Report of the Society for 1877:

Visits to families	2,103
Visits to sick	1,905
Cottage meetings conducted	143
Visits to Maria Camilla Training School[29]	27
Visits to Workhouse	26
Visits to the Sailors' Home	122
Visits to the Soup Kitchen	11
Tracts distributed	4,282
Exchanges of Town Mission Library Books	700

John (3) carried out this formidable volume of work during the year before he was struck down with paralysis.

The manner in which John (3) viewed his commission as a scripture reader and the conditions in which his work was carried out is contained in two verses from his poem *The Bible Reader*:

No blade with battle gore
Or rifle, does he bear
His scimitar, the scriptures;
His mail-coat, earnest prayer.
And forth he goes to conquer
Upon the field of sin.
And many a noble trophy
For Jesus Christ to win.

He reads where darkness gathers,
And ignorance resides;
Where, like a careless heathen,
Neglect unwash'd abides.
He reads where sickening vapours
Rise on the alley air,
Content if Christ his Master,
Be present with him there.

Again, also in his *Monro*:

In hollow attics near the rended roof,
In cellars grim, as sea-waves washed the walls,
In squalid places where peace stood aloof,
And day and night beheld intemperate brawls,
In chambers where the obscene insect crawls,
And lewdness burrows in a broken bed,
On wandering wights in gentle tones he calls,
With pitying pleadings for the poor mislead,
And from the Holy Book the words of life he read.

In retrospect one wonders if the change of occupation by John (3) from miner to scripture reader was, in the final analysis, beneficial to his health; might not 'neglect, unwashed and sickening vapours' be even worse than 'the heat, the cold, the sulphur and the slime'?

Presumably because of the deterioration in John's (3) health, together with the volume of work involved, an assistant, W.H. Moss, was appointed by the Society in 1878. Around this time the Town Missioner was Joseph Knight. W.H. Moss remained as an assistant to John (3) up to the time of the latter's death in 1884, but apparently was not selected to follow him, as in March the same year the committee appointed John Lomas to fill the vacancy. John Lomas had previously been a captain in the Salvation Army.

Whilst no report has been located to prove when the Scripture Readers' Society ceased to continue its work, it would appear to have been around 1884–85. No reports seem to have been published beyond that date. Indeed, in

1885 we find that the Town Missioner was now John Lomas. This leads to the conclusion that a lot of the work of these two societies was in fact a duplication, and so instead of continuing with the two parallel organisations it was decided to streamline the operation. The Town Mission still existed thirty-three years later in 1917.

John (3) came to love Falmouth with its beaches, walks, inlets and views of the estuary. In 1865 when Edward Stoneman Tregonning wrote his *History of Falmouth* he expressly requested John (3) to write a poem which would extol the virtues of the town and port. Some verses are given below:

I saw it first when April shoots
Were shining on the tree,
And daisies, gladdened by the sun,
Looked up from lawn and lea.
I left my home when but a boy,
And, crossing mead and moor,
Gazed I upon the harbour waves,
Which kissed the pleasant shore.

I never shall forget when first
It burst upon my view,
And from a neighbouring carn I saw,
Its ships and waters blue,
And tower and terrace, ocean girt,
Which met me from the hill.
'Twas beautiful; 'twas beautiful!
And so is Falmouth still.

Oft from the street I turn away,
As peals the solemn bell,
When eve, with glow worms in the moss,

Sits musing in the dell.
And O how sweet it is to stand
Upon the pebbly shore,
And hear across the gathering dusk,
The dripping of the oar!

Here lie, the Docks, those wonder works[30]
Of labours kingly hand;
And here the Railway sends its stores[31]
The marvel of the land:
And here the Telegraph wire
Runs conquering space and time
O, grandeur of the grandest age,
And wonder most sublime!

Publication of Works and List of Writings

A poem which John (3) had written entitled *The First Primrose* appeared in a magazine and came to the notice of Dr George Smith of Trevu, Camborne,[32] whereupon John (3), was invited to Trevu. George Smith, although twenty years older than John (3) had a lot in common with him in that he was the son of a carpenter from Condurrow, a hamlet approximately half a mile from Beacon, and the birthplace of John's (3) mother. George Smith also by persistence, native ability and a deep desire for self-improvement had risen from humble birth to become a highly respected scholar, writer and Wesleyan Methodist Layman. A suggestion has been mooted, though not proven, that Dr George Smith and Christian Smith, John's (3) mother, were related and it is just possible that they may have been second cousins. Be that as it may, George Smith took considerable interest in John (3)

7 Wellington Terrace (now modernised) in which John Harris first lived when he came to Falmouth in the Autumn of 1857

84 and 85 Killigrew Street, Falmouth. It was the right-hand house, number 85, in which John Harris lived from before 1871 until he died in 1884.

from this time and continued to do so throughout his, the former's, life. Following several visits to Trevu, John (3) plucked up courage to tell Dr Smith that he would like to publish some of his poems but was unsure as to how to proceed. Dr Smith advised him to copy some of his best poems and promised to pass them to his friends to obtain their opinion. The result being that a collection of blank verse and rhyme called *Lays from the Mine, the Moor, and the Mountain* was published by subscription in 1853 and dedicated to George Smith who had dealt totally with the business aspects of publication on John's (3) behalf. In fact, all his books were published by subscription or forward ordering.

At the start of his preface to this first book John (3) said, 'The following pages are presented to the world, not with any pretension to high poetical merit, but as the first compositions of an uneducated working man.' He added in the second edition 'and as the simple effusions of one who daily toils in the darkness of the mine.' The following list, though not necessarily exhaustive, contains the major bulk of the written work of John (3):

1. *Lays from the Mine, the Moor, and the Mountain*
Published in 1853 by Simpkin, Marshall & Co. of London. It contains two lengthy blank verse poems and forty-two minor ones including three humorous pieces.

2. *Lays from the Mine, the Moor, and the Mountain*
Published in 1856 by Alexander Heylin of London and said to be a second edition of the 1853 book of the same title, but in fact contains an additional thirty-two poems. This book was also dedicated to Dr George Smith.

3. *The Land's End, Kynance Cove, and other Poems*
Published in 1858 by Alexander Heylin, twelve months after John (3) had moved from Troon to Falmouth. His younger brother Benjamin was a subscriber for one copy.

4. *The Mountain Prophet, the Mine, and Other Poems*
Published in 1860 by Alexander Heylin. Brother Benjamin again subscribed for one copy.

5. *A Story of Carn Brea, Essays and Poems*
Published in 1863 by Hamilton, Adams & Co. London. In this book John (3) for the first time includes some notes on his life under the heading 'Peeps at a Poet'. Brother Benjamin subscribed once more, his last prior to leaving for North America.

6. *Shakespere's Shrine, an Indian Story, Essays and Poems*
Published in 1866 by Hamilton, Adams & Co. Here again John (3) included a brief résumé of his life up to the point where his fortunes as a tributer had somewhat improved.

7. *Luda; A Lay of the Druids, Hymns, Tales, Essays and Legends*
Published in 1868, again by Hamilton, Adams. Caleb Cliff, a major poem, is written in dramatic form.

8. *Bulo; Reuben Ross; A Tale of the Manacles; Hymn, Song and Story*
Published in 1871 by Hamilton, Adams, and dedicated to Robert Alexander Grey,[33] Governor of St Thomas and St Bartholomew Hospitals. Bulo, Reuben Ross, Meena - A Tale of the Manacles and Rando Reef, all major poems in this book are also written in dramatic form.

9. *The Cruise of the Cutter and Other Peace Poems*
Published in 1872 by Partridge & Co. London, and dedicated to Baroness Burdett Coutts.[34] A portion of the preface reads: 'The following simple poems have been written with a desire in the author's heart to spread the principles of Peace, and accelerate in some humble way the desired consummation of the beating of swords into ploughshares, and the spears into pruning-hooks, when men shall learn war no more. It is surely the duty of Christians of all denominations, of all colours and of all clans, making the Bible their guide-book, whose holy utterances are peace on earth and goodwill towards men, to labour for the spread of this precious truth, when man shall meet his BROTHER everywhere, and the dreadful voice of war shall no more be heard.'

10. *Wayside Pictures, Hymns, and Poems*
Published in 1874 by his former publishers, Hamilton, Adams and dedicated to Robert Alexander Grey, to whom is also inscribed an eleven-verse dedicatory stanza. This book contains a selection of the poems of John (3) up to that time, including one hundred and five hymns and fifty peace poems. The frontispiece carried a photograph of John (3).

11. *Walks with Wild Flowers*
Published in 1875 by Hamilton, Adams and dedicated to Baron Northbrook,[35] at that time Viceroy and Governor General of India. At the end of each poem there is included a brief botanical description relative to the particular flower, and presumably obtained from Ann Pratt's *Wild Flowers* to whom he made a suitable acknowledgement. The book is also illustrated with woodcuts of the various wild flowers upon which the poems are based. The woodcuts were the

first works of the younger son of John (3), John Alfred, who suffered from curvature of the spine which necessitated, at this time, his working in a reclining position.

12. *Tales and Poems*
Published in 1877 by Hamilton, Adams & Co. and also illustrated with woodcuts by John Alfred. This book is mainly prose but also contains thirty-two poems.

13. *The Two Giants*
Published in 1878 by Hamilton, Adams, and printed by John Gill of Penryn. It is dedicated to Earl Northbrook with woodcuts by John Alfred.

14. *Monro*
Published in 1879 by Hamilton, Adams, and printed by John Gill. The woodcuts are again by John Alfred, and it is interesting that page 143 carries a woodcut of the back of the Shakespeare Tercentenary Gold Watch which John (3) had won. The three parts of the poem *Monro* are, with certain additions and flights of fancy, the story of the life of John (3).

15. *Linto and Laneer*
Published in 1882 by Hamilton, Adams, and printed by John Gill. There are only a few woodcuts by John Alfred which possibly indicates that he was now away taking a course in photography.

16. *My Autobiography*
Published in 1882 by Hamilton, Adams, and printed by John Gill. It also contains nineteen poems and numerous footnotes, together with a picture of the author. A second edition was published in 1883.

17. *Last Lays*
It was published in April 1884, by James Howard and John Alfred the two sons of John (3), three months after his death which occurred on 7 January. Prior to his death John (3) had completed the whole manuscript, including the preface, and had initiated the publishing procedures. It was printed by John Gill, and most of the poems had been written after 1882.

It has to be admitted that a certain number of poems and prose were repeated in different books, and this is especially so in the case of major poems. Other poems were shortened or added to, and there are a couple of instances where quite different verses were presented under the same title.

Of the earlier books published under the aegis of Dr George Smith, it appears that he subscribed for twenty

books of each publication! The Thomases, Managing Agents of Dolcoath, together with certain of the county families, other rising Camborne industrialists and friends all subscribed for several copies each, thus encouraging and firmly demonstrating their belief in John's (3) ability. The subscriptions of this group of people possibly accounted for one-third of each addition.

Overall, John (3) obtained very little profit from the sale of his books. He accumulated as he said, 'A score or two pounds' but it seems he lost this through some problem with one of the London-based publishers. During the period 1860 to 1878 he only received three pounds one shilling and one penny from this source. Despite this he did manage to accrue from about 1872 a certain amount of capital as a result of literary awards and grants with which he had been honoured. On the death of Dr George Smith on 30 August 1868, the onus fell on John (3) to arrange for future publication, but due to his inexperience in business matters it cost him dearly; and so in the same year he sought and obtained the assistance of his friend, John Gill, the printer of Penryn. This proved to be a satisfactory arrangement and, as will have been seen, continued throughout the remainder of his life.

From 1875-76, Mr J.E.M. Vincent, the editor of two weekly newspapers, at Leamington, Warwickshire, engaged John (3) to write for him. His most ambitious writing for the papers was a serial of sixty-three chapters called *Mountain Mat and His Three Sons*.

John (3) also published a series of three pamphlets which he wrote especially for Earle's Retreat Home at Falmouth:

1. *The Earnest Enquiry* 1879
2. *John the Baptist, the Strange Preacher* 1881
3. *The Lowly Lifted or Lessons from the Life of President Garfield*

In addition he contributed to the following periodicals:

The Band of Hope	*The Family Friend*
The British Workman	*The Friendly Visitor*
The Souvenir of Modern Minstrelsy	

Between 1863 and 1879 John (3) wrote numerous tracts for the Religious Tract Society and the Leominster Tract Society, the bulk of which are listed below, commencing with those for the former society:

The Converted Miller and His Daughter	*Nancy Grey*
Old Roger Rough the Cornish Streamer	*Betsy Blight*
A Sinner Lord I Come to Thee	*The Miller's Wife*
Widow Erne and Erry, a Christmas Story	*Old Frankey*
Naught Hast Thou, Poor Child of Sin	*Believe and Live*
Frank Fraddon and His Father	*Dame Dritton*

Daniel Doner the Pedlar	*Dan Dugal*
Rob the Coal Porter	*Batta Bate*
Ellen and Her Father	*Kit Bowden*
Lost among the Dikes	*The Two Sticks*
Mary the Mining Girl	*The Miner's Wife*
Old Jasper's Eagle	*The Storm Silenced*
The Power of Faith	*The Crippled Miner*
Rilla Rock the Maid of the Moor	
(a pamphlet)	*Uncle Dick's Story*

For Leominster Tract Society:

Widow Watt	(rhyme)
Old Robin Green	"
Edmund Ivy the Fisherman	"
Isaac Moore	"
The Mysterious Basket	"
Watt Wallace	"
Escape from the Mine	(prose)
The German	"
The Prodigal's Return	"
I'm Going Up	"
Light in a Dark Cellar	"
The Blind Sailor	"
The Old Ship Carpenter	"
Lord's Apple Tree	"
The Cornish Fisherman	"
The Dairy Women	"
This Man Receiveth Sinners	"
Tommy the Fisherman	"
The Orphan's Printing Press	"
Repent	"
The Door on the Latch	"
God Hears	"
We've Got a Saviour	"
The Soldier Sceptic	"
The Blacksmith's Wife	"
Old John the Ragman	"

At the request of John Gill, a series of four-page tracts under the overall title Peace Pages for the People were written by John (3) during 1873-74. They carried wood-cut illustrations by John Alfred, and the writer was paid one pound for each tract:

Watt Willow	*Solomon Sloop*
Rod Roughter	*King Harry Ferry*
Joseph Price	*Jane Mansfield*
George Smith	*The Bengal Famine*
Michael Verran	*Joseph Sturge*
The Soldier's Mother	*The Young Calculator*

Second Series:

Elihu Burritt	*French Gratitude*
Conscription	*Widow Ward*
Women's Work	*Abner Grey*
Thomas Jones	*Barbouilly the French Barber*
Dame Terril	*William Sullivan and the Indian*
The Syrian Host	*Old Davie the Miller*

It is recorded that in one year John Gill printed nearly a quarter of a million of these peace tracts, some being translated into German and some were reprinted in America. The concept of religious tracts was sponsored in the nineteenth century by various denominations of the Church, Temperance Societies and middle-class society. The intention was to divert the working class away from intemperance, impiety, evil practices, Sabbath breaking and illiteracy. The stories or verse were generally based on true-life situations and everyday occurrence in the lives of the working class and were written in simple language. What better than to have them written by a working-class author and poet such as John (3)?

The *Penryn Advertiser*, a weekly newspaper started by John Gill on 8 June 1867, frequently included over the years selected poems by John (3).

After studying such a formidable list of books and writing, of itself a positive achievement, we can reflect on the lack of a formal education by John (3), his lack of contact with people of equal ability who could advise and encourage, his lack of opportunity to travel, his lack of a wide reading opportunity, his lack of funds and his twenty-four years of drudgery in the mine coupled with his twenty-six years of toil among the poor in Falmouth, and this volume of writing was carried out in addition to these daily duties. Then consider how, despite all these drawbacks, he could apply such sensitivity to the written word. He says in his autobiography that he felt 'as solitary as a stranger among my own people without a single friend to direct me.' Small wonder that he withdrew into himself. In his poem *The Mountain Boy* he tells us of his solitary cultural existence and loneliness:

From busy man he stole
To nature's altars rude,
And gave his thoughtful soul
To muse with Solitude.

O'er silent glens and glades,
Where lovelorn rustics sigh,
Through evening's solemn shades,
All lonely he would hie.

And yet, standing on Bolenowe Carn he exultantly exclaims:

> This mountain is my world, these crags my throne,
> And glancing fairies are my retinue;
> The night-bird is my poet, and the rill
> My sweet musician trickling down the rocks.

from *The Mountain Prophet*

Following publication of the second edition of *Lays from the Moor, the Mine and the Mountain* in 1856, The *Athenaeum* commented, 'His writing to any other age would have been a marvel, and it is a phenomenon even in our own.' Some 120 years later D.M. Thomas in his introduction to *Songs from the Earth* said, 'Through native genius, he still achieved against all odds, a body of poetry as fine as any but that of the half dozen great poets of the Victorian age.'

One has to admit that in his writing about himself John (3) does, on occasions, become somewhat self-centred, but interestingly none of the contemporary press or critics mentioned it, unlike several writers of more recent years. Almost inevitably the harshest critic has been Sabine Baring-Gould, who in his *Cornish Characters and Strange Events* (1908) said of John (3) 'Moving in his little circle, surrounded by the ignorant, it is no wonder that John Harris was puffed up with vanity, and thought himself a poet... he calls himself a Miner Poet, but he is not even a Minor Poet.... When he steps up into his florid car as chauffeur at the Battle of Roses at Nice he is intolerable.'[36] Once again Baring-Gould appears to have been unaware of the facts of the struggle through which John (3) had emerged, and obviously had only read a limited portion of his work. He did, however, admit that 'John Harris could write smooth lines and had a tender appreciation of the beauties of nature.' Additionally in the preface to his book it appears that Baring-Gould was unaware that John (3) had merited inclusion in the *Dictionary of National Biography*. It is a pity that Baring-Gould was not as generous as his relative, Thomas George Baring - Lord Northbrook.

In the context with egoism, whatever John (3) wrote about himself, his progress and comparison to others, it was done in innocence, in that he was truthfully and justifiably portraying a pride in his achievement. Should he not be proud of his progress in self-improvement and in the quality of his writings? The answer to this question must surely be in the affirmative. One is reminded of the comments of a present-day scholar and eminent historian, who says in his autobiography 'No doubt there will be critics silly enough to complain of the egoism of this book. But what is the point of an autobiography if it is not about the "I" who wrote it? The only question is whether the "I" is interesting.' This must be the ultimate in answering Baring-Gould's criticism. One could certainly claim that John (3) had something to be egotistic about, but whatever may be said one should never doubt the sincerity of John (3) in writing about himself. Self-satisfaction was not his forte, rather the simple desire to walk humbly with God.

Perhaps finally one should mention the statement of Bickford H.C. Dickinson in his book *Sabine Baring-Gould, Squarson, Writer and Folklorist* which says 'His ironic pen earned him enemies'. And Bickford Dickinson was Sabine's grandson!

Other Offices Held in Church and Community

John (3) became Superintendent of Black Rock Sunday School some time after his marriage in 1845. The hamlet of Black Rock lay some two miles south of Troon. He was also librarian of Troon Wesleyan Sunday School.

He became a teacher in Troon Sunday School in 1836 when sixteen years old. In the second quarter of 1853 he became a local preacher 'on trial' in Camborne Wesleyan Circuit, and by 1854 was a 'fully accredited' local preacher. From Plans of Preachers' Appointments it can be seen that he averaged eleven to twelve appointments each quarter; and as was the custom, and of necessity, he walked to all his appointments. The church at the greatest distance necessitated a round trip of almost eight miles. John (3) also records that 'I frequently had in addition to preach twice a day on Sunday, finishing my labours about ten o'clock at night. This course of rather severe sabbath discipline was cheerfully pursued almost up to the time that I became a Scripture Reader at Falmouth.' The foregoing suggests that he must have accepted additional appointments to those listed on the circuit plan.

On 6 May 1879 John (3) became a Quaker and joined the Society of Friends at Falmouth. The membership list of the Society for the period 1837-80[37] states that his membership was acquired 'by convincement'. He no doubt became very impressed with the Quakers with whom he had made contact at Falmouth - the Fox family and his friends John Gill and Lovell Squire to name a few. A poem that he wrote soon after he joined the Society extols the virtues of these Friends, in that when he badly needed friends, help and comfort they did not hesitate or stand aloof. It seems that their actions and understanding of the reason and cause of his sorrow became the deciding factor in his decision to become a Quaker. The cause of his deep sorrow and that of his family was due to disappointment in his son-in-law, who had been accused of committing forgery and had absconded. The poem entitled *The Friends* is appended in its entirety:

Who came to me when skies were dark,
And high waves rolled upon my bark
From iron ridges sheer and stark?
                              The Friends.

Who cheered me when the form of Gloom
In sable vest passed through my room,
Like one in trappings of the tomb?
                              The Friends.

Who sat beside my stricken hearth,
When sorrow's bitterest tears had birth,
And wild weeds wrapped the reeling earth?
                              The Friends.

Who came with quiet, noiseless pace,
With love-words, when no other face
Or foot of man stole near my place?
                              The Friends.

Who gave me sympathy in woe,
And strove to ease the fearful blow
Which in a moment laid me low?
                              The Friends.

Who took my hand in Christian cheer,
When hills were steep and dales were drear,
And red-eyed Grief was cowering near?
                              The Friends.

Who prayed for me with simplest grace,
While yet the tears were on my face,
Approaching Heaven's own dwelling place?
                              The Friends.

Who bade me trust in Him the more,
Although the waves of trouble roar
In anger on the shaken shore?
                              The Friends.

Who raised the reed with broken stem,
And bade me touch His garment's hem,
So that my heart is drawn to them?
                              The Friends.

6 November 1876

John (3) had some years earlier visited the quaint thatch-roofed Friends' Meeting House at Come-to-Good, Feock, built in 1710 it is still used today. It is said to be the only thatched Quaker Meeting House in Britain.[38] John (3) was most impressed with its simplicity and rural setting and composed a poem about it:

I, knew not, though I've lingered long,
Through dear Cornubia's glades of song,
The tinkling stream fair-fringed with moss
By crag and carn and curious cross,
That our own land of wild and wood
Owned sweet sequestered Come-to-Good.   Verse 1

O Come-to-Good! O temple meet
To bow in silence at His feet!
O fitting place for bard to dwell,
And wake the mysteries of his shell.
Where bank and bower, and lawn and lea,
And wood and water, tell of Thee.   Verse 6

Following the removal of John (3) to Falmouth, it appears that with his huge workload as scripture reader it was not possible for him to undertake preaching appointments on a regular basis in the Wesleyan Circuit there. Although it has not been possible to locate minutes of the Local Preachers' Meeting from the last quarter of 1857 to the last quarter of 1865, no mention of him is contained in the minutes from 1865[39] to the time of his death in 1884. Had he been a member of the meeting in May 1879 when he joined the Quakers it would most certainly have merited an entry in the minutes. However, despite the large number of cottage meetings he conducted as a scripture reader he did on occasions take services in the chapel attached to Earle's Retreat.

John (3) was appointed a Governor of Earle's Retreat at Bowling Green Hill, Falmouth in 1869. His signature may be seen in the bound volume of their Conditions, Rules and Regulations drawn up by George Earle[40] in 1670 for the government and management of the Home. Indeed, he took a great interest in this institution which still continues its charitable work today. The poem by John (3), *Earle's Retreat*, is a tribute to George Earle.

At the opening of Clare Terrace British School by Miss Fox of Penjerrick on 2 May 1882 the scholars sang a hymn which had been written expressly for the occasion by John (3). One can imagine the immense pleasure he must have derived in playing a little part in organised education being made available to all children.

By 1855 it seems that John (3) was considered by the family to be a person of some merit, because in that year he became a witness to the Will of his uncle by marriage, John Rule, a miner, who had married at Camborne Church on 16 May 1812 Susanna Smith of Beacon, an elder sister of Christian, mother of John (3).

Society of Friends. Cornwall Record Office Ref. SF 146 Falmouth Monthly Meeting Membership List 1837-1880. Folio 59.

Name:	John Harris	
Description:	Scripture Reader	
Residence:	Falmouth	
Membership acquired:	How:	By convincement
	When:	6 May 1879

THE WESLEYAN METHODIST PLAN
OF THE
CAMBORNE CIRCUIT, 1853.

Names of Places AND HOURS OF SERVICE. "Take heed how ye hear."	JULY 17 — 1 Kings 13 / John 5	24 — 1 Kings 18 / John 12	31 — 1 Kings 21 / John 19	AUGUST 7 — 2 Kings 5 / Acts 5	14 — 2 Kings 10 / Acts 12	21 — 2 Kings 19 / Acts 19	28 — Jerem 5 / Acts 26	SEPTEMBER 4 — Jerom 35 / Matt 5	11 — Ezek 14 / Matt 12	18 — Ezek 14 / Matt 19	25 — Ezek 20 / Matt 26
CAMBORNE WESLEY CHAPEL 10½	3	1	2	3 B	9	2	3	1 B	2	3q	1
6	2	3	8	2 s	3	6	2l	3 s	1	2 S.A	3
Thursday 7	2	3	13	2	3	24	2	3	1	2	3
CAMBORNE CENTENARY CHAPEL 10½	29	23	9	6	13	8	16	6	24	31	9
2½	13	31	14	3	24	30	9	11	13	17	11
Tuesday 7	2		P		3		2		1		
TUCKINGMILL 10½	2	3	6	2 B	3	27	2	3 B	1	2q	3
6	3	1	2	3 s	11	2	3l	1 s	2	3 S.A	1
Wednesday 7	2	3	21	2	3	22	2	3	1	2	3
TROON 2½	24	19	15	18	4	14	20	26	31	23q	13
6	1	11	11	17	2 s	9	6	8l	3	16q	10
Monday 7	P	2	3	P	2	3	P	2	3	1	2
POOL 6	17	2	28	8	6	3 s	11	15l	27	1q	18
Thursday 7	3	P	2	3	P	2	3	1	2	3	1
PENPONDS 10½	26	30	s.s.	13	29	16	33	2 s	12	14q	27
6	24	6	s.s.	5	21l	17	18	11	10	9q	34
Tuesday 7	2	3	P	2	3	P	2	3	1	2	3
FOREST 10½	1	21	13	31	2 s	15	26	21	3	18q	4
6	10	22	30	11	19	14	20l	27	24	12q	17
Wednesday 7	3	2		P		3		2		1	
KEHELLAND 10½	31	17	33	s.s.	26	23	30	32	22	20q	12
6	23	10	21	s.s.	24	28	15	2 s	14l	11q	6
Friday 7	2	3	P	2	3	P	2	3	1	2	3
ILLOGAN DOWNS 2½	28	14	3	20	23	12	13	19	30	15q	2 s
6	21	27	10	22l	18	11	32	9	17	6q	31
Tuesday 7		P	9		2		1		3		
PENGEGON 2½	30	24	28	21	14	19	3 s	4	33	13q	23
6	22	29	15	27l	12	26	34	16	31	10q	5
Friday 7	P	13	3	P	2	17	P	2	3	24	1
ILLOGAN HIGHWAY 2½	21	27	31	30	33	11	5	15	23	24q	14
6	26	14	3	20	10l	32	13	19	18	34q	2 s
Monday 7	2		P		3		2		1		3
TRESWITHAN 2½	P	P	P	P	P	P	P	P	P	P	P
6	15	26	32	29	27	10l	24	5	26	21q	32
Wednesday 7	P		3		2		P		3		2
ROSCROGGAN 2½	15	11	5	23	32	22	24	17l	28	21q	31
Friday 7	3		2		P		3		2		1
PLANTATION 10½	33	4	19	12	s.s.	24	29	13	26	30q	16
Tuesday 7	3		2		P		3		2		1
BEACON 2½	27	8	23	28	17	33	26	29	19	20q	24
Wednesday 7		P		3		2		1		3	
TREGAJORRAN 2½	18	2	22	15	5	3 s	21	12	11l	1q	29
6	27	9	31	28	14	19	10	34	32	20q	24
Thursday 7		2		P		3		2		1	
CONDURROW 10½	13	18	26	10	19	31	12	10	16	22q	21
Friday 7		2				3					
BLACK ROCK 6	11	13	24	9	30	18	27	22	34	8q	19
CARTHEW 2½	20		24		15		31		3 T		33

Names and Residences OF THE Itinerant & Local Preachers. "Preach the word."

1	Watson	...	Camborne
2	Hooley	...	ditto
3	Blencowe	...	Tuckingmill
4	Thomas	...	Troon
5	Bennett	...	Kehelland
6	Smith G	...	Camborne
7	Oatfield	...	ditto
8	Thomas C	...	ditto
9	Lean	...	ditto
10	Vivian E	...	Tuckingmill
11	Tonkin	...	Pool
12	Vivian W. 1st	...	Tuckingmill
13	Smith W	...	Camborne
14	Uren	...	Illogan Downs
15	Willoughby	...	Pool
16	Allen	...	Camborne
17	Thomas Jno	...	ditto
18	Slater	...	Pool
19	Roberts	...	Forest
20	Opie	...	ditto
21	Vivian W, 2nd	...	Tuckingmill
22	Trestain	...	ditto
23	Floyd	...	Camborne
24	Vincent	...	ditto
25	Nancarrow	...	Pool
26	Chirgwin	...	Camborne
27	Bishop	...	Pool
28	Williams	...	ditto
29	Smith W. B	...	Camborne
30	Tredinnick	...	ditto
31	James	...	ditto
32	Bond	...	Roscroggan

ON TRIAL.

33	Cocking	Camborne 3 P.
34	Harris	Troon ... 2 P.

REFERENCES.
1. 3 P. Third Plan.
2. 2 P. Second do.

N.B. The Local Brethren are expected to fulfil their own appointments, or if unavoidably prevented, to endeavour themselves to get them supplied, by their brethren, who are regularly appointed during the current quarter on their own plan, before applying to the Superintendent to procure a substitute for them.

Quarterly Fast Day on Friday September 30th.

References.

1	B.	Baptism.
2	S.	Sacrament of the Lord's Supper.
3	L.	Lovefeast.
4	Q.	Quarterly Collection.
5	T.	Tickets to be renewed.
6	P.	Prayer Meeting.
7	S.A.	Sabbath School Address.

NOTICES.

1. In presenting their Children for Public Baptism, the Parents are requested to observe the days appointed for the ordinance, as much as possible, and to give previous intimation of their intention. This ordinance will be confined to the Children of the *Members of Society*, and of those who *regularly attend our Ministry.*—Both Parents are expected to be present on such occasions.

2. The Quarterly Meeting will be held at Camborne on Wednesday September 28th. The Circuit and Society Stewards will meet for the transaction of their financial business, at 3. Tea will be provided for all the members of the Quarterly Meeting at 5 o'clock.

3. The Local Preachers' Meeting at Camborne, on Tuesday September 20th to commence at 3 o'clock. Punctual attendance at the *commencement* of the Meeting is particularly requested, as Mr Smith's Lecture will commence at half-past 6 o'clock.

4. The Society Stewards will give notice of the Sacraments, Lovefeasts, and Collections, on the previous Sabbath, and will forward the Connexional Collections to the Superintendent, as soon as possible.

NEWTON, PRINTER, CAMBORNE.

CAMBORNE CIRCUIT.

PLAN OF THE WESLEYAN PREACHERS.

1855.

Places.	LESSONS.	Ezekiel 14. 3. Mark	Ezekiel 20. 10. Mark	Daniel 3. Luke 1 to 39.	Joel 2. Luke 7.	Habk. 2. Luke 14.	Prov. 2. Luke 20.	Prov. 11. John 3.	Prov. 13. John 10.	Prov. 15. John 17.	Isaiah 4. John 7.	Isaiah 5. Acts 9.	Isaiah 25. Acts 16.	Isaiah 30. Acts 23.	Isaiah 9 to v 8. Luke 2 to v 16
	Time.	SEP 30	OCT 7	OCT 14	OCT 21	OCT 28	NOV 4	NOV 11	NOV 18	NOV 25	DEC 2	DEC 9	DEC 16	DEC 23	DEC 25
CAMBORNE WESLEY CHAPEL	10½	2	1B	2	1	2	1BK	2	1	1	1B	2	1q	15	1
	6	1	2	5	2	1s	2K	1	2l	1	2s	4	2q		2
Thursday	7	1	2	1	2	1	2	1	2	1	2	1	2	1	
CAMBORNE CENTENARY CHAPEL	10½	18	28	17	21	10	25K	7	21	14	8	4	24q	5	
	2½	5	22	11	28	24	6K	27	18	12	20	(7)	23q	9	6
TUCKINGMILL	10½	1B	2	1	8	1K	2B	1	2	1	2B	1q	2	1	2
	6	2	1	15	1s	2K	5	2	1	2	9	2q	1s	4l	1
Wednesday	7	2	2	1	1	2	2	1	1	2	1	2	1	2	
TROON	2½	28	27	26	6	5K	17	25	24	16	5	26q	27	8	
	6	19	8	4	29	18K	3	28	8l	4	14	1q	10	24	27
Monday	7	2	1	2	1	2	1T	29	1T	2	1	2	1	2	
POOL	6	(7)	26	2	20	8	4	29	9l	24	15q	19	5	6	8
Thursday	7	2	1	2	1	2s	1	2	1T	2T	1	2	1	2	
PENPONDS	10½	10	20	19	4	26	14K	15	28	25	27q	10	(7)	2	
	6	6	5	24	27	9	26K	23	29	21	4q	11	16l	26	
Tuesday	7	28	1	18	2	4	1s	10	2T	29	1T	24	2	29	
FOREST	10½	17	23	3	2	17	4K	28	10	9	29	24q	14	(7)	
	6	29	19	27	14	16	21K	8	15	6l	1s	23q	20	19	17
Wednesday	7		1		2		1T		2l		P		2		
KEHELLAND	10½	26	14	22	(7)	23	20K	5	25	(7)	4	16q	12	24	
	6	8	16	9	18	28	25K	4	21		6q	17	2	29	
Friday	7	2		1		2		1T		2T	1		2		
ILLOGAN DOWNS	2½	13	25	18	20	11	29K	14	12	8	26	15q	19	11	
	6	9	4	1	19	15	8K	24	(7l)	18	10	4q	22	23l	(7)
Tuesday	7	1		2		1s		2T		1T	2		1		
PENGEGON	2½	14	29	21	16	12K	11	20	30	14	17	1q	8	21	
	6	10	6	21	4	12K	9	22	26	28	(7l)	25q	8	29	10
Friday	7			1					2T		1T				
ILLOGAN HIGHWAY	2½	22	9	14	12	15K	10	21	20	11	23	12q	30	10	
	6	4	(7)	12	26	13K	1s	6	19	8	18	8q	9l	10	21
Wednesday	7	1		2		1		2T		1	2		1		
TRESWITHAN	2½	25	10	23	24	(7K)	26	16	5	25	28	20q	26	21	19
	6														
Tuesday	7							1T							
ROSCROGGAN	2½	21	18	10	30	19K	24	26	14	22	8	5q	15	18	
	6	15	11	25	12	29	23	4	6	22	20	9q	6	11	26
Monday	7							2T							
PLANTATION	10½	23	15	17	25	22K	27	12	30	23	6	18q	28	14	
Tuesday	7											2T			
BEACON	2½	3	13	8	5	10K	30	12	15	5	29	27q	3	13	
Wednesday	7										1T				
TREGAJORRAN	2½	30	24	2	11K	6	22	9	19	15	10q	21	25	27	
	6	18	12	28	10K	14	19	(7)	23	26	11q	22	18	12	23
Tuesday	7	2		1		2		1T		P		2			
CONDURROW	10½	12	21	29	9K	25	12	27	13	29	22q	11	21	28	
CARTHEW	2½		30		23K		16		21		14q		29		

Names.

1 Wood, T. S. .... Camborne
2 Nance, J. ... Camborne
3 Thomas ... Troon
4 Smith G ... Camborne
5 Thomas C ... Camborne
6 Lean ... Camborne
7 Vivian E ... Tuckingmill
8 Tonkin ... Pool
9 Vivian W. 1st Tuckingmill
10 Smith W ... Camborne
11 Uren ... Illogan Downs
12 Willoughby ... Pool
13 Allen ... Camborne
14 Thomas Jno ... Camborne
15 Slater ... Pool
16 Roberts ... Forest
17 Opie ... Forest
18 Vivian W, 2nd Tuckingmill
19 Trestain ... Tuckingmill
20 Vincent ... Camborne
21 Chipman ... Pool
22 Bishop ... Pool
23 Williams ... Pool
24 Smith W. B ... Camborne
25 James ... Camborne
26 Bond ... Roscroggan
27 Harris ... Troon
28 Berryman ... Penponds
29 Lean ... Camborne

ON TRIAL.

30 J. M. .... Tuckingmill.

REFERENCES.—B. Sacrament of Baptism. —S. Sacrament of the Lord's Supper.— Q. Quarterly Collection. K. Kingswood and Woodhouse Grove Schools Collection. T. Tickets.—P. Prayer Meeting.—Quarterly Fast October 5th.

The Society Stewards will give the requisite Notices at their respective Chapels, and also remit the Connexional Collections to the Superintendent as soon as possible after they are made.

The Quarterly Meeting will be held at Camborne, on Wednesday 26 December. The Circuit Stewards will be in attendance to meet the Society Stewards at Three p.m. Tea will be provided for all the Members of the Quarterly Meeting at Five o'clock.

The Local Preachers' Meeting will be held at Camborne, on Monday December 10th, to commence at Three o'clock.

Every Preacher is expected to attend his OWN appointments, or if UNAVOIDABLY prevented, to procure HIMSELF a duly accredited substitute.

The Local Preachers being deeply impressed with the importance of a due fulfilment of the appointments, and the mischievous influence of the neglect of them, unanimously agree, that if any brother shall be found to have been absent from his appointment, without furnishing reason, which the Local Preachers' Meeting shall deem satisfactory, he shall have his name placed at the bottom of the plan, until it shall be judged proper to restore him to his former place.

NEWTON, PRINTER, BOOKBINDER, BOOKSELLER, STATIONER, &c., CAMBORNE.

Awards and Grants

In 1864 on the tercentenary of the birth of William Shakespeare, the city of Coventry held a competition for the best commemorative poem in praise of the great Bard. The adjudicators were Lord Lyttleton, G. Dawson MA, and C. Bray Esq.

In his autobiography John (3) describes how he came to enter the competition and his surprise at winning it. 'The winning of the Tercentenary Prize happened thus. A rhyming friend of mine, Mr W. Catcott[41], sent me an advertisement out from a London journal wherein was offered the prize of a gold watch for the best poem on the three hundredth anniversary of the birth of Shakespeare, advising me to compete for it. I consulted my wife about it, and she thought it would be well to try. So try I did, writing and copying my ode in two evenings by the kitchen fire when the children were sleeping in bed. I complied with the requirements of the committee, sending my poem with a motto only and my own name with a similar motto in a sealed envelope. Before posting it however I read it to my wife, and she spoke encouragingly of it. It would be nearly three months before the poem would be examined by the adjudicators, and so we had to wait. Time passed, and I had forgotten the day of the competition, going out at my Bible reading. When I came in, my wife called to me from the top of the stairs, "You have won the prize - the gold watch." And sure enough there was a telegram asserting that I was the successful competitor out of upwards of one hundred. I was invited to Coventry to participate in the presentation; but that could not be so. For this entertainment great preparation had been made. Flags were hung in the streets, and the shopkeepers closed their shops at five in the evening. The Corn Exchange was pleasingly decorated. The back of the orchestra was ornamented with crimson drapery, the city arms and choice flowering shrubs. In the centre was a facsimile of the bust of Shakespeare over his grave in Stratford Church. Wreaths, garlands and flags were arranged about the hall in tasteful profusion and the pillars were ornamented by scrolls, inscribed with the names of Shakespeare's works. The Mayor of the city, the Mayor's crier and mace-bearer wore their official costumes, and his worship announced from the platform that the first prize had been gained by my poor self.'

Although unable to attend the ceremony at Coventry, John (3) did visit Bristol, Clifton, Hereford, Worcester, Gloucester, Malvern, Birmingham and Stratford-upon-Avon later in the year, the only occasion on which he left his native county. Of Stratford, John (3) said, 'The place bound me with a wondrous spell.'

The ode contains nineteen verses and records John's immense delight and pleasure of his first introduction and reading of Shakespeare; the final verse expresses the feelings and gratitude of English-speaking peoples for the life and works of Shakespeare:

> And so, great bard, to-day
> We weave thy natal lay,
> And cluster gratefully around thy name:
> England will ever be,
> Dear Shakespeare, proud of thee,
> And coming ages but augment thy fame.

The manuscript entry of the poem was framed and mounted by Mr J.E.M. Vincent, who presented it to the

The thatched Quaker meeting-house at Come-to-Good, Feock, Cornwall.
Photographs taken June 1995

museum at Stratford in 1870.

Of the facsimile of the Shakespeare poem, James Howard Harris, the elder son of John (3), records in the biography of his father, 'It was copied in his characteristic and artistic handwriting.'

The following report from the *Falmouth Packet* newspaper of 14 May 1864 included a copy of the letter from Coventry which was enclosed with the gold watch. It certainly emphasizes how splendid the watch was, and the excellence of its makers: 'The Shakespeare Prize. The first prize was awarded to Mr J. Harris, author of *A Story of Carn Brea* etc on Saturday last, with the following letter from Coventry. "May 6 1864. Dear Sir, I send by tonight's post the gold watch awarded to you for your poem. Please send me word whether you receive it safe and sound. The watch is manufactured by one of the first of English firms, Messrs Rotherham, who have acted very liberally and made it worth twenty instead of fifteen guineas, the amount which they will be paid for it. The watch presented to the Princess of Wales was manufactured by this firm, who constantly employ upwards of two hundred hands in the different branches of the watch trade. I hope it will be satisfactory to you. I am Sir, Yours very faithfully, J.M. Vincent." The gold watch is really a handsome one. On the centre of the case is a beautiful engraving of Shakespeare surrounded with a wreath of leaves, encircled with the words "The Tercentenary of Shakespeare Coventry 1864." Inside the case are engraved those well known lines from the great bard:

To-morrow, and to-morrow, and to-morrow
Creeps in this petty pace from day to day,
To the last syllable of recorded time.

The watch reflects much credit on the great firm of Rotherham and is also an honour to the writer of the Shakespeare Tercentenary Prize Poem.'

Eight years later in 1872 John (3) received an annuity of £50 from the Royal Literary Fund, and although it is not perfectly clear this seems to have continued at least until 1875.

In April 1877 the Earl of Beaconsfield, Benjamin Disraeli, granted John (3) the sum of £200 from the Royal Bounty Fund through the efforts of Mr W.H. North, John Tremayne MP, the Earl of Mount Edgcumbe and the Right Honourable John Bright. These monies were invested in the Cornish Naval Bank, a branch of the Cornish Bank at Truro which was suspended on 4 January 1879 resulting in a loss, according to John (3), of a fair portion of it. The initial reaction of John (3) to this calamity is easy to understand, but how in retrospect he continued to be concerned is not clear. Admittedly it was

the first investment he had ever made and of course he was totally inexperienced in financial matters. In the event the Bank's Receivers announced within weeks[42] that realisation of the bank's assets together with personal assets of the partners, they were in a position to offer payments by instalments of sixteen shillings in the pound. By 1883 nineteen shillings in the pound was paid to all creditors and the final shilling some time later. It can, however, be accepted that the final payment may not have materialised until after the death of John (3). Apparently the suspension had been due to a run on the bank, where deposit monies had been invested in securities which could not be realised at short notice. As it happened the bank was reconstructed as a Limited Liability Company and opened as the Cornish Bank on 12 March 1879. It seems probable that the investment had been made on the recommendation of his friend John Gill, because it is recorded that the latter was greatly concerned at the time of suspension because he had invested in the bank for a friend.

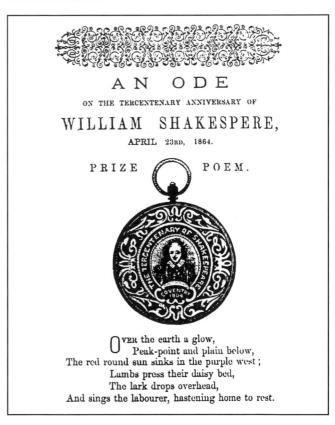

The back view of the watch presented to John (3). The opening verse of the Prize Poem is also included. The above copy is taken from Monro where it formed the frontispiece for the poem which was incorporated at the end of the book. The present whereabouts of the watch is unknown, although it must presumably have been passed down to the poet's immediate descendants.

In December 1881 the Right Honourable W.E. Gladstone, the then Prime Minister, granted John (3) £100 from the Civil List through the efforts of Earl Northbrook and T. Webber Esq.

Whether or not the confidence of John (3) was sufficiently restored to again invest in the Cornish Bank is not certain. Whatever he may have done with this slowly accumulating capital, there is no doubt that he would have been very prudent and would have spent very little of it. Besides the foregoing grants his income was obviously helped by his earnings from writing occasionally in weekly newspapers and periodicals, and more particularly the numerous religious tracts. It can also be assumed that he had some small rent from his cottage at Troon Moor until 1869 when probably he also received some payment for the unexpired portion of the lease. In fact, and not surprisingly when added together, when he died in 1884 he was worth just over four figures.

Will of John (3) and certificate of Probate to his wife Jane

Recognition

From the time of publication of the first book, the Victorian press were generous in their praise of the efforts of John (3), but winning the Shakespeare Prize was the pivot or turning point in acceptance of his place as a poet when he gained a somewhat wider although still limited following.

Very shortly after the award John (3) was invited to speak at a platform meeting in connection with the opening of the extended chapel and new school room of Troon Wesleyan Methodist Society. This took place on 31 May 1864 under the chairmanship of Capt. Charles Thomas, manager of Dolcoath Mine. Those present with him on the platform were: Dr George Smith, who had encouraged and assisted in publishing his books; Capt. Josiah Thomas, son of Capt. Charles, and who succeeded the latter as manager of Dolcoath; Mr Mark G. Pearse, chemist and father of Rev. Mark Guy Pearse (Mark Guy to Cornish Methodists); and Rev. John Rhodes, Rev. Featherstone Kellett, Rev. John Parkes and Rev. James Nance. Undoubtedly John (3) must have felt a degree of satisfaction at being invited to speak on equal terms with this distinguished platform. At this meeting Dr Smith voiced an objection to recent newspaper reports in connection with the Shakespeare Prize where John (3) was referred to as John Harris of Falmouth. Dr Smith reiterated, 'He's not John Harris of Falmouth. He is OUR John Harris, and we mean to keep him.'

In his *Poets of Methodism* (1875), Rev. S.W. Christophers devotes a whole chapter of twenty-two pages to John (3) under the title *A Bard from the Mine*. Here, the author writes in a descriptive manner quite similar in some respects to John (3) and in an allegorical context. Strangely it was generally written in the past tense although John (3) did not pass away until 1884.

Early in 1879 John (3) was elected a Fellow of the Royal Historical Society. A note of this award in the *West Briton Newspaper* of 17 April that year reads as follows: 'We understand that the Council of the Royal Historical Society have unanimously and unsolicited conferred on Mr John Harris, the Cornish Poet, the title of FRHS as being distinguished in letters.'

A year later John (3) was the recipient of congratulations from Professor H.W. Longfellow after the latter had read *Monro* which had been published in the same year.

In 1882 John (3) merited a 600-word entry in the *Dictionary of National Biography*, a distinction only accorded to a few Cornishmen.

In the same year, two years prior to John's (3) death, his friend John Gill gave a lecture at the instigation of the Governor of Earle's Retreat entitled 'John Harris the Cornish Poet'. Shortly after the death of the poet the lecture was published jointly by John Gill and the poet's younger son John Alfred (1).

In 1885 James Howard Harris, the elder son of John (3), published *John Harris the Cornish Poet*. Much of the information was the same as that contained in *My Autobiography* but there are certain further details which help to form a more complete picture of his father.

Quite lengthy references to John (3) are contained in Boase's *Collectanea Cornubiensis* of 1890 and also Boase and Courtney's *Bibliotheca Cornubiensis* published in 1894.

Some time after the Second World War, Mrs T.E. Rapson[43] donated a plaque which was affixed to the house at 84 Killigrew Street, Falmouth with the inscription:

John Harris
The Cornish Miner Poet
Lived here from 1853 until
his death in 1884.

Unfortunately the plaque was placed on the wrong house, as it was in number 85 that John (3) lived during the latter portion of his life, and also where he died. Additionally, he did not move to Falmouth until the autumn of 1857, and to number 85 before circa 1866.

Recent years have witnessed a renewed interest in the life and works of John (3) resulting in certain events and publications:

The Granite Kingdom - Poems of Cornwall, an anthology, was edited by D M Thomas and published in 1970. Containing sixty-seven poems, thirteen were by John (3).

Songs from the Earth - Selected Poems of John Harris Cornish Miner, 1820-84, also edited and with an introduction by D.M. Thomas, was published in 1977. To mark the publication of this book, an evening of Cornish Poetry was arranged by D.M. Thomas who, with Charles Causley, read works by John (3) and themselves. This event took place at Redruth Community Centre on 1 March 1977 and was sponsored by Lodenek Press of Padstow, publishers of the book, John Oliver, bookseller of Redruth, and the National Poetry Secretariat.

Cornwall in Verse, edited and introduced by Peter Redgrove, was published in 1982 and contains six excerpts from the works of John (3).

On 19 March 1984 Professor Charles Thomas[44] delivered a lecture to the Cornish Methodist Historical Association at the County Museum, Truro, entitled 'John Harris - Miner Poet of Bolenowe 1820-1884'. Professor Thomas has always evinced a great interest in Bolenowe, its families of the eighteenth and nineteenth centuries and John Harris, and has written a number of articles on these subjects.

On the occasion of the 100th anniversary of the death of John (3), a wreath of bay leaves was laid on his grave in Treslothan Churchyard by Professor Thomas, then Director of the Institute of Cornish Studies, and his relative Richard Henry Thomas of Bolenowe; the vicar, Rev. Sutcliffe, offered prayers. The inscription on the wreath read:

John Harris of Bolenowe
b. 14 October 1820 d. 7 January 1884.
A True Poet and Christian
Placed in Memory
by the Thomases of Bolenowe
7 January 1984

The wreath-layers had speculated as to whether anyone in Cornwall would also remember. John (3) certainly hoped they would and had written a second poem entitled *The Request* in which he asked for wild flowers to be put on his grave:

I hear far off diviner songs
Than ever filled my soul
When boyhood roved, with careless feet,
Where clearest waters roll.
The echoes float with silver tongues
O'er dearest lake and lea:
So, Cornwall, I have in my heart
One thing to ask of thee.

'Tis not a great thing, is it now,
That I would humbly crave?
A few of Cornwall's hedgerow gems
Upon my village grave!
The wild rose from the crooked lane,
Beside the mossy well,
The cowslip and the violet,
The primrose from the dell.

I've loved them long, I've loved them much,
And now I love them more,
And surely I shall love them still
When life and toil are o'er.
So through the mist of gathering tears,
By holiest feeling led,
I ask that thou would'st nurture there
The wild flowers o'er my head.

And when the dusk is on the hills,
And in the listening vales,
And the bat round the belfry-caves
In airy circles sails.
I'll stoop from emerald heights unknown,
Where love for ever sings,
And fan upon my silent grave
The wild flowers with my wings.

A few of the poems of John (3) have been set to music:

(1) *The Winding Wye* by Shirley Kelder

(2) *Jane's Epistle to her Uncle*
Jane finding a Primrose in February
A Lullaby for Jane
My Infant Daughter falling asleep on my Knee

The music for these poems was arranged by Geoffrey Self of Redruth and was first performed on 1 August 1985 at Trelowarren House, near Helston, as part of the '1985 Season of Music at Trelowarren' and 'European Music Year'. The artistes were Margaret Bird, soprano, and Peter Bone, guitar. It is interesting to reflect on the reaction of John (3) had he heard the strains of the guitar set to his poems, but one feels assured that he would have been as delighted as those of us who were privileged to attend the performance. The Jane of the poems was the elder daughter of John (3).

Included in 1985 was a reference to John (3) in *The Oxford Companion to English Literature* edited by Margaret Drabble.

On 21 November 1986, and repeated on 4 November 1988, a television programme entitled 'Mystic Melody' was broadcast by BBC South West. The script was written and narrated by D.M. Thomas, the Cornish poet and novelist of best-selling fame, who grew up almost within sight of Six Chimneys. This celebration of the works of John (3) was a superb and sincere performance with the poems *The Burial* and *Gyllyngdune* set to music by Michael Head and sung by Wendy Eathorne soprano, also born in the locality and a renowned opera singer. *The Burial* was

Concerts for 1985 Summer Season

June 6th	TRESILLIAN LADIES CHOIR - Concert includes Cornish poetry ★ Includes Buffet Supper ★
June 13th	CHIMBA CHAMBER GROUP - Woodwind Concert
June 20th	LYDIAN STRING QUARTET - Royal Academy of Music students
June 27th	NO CONCERT (replaced by concert on Sunday 22nd)
July 4th	DUCHY OPERA SOLOISTS - Opera Highlights, Voices and Piano ★ Includes Buffet Supper ★
July 11th	TERENCE NETTLE AND ALAN CLAY - Violin and Piano
July 18th	RAYMOND TRETHEWEY & FRIENDS - Baritone, Soprano, Violin and Piano
July 25th	TRIO ZAFARAN - Clarinet, Soprano and Piano Martha Kingdon-Ward, Patricia Boynton, Paul Comeau ★ Includes Buffet Supper★
August 1st	MUSIC THROUGH THE AGES - Adele Berntzen, Margaret Bird, Peter Bone, Martin Hall - Mezzo-Soprano, Soprano, Guitar, Keyboard
August 8th	ELIZABETH & HOWARD ROOKE - Piano Duettists
August 15th	ALISON JANE - Solo Piano
August 22nd	PARNASSAS ENSEMBLE - String consort from the Royal Academy of Music
August 29th	THE SHEPPARDS & TESS SWAN - Violins, Cello and Piano ★ Includes Buffet Supper ★
September 5th	CELTIC BRASS ENSEMBLE

These concerts are arranged by the TRELOWARREN FELLOWSHIP, a Christian group of several denominations which uses part of Trelowarren House. It encourages deeper appreciation and enjoyment of any aspect of spiritual or artistic activity. You are welcome to become a Member. We are especially keen to encourage young musicians, so please tell us if you know any who would like to perform here.
FELLOWSHIP members wearing STEWARD badges will gladly help you to feel at home at all concerts. Please ask if you would like more information, or would like to be kept informed about future concerts.
THE STEINWAY GRAND PIANO used at Trelowarren is provided with generous help from the RADCLIFFE TRUST and LADY VYVYAN.
Responsible musicians are welcome to play this piano - occasionally or regularly - by arrangement with the Warden (Mawgan 366).

TRELOWARREN FELLOWSHIP

1985 Season
Music at Trelowarren

Thursdays at Eight

Programme

Reproduced by kind permission of Geoffrey Self, the Composer

enacted by children from Carnkie Junior School in a never to be forgotten performance.

In 1987 Roger and Esther Race included a short but informative article on John (3) in their booklet *Cornish Company*.

More recently, in 1994, Paul Newman in his book *The Meads of Love* has produced a masterly analysis and assessment of the poetry of John (3) and his struggle against the odds. Publication by Dyllansow Truran was preceded by a Conversation Piece by the Author and D.M. Thomas which took place in the City Council Chamber at Truro, and organised by the Cornish Literary Guild.

Quite frequently short articles appear in various periodicals and newspapers which serve to draw attention to the Miner/Poet but by their nature do not tend to present an in-depth picture.

From the foregoing it will be seen that interest is being renewed and is growing, which is much in line with the hope of John (3) as expressed in his preface to *Carn Brea* in 1863:

Go little book from this my solitude,
I cast thee on the waters, go thy ways,
And if, as I believe, thy vein is good,
The world will find thee after many days.

The Chapel at Trelowarren House where some of John Harris' poems were sung by soprano Margaret Bird in August 1985 accompanied by Peter Bone on the guitar.

The photograph is reproduced by kind permission of Sir Ferrers Vyvan Bt. of Trelowarren

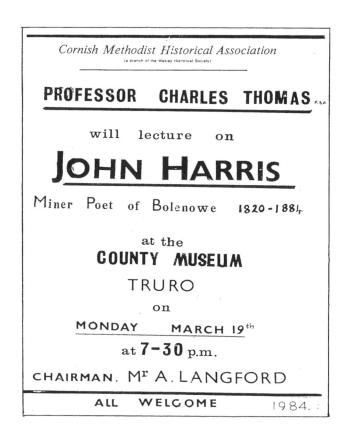

Poster for the Exhibition arranged by Tina Pentney in 1996

Book launch at Camborne on 16 May 1995 of The Meads of Love, the Life and poetry of John Harris 1820-84, by Paul Newman.

Photograph L-R. Jim Thomas - Area Director Lloyds Bank who sponsored the ceremony; Professor Charles Thomas; Arthur Langford, great-nephew of John Harris; Mike Rattue Local Manager Lloyds Bank. Seated - Paul Newman, holding a photograph of John Harris.

Jane Rule Harris

Jane, the eldest child of John (3) and Jane Rule, was born 1 April 1846 and baptized at Treslothan Church the following July.

She was born in the two-roomed cottage at Polgine, Troon, where the family lived for a couple of years after her birth until they moved to the cottage that her father had had built at Troon Moor. Young Jane, as we have already discovered, was one of the three lives on the lease of the cottage.

Jane would have been eleven years old when they moved to Falmouth but no record of her education has come to light, although the 1861 Falmouth census listed her as attending school when she would have been fifteen. The 1871 census does not indicate her occupation and so it would seem that she was at home, where no doubt her mother required assistance in caring for the youngest member of the family, John Alfred, who had been born with curvature of the spine.

During her childhood years at Troon, Jane and her younger sister Lucretia often accompanied their father on his poetry-making nature walks and rambles. The company of these children gave John (3) immense joy and pleasure and he wrote a number of poems about and for them. Actually he wrote upwards of twenty about his four children. Two of these poems especially about Jane are included here:

A Lullaby for Jane

Hush, my darling! hark, my child,
To the cold winds roaring wild
Through the hollow, round the height,
On this wintry market-night.
Let us strive to heed it not,
Shelter'd in our humble cot,
Puss and I and little Jane,
Waiting for Mamma again,
Who has promised home to bring
To her babe some pretty thing.
Hush, wild wind! shine out, fair moon!
That kind Mamma may haste here soon,
Through the long, the miry lane,
With some pretty things for Jane.

Jane finding a Primrose in February

Ho, Ho, pale flower, what strange mishap
Could throw thee here on Winter's lap?
Jane saw thee by the village way
Look up with yellow eye,
'Mid cold snow-heaps that round thee lay
Beneath a frowning sky:
And so she gather'd thee, and brought
The treasure where the snows are not.

She knew the biting, blustering storm
Would rave upon thy lovely form,
And pity could not bear to see
The little stranger pale
The savage sport of Winter's glee,
Rock'd by the frigid gale;
She could not leave thee thus alone,
And so she made thee all her own.

She deem'd the pleasant lays of Spring
From thy sweet lips were murmuring;
And as she gazed on thy wan face,
And thought of days to come,
She pluck'd thee from thy native place,
And bore thee to her home,
'To whisper hope' when griefs o'erpower,
And skies grow dark, and tempests lour.

Perchance she thought sad sorrow's tear
Did on thy yellow lids appear,
And so she could not leave thee there,
By cruel blasts defiled;
Batter'd with hail and chilling air,
In Winter's footprint wild.
She could not leave thee 'neath such skies;
And now thou art her cherish'd prize.

If it were some unheeding boy
Who pluck'd thee in his freak of joy,
We might be angry with the lad
Who thus had stripp'd the bower;
And it might make our bosoms sad
To lose thee, favourite flower;
But when 'tis Jane who roams the Mead,
We only love her for the deed.

Farewell, pale flower; thy reign was brief,
To see but not to savour grief,
On wintry wild to ope thine eye,
'Mid ice and chilling sleet;
To taste the bliss of life and die
Thus early, village sweet;
To lose thy place in Spring's loved throng,
And bloom a summer life of song.

During her late teens or early twenties, Jane became acquainted with Jonathon Worsdell of Penryn and they were married at Treslothan Church 11 May 1871 by Rev. George T. Bull.

Unlike her parents' marriage ceremony, there were many more people present. The register was signed by her father, the bridegroom's brother Henry and three

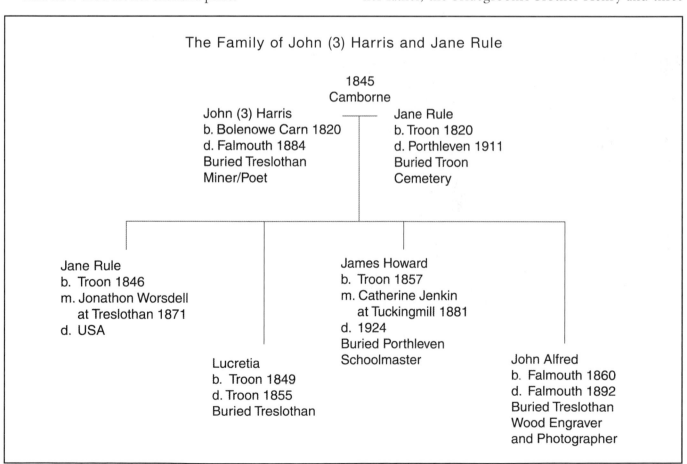

The Family of John (3) Harris and Jane Rule

1845
Camborne

John (3) Harris
b. Bolenowe Carn 1820
d. Falmouth 1884
Buried Treslothan
Miner/Poet

Jane Rule
b. Troon 1820
d. Porthleven 1911
Buried Troon
Cemetery

Jane Rule
b. Troon 1846
m. Jonathon Worsdell
   at Treslothan 1871
d. USA

Lucretia
b. Troon 1849
d. Troon 1855
Buried Treslothan

James Howard
b. Troon 1857
m. Catherine Jenkin
   at Tuckingmill 1881
d. 1924
Buried Porthleven
Schoolmaster

John Alfred
b. Falmouth 1860
d. Falmouth 1892
Buried Treslothan
Wood Engraver
and Photographer

other friends. Jonathon was about two years younger than Jane, the eldest son of Jonathon and Ann Ackerly Worsdell. Both father and son were described as curriers (to dress or treat leather). Jonathon senior had a business in Lower Market Street, Penryn, and also at 13 Market Street, Falmouth, and Jonathon junior was employed by his father as was his brother Henry. Another younger brother, Alfred, was a carpenter and subsequently emigrated to America and enlisted in the American Army in 1881; he served in the 12th Regiment of Infantry for six years and was honourably discharged in 1886. Alfred later became an American citizen, being attested by Jonathon junior as being of good moral character.

The first child of Jane and Jonathon, John Alfred, was born 31 March 1872 at which time the family was living at Clifton Place, Falmouth. Registration of the birth was made by Jane.

Between the date of John Alfred's birth and the birth of their second child, Beatrice Jane, on 13 October 1873 the family had moved to South Hinksey, Berkshire.[45] This suggests that Jonathon had ceased to work for his father, possibly because his earnings were insufficient to provide for a growing family. Among some Cornish business owners there was a tendency to assume that their offspring, when employed in the business, did not require much in the way of remuneration based on the

assumption that their children would inherit the business in due course of time! We know that Jonathon did not return to his father's business after the family returned to Falmouth where their third child, Henry Howard, was born on 13 January 1876. In fact, he set up in business on his own account at 97 Killigrew Street.[46] From this address on 18 and 25 March 1876 Jonathon placed an advertisement in the *Penryn Advertiser* (whose editor and owner was John Gill) which read as follows: 'Wanted respectable youths as apprentices to the currying trade, also at clicking in boot upper trade, also girls as apprentices in boot upper trade.' However, Jonathon junior's attempt to have his own business was doomed to failure as on 23 November 1876 the following notice appeared in the *West Briton* newspaper: 'On 10 ultimo, Jonathon Worsdell, jnr., of Falmouth, Currier etc. a bankrupt, charged on a warrant with having forged a certain undertaking for payment of money, to wit, any dishonoured bills of the said J. Worsdell the younger. He is 28 years of age, 5 feet 8 or 9 inches high, medium build, fair complexion, very pale, light-brown hair, blue eyes, slight whiskers on upper part of cheek and no moustache, a large mouth and prominent lips. £50 reward will be paid by Mr Chirgwin of Truro, the trustee of the estate of the said J Worsdell, jnr., to any person giving such information as shall lead to his apprehension. Information to be given to

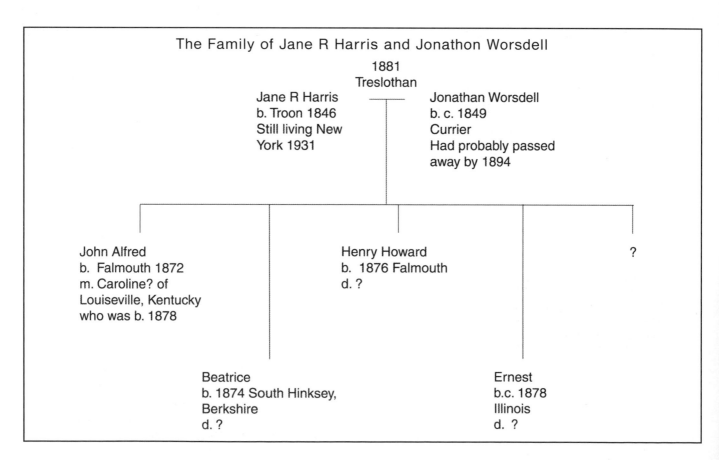

The Family of Jane R Harris and Jonathon Worsdell

1881
Treslothan

Jane R Harris
b. Troon 1846
Still living New
York 1931

Jonathan Worsdell
b. c. 1849
Currier
Had probably passed
away by 1894

John Alfred
b. Falmouth 1872
m. Caroline? of
Louiseville, Kentucky
who was b. 1878

Henry Howard
b. 1876 Falmouth
d. ?

?

Beatrice
b. 1874 South Hinksey,
Berkshire
d. ?

Ernest
b.c. 1878
Illinois
d. ?

Sergeant Bourne, of the Falmouth Borough police.' It would appear from this that Jonathon junior had been declared bankrupt prior to his return to Falmouth. As can be imagined this turn of events came as a considerable shock to John (3) and his family, but as will be remembered it was his Quaker associates who provided him with solace and comfort and this concern by these friends caused him to immediately compose the poem *The Friends*.

Following promulgation of the notice we find that in mid-1877 Jonathon senior transferred the Penryn business to his son Henry, but despite much publicity regarding the transfer the arrangement did not stand the test of time. Henry also emigrated to America where he died in tragic circumstances on 23 December 1897 in Quincy, Massachusetts, being run over by a train.

It has not been possible to obtain the precise facts, but it seems that Jonathon junior probably boarded a fishing boat at Falmouth and slipped across the channel to France. We know from information contained in an application by his son John Alfred Worsdell for an American passport to visit England in 1909 that the latter stated that his father had embarked at Le Havre for America. We know that Jonathon eventually settled in the USA.

John Alfred Worsdell and son Alfred John Worsdell.
Original photograph by H & J C Burrows,
Camborne 1909

Jane Rule Harris
Original photograph taken by her brother
John Alfred (1) Harris

But what of Jane and the children? Again it has not been possible to locate their names on a ship's passenger list, but it seems probable that once Jonathon had arrived in North America he sent for them to join him. Yet again we turn to a poem by John (3) which he called *The Last Lullaby*, composed in August 1877. From this date it can be assumed that at some time within ten months of Jonathon absconding the family were together again. Perhaps what is more important is that Jane forgave him and remained with him! The poem comprised four verses which, excepting the first verse, is quoted below:

> The evening star shone o'er the lake,
> And a mystic melody filled the brake;
> The brooklet murmured along the dell,
> Where the glow-worms glittered beside the well;
> And still that young wife's last refrain
> Flowed forth a-near the lattice-pane,
> So softly sad, so meekly mild:
> 'Lulla-by, baby! sleep, my child!'

> Ah! marvel not that my soul is stirred;
> My daughter's voice was the sound I heard,
> Which haunts me still when the day is dim,
> And the fields o'erflow with the milkmaid's hymn:
> For she's gone, she's gone to the western land,
> Where the lakes are broad and the forests grand,
> To sing where the dark pines fringe the wild,
> 'Lulla-by, baby! sleep, my child!'

But God is there, where the eagle soars,
And the grand Niagara ever roars;
Where the boundless prairie strangely swells,
And the red man roams through the pathless dells.
Yes, God is there; and her heart will rise
To Him, when the white moon fills the skies;
And her nursery chant shall murmur mild:
'Lulla-by, baby! sleep, my child!'

Jonathon applied for American citizenship on 22 September 1886, which was granted on 5 October 1888. Besides the foregoing he was also included on the 1892 Registered Voters and Poll List for Cook County; the family were then resident at 216 Humboldt Park, Precinct 9, Chicago where they had lived since 1886.

**Jane (Rule) Harris wife of John (3) (Standing)
Jane R Harris her elder daughter (Seated)**

Original photograph taken by John Alfred (1) Harris circa 1876

According to the 1880 Cook County census they had a further son, Ernest, born in Illinois circa 1878. Whether this birth completed their family is not known.

An article in the *Penryn Advertiser* of 14 July 1894 indicates that Jane moved in that year to Columbus (presumably Ohio), so it would seem to be in order to assume that Jonathon had passed away by this time. Probably one or other of her children or family friends were at that time living in Columbus. The article clearly demonstrates that Jane had continued to abide by the lessons and precepts learned in her youth:

Presentation to a Cornish Woman

At Chicago, United States of America recently Mrs Worsdell (daughter of the late John Harris, Cornish Poet) on the occasion of her removing from Chicago to Columbus, was presented by the Ladies of St George Lodge, of which she is a member, with a handsome gold badge in the shape of a Roman Cross attached to a bar with her name and the name of the lodge engraved on it. The presentation was made by the President, Mrs Dale with a memorial which was signed by the ladies of the lodge as a token of their love and respect for her as a useful member among the sick and poor in her district. The ladies of St Luke's Church Guild also presented her with a beautiful quilt which they had worked for her. The presentations were made at the residence of Mrs Baragwanath who gave a luncheon at the farewell meeting which was fully attended and all united in wishing her health and prosperity in her new home.

It should be recorded that apparently Jane had attended the Friends' Meetings at Falmouth prior to leaving for America. There is a pencilled note to this effect in the Monthly Meeting List.

Jane did not long remain in Columbus, for in Mark Smith Harris' diary it is noted that by 1897 she was living at 429 Eighth Street, Brooklyn, New York. She was still resident in Brooklyn in 1931 and it was here that her eldest son was also living.

In mid-1909 Jane came over from New York to visit her relatives in Troon and the village in which she had been born. Jane was accompanied by her eldest son, John Alfred Worsdell and his wife Caroline together with their young son, Alfred John, who had been born in Brooklyn, New York, on 6 March 1902. According to the *Cornish Post and Mining News*[47] Jane's mother had come up from Porthleven and stayed with her at the home of Mrs Thomas Carter in Troon.

Lucretia (1) Harris

Lucretia, the second daughter of John (3) and Jane, was born 10 august 1849 in the house at Troon Moor that her father had had built. She was baptized at Troon Wesleyan Chapel on 18 February 1850. John (3) wrote a poem about her when she was only a week old, and the last line of the following verse was more true than he must have realised at the time:

> Thou camest with the crystal stars, even when
>   thy tuneful sire
> Was wandering o'er poetic heaths with his
>   untutor'd lyre.
> Ah! hadst thou not a loving smile, upon thy
>   happy face,
> As if a cherub for a while had left its holy place?

As previously mentioned, John (3) took her for rambles with her older sister Jane. Indeed these two little girls became his inseparable companions on his walks when seeking inspiration for his poetry making. A poem which John (3) wrote much later describes their waiting for him to come home from his work at Dolcoath and their excitement at his coming:

> Where'er I go, whate'er I do,
> A vision meets mine eye
> From the far valleys of the past,
> Flecked with the summer sky.
> It comes in days of quiet trust,
> It comes in wind and rain,
> It comes when harvest crowns the earth –
> The faces at the pane.
>
> When toiling in the darksome mine,
> As tired as tired can be,
> How has the glad thought cheered my soul, –
> My children watch for me!
> And as I oped the garden gate,
> Which led into the lane,
> How danced my heart to see once more
> The faces at the pane!
>
> Two little girls, with gleaming eyes,
> With soft and shining hair,
> And sweetest prattle on their lips,
> Were watching for me there.
> One in the grave is sleeping now,
> And one has crossed the main;
> Yet still I see, where'er I be,
> The faces at the pane.

> And when I brought some hedgerow fruit,
> Or darling hedgerow flowers,
> Which they were early taught to love,
> Their kisses came in showers.
> O, precious were those distant days,
> Which may not come again,
> Made brighter, fairer, fresher for
> The faces at the pane.
>
> Old age has bound me in its bands,
> And o'er the solemn sea
> I seem to hear mysterious sounds
> From unknown lake and lea.
> But through the cares that lie behind,
> Along the murky plain,
> I see, as if but yesterday,
> The faces at the pane.
>
> Few retrospects have greater joy,
> Now life is waning fast,
> And fewer visions sun my soul
> Like this from out the past.
> And thank I Him who giveth much
> Our gratitude to gain,
> Not least among his greater gifts
> The faces at the pane.

from The Faces at the Pane

Unfortunately the joy of John (3) at Lucretia's presence was short lived as she contracted pneumonia and after a short illness of seven days passed away on 23 December 1855. She was six years and five months old. The funeral was held on Christmas day which must have increased the poignancy and grief of John (3) and his family. The burial was in the graveyard at Treslothan Church, consecrated just eight years previously in 1847; from this time the grave locations of the Harrises became reasonably certain, unlike that of Lucretia's grandfather John (2) and her great and great-great grandparents.

John has very discerningly expressed his feelings at the death of Lucretia in a poem of that name, and also his pleasure at her grave being in the peace and tranquillity of Treslothan Churchyard:

> And art thou gone so soon?
> And is thy loving, gentle spirit fled?
> Ah! is my fair, my passing beautiful,
> My loved Lucretia number'd with the dead?
> Ah! art thou gone so soon?
>
> I miss thee, daughter, now,
> In the dear nooks of earth we oft have trod;
> And a strange longing fills my yearning soul
> To sleep with thee, and be, like thee, with God!
> I miss thee, daughter now.

I miss thee at day's close,
When from my labour I regain my cot,
And sit down sadly at the supper-board,
Looking for thee, but, ah! I see thee not:
I miss thee at day's close.

When I and little Jane
Walk hand in hand along the old hill's way.
Shall we not feel they cherub-presence, love,
Singing our psalms in the twilight grey?
I soon shall go to thee.

Hush, murmuring spirit, hush!
It is the Lord, He only, who hath given;
And He hath taken - blessed be His name -
The gem, which fell from paradise, to heaven;
I bow and kiss His rod.

from *On the Death of My Daughter Lucretia*

'Tis where the tree-tops wave,
And gleam with glory 'neath the summer's sun,
And gentle breathings steal among the boughs,
When busy day is done.

'Tis where the village church
Among the dews its solemn shadow throws,
When silvery lyrics o'er the dingles float,
At evening's gentle close.

Above it shine the stars,
Around it woods and rocky mountains rise:
O, let it be the poet's sepulchre,
When death has seal'd his eyes!

from *Lucretia's Grave*

James Howard Harris

James Howard, the third child and elder son, was also born in the cottage at Troon Moor about six months prior to the family moving to Falmouth. He was born 15 January 1857 and baptized at Troon Wesleyan Chapel on 17 April the same year.

Howard was to be no exception to the habit of John (3) in writing poems about his children; he wrote the first poem about Howard on the occasion of his first birthday, just in time for its inclusion in *The Land's End, Kynance Cove and Other Poems*. The first two verses read:

'Tis pleasant, on thy natal morn,
The first birthday since thou wert born,
To pause amid life's busy scene,
With clouds and sunny streaks between;
And carol with a father's joy
A song for thee, my first-born boy.

Thy mother, with the tenderest love,
Hangs fondly o'er her smiling dove;
And as thou chatterest in thy glee,
'Tis like Apollo's lute to me.
Accept thy sister's tiny toy,
On this thy first birthday, my boy.

Howard received his formative education at Kimberley Classical School[48] in Killigrew Street, Falmouth. The school subsequently changed its name to Kimberley Grammar School, and stood on the site of the present Technical College. It was under the Headmastership of J. Broad Ede FRGS, and its curriculum offered a course of study comprising, French, Latin and English Languages, mathematics including Euclid, algebra and mensuration, political geography, ancient and modern history, analysis and composition, mapping, penmanship and religious instruction. Certainly a far cry from that which had been available to his father!

In 1872 when fifteen years old, it is recorded[49] that Howard took the examination papers at Kimberley Classical School, not for a prize but for the honour, and came out first in several of the subjects, and that he was to be engaged after the Christmas vacation as Assistant Teacher in the school. In fact, in 1873 Howard was listed as Assistant English Master.

Howard also studied geology as an adjunct to his other studies, probably resulting from a desire to learn more of the structure and mineralisation of his native county, about which no doubt he had been an avid listener to his father's descriptions of the occurrence and crystalline structures of the copper and tin ores in Dolcoath. In mid-1875 he took the South Kensington (Imperial College) advanced examination in geology, through Penryn

Science and Art Classes, and obtained a second-class certificate.

Following his stint as Assistant English Master at Falmouth, Howard entered for a course of study at Exeter Diocesan Training College, which later changed its name to St Luke's College.

On completion of his course at Exeter, Howard applied to the newly-formed (1876) Sithney School Board[50] for the position of Master of Trannack Board School, but he was unsuccessful. Nothing daunted he then applied for the same position at Porthleven Board School and was awarded the appointment effective from 25 March 1878. In this appointment he was more fortunate in the matter of salary because Porthleven was worth £100 per annum, whereas Trannack was worth only £90.[51] Howard duly opened the school on 8 April 1878 and reported the following in the school log book: 'I James Howard Harris late of the Training College Exeter, opened this school today. Mr James (clerk) and Mr Rowe (member) of the Sithney School Board were present. The premises were formerly known as Porthleven Wesleyan Sunday School but hereafter the Porthleven Board School.' There were ninety-two pupils on the roll.

Just over five months later, on 27 September, Howard applied to the Board for permission to use the school for evening classes and received their unanimous approval. It is recorded by Rev. Rex Hurral, then Vicar of Porthleven[52] and one of the School Governors, that on 9 October 1893 the Board School began evening classes for those too old to come to school in the daytime. It began with thirty-nine young men and eighteen young women who came to learn the basic elements of education. One assumes the foregoing to be an extension of the classes which Howard had first started in 1878. A further innovation by Howard was the introduction in October 1878 of a lending library for the pupils. The books were obtained from the Religious Tract Society and Howard loaned a bookcase in which to keep the books. At the presentation of prizes at the school in December 1878, it was noted that the examiner's report reflected credit on the Master, and by July 1892 Howard's salary was increased to £120 per annum.

In an interesting entry in the school log book for 21 June 1878 Howard noted: 'Several boys temporarily left school to take part in the approaching pilchard fishery.' The entry is evidence that although compulsory attendance was introduced in 1876 it was not enforced until 1882.

Recollections and impressions of Howard have been recorded by some of his pupils: the late Bert Cowls remembered that Howard was very patriotic. On Empire Day Howard would give them a talk on 'The Great Traditions of the British Empire' coupled with the pupils singing *Rule Britannia* and then writing an essay about their pride in the Union Flag. Bert also recalled that during the First World War, Howard would read the latest war news to the whole school at assembly. Bert was also grateful for the opportunity to study in Howard's evening classes.

Mrs Joseph Williams, née Susie Pascoe, recalled that Howard was a very strict disciplinarian and always insisted on being called Master. His strictness was very noticeable on Monday mornings after he had taken preaching services on Sunday! She had private tuition from Howard and became an Assistant Teacher in the Infants' School, and treasured an evening class prize she received from him. During her studies her parents bought a bookcase for her from Howard; when it was delivered to their house they found that he had included fifteen volumes of Shakespeare for her!

Fred Lavin Matthews also recalled that at assembly each morning Howard always chose the same hymn, *New Every Morning is the Love*. He remembered Howard as a keen gardener and had a boyhood mental picture of espalier apple trees trained against the garden walls of Pendower, the house which Howard had had built just after the turn of the century and subsequently moved into circa 1907 from his original home in Peveral Terrace.

Howard retired from the school in 1922 having served for forty-four years. Some time after his death his children presented the school with a silver cup as a memorial to their father. Currently the cup is awarded annually to the scholar of the Junior and Infants' School in the third of four age groups for proficiency in handwriting.

Besides being a Methodist Lay Preacher, and like his father before him walking to all his appointments, he was active in the society at Porthleven and also had a literary bent. Howard contributed to *Review of Reviews* and other periodicals, together with the *Cornish Telegraph*. In 1884 he published *John Harris the Cornish Poet - The Story of His Life* which was an updated, but generally similar in detail to, *My Autobiography* by his father. For some inexplicable reason the author's name is recorded on the title page as *John* Howard Harris! In June 1889 Howard edited an article for *Camborne Wesleyan Circuit Magazine and Monthly Greeting* entitled Early Days of Methodism in Troon. This article was based on the diaries of Capt. Jimmy Thomas of Bolenowe, the man who opened his library doors to Howard's father; the diaries had originally been copied by Mark Smith Harris, Howard's uncle and the writer's grandfather.

Howard also wrote a little poetry. Two of his poems, *A Cornish Welcome* and *Woven Fancies*, being published in 1892.[53] Howard became joint editor with Rev. John Barnes of Redruth of the *Cornish Methodist Church Record* which they first published in January 1893. He was also joint author with Martin Veall of *Porthleven - Scenes from the History of a Cornish Fishing Village* published in 1885.

Elected a Fellow of the Royal Historical Society on 15 December 1892 he resigned, for what reason it has not been possible to ascertain, on 19 March 1908. Howard also merited an eighty-one word entry in *Collectanea Cornubiensis* - G.C. Boase, 1890.

At Tuckingmill Parish Church on 4 August 1881, Howard married Catherine Jenkin of Roscroggan near Camborne. Catherine was the daughter of Henry Jenkin, a farmer. At her marriage Catherine was said to be a school mistress. She was in fact a certificated teacher and probably had attended Truro Diocesan Training College, but unfortunately there appears to be no extant records of the period when she would have been a student there.

On 28 October 1887 Catherine was appointed Assistant Teacher at Porthleven Board School at a salary of £30 per annum, and on 13 September 1890 she became Mistress of Porthleven Infants' School, when her salary was increased to £70 per annum. Catherine remained in this capacity until her retirement in 1911.

A devout Christian and Society Class Leader, Catherine's life was not without its sorrows for she lost two daughters, Elizabeth Jane Mildred and Vera Jane,

as infants at one year and one year eight months old respectively. Catherine led a busy life. For nineteen of her twenty-two years service at Porthleven Infants' School she, in addition to caring for her immediate family, cared for her mother-in-law Jane, the wife of John (3). Jane was seventy-one years old when she came to live with Catherine and ninety when she died. Three of Howard's and Catherine's children outlived their parents. Catherine Winifred (Winnie), their first child, was born with a deformity of the hip which necessitated her wearing special footwear for the whole of her life. Winnie was, however, a pianist of considerable talent and spent a lot of her time as a young woman organising concerts in aid of various chapel funds. Winnie married William Polglase, a shoemaker of Porthleven, in the spring of 1906. Her father had a bungalow built for the young couple at Breage village where they resided all their married life. The bungalow was named Pendower, the same name as the house Howard had had built for himself at Porthleven. There were no children of the marriage. Winnie died at Breage on 14 May 1963 and was buried at Porthleven. William lived on for another eight years, passing away on 23 May 1971 and was interred with Winnie in their beloved Porthleven.

Howard and Catherine's third child, Cora Milicent,

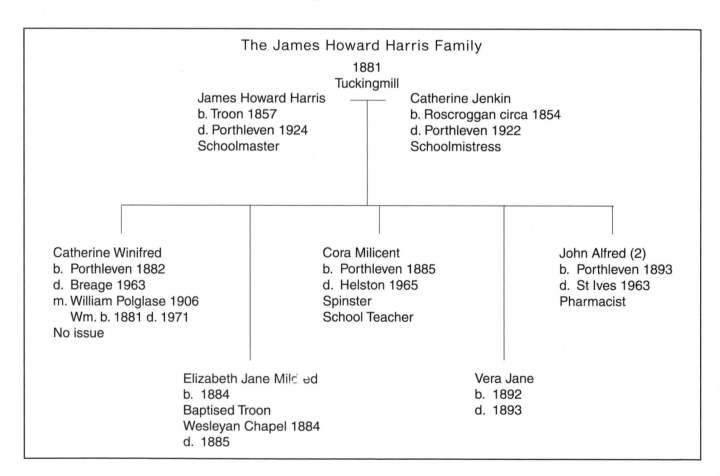

The James Howard Harris Family

1881
Tuckingmill

James Howard Harris
b. Troon 1857
d. Porthleven 1924
Schoolmaster

Catherine Jenkin
b. Roscroggan circa 1854
d. Porthleven 1922
Schoolmistress

Catherine Winifred
b. Porthleven 1882
d. Breage 1963
m. William Polglase 1906
    Wm. b. 1881 d. 1971
No issue

Cora Milicent
b. Porthleven 1885
d. Helston 1965
Spinster
School Teacher

John Alfred (2)
b. Porthleven 1893
d. St Ives 1963
Pharmacist

Elizabeth Jane Mildred
b. 1884
Baptised Troon
Wesleyan Chapel 1884
d. 1885

Vera Jane
b. 1892
d. 1893

was born on 7 October 1885, just five months after the death of their second child, Elizabeth Jane Mildred. Cora attended Porthleven Board School and on 2 October 1899 was appointed by the Board as a Probationer Teacher at the school and awaited confirmation of the appointment by H.M. Inspector. A timetable of her studies had been arranged by Howard, which also awaited the Inspector's approval. By 1900 she was listed as a paid monitor. In her quarterly pupil teachers' examinations 1902–03 she did very well, averaging over 80% marks, Howard having prepared her for the examinations. In due course she was appointed as a teacher in the Infants' School, and remained there until her father's retirement when she obtained an appointment at Mullion Council School and lived in a small bungalow on her own at Poldhu by the bridge. The bungalow is no longer extant. Cora never married. Some of her pupils at Mullion still remember her with affection and esteem. In the eventide of life Cora suffered a stroke and leaving Poldhu went to live with Winnie and William at Breage. Later she became a patient at Meneage Hospital, Heston, where she died on 19 September 1965. Cora was also brought back to her home village for burial and was interred with her only brother John Alfred (2) Harris.

Howard and Catherine's only son, John Alfred (2), was born at Porthleven on 26 August 1893 and grew up in this delightful fishing village, becoming very interested in all matters connected with the sea. Mrs Joseph Williams remembered a large photograph at Pendower of John Alfred (2) as a boy kitted out in oilskins and sou'wester. John Alfred (2) trained and qualified as a pharmacist and served in the army in the First World War, seeing service in Germany and Italy. It was perhaps inevitable that he would later find employment on board an ocean liner. Eventually up to the time of his death he was employed by Sampsons (St Ives) Limited, Pharmacy, of Market Place, St Ives, Cornwall, and lived during this period at Lelant. He died suddenly at the pharmacy on 19 December 1963 and was laid to rest at Porthleven. In the interest of authenticity it should be noted that the year of death recorded on the gravestone is incorrect. It should read 1963 not 1964.

Catherine died 26 February 1922 and although she had been in failing health for some time her death was unexpected. There were marked expressions of sympathy from the whole village and especially from her ex-pupils. The procession to the Wesleyan Chapel was headed by members of her Society Class, and interment took place at Porthleven.

Howard lived on for another two years but died on 29 May 1924 aged sixty-seven. He had been on holiday in the Lake District and had preached at a small village chapel there exactly one week prior to his burial. Additionally he had been planned to preach at Porthleven on the day of his burial. At the funeral service Rev. E.J. Chappell spoke of Howard's sterling qualities as a local preacher, citizen and schoolmaster. The procession to the graveyard was headed by almost all the local preachers in the circuit and there was a large and representative attendance of the people of his adopted village and from the district round about.

James Howard Harris

'Pendower', the house that James Howard Harris had had built for his family circa 1906 at Pendeen Road, Porthleven

John Alfred (1) Harris

John Alfred (1), the second son and fourth child of John (3) and Jane, was born at 7 Wellington Terrace, Falmouth, on 17 February 1859.

Doctor John Alfred Langford[54] of Birmingham was a friend of the family and an avid supporter of the poetical talents of John (3); it seems that the new arrival in the poet's family was named after him. However, it may be that it was solely the Alfred which was derived from this source; certainly Alfred was a new name among the Harrises.

Like his brother Howard, Alfred received his formative education at Falmouth Classical School but which by this time had changed its name to Grammar School. In December 1872 it is recorded that at the Kimberley Grammar School Prize Day Alfred was awarded a third-class prize for writing.

Alfred was afflicted from birth with curvature of the spine; this deformity undoubtedly presented a problem in selecting an occupation where the work would be such as could be carried out with this disability, and so Alfred decided to teach himself the art of drawing and cutting sketches on wood blocks. From 1875 onwards Alfred's woodcuts were used to illustrate his father's books and tracts. Additionally we find that Alfred advertised in the local press to the effect that he carried out 'Wood engravings of all kinds of machinery, shop fronts and book illustrations, cut in blocks for printing and photographs'. Alfred's first woodcuts appeared in *Walks with Wild Flowers* by John (3) and in the preface to the book John (3) wrote, 'Rude as they may be considered to appear, I hope they are an earnest of more successful efforts, and will win my feeble boy many friends.' Later, when in 1885 his brother Howard and Martin Veall published *Porthleven, Past and Present*, the woodcut of the First Porthleven Methodist Meeting House was produced by Alfred.

In order to carry out the actual wood cutting Alfred had to lie in a recumbent position because of his deformity and this posture must have presented problems.

Alfred also turned his attention to portrait photography, probably to increase the income of the family, especially when in April through to June 1878 his father lay ill and remuneration from the Scripture Readers' Society was reduced from £30 to £15 per annum. At this point, and for his new interest, Alfred took over his father's study for use as a studio.

It appears that for the next few years Alfred experimented by taking photographs of his family and friends, and then having some basic knowledge of the subject became articled to an Exeter photographer. Having completed his training, by early 1883 he placed his first advertisement in the *Penryn Advertiser* on 18 January announcing

Examples of the woodcuts which John Alfred (1) made to illustrate seven of his father's books.

that he had set up in business as a photographer in 'A newly erected Studio of Photographic Art' (his father's study) at his father's residence, 85 Killigrew Street, Falmouth. Specimens of his work were on view in the showroom and 'All Sitters were to be taken by the new Instantaneous Process!' Later his advertisements included the taking of photographs of children and animals. Considering the camera had only been invented in 1839, and photography only became a commercial proposition in 1860, Alfred was setting up in a relatively new profession.

Alfred attended the Quaker meetings at Falmouth and became much involved with Falmouth Adult School of which George Henry Fox was Superintendent. Meetings of the Adult School took place on Sunday mornings and Wednesday evenings and were held in the Friends' Mission Room in New Street. The Adult School had been established in 1884. Instruction was given in reading, writing and the Bible. A library, savings bank and sick-benefit fund were also connected with the school. Alfred was an Officer and Librarian. His obituary in 1892 stated that 'He worthily discharged this office and was well respected by the men', the latter having some time prior to his death presented him with a testimonial for his services.

Alfred possessed a certain literary talent, and he composed a seven-verse poem extolling his father's virtues on the occasion of the latter's death. He wrote many articles for local newspapers and contributed two poems for John Gill's second series of *Peace Poems* viz *The Lifeboat* and *A Soldiers Story.* There is extant, in his own handwriting, a song he wrote to his friend and neighbour William Walton, a tea dealer of 99 Killigrew Street. Alfred's seven-verse poem *Lay of the Bereaved* (one verse of which is included in the following chapter) was included in *Poems of Cornwall.*

Alfred's last advertisement for his photographic business appeared in the *Penryn Advertiser* on 9 May 1891. Somewhere between this date and the end of the same year he visited the United States, presumably to see his sister Jane Worsdell and her family who at that time were residing in Chicago. Shortly after his return from America, Alfred was stricken with pneumonia from which he did not recover, and died in his forty-third year on 20 January 1892 at 85 Killigrew Street. It seems that his niece Beatrice Jane Worsdell travelled back from America with him, for she attended his funeral.

Alfred was buried with his father and young sister at Treslothan churchyard. Only two years previously Alfred and John Gill had visited the grave of John (3) and repeated the following stanzas from the concluding verses of *Monro* as a testimony to John (3), which John Gill described as a 'Remarkable description of the reality of the Poet's vision':

And when the pulse of life shall throb no more,
At His command, and its red currents freeze,
When silence comes, and busy day is o'er,
Monro would sleep beneath her whispering trees,
Where sing the birds, and hum the homeward bees,
And blush the flowers when Spring is passing by,
As notes unnumbered float upon the breeze,
And he will watch her from the upper sky,
And at eve's musing hour will sometimes
   near her fly.

Farewell! farewell! A voice is in his ear,
That time's fleet hour-glass is expending fast,
The glittering grains run faster year by year,
With soundless drop, and soon will fall the last.
O thou who through the gloomy grave hast past,
Send Thy good Spirit to renew our own!
May doubt and fear for ever be outcast,
And then uplift us to Thy glorious throne,
Where faith expands no more, and perfect
   love is known.

His task is ended, and he feels like one
Whose boat is rocking 'neath the island trees,
Where gorgeous birds are fluttering in the sun,
And harps ring sweetness on the sauntering breeze:
The hills and vales, where hum the honey bees,
Are those he laboured to discover long,
Sailing hope-beckoned over unknown seas,
Though fierce winds blew, and beat the
   billows strong.
Once more farewell! farewell! Thus closeth
   Monro's song.

The reverse detail on photography by John Alfred (1)

In addition to the officers over forty members of the
Adult School attended Alfred's funeral. They had sung a
hymn at 85 Killigrew Street before leaving and again at
the graveside. The rendering of these hymns was long remembered by the family.

Alfred merited mention under his father's listing in
the *Dictionary of National Biography* and again in the same
manner in *Bibliotheca Supplement*.

Written expressly for my respected
friend Mr Walton, hoping he may
live many years to sing his song
and to carry his famous TEA through
the green lanes of dear old Cornwall.
            Alfred Harris.

The note written and signed by John Alfred (1) Harris, and
enclosed with the Song he had composed, Christmas 1886

A Newly-erected Studio of
Photographic Art

ALFRED HARRIS
(Son of *John Harris*, author of the
Tercentenary Shakespere Prize Poem and
other Works,) begs to acquaint the
inhabitants of
FALMOUTH, PENRYN,
and the Neighbourhood, that, after being
articled and acquiring other experience
in the neighbourhood of, and in the
City of Exeter, he has commenced
business as a
Photographer
At his Father's Residence,
Killigrew Terrace, Falmouth,
(Opposite St. Mary's Church,)
Studio hours from Nine a.m. till dusk.
•.• Note the Address—
      85, Killigrew Terrace, Falmouth.

The advert which Alfred placed in
the Penryn Advertiser 13 January
1883

Death and Burial

John (3) suffered a stroke on Sunday evening, 14 April 1878. He was in his study at the time. As a result of this illness he did not resume his duties as a scripture reader until 17 June the same year. Obviously his health was failing, but when in November 1883 he was visiting Earle's Retreat he misjudged a step on the stairs and fell backwards, which left him very shaken and frail. Then, when recovering from this shock, he suffered an attack of bronchitis from which in his feeble condition he was not to recover. No doubt the bronchitis was exacerbated by his years spent in his occupation as a miner. He died on 7 January 1884 at his home at 85 Killigrew Street in his sixty-fourth year.

He had long since made it known that he wished to be buried at Treslothan, where his little daughter Lucretia had been laid to rest in 1855. In his major poem *A Story of Carn Brea*, published in 1863, he wrote these lines:

One sweet spot
Is ever with me, as your echoes float,
Above the tree-tops, like the sweep of wings
A little grave it is among the hills,
Beside a Gothic Chapel, and I seem
To hear the tread of those who haste to prayer,
Through primrose lanes, although I'm far away.
Here I have long desired to sleep at last
When life, with all its cares, is at an end,
Among the honest, pious villagers,
Just at the foot of my old granite mount.

The coffin was of polished Danzig oak and the breastplate simply recorded his name and age. A beautiful and thoughtful act had been performed by the poet's nephew Jacob (2) Harris, the son of one of John's (3) younger brothers, Mark Smith Harris. Jacob (2) was assisted by his friend Tom Carter and they lined the grave with wild flowers. How this little act would have delighted John (3). Jacob (2) was just nine years old and his friend Tom was of similar age.

The service at the graveside was of the most simple form, as befitted a Quaker, and was conducted by his old friend Rev. George Bull, who had formed the little poetry-reading group about forty years earlier and who, some nine years later, was laid to rest about ten yards from John (3). The mourners were few in number but included his wife Jane, his two sons, his brother Mark, his sister Kitty and Mark's wife; these were the sole mourners of the immediate family. His faithful friend John Gill was also there. The Scripture Readers' Society was represented by Rev. Gardiner and the Assistant Reader, W.H. Moss. Messrs N. Sara, R.H. Earle, Mrs Dymond, Mr E. Lovey and Mr Dunn represented the societies with whom John (3) was associated. The small attendance of Quakers was apparently due to them being at their Quarterly Meeting in Plymouth. Villagers from Troon who attended included Mr and Mrs E. Prideaux, Mr and Mrs T. Carter and Mrs W. Rule.

Capt. James Thomas of Bolenowe, who had given John (3) access to his library, had been buried at Treslothan and his grave lay fifty feet south-south-west of John (3).

At the death of John (3) his wife Jane received a letter from the Secretary of the Scripture Readers' Society of which the following is an extract: 'The Committee cannot but express their own sense of loss in the removal of him whose work and patience, and piety, together with his exceptional gifts of poetry and song, had won for him the admiration and affection of all whom he had come into intimate relation.'

Both of the sons of John (3) composed a poem in memory of their father and included them in the final pages of *Last Lays*. The final verse of Howard's poem reads as follows:

Tho' form and face are resting now
Within the churchyard shade,
Tho' spring-tide buds may ope and spread,
Their blossoms droop and fade,
Yet 'mid life's unceasing change
My heart will still rejoice,
If 'mong the links of duty's chain
I hear my father's voice.

Likewise the fourth verse of the poem by John Alfred (1) reads as follows:

The world, perchance, will miss thee not
Nor heed thy simple minstrel lays;
But He who knows the smallest sparrow's fall
Did heed thine unobtrusive ways:
Well pleased His child should sow the precious seed,
And scatter Gospel rays.

And there he lies, as he wished, 'Among the honest, pious villagers (about 1,300 in all) just at the foot of his old granite mount.'

His wife Jane continued to live at 85 Killigrew Street with John Alfred (1), but following the latter's death in January 1892 she went to live at Porthleven with Howard and his family. She died there on Friday, 17 January 1911, quite suddenly at the ripe old age of ninety. Jane was buried at Troon Cemetery, where her polished granite headstone is a replica to that of the poet at Treslothan. John Alfred (1) had been buried with his father in the grave at

Treslothan, and on the assumption that Lucretia was also interred in this grave, one assumes the grave had reached its capacity. Also bearing in mind that the churchyard had been closed to new grave burials in 1882, there was no alternative but Troon Cemetery if she was to be buried in her native locality.

A Selection of the Works of John (3) Harris FRHS

His Perception, His Sensitivity and Intense Love of Nature

I love thee, Night, when thy majestic brow
Glitters with star-light as it glitters now;
When Cynthia pours on all her silvery flood,
The mine and meadow, valley, hill and wood;
When contemplation leaves her lone retreat,
And climbs the white crags where the Muses meet;
When Peace broods o'er the earth; when hope is high,
And heaven seems shining through the far-off sky.

Night

As by the stile I pleased did stand
The waves stole up and kiss'd the land;
The swallow wheeled among the trees,
And rushes whisper'd with the breeze;
A murmur ran along the shore,
As flash'd and dipp'd the boatman's oar;
The white gull rose with shining beak,
And left his note in Sailor's Creek.

Sailor's Creek

O, many years have passed away since then,
And many images of by-gone days
Lie in the chambers of forgetfulness
Mid skeletons dust-covered;

The Mountain Prophet

Ye living boundary-lines,
Where pensive thought reclines,
And gentle song in moss of ivy bower
Trills strains of music rare
Upon the upland air,
All hail, ye temples where the Muses cower.

The briony is here,
And many a wilding deer,
And gentle whispers heard not in the street,
And fays at eventide
On the long grasses ride,
Or climb the mosses with their velvet feet.

Hedges

How beautiful the sounds of nature are
To a blind captive, wandering in the dark!
How soul-reviving is this gentle breeze
Straying along those rocks so musical.

The Blind Miner and his Daughter

Chaste, lovely little things!
Dame nature nurses you;
Ye quaff the breeze that murmurs by,
And drink the falling dew.

To a Cluster of Primroses

Treslothan Church
Built 1842. First registers date from 1845

The grave of the Poet, his daughter Lucretia and his son John Alfred

The grey-bearded man, clad in rags as he goes,
And the water-cress girl, with frost in her toes,
I saw them today creeping down the dark lane,
And they trembled with cold, and were
  weeping with pain.

Winter

Ah, world, how changeful art thou! Morning dawns
On Hopes in embryo, withering ere the Eve
Draws her grey cloak around her. All things here
Have marks of change upon them, and a sigh
Is ever creeping at the heels of Joy.

A Story of Carn Brea

Summer was past, and in the leafless wood
Autumn lay down to die.

A Story of Carn Brea

How gently it falls from the quiet sky,
On the lovely mead and mountain high!
No trace of wind, no rush of gale,
No echo of storm in the leafy vale.
But soft as a fairy tapping the pane,
When the moon is full, is the Summer Rain.

Summer Rain

Night waned away in silence; then the morn
Broke like a mystery o'er the ancient hills
And fill'd the vales with music.

The Mountain Prophet

There is a melody that floats to me
When eve is on the moor,
And the wind stealeth through the leafy tree
Beside the river's shore.

Like waters ebbing, down the cadence glides
The broad way of the moon,
Over the wide flat where the heron hides,
And night-birds sob their tune.

I strive to give it utterance in my lay,
But cannot catch the strain,
Which like a sceptred monarch stalks away,
And it is all in vain.

From the old woods it comes, the waters clear,
The swallows in their flight,
The mystic portals of the opening year,
The chambers of the night.

Is it an echo of the lyres of love,
Which angel forms possess,
Borne earthward down the grand star-tracks above,
That I may not express?

I know not. Yet I hear it evermore,
Which time can not destroy,
Sweet sounds of song the hills and valleys o'er
Earth's most delicious joy.

Mystic Melody

One hand was splinter'd, half the fingers gone,
And the dried wrist, all blacken'd with the blast,
Seem'd like a moving cinder of charr'd wood.

A Story of Carn Brea

An observation of a miner who had suffered the loss of
his sight and damage to his limbs whilst working underground, and led by his little daughter, played a violin
around the villages. This being the only means of liveli-
hood for the miner.

There's more divinity in the still thicket,
Forests, and fens, and fields,
Where waters murmur by the woodland wicket,
Than oft the pulpit yields.

The Traveller's Joy

Hail to thee, little flower,
Within my mountain-bower,
Smiling among the wiry broom,
Like Hope's bright star 'mid clouds of gloom!
I bend me o'er thy sweet blue eye,
Dropping salt tears I know not why,
Feeling a warm inspiring fire,
Sweeping my fingers o'er my lyre,
Singing within my heathy bower:
Hail, Hail to thee, Spring's early flower!

The First Violet

Bird of bright and glossy wing,
Coming to us in the spring!
Dost thou love this nook so rude?
'Tis the cave of solitude.
Here I've linger'd many an hour;
Bird, this is the poet's bower!
Float around me, little stranger;
Float around me, there's no danger.
Startling sounds won't here alarm thee:
Can a poet's musings harm thee?
Other birds, the woods among,
Cheer us with their summer-song;
But thou'rt welcome, little swallow,
Floating round my heathy hollow.

To the Swallow

I met thee on the rough hill's brow,
And in the valley there art thou!
Our Cornish hedges thou doest gem
With gold cups on thy wiry stem;
And by the North Sea's dreaded shore,
Thou listenest to the ocean's roar.
By murmuring stream and hamlet fair,
I see thee smiling everywhere!
But, heath-flowers on my mountain's side,
I love you more than all beside!

The Heath

Sweet little nursling of the storm,
Why dost thou look so pale?
How is thy tender, fragile form
Shook by the wintry gale?

Art thou a spirit of the flowers
Which once this hedge-row lined,
Come back to tell of other lands,
Where thou hast been enshrined?

Dost thou not, little shivering one,
Sweet hopes and memories bring,
The earliest of ten thousand buds,
The harbinger of Spring?

Art thou not come to glad my sight,
Now adverse fortunes frown,
A momentary comforter
A star in Winter's crown?

I fear the ruthless frost will come,
And kill thee, little sweet!
Too early hast thou found our home
Within this wild retreat.

Come, sing a song of far-off lands,
Before the snows have birth,
And the hoarse whirlwind howl thy dirge,
And smite thee to the earth.

Sweet one, the earliest and the best!
Thy moments are but few;
Thou shouldst have come with other flowers,
To drink the April dew!

But thou art like the child of song,
Who blossoms ere his time;
Whose soul, too darling, falls before
The rigour of its clime.

A Primrose in Winter

In this cold region of neglect,
Perchance thou would'st have known
The agony to ask for bread
And only get a stone.
For poverty's true friends are few,
He struggles, like the mole,
Who digs his tunnel in the dark,
Though genius gilds his soul.

The Ayrshire Ploughman
(Robbie Burns 1759-96)

'Twas called by us the Under Field,
And there the lambkins played,
When violet-fairies donned their shield
In many a mossy glade.
But nought to me was half so dear,
Which loving Nature dowers,
As this small meadow by the mere
All white with daisy flowers.

Nor will it fade from memory's eye,
From memory's treasured store,
Till darkness shadow earth and sky,
And life itself is o'er.
A bliss by hidden hands unsealed,
To cheer my latest hours,
Is that hill-sloping Under Field
All white with daisy flowers.

The Daisy Meadow

That summer-eve was beautiful,
As round the peasant's board,
The father and his family
Knelt down with one accord,
And for the mercies of the day
Kind Providence adored.

How sweetly does their evening hymn
Float down the silent vale,
O'er which the Twilight gently draws
Her soft subduing veil,
And Philomela stops to hear
It trembling on the gale.

Evening Family Worship

'Tis eve, 'tis calm; the winds are still;
Not e'en a whisper walks the hill,
In silent groups the lilies lie,
Nor trembles as the stream steals by.

Luda - A lay of the Druids

He loved the golden sunshine,
The blue sky and the sea,
The clouds at solemn sunset,
The flowerets on the lea;
The birds and trees and rivers,
His cot upon the height,
The face of man and maiden,
And all things pure and bright.

You might have seen him wander
Along his father's lease,
Communing with the ivy,
And whispering with the breeze;
The swallows his companions
In many a sacred nook;
The hedges were his study,
And nature was his book.

A Rhyme for Edward Bastin

The ability of John (3) to perceive in the seasons, the flowers, the moors, the hills and valleys, the sun, moon and stars, the wind and rain, ponds, streams and rivers, together with his vignettes of human emotions, desires and problems, all demonstrate his depth of observation, expression and his descriptive powers.

His Desire for Solitude

And is there not, in all the earth,
In ocean, or in air,
A spot where Peace delights to dwell?
O lead the wanderer there!
Yes, many such, I'm sure, there are
In this fair world of ours,
Hung round with crystal innocence,
And gemm'd with tearless flowers.

O for a Cot in Some Lone Place

I'm fond of travelling old deserted paths,
Searched with the winds and soft with solitude.

Kynance Cove

From busy man he stole
To Nature's altars rude,
And gave his thoughtful soul
To muse with Solitude.

To ramble was his choice
To Contemplation's lair,
Where zephyrs have a voice
To charm the ear of Care.

The Mountain Boy

To walk by falling waters,
And little lonely rills,
Which murmur 'mid the rushes
Among the watching hills:
O, here the swallow glideth
By many a fairy grot:
How sweet in solemn silence
To be where man is not.

The murmur of the forest,
The woodbine and the rose,
The thorn and tangled thicket,
Along the dingle flows.
No music is like Nature's,
By bird and breeze begot:
How much the soul may profit
To be where man is not.

O, could my wish be granted,
My dwelling-place should stand
Alone amid the mountains,
With woods on either hand,
Where limpid runnels ripple,
And thrush-notes link the thought;
Contented thus for ever
To be where man is not.

To Be Where Man is Not

The day is come I long have woo'd:
'Tis April's budding hour,
And I, with sister Solitude,
Am seated in my bower.
Across the lawn the zephyr's chime
Melodiously doth sweep;
But, though it is the budding-time,
I steal away to weep!

The lark is shouting in the sky,
The redbreast on the wall,
And, in the Forest Moor hard by,
I hear the cuckoo's call:
The sparrows on our old cot
Their merry-makings keep;
But, though they seem so musical,
I steal away to weep.

The furze-bush waves its golden bells
Where panting breezes run,
And every little daisy tells
A story to the sun;
Blue violets, 'neath the hawthorn-tree,
And nodding cowslips peep:
But, though a thousand flowers I see,
I steal away to weep.

Around I hear the shout of joy,
Yet shun the merry choir:
A mother loves her singing boy,
A sister and a sire;
A loving wife, a daughter dear,
Around my heart-strings creep:
But like a banish'd man I'm here,
I steal away to weep!

And when my comrades smile so gay,
So jubilant and glad,
I wonder why I turn away,
And seem so very sad.
I wonder why within my bower
Alone I love to creep,
And, though it is the budding-hour,
I steal away to weep.

I Steal Away to Weep

It will be seen that the contradiction between the absolute enjoyment of family and friends by John (3) and his
persistent desire for solitude is nothing short of an enig-
ma.

The Mining Scene

Hast ever seen a mine? Hast ever been
Down in its fabled grottoes, wall'd with gems,
And canopied with torrid mineral-belts,
That blaze within the fiery orifice?
Hast ever, by the glimmer of the lamp,
Or the fast-waning taper, gone down, down,
Towards the earth's dread centre, where wise men
Have told us that the earthquake is conceived,
And great Vesuvius hath his lava-house,
Which burns and burns for ever, shooting forth
As from a fountain of eternal fire?
Hast ever heard, within this prison-house,
The startling hoof of Fear? the eternal flow
Of some dread meaning whispering to thy soul?
Hast ever seen the miner at his toil,
Following his obscure work below, below,
Where not a single sun-ray visits him,
But all is darkness and perpetual night?
Here the dull god of gloom unrivall'd reigns,
And wraps himself in palls of pitchy dark!
Hast ever breathed its sickening atmosphere?
Heard its dread throbbings, when the rock has burst?
Leap'd at its sneezings in the powder-blast?
And trembled when the groaning, splitting earth,
Mass after mass, fell down with deadliest crash?
What sayest thou? - hast thou not? Come with me;
Or if thou hast, no matter, come again

Don't fear to trust me; for I have been there
From morn till night, from night till dewy morn,
Gasping within its burning sulphur-cloud,
Straining mine eyes along its ragged walls,
And wondering at the uncouth passages
Dash'd in the sparry cells by Fancy's wand;
And oft have paused, and paused again, to hear
The eternal echo of its emptiness.

Christian Heroism

A mine spread out its vast machinery.
Here engines, with their huts and smoky stacks,
Cranks, wheels, and rods, boilers and hissing steam,
Press'd up the water from the depths below.
Here fire-whims ran till almost out of breath,
And chains cried sharply, strain'd with fiery force,
Here blacksmith's hammer'd by the sooty forge,
And there a crusher crash'd the copper ore.
Here girls were cobbing under roofs of straw,
And there were giggers at the oaken hutch.
Here a man-engine glided up and down,
A blessing and a boon to mining men:
And near the spot where, many years before,
Turn'd round and round the rude old water-wheel,
A huge fire-stamp was working evermore,
And slimy boys were swarming at the trunks.
The noisy lander by the trap-door bawl'd
With pincers in his hand; and troops of maids
With heavy hammers brake the mineral stones,
The cart-man cried, and shook his broken whip;
And on the steps of the account-house stood
The active agent, with his eye on all.

Below were caverns grim with greedy gloom,
And levels drunk with darkness; chambers huge
Where Fear sat silent, and the mineral-sprite
For ever chanted his bewitching song;
Shafts deep and dreadful, looking darkest things
And seeming almost running down to doom;
Rock under foot, rock standing on each side;
Rock cold and gloomy, frowning overhead;
Before, behind, at every angle, rock.
Here blazed a vein of precious copper ore,
Where lean men labour'd with a zeal for fame,
With face and hands and vesture black as night,
And down their sides the perspiration ran
In steaming eddies, sickening to behold.
But they complain'd not, digging day and night,
And morn and eve, with lays upon their lips.
Here yawn'd a tin-cell like a cliff of crags,
And Danger lurk'd among the groaning rocks,
And oft times moan'd in darkness. All the air
Was black with sulphur, burning up the blood.
A nameless mystery seem'd to fill the void,

And wings all pitchy flapp'd among the flints,
And eyes that saw not sparkled mid the spars.
Yet here men work'd, on stages hung on ropes,
With drills and hammers blasting the rude earth,
Which fell with such a crash that he who heard
Cried, 'Jesus, save the miner!' Here were ends
Cut through hard marble by the miners' skill,
And winzes, stopes, and rises: pitches here,
Where work'd the heroic, princely tributer,
This month for nothing, next for fifty pounds.
Here lodes ran wide, and there so very small
That scarce a pick-point could be press'd between;
Here making walls as smooth as polish'd steel,
And there as craggy as a rended hill:
And out of sparry vagues the water oozed,
Staining the rock with mineral, so that oft
It led the labourer to a house of gems.
Across the mine a hollow cross-course ran
From north to south, an omen of much good;
And tin lay heap'd on stulls and level-plots;
And in each nook a tallow taper flared,
Where pale men wasted with exhaustion huge.
Here holes exploded, and there mallets rang,
And rocks fell crashing, lifting the stiff hair
From time-worn brows, and noisy buckets roar'd
In echoing shafts; and through this gulf of gloom
A hollow murmur rush'd for evermore.

The Mine

He was a tributer; a man who work'd
On speculation, digging through the ground
In search of ore, the sweetener of his toil.
If found, he flourish'd; if not found, he fell;
Nor fell alone, fell wife and family.

A Story of Carn Brea

Copper has colours different in the ores,
As various as the rainbow, black and blue
And green and red and yellow as a flower;
Gold-coloured here, there dimly visible,
Though rich the same in measure and in meed.
'Tis found alike where glittering granite gloams,
Where killas darkens, and where gossans shroud,
And oft where wise ones write it cannot be,
Thus wisely scattered by the Hand Divine.
Tin is more secret far, with duller eye
Oft hiding in the river's shingly bed,
Or the flint's bosom, near the central fires,
In chambers wide, or veins like silken lace;
So that the labourer, stumbling on a start,
Wipes his hot brow, and cries, 'Lo, here is tin.'

The Mine

His Love and Respect for His Birthplace and Home

Once more, and yet once, old hill,
I kneel upon thy crest;
Of all those mountain-peaks around,
Thou art the brightest, best.
The flowers that gem thy rustling locks,
And stud thy forehead fair,
Are peering from among the rocks,
To me beyond compare.

To the Old Hill

Till life's last hour, my heather-cover'd carne
Will share a large place in my inner self.
The very stones are precious in my sight,
And the peat hedges thrill like chords of song.
My spirit, panting through the universe,
Floats back to it, and settles down in peace.

The Mountain Prophet

Beautiful vale, with thy rippling stream!
How like a picture of youth dost thou seem!
Blushing with hope-buds, and sparkling
  with flowers,
And gushing forth harp-notes from all
  thy bright flowers!
Beautiful vale, with thy rippling stream,
How like a picture of youth dost thou seem!

On my dear native hill I sit midst the heath,
Gazing down on the tree-covered village beneath,
Where oft I have play'd in the spring tide of youth,
When Nature's sweet voice was the music of truth.
Like birds from their nests thy white cottages
  gleam,
Beautiful vale, with thy rippling stream!

The swallow floats round, as the grasshopper sings,
And brushes the locks of my mount with her
  wings!
The sky-lark is mounting to heaven, with its song
Overflowing the dell, as it flutters along;
And with mirth and with music thine avenues teem,
Beautiful vale, with thy rippling stream!

A thousand past scenes, too numerous to speak,
Rush into my eyes, and roll over my cheek.
I think of a brother with whom I have play'd.
A sister who sat with me under the shade.
They have cross'd the wide sea; but surely they
  dream
Of my beautiful vale, with its rippling stream!

To My Native Valley

The dear old carn, the dear old carn,
A few feet from my father's barn,
Where hummed the bees in summer hours,
When sunshine oped the heather flowers!
Though bowed with age, neglect, and ill,
Through tearful eyes I see thee still.

And when the winter snow came down
Upon the fields and highland brown,
Then redbreast sought our rustic door,
Hopped on the hatch-knob and the floor.
I hear his bright bill tap the pane,
And see him eat his crumbs again.

The storm that roared around the crags,
The breeze that murmured through the flags,
The lambs that gamboled in the mead,
The snipe that rustled from the reed,
The lark that carolled o'er the hay,
Are with me in my chair to-day.

The horse that pulled the hazel plough,
The gate through which I drove the cow,
The moorland pool where swallows played,
The lily-leaves that loved the shade,
The bird that swept the river's shore,
Are with my spirit evermore.

But more than all, my bower of green,
Where first I wooed my rhyming queen,
When moonlight silvered o'er the lake,
And fays were feasting in the brake,
When Nature crowned her singing boy,
And still it gives me purest joy.

I cannot doubt, when life is o'er,
And I have gained the other shore,
On rays of light I oft shall drop
Upon my dear old mountain top,
And praise Him with angelic swell
That He had ordered all things well.

The Dear Old Carn

There is a spot I love full well,
Whose worth can not be told,
Whose price to me is dearer far
Than silver-hoards or gold.
Gems in compare are roughest stones,
And Jewels lose their pride,
Nor lands nor castles equal it,
My own, my dear fireside.

When youth was green this love was mine,
A nature-given store,
Which strait and storm could not suppress,
And years have made it more.
No spot of this revolving earth,
Which sea and stream divide,
Can ever hold a gem so dear
As is my own fireside.

My Own Fireside

The wintry storm is over; its wrecks are
  strewn around;
Uprooted trees and cottages are prostrate
  on the ground,
Deserted sheds, that quaked to hear the
  tempest-spirit's call:
But one there is, my dear old home, more
  desolate than all.

And here, on England's holy-day, old
  gathering friends would come,
And sip the peace-cup joyously within my
  mountain home;
Here strangely talk'd the eve away with
  legendary lore,
Until the minstrel's harp-strings twang'd:
  they'll gather there no more.

The blast has come, the parting blast: how
  wildly did it roar!
I look'd, my dear old home was gone!
  'Twill be a home no more!
And since all things are perishing beneath the
  solemn sky,
O may I seek a happy home more permanent
  on high!

The Fall of the Old House

Sorrow may touch my spirit,
And weigh my vigour down,
As in this world of trouble
I meet with smile and frown.
But one spot is with me,
Wherever I may go,
Where flowerets gem the hillocks,
And shining waters flow.

I turn to it in summer,
And when the autumn gleams,
When surly-sounding winter
Flings frost upon the streams;
And when the spring is budding,
And blue bells seek the light,
When larks sing o'er the meadows,
And it is ever bright.

And if through man's unkindness
I turn aside to weep,
O, then its crystal waters
Flash down the rocky steep.
And daisies gleam with gladness,
And fairies mount their steeds,
And gallop o'er the cowslips,
Unseen in other meads.

And when the world's great wrangle
Assails me near and far,
Amid the twisted jangle
It shineth like a star.
And in the sunset glory
Which gilds this hallowed height
The holy angels gather
In robes of purest white.

A mother taught her offspring,
A father struggled there,
And sounds which poets gather
Fill up the fragrant air.
And, as I journey onward,
It glitters more and more,
As if it caught the radiance
Of the eternal shore.

My birth-place! O my birth-place!
I thank the Lord for thee,
Where town nor city staineth,
But all is fair and free:
Where Nature loves her children,
In weeds of mystery clad,
And music heals for ever
The sorrowful and sad.

My Birth-place

Impressions of the Places He Visited

I've been to fairy-land, and seen the fays
Invested in their workshop. Scenes were here
That held a poet captive with their charms,
And mock'd his fancy like a thing of gloom.
The wondrous cliffs were polished with the waves,
And flash'd and flicker'd like huge mineral walls
Their scaly sides were clothed with leafy gold,
And burn'd with beauty in the light of day.
The sands that lay on this Elysian cove
Were all ring-marked with painted serpentine.
The hollow caves the waves had fretted out
Were dash'd with images of flowery hues;
And on the rocks, like beautiful psalm-leaves,
Were odes of music lovely as the light,
Trill'd by the sea-nymphs in their watery robes.

Why seek for beauty in the stranger's clime,
When Beauty's state-room is the gay Kynance?
Why seek for visions courted by the Muse,
When Kynance opens like a mine of gems?
Why seek for language from the waves' white lips,
When ocean fills this pictured Cove with hymns?
Why seek for caverns striped with natural lays,
When they are gouged here by the surging sea?
Why seek for islands girdled with the main,
When Kynance holds them in her feathery folds?
So mused I in the sea-damp Drawing-room,
While through the Bellows rush'd a flood of song.

Kynance Cove

Note: The first visit John (3) made to Kynance
Cove was during the harvest time of 1855
when a neighbour loaned him a horse-
drawn conveyance.

For me the rocks have language,
When gazing on those lichen'd chroniclers,
So stony still, like giants clad in mail.

I walk'd the storm-swept, heather-hung Land's End,
And mused within its sea-washed galleries,
Whose granite arches mock the rage of time.
I revell'd in the mystery of its shades,
And my soul soar'd up on the wings of song.
I treasured up the lore the sea-gulls taught,
Which in white clouds were cooing to the breeze,
I quaff'd the music of this granite grove,
And read rude cantos in the book of crags,
Stretching me in the theatre of heath,
When morn was breaking, and the
  light-house seem'd
An angel in the waters, and the rocks
Rang to the music of a thousand throats.

The Land's End

Note: John (3) first visited Land's End in August
1856. It was the first time that he had spent a
night's rest away from home. He was thirty-
six years old. A corresponding friend, Mr
Henry Gill of Tiverton, Devon, sent him a
pound note with which he and Jane decided
to spend on the visit to Land's End. After
walking from Troon to Camborne where
they caught the train to Penzance, they then
walked the final ten miles to Land's End, returning by the same means the following
day.

How pleasant here at cool of day
Along the winding walks to stray,
Where ebbs and glows the murmuring main,
Whose music fills the woodbine lane,
High on the beach with shingles strewn,
As rise thy vespers, Gyllyngdune.

When last I chanced to ramble here,
The winds were still, the skies were clear;
Two lovers sat upon a seat,
With ocean shining at their feet,
Whispering their loves beneath the moon,
Which filled with silver Gyllyngdune.

Gyllyngdune

Note: Gyllyngdune is a public garden on the sea-
front at Falmouth.

I first beheld it when the wintry clouds
Were rolling grandly through the murky air;
And flocks of starlings, wheeling to their home,
Like sound of many waters, murmured there.
Here graceful trees, the green, the rich, the rare,
So chastely grouped, in fairy fringes stand;
And limpid rills, and crystal waterfalls,
Are breathing song like notes from angel-land.
Old Winter here is reft of his command,
Here roses bloom, and fragrance fills the breeze;
Here forest-birds from off a friendly hand
Pick their full meal, and flutter 'neath the trees.
If such, Penjerrick, by thy winter scene,
How Eden-hued in summer's richer sheen!

Penjerrick

Note: Penjerrick was at this time the country residence of Robert Were Fox, FRS.

I love it for its rustic dress,
Its spirit-speaking loneliness,
Its fences quaint, its footpaths rude,
Its silent fanes of solitude.
Whose sea-notes soothe the strife of care,
Which murmur not where cities glare.

I love it for the lark that sings,
And soars with sunlight on his wings,
Whose music fills the listening land,
And trembles o'er the shining sand,
While holy feelings fill the breast,
Replete with rapture unexpressed.

I love it for the healthy breeze
Long-lingering over solemn seas,
Which fans my brow as here I roam,
Where cliff-flowers hang o'er fields of foam,
And Silence on yon craggy stair
With folded hands invites to prayer.

Perranporth

Note: Perranporth - a seaside village on the North
Coast of Cornwall.

Then the steam-horse bore him
One sky-pleasant day
Out of old Cornwallia,
Many miles away;
Onward, onward ever,
Charmed with sight and sound,
Till his feet at Stratford
Pressed the classic ground.

Out of Cornwall

Note: The only occasion on which John (3) left
Cornwall was just after the award for his
Shakespeare Tercentenary Poem, when in
company with a certain William Hooper,
who presumably organised the tour, he
visited Bristol, Clifton, Bath, Hereford,
Worcester, Gloucester, Malvern, Birmingham and Stratford-upon-Avon.

Saw he, too, the chancel
Where the poet sleeps,
By his own dear river
Which for ever weeps.
Saw he hill and valley,
Meadow, tree, and plain,
And 'sweet Anne's' dear dwelling
By the twisted lane.

Saw he these and wondered
Saw he these and wept,
Holy as a vision
Coming when he slept.
Every little daisy,
Like a hermit then,
Spoke of William Shakespeare,
Shakespeare king of men.

Shakespeare's Shrine

I stood before it with a joy
Almost akin to pain,
Nor can I hope, throughout life's race,
To drink so deep again
As when I pulled the rude bell-wire,
Which dangled by the door
Of Shakespeare's house in Henley Street,
And stepped the threshold o'er.

The old walls seemed to speak to me
With a mysterious sound;
And lyre-chords echoed in mine ears,
As I stood gazing round.
I bared my head, I know not why,
And tears ran down my face;
I felt I was stealing through
A sacred solemn place.

Yes, here he piped, and here he played,
Upon this self-same floor;
His hands have often touched these walls,
Now widely written o'er.
And here he slept, when moon and stars
In Night's dark mantle came;
Watched by the Genii of the muse,
And the bright form of fame.

O boy, O bard, O house of fame,
O spot to Britain dear!
From every sea, from every land,
The pilgrim journeys here.
How did my thankful heart o'erflow,
When on that blessed morn
I breathed within the written walls
Where Shakespeare's self was born!

Shakespeare's House

I feel it much to meet
In shades so solemn. Tears are on my face;
The dust of Shakespeare is beneath my feet;
O, what an honoured place!

Shakespeare's Tomb

O Shottery, dear Shottery!
Sequestered in the dell,
Far-famed for sweet Anne Hathaway,
I feel I love thee well.
For thou hast hedges like my own,
With little glens of green,
Where primroses smile out in spring,
With violets between.

O Shottery, dear Shottery!
I oft have thought of thee,
When reading Shakespeare in my youth
Under the hawthorn tree;
Nor did I dream in those joy-days
To see thee with mine eye,
And tread thy ever-hallowed ground
Under the bluest sky.

Shottery

The Wye, the Wye, the winding Wye!
Beneath a cold November sky,
I first beheld its waters clear,
And heard the music of its flow,
As through the vales it wander'd slow
With many a song, and many a sigh,
The Wye, the Wye, the winding Wye.

The Wye, the Wye, the winding Wye,
With happy Hereford close by!
And whether sleep the eyelids seal,
Or busy-hands press round the wheel,
Should pleasures cheer, or sorrows lower,
Thou murmurest of thy Maker's power,
Who never leaves thy channels dry,
The Wye, the Wye, the winding Wye.

The Winding Wye

His Home Town and Native County

I well remember, in my childish days
Thy name was like a magic word to me,
Replete with strange emotion! Not a lip
That syllabled the word but seem'd to be
More than a common hero; and I thought,
If I could stand upon thy threshold-stones,
And peep into thy streets of burnish'd brass,
'Glittering and flashing' in the golden sun,
Why, I should see just all the world at once:
O Camborne! what a blessed sight for me.

Thou hast thy halls of learning, and thy men
Of wonderful renown; thou ownest too
Thy seats of science, and thy mounts of power,
Thy dens of discord, and thy bowers of bliss,
Thy hallow'd fanes, and dungeons dark and deep.
Thou hast, within thy borders, master-minds,
Rare spirits, of the modern mining school,
Who, mole-like, dig their way into the earth,
Yoking the elements in brotherhood,
To belch the flashing diamond into light,
And vomit forth the backbone of the world!

Camborne

When moonlight-shafts fell on thy meres,
And fairies thronged thy wells,
How oft I've heard the queen of song
Within thy flowery dells!
And where thy mineral stores lie hid
Beneath the pall of night,
Mine ears have caught unuttered strains
From many a tinselled sprite.

Twilight with me, twilight with thee:
Yet still thy waters roar,
And great ships come and great ships go
With many a precious store.
Thy mountain-tarns are sacred sites,
Thy peaks are holy ground,
Where angels gather in the dusk
When psalms are floating round.

From schoolboy tasks to fading age,
Thy reeds and rocks among,
Muse-led, my earnest life has been
An era of strange song,
My theme - thy beauties unsurpassed
On sea-side, mead, and moor,
Where fairest damsels sing thy fame
By many a rustic door.

Twilight with me, twilight with thee:
Yet will I sing thy worth
Until thou yieldest me a grave
Within my mother earth.
The flowers are fair in other lands,
And clear the waters fall,
But old Cornwallia is the best
And brightest of them all.

Cornwallia

Kynance Cove

Cornish Legends

At Chapel Porth a stain of red
Shows where the Giant Bolster bled;
And in the vale is seen the stone,
With lowly lichen overgrown,
Which bears upon its rugged side
His finger-marks both deep and wide,
Made as he strode one sultry day
From the bold Beacon to Carn Brea,
And stoop'd to drink out of the well,
As Cornish early legends tell.
Six miles, if you can measure right,
This stride would be from height to height.
Among our giants huge and tall
He was the mightiest of them all.

Great Bolster fell in love, they say,
With good St Agnes o'er the way;
And generous was the saint and fair,
Possessing numerous virtues rare.
He follow'd her with sighs and groans;
The mountains trembled with his moans.
The lovely lady listen'd not;
The giant raged with passion hot
She warned him not to woo her more;
For he was married long before.

A recent photograph of Penjerrick, one of the homes of the Fox family.
It was here that John (3) was invited soon after his appointment as Scripture Reader at Falmouth and where he took tea with the family out of a silver teapot, the silver from which it was made having been raised in Dolcoath Mine.

Her prayers and tears were all in vain:
He urged his suit, and urged again,
Till she resolved some plan to try
To rid her of the giant high;
Demanding, by the Powers above,
A stronger token of his love,
That, if he fill'd with his own gore
A rugged hole a-near the shore,
Then she no more his zeal would tire,
But freely grant him his desire.
The cunning saint full well knew she
The hole was open to the sea.

This huge bestrider of the hill
Supposed he could the chasm fill
At Chapel Porth, beside the main,
Which ebbs and flows and ebbs again,
And not be weaker for the loss;
And so he stretch'd his arm across,
And cut the vein. Out rush'd the gore,
Dash'd down the whole with seething roar;
And yet the hollow would not fill,
Though he was bleeding, bleeding still;
And gory were old Neptune's locks,
And crimson waves broke on the rocks.
Hour after hour, with ruddy roll.
The life-stream hurried down the hole.
Hour after hour the blood flow'd on,
Until great Bolster's strength was gone.
Too weak was he to staunch the wound,
Too weak to struggle from the ground;
Too weak to roll, too weak to rise,
A film kept gathering o'er his eyes
And with a storm of dreadful throes
Ended great Giant Bolster's woes.

Giant Bolster

Low lies beneath the western wave
A city in its watery grave;
And many a chronicler will tell
What once fair Lyonesse befell:
How rose the sea with sullen frown,
And beat the rocky barriers down;
Then roll'd o'er mead and orchard glade,
And home's loved hearth where childhood play'd,
Entombing on its march sublime
Grey stooping age and manhood's prime,
Loved beauty bright and genius rare,
And grief with matted locks and spare,
And tower, and church, and mansion heap,
Within the chambers of the deep;
For which, when rolls the tempest tone
The rough Land's End sends out its moan.

Amid the rising, flashing spray
A horseman gallops fleet away.
On, on he flies, not looking back,
Dashing the water from his track.
Each side the rising waves he sees,
Which reach even now the horse's knees.
He spurs the brute, and jerks the rein,
And shouts and shouts its name again,
Until with many a spring and bound
He gains at last a higher ground;
And, looking out along the shore,
His precious home is seen no more.
A watery waste is everywhere,
Except a few rocks here and there;
And Perranuthnoe safe from harms
Receives Trelawney to its arms.

The Buried City

A little river strange and clear
Beside the chapel flows:
Then suddenly adown the rocks
A waterfall it goes.
And much the music which it makes
From morn till pensive eve,
As it drops o'er mid fern and flower
Into the rocky Kieve.

Cornwallia boasts no fairer spot
In all her wide domain:
The very rocks are legend-mark'd,
And rife with legend stain
The grasses bending o'er its brim,
The mosses shining round;
The winds with hymns of olden times
Make it enchanted ground.

And here the good St Nectan dwelt
In his religious cell;
Within his tower upon the rocks
He placed a silver bell.
Its solemn notes the sailor heard
Clear sounding down the glade,
And flowing o'er the salt sea wave;
Then cross'd himself, and pray'd.

The evening sun was sinking down
The crimson western sky,
When by the Kieve St Nectan lay
Upon his bed to die.
They brought his silver bell to him;
He rang it thrice, and sigh'd,
Then dropp'd in the crystal Kieve,
And closed his eyes and died.

Two ladies from a distant land,
In foreign garments dress'd,
The dead saint and his sacred store
Placed in an oaken chest.
His solitary grave was dug
Within the river-bed,
And evermore the waters clear
Are murmuring o'er his head.

Within the chapel of the saint
These lonely sisters hide:
No fellowship had they without,
And here at last they died.
Of lofty parentage they seem'd,
And no one knew their name,
Or cross'd the threshold of their cell
To glean from whence they came.

A mystery hides their sleeping-place
In fair Glen Neot dell,
A-near the mossy waterfall
Where lies the silver bell.
Still mystic murmurs fill the glen,
And tremble on the air,
As from the holy hermitage
The nuns come forth to prayer.

St Nectan's Kieve

Note: St Nectan was assumed to have built his fifth-
century oratory by a stream near Tintagel in
North Cornwall.

Near a century since in the west
Sank a beautiful lady so pale;
And they solemnly laid her to rest
In a vault by the church in the dale.

One night, when the darkness was deep,
The sexton contrived to be there,
Where the dead in the charnel-house sleep,
To rob her of jewels so rare.

In his mouth mid the lantern-light dim
Her lily-white finger placed he,
When her strange eyes she open'd on him,
And up in her coffin sat she.

He mightily stagger'd with dread,
Half-blinded he rush'd from the yard;
His lantern he left with the dead,
And down the deep hollows ran hard.

Away by the orchard he flies,
And on by the ruin he reels,
While the hair on his forehead doth rise,
And the spirit seems still at his heels.

In her white shroud the lady arose,
And quickly she cross'd the tomb-door;
Then out of the churchyard she goes,
And over the tenantless moor.

The lantern she swings in her hand
Like will-o'-the wisp in the reeds,
And soon at the hall-door doth stand
Of her own mansion-house in the meads.

At the lattice her lord doth appear,
And gazes he into the gloom:
'My own dearest treasure, I'm here;
Your Laura, escaped from the tomb!'

How pale grew her lord at the sound,
And the servants were fill'd with alarms!
She soon in love's fetters was bound,
Lock'd fast in the nobleman's arms.

And many years' sands saw they run,
And dry leaves their valley-path strew:
Kind Providence gave them a son,
And he was the heir of Renew.

The Heir of Renew

His Humour

I know not how this custom came
Which all my clansmen love to name.
They've told me by the embers seated,
Our parish church was then completed;
And since that time, when comes the day,
A feast awaits both old and gay.
This vague tradition may be true;
I've seen no record, pray, have you?
To explain the mystery of the matter:
All hail, once more, the smoking platter,
The sirloin rich, and sweet fowl-pie[55]
Cook'd in the chimney wide and high!
For weeks before the welcome morn,
The rosy youth and age forlorn,
And she who sang in woe or weal,
Whilst turning round her spinning-wheel
'Mid shining cans and bucket handles
And tin-case where she kept her candles,
These chattering ones, for weeks, at least,
Have preach'd long sermons on the feast.

And mother, too, kind hearted dame,
Full fourteen days before it came,
Invited us to come and take
A rich repast amid the brake.
On Friday eve they kill'd the lamb,
Which in the summer miss'd its dam.
And Jem's grey duck, too, lost its head;
It hung up in the pantry dead;
A well-fed drake which, by and by,
Would make a sweet delicious pie.

The lagging morning came, and we
Met round the old hearth, red with glee,
To chat, and read, and sing, and rhyme,
Till came the long'd-for dinner-time;
And then, at mother's welcome call,
We sat within our ancient hall;
And, in the not unpleasant clatter,
Two legs were served upon a platter.
When father took his usual place,
Though ill, he rose, repeated grace;
And, mid melodious murmurs rife,
I used the keen-edged carving knife.
O what a feast was ours! A sight
To fill Sam Martin with delight.
Like kings and princes did we dine,
And water was our strongest wine.

The Parochial Festival

Note: The foregoing verses give us an insight of the
          Harris family preparing for and their enjoy-
          ment of the special food on the occasion of
          Camborne Feast, which is held on the near-
          est weekend to 11 November.

One morn a poor youth went away to the mine,
Not late, no nor early, betwixt seven and nine;
His bag held his dinner, 'in which he took pride,'
Down deep in his pocket, and thumping his side.

He tripp'd down the mountain, and over the lea,
And through the long lanes, singing loud in his glee;
Now blessing the flowerets, now pausing to mark,
And clapping his hands at the song of the lark.

He keeps his left elbow so close to his side,
One would think that in fancy he stroll'd
  with his bride.
O, no; 'tis his pasty he's hugging so tight,
For fear he should lose it, or some one should bite.

The ploughmen and ploughboys that work
  on the farm
Have seen him walk onward, and look'd at his arm,
And thought he had copper or silver, and hid it;
O, no; they were wrong; 'twas his pasty that did it.

A pasty! a pasty! I grant that the name
Has never roll'd far on the chariot of Fame.
Of Hebrew or Latin small knowledge had he;
But a pasty - he knew it as well as could be.

He passes the blind man's, and goes near the mill,
And walks by the stream on the side of the hill,
Steps round the wide tin-pits which darken
  the moors,
Soon reaches the mine, and is on his own floors.

He throws off his coat, one might think he
  would sweep
The work of ten tinners, ay, off at a leap.
His eyes how they pierce you, his words how
  they ring!
I doubt if a blackbird were gayer in spring.

He walks on so briskly, the weight of a barrow
Seems nothing for him, he is blithe as a sparrow;
The thought of his pasty inspires him like wine,
And he longs for the great bell to call him to dine.

On a cobbing-house yonder he fixes his eyes;
For there in his jacket the dinner bag lies,
Full up to the top. 'O soon I shall meet it;
And then what a pleasure it will be to eat it!

Come, Mary, go on, let us strive to be winner;
A few barrows more, and then we shall have dinner.'
Ding dong goes the bell: like an arrow he sped,
Where his pasty was left in the wood-cover'd shed.

Stock-still in the corner he trembles and sighs,
And the great shining tears are half out of his eyes.
His comrades were shouting and laughing aloud;
But he looked like Sorrow closed under a cloud.

But why all this sadness? His dinner was gone!
He search'd; but he found not. His comrades
  laugh'd on:
At last they relented, and said they would try
To find out his pasty, and not let him die.

O could you have seen the poor fellow this while!
The drollest comedian could not make him smile.
He paced up and down, with eyes fix'd on the roof,
With comrades and every one standing aloof.

Now he's out at the door, he looks this way and that,
He shrugs up his shoulders, he picks up his hat;
He views every stamp-boy that swallows his crust,
And wrings his hard clutches, and kicks up the dust.

'No dinner to-day, what sad tidings for me!
Before I leave work O how faint I shall be!
Have pity upon me I wonder who will,'
But see they are coming down over the hill.

'A sight of my pasty new life would impart,
And sunshine again would be filling my heart,'
He sigh'd as he spoke, and then laugh'd with a stare;
For his dinner unbroken was brought to him there.

A hoax had been play'd by his mine-mates in toil,
At the trifling expense of this son of the soil,
Who leapt at his bag like a hound at a hare,
And shriek'd in his gladness, 'O never despair!'

The Lost Dinner

Poor weather-beaten silker, how slight thou'rt
  looking now,
From what thou wert seven years ago, when
  perch'd upon my brow!
Thy shagless top, and silkless brim, how piteous
  to behold!
And sides, that look crush'd cruelly together with
  the cold!

Thou didst not always look like this, poor,
  ragged, wrinkled wight!
When thou wert brought from Paris here, thou
  wast a beauty quite;
Thy glossy silken self might then grace even a
  captain's brow;
But Time hath torn thee in his rage! thou'rt sadly
  alter'd now.

Change after change has altered both my old silk
  hat and me,
Since first we met, ay, proudly met, elate in
  youthful glee;
But signs have been for months gone by that
  thou wouldst surely fall,
While hanging to thy wonted nail, escutcheon'd
  in my hall.

I know not who thy maker was, nor what his
  name might be:
For once he did out-do himself, when he had
  fashion'd thee.
A Paris hat to stand the rust and rub of such an age
Adds glory to the Frenchman's name, unknown in
history's page!

Peace to the memory of the man who smooth'd
  thy curly brim;
And may ten thousand silkers more, like thee,
  be made by him!
I lost his honourable name before my song
  was penn'd;
But he deserves to blaze in print for blocking
  thee, old friend.

In peaceful bowers thou'st been with me, far from
  the busy town;
And many a thoughtless canzonet I've scribbled
  on thy crown.
I wore thee on my bridal-day, that sunny day
  of days;
But Time hath cudgell'd thee in ire, and knock'd
  thee several ways.

To My Old Silk Hat

I rose to-day, put on my hose,
My handkerchief, and all my clothes;
And, with my porringer and spoon,
I ate my mess of milk. Full soon,
With brother Will, a stout young chap,
We levell'd down the old field gap,
The horse traced in, and all away
With forks and rakes about the hay.
Dad built the load; we work'd amain,
Expecting it would shortly rain;
Then drove the laden wain along
With many a shout, and many a song.
Well, then 'twas who will build the rick?
Shall Will, or Sam, or Matt, or Dick?
Or Jem. As he's a clever lad?
O no, the lot must fall on Dad.
So he began to work away,
When we upset the load of hay;
Then, turning the red horse about,
We from the corn-close hastened out,
And trotted down the narrow lane,
And soon we had a load again;
Threw up the ropes, and driver John
With chirp and whistle, drove him on;
While mother in the field did stay
Behind us raking up the hay.
Ann trod the dry grass on the stack,
Her hair and bonnet, too, hung back;
And father pull'd with might and main,
And driver John re-loaded quick,
That soon we built and thatch'd the rick.

Hay Carrying

Toss, toss the hay!
Who will, may dig the shining ore;
Who will, may toil on foreign shore;
Who will, may dye their blades in gore:
We'll toss the hay.

The Haymaker's Song

Generally the foregoing poems were written by John (3) in his younger days solely to amuse his younger brothers and sisters, his paper being the reverse side of tea wrappers.

Hymns

John (3) wrote almost one hundred hymns. Except for some which were included in the Earle's Retreat Hymnal, no others have been included in any collection, and until the end of his life this was a great disappointment to him.

Tune: Petra   Matthew XV and XXV

This shall be my prayer today;
Help me, Saviour, on my way,
Guide me by Thy Spirit's might,
Fill me with Thy heavenly light,
Let my footsteps ordered be
Every moment, Lord, by Thee.

Help me in my daily task;
For Thy presence, Lord. I ask.
Should my spirit be distrest,
Quickly come and give me rest.
Show me Thy forgiving Son,
Teach me what His love has done!

Help me, Thou who hearest prayer,
In the smallest earthly care,
In temptation's trying hour,
In the winds that blight the flower,
In the storm that rocks the tree,
In the feeblest work for Thee!

Help me in my prayer of praise,
Which my heart would daily raise,
For the mercies I receive,
New at morning, noon, and eve,
Coming from Thy loving hand,
More in number than the sand.

This shall be My Prayer Today

Tune: Wellspring   Malachi Chap. 3 Verse 1

In the place prepared for Thee,
Hear us, mystic Trinity:
Lowly at Thy feet we fall,
Hiding nothing, owning all;
Seeking pardon for our crimes,
Acted o'er so many times.

O forgive our wanderings wide
For the sake of Him who died;
Show us Thy forgiving face;
Now enrich us with Thy grace.
Wash us in the purple tide,
Flowing from the Saviour's side.

May we at this solemn hour
Feel the Spirit's healing power;
In the silence of the soul
Worship Him who fills the whole,
Looking off from earthly love
To our great High Priest above.

Dear Redeemer, Prince Divine,
On our natural darkness shine;
With Thy erring children stay;
Speak our numerous sins away.
May we feel that Thou art nigh,
Jesus Christ is passing by.

Tune: Charterhouse   Hebrews Chap XII
                                    Verses 1 & 2

Prince of Princes, give us grace
To pursue the heavenly race,
Never in our duties slack,
Never, never looking back,
Life and all things to resign,
Striving for the faith Divine.

Grant us patience day by day,
Step by step along our way:
Guided may we ever be
In the path marked out by Thee:
From our fears and doubtings cease,
Striving after perfect peace.

Lift we now our anxious eyes
To the Ruler of the skies:
O descend our souls to bless,
Clothe us with Thy righteousness.
Let Thy power to us be shown,
Then transport us to thy throne.

Lead us on through pastures new,
With the Prince of Life in view.
He the Author, He the End,
Jesus Christ the sinner's Friend;
Who will give us here His love,
And the rest of heaven above.

Prince of Princes, Give us Grace

Tune: Euphony   Luke Chap.
2 Verses 11 & 14

The King is come, foretold so long:
The earth is now one strain of song:
O'er town and tower the billows swell,
O'er mead and moor, o'er down and dell:
The wilds rejoice, in glory clad,
And every mountain-top is glad.
Behold Him in a manger laid:
The star appears in heaven's high glade:
The shepherds hear the angelic strain,
And leave their flocks upon the plain;
While overhead bright seraphs sing,
In honour of our Saviour King.

O precious, precious guiding Star,
Which cheers the sinner's eye afar,
And lights us through the deeps of time
To regions holy and sublime!
O may we our best offerings bring
In honour of our Saviour King.

Still swells the song through every sky,
'All glory be to God on high!
Goodwill to men: from shore to shore
Let peace prevail for evermore.'
And rivers roll and forests ring
In honour of our Saviour King.

The King is come, Foretold so Long

Tune: Te Laudant Omnia   Matthew Chap.
XI Verse 29

Ever learning may I be
Living lessons, Lord of Thee,
From the ever-cheering light,
From the mystery of the night,
From the stars that spread Thy fame,
Whispering through the heavens Thy name.

Let me learn from all things here,
Bird and brook and floweret dear,
Valley low and mountain high,
Ocean vast and spreading sky,
Meadow green and forest tall;
For Jehovah made them all.

Let me in the knowledge grow
How Thou didst abide below,
Wear Thee ever in my heart,
Meek and lowly as Thou art,
Who the scoffer's insult bore,
And the crown of mockery wore.

Let me learn from hour to hour
More and more Thy saving power,
More and more Thy counsels sweet,
Sitting lowly at Thy feet;
On Thy steadfast truth rely;
Learn to live, and learn to die.

Ever Learning May I Be

It seems fitting to close this small selection of hymns with extracts from a poem which John (3) wrote and called *A Sermon in Prayer*:

My text shall be – Do good to all,
The bondman and the free,
To him whose feet may often slide,
And good shall come to thee.
Give not thy casket to a thief,
Thy secret to a liar,
And rather suffer stripes than stain
The honour of thy sire.

Let no hypocrisy be thine,
In market, church, or shop;
Appear exactly what thou art;
Let all deception drop.
The painted bubble in the wind
Is almost sure to burst;
Of all the creatures God has made
The hypocrite is worst.

Judge not thy neighbours hastily,
For fear that thou may'st err;
Thou canst not tell how fierce the fight
Which did his pulses stir.
For in temptation's fiery hour,
When scorn is on the lip,
If thou wert sorely pressed like him,
Thy feet, perhaps, might slip.

Find out thy work, and follow it
With earnest trusting care,
And fit success shall come at last,
A satisfying share.
No rod from Vulcan's blazing forge,
Which northern tempests fan,
Was ever heated hot enough
To brand the lazy man.

And do not run in debt for clothes,
Or even daily bread,
Nor waste the gifts which God has given
By lying late in bed.
Be prompt at duty's earnest call,
Thy country's laws obey,
Nor let to-morrow find undone
What thou should'st do to-day.

Conclude I now, Keep passion down,
Let conscience rule thy breast,
Of all the gifts on thee bestowed,
Give Him thy very best.
Make Bible-promises stay,
Let not thy praying cease,
But thank thy Maker day by day,
So shall thy end be peace.

Acknowledgement is made to Mr Colin Anthony, Organist of Stithians Methodist Church, for selecting appropriate tunes from *Hymns and Psalms*, the current Methodist and Ecumenical Hymn Book - Methodist Publishing House 1983.

War, Peace and Intemperance

'Tis night:: along the sky huge meteors walk,
Like giants flashing with a thousand blades.
Behind them, on those clouds of gory red
Ride hosts of horsemen, and their flickering swords
Clash and re-clash upon the ear of Night;
And down the sides of those dark rolling hills
Rush streams of human blood, with fire and smoke.
Unearthly sounds are muttering through the dark:
Men shiver in the streets, and talk of woe:
Dogs howl, the ravens scream, and funeral songs
Wail through the midnight with the voice of death,
Awful prognostics of the coming storm.

The War-fiend

The ground was red with gore,
Red waves roll'd on the shore;
Uncoffin'd armies stiffen'd where they fell;
Cities and towns were void,
Deserted, sack'd, destroy'd,
And creeping things did in their ruins dwell.

The Last Warrior

I sometimes tell my little boys
What I should like to see.
No drunkard reeling from his shed,
No dark oppressor's hand,
No sound of war or tyranny
From farthest land to land,

No beggar shivering in his rags,
But men be brethren all;
And peace and plenty reign throughout
This sublunary ball.

A Home Idyll

Hail labour's noble line,
In meadow or in mine,
Whether ye lay the rail, or ride the wave:
Ye are a nation's health,
Ye are a nation's wealth,
Her treasure ye, the bravest of the brave.

Shout in the reign of Peace,
When tyranny shall cease,
And not a bullet cuts the feverish air;
When the green corn shall rise,
And ripen 'neath all skies,
And man shall meet his brother everywhere:

Prologue for Penny Readings

I had a vision yester-eve,
Of blossoms white and rare,
A little child the lion led,
The wolf and lamb were there:
No tent of war was on the plain,
The sounds of strife did cease,
And through the air an angel sang,
'It is the reign of Peace.'

Old John

The rushy vale, the mountain brown,
The swallow wheeling o'er the down,
The solemn tarn, the echoing moor,
The boulders on the great sea shore,
All whisper, where the echoes flee,
'O, live in peace, where'er you be.'

Live in Peace

Where the woodbine and whortle arose,
And held their sweet cups to the sun,
I sat in a dingle of rose
When an evening of June had begun:
And far o'er the rock-covered wold,
Where the glory of sunset did lie
In currents of crimson and gold,
A vision arose on mine eye:

A country of meadow and stream,
With valleys of palm-tree and vine,
Where corn in its richness did gleam,
And fattened the beautiful kine;
The ploughman was on the wide mead,

The milkmaid was under the tree,
The shepherd was tuning his reed
Afar in the bountiful lea.

Here Peace, in a halo of light,
Her sway o'er the populace spread:
No clamour arose on the night,
No cry of the orphan for bread.
The sword and the battle-axe then
Were changed to the glittering share,
And songs from the bosoms of men
Swelled on the millennium air.

No brother chased brother to death,
No master did fetter the slave,
No chief-trump received the warm breath:
O, War had gone down to his grave.
And over the nations a joy,
For ever fresh honours did win,
Which rifles would never destroy,
The kingdom of love had set in.

A Vision

Where four roads met in quaintness
Upon the hedgeless moor,
A lame old man instructed
The children of the poor.
And, hanging in his school-room,
Was many a curious board,
'Why cannot wrongs be settled
Without the flashing sword?'

'Tis said, by those who knew him,
That strips were his disdain;
He never beat a pupil,
He never used the cane.
Yet rich became his scholars
From Wisdom's golden hoard:
Why cannot wrongs be settled
Without the flashing sword?

And still the utmost order
Prevailed throughout the place;
He had some word of comfort
To cheer the rising race:
And sang they morn and even,
How Peace should be restored,
And every wrong be settled
Without the flashing sword.

Forth went that old man's pupils
Along their several ways,
With Peace-stars on their banners,
Throughout the after days.

Each strove for arbitration,
Of which we are assured,
When wrongs shall all be settled
Without the flashing sword.

The Lame Schoolmaster

Is there nothing for man but the gun and the sword?
Why cannot disputes be settled by word?
Why cannot the errors to which we are prone
Be righted for ever by reason alone?

The Sharpshooter's Victim

If men were wise, they'd sow the land,
And seek the earth's increase,
Destroy the instruments of War,
And follow after Peace.
Whose home is where the vine-leaves spread
Around the pastoral walls,
And lowing herds adorn the fields,
And oxen fill the stalls.

If men were wise, no martial blade
In soldier-hand would gleam,
But Peace would carol in her bower
By lake and gentle stream:
The flowers of Paradise would bloom
In every earthly home,
And Trees of righteousness abound.
O God! when will it come?

If Men were Wise

O God of Gods, assert Thy strength!
Uplift Thy might hand!
May War and Drunkenness no more
Deface the lovely land!
Let truth and righteousness prevail,
And love's all-powerful leaven
Transform the erring universe,
And earth be bathed in heaven!

Two Giants

How are the mighty fallen!
How are the weak beguiled!
How strong drink robs the father
Of love for wife or child;
Shattering domestic concord,
As if by furies hurled,
In a destroying tempest,
Across the wailing world.

Alvina

His Final Poem

I stand like one upon a reach of elms,
By the Great River's shore,
Listening for voices from untrodden realms,
Which thrill me evermore.

My staff is lying by a mound of flowers,
My weary feet at rest,
The echoes haunt me in song-ringing showers
From regions of the blest.

A mystic Hand comes through the fading light,
Which I but dimly see,
And takes my lyre, and bears it out of sight,
The Hand that gave it me.

The sky-taught bird, and lesser shining shapes
That in the hedgerows dwell,
Or gather to the concert of the capes,
Breathe forth their sad farewell.

My last lay holds a benediction bright
For friends and patrons kind,
Who filled my hemisphere with purer light,
Which leaves a glow behind.

My Last Lay

(Respectfully inscribed to 'My Patrons and Friends')

4. William B. Harris

William B Harris
1822–92

On the reverse of the original photograph is written:
To my Mother Kitty Harris. Wm B. Harris

Early Life

William, the second child of John (2) and Christian (Kitty), was born at Six Chimneys on 11 April 1822 and baptized at Camborne Parish Church on the 27th of the same month.

William and John (3) grew up together and were inseparable companions and as youngsters shared the same bed. From poems which John (3) wrote about their boyhood it is evident that they very much enjoyed their simple rural upbringing; they had happy times together, getting into various scrapes! Two of these episodes are depicted in poems by John (3) which he wrote later in life as a means of acquainting his small daughter Jane with the pitfalls and joys of his and William's boyhood. Two of these poems are as follows:

The Two Boys and the Lamb

A little lamb was feeding upon the mountain side,
Among the grass and meadow-flowers that sparkled
  far and wide;
A little snow-white lamb, so innocent and free,
Leaped up to kiss the sunshine in my father's daisy-lea.

Two little boys were playing, with wheelbarrow
  and spade,
Where this white lamb was leaping in the
  bright daisy-glade.
Sometimes they carolled lightly, sometimes they
  both would sigh,
And, in a moment, they would weep, perhaps
  they knew not why.

These two delicious urchins, myself and Uncle Will,
Here dreamt away our childhood upon our
  native hill;
We carolled in the sunshine, we chatted in the shade:
We played beneath the hawthorn, in snow-white
  flowers arrayed.

We had a little iron pick to dig the mountain earth;
Some genius of uncommon strength had surely
  given it birth!
We ran and struck this little lamb with it upon
  the head,
And, in an instant, down it fell: we thought it
  must be dead!

The pretty white unconscious thing we in the
  barrow placed,
To wheel it somewhere out of sight, and bury it
  in haste.
We trembled lest the owner's eye our wickedness
  should see;
We looked behind, we looked before: alas! how
  sad were we!

At last we tripped it on the heath, sheer o'er the
  barrow's side;
It felt the shock, and off it ran in mazy circles wide!
We clapped our hands, we sang for joy, we danced
  in rapturous glee:
If we had got a thousand pounds, we could not
  happier be!

We promised, creeping hand in hand our father's
  meadows o'er.
That we would strike a little lamb in such a way
  no more!
We never did. Go where I may in Nature's wildest
  bowers,
I never shall forget the lamb we struck among the
  flowers.

This is a simple circumstance, I grant it, little Jane:
But 'tis a wicked thing to cause unnecessary pain.
The smallest worm you tread upon, the little fly
  you kill,
Feels equally as keen a pain as I or Uncle Will.

The Truant Schoolboys

There is a little rivulet,
Within a shadowy dell,
Which has been murmuring, on and on,
For years: I know it well:
For, when a very little boy,
I played beside its brink,
And saw the little singing birds
Hop from the boughs and drink.

I think I love this little stream
Far more than any other,
Because it tells me, even now,
Sweet stories of my brother.
It tells me of your uncle, dear,
Who, in a far-off land,
Will oft look back upon the time
We frolicked on its sand.

I well remember now the day,
A long, long time ago,
When we left school before the hour,
'Twas very naughty though!
To go and catch the little fish,
And make them die with pain,
On purpose to amuse ourselves:
'Twas naughty, little Jane!

We tarried till the sun had set,
And then the stars came out,
But we, beside this little stream,
Were watching for the trout.
Up rose the yellow harvest-moon:
We saw her in the rill,
And turn'd our faces to our home
Upon Bolenowe Hill.

We stopped, when half-way up its side,
To wipe the mud away:
'Twas then we felt how sad we were,
What we had done that day,
Deceived our parents, left the school,
And told our master lies,
And killed those pretty little fish:
The tears came in our eyes.

How very sad we crept along!
Our cottage came in sight;
We heard our own sweet mother's voice,
We saw the taper's light.
We trembled; for we were afraid
To stand before our sire;
We knew we had incurred that day
His greatest, heaviest ire!

Our hands were lifted to the latch,
Now trembling more and more,
And soft as ever fairy did,
We stepped across the floor,
And cowered beneath our mother's wing,
With love's sweet odour wet;
And how she acted to us then,
I never shall forget.

And when the waxing harvest moon
Shall rise above the hill,
All bright and beauteous at her full,
I'll take you to the rill,
And show you where, years, years ago,
Your singing father strayed,
Beside this murmuring rivulet,
And with your uncle played.

Another escapade in which these two boys participated is included in John's (3) autobiography and must have taken place when William was just over four years old: 'Six years had scarcely passed, when my brother and I, without the consent of our parents went to fish in the nearest stream. It was the month of March, and still cold. I remember it as if it only transpired a week ago. Now and then a lark soared into the ether, and we shaded our eyes with our hands to watch it and hear its song. But we were not happy, having gone without leave. We caught an exceedingly large trout, and in doing so wet ourselves to the skin. Evening was approaching, and I asked my brother to go home. He seemed stupified in his drenched garments, and did not care to move, so I took him by his hand and led him up the hill. In this way we reached the outer hedge of my father's farm, and then he suddenly stopped, lay down on the bank, and begged me to let him sleep. Young as I was, I knew he was seized with cold, and that if left alone he must die. So I took him on my back, though I could scarcely trudge under him, and went on. The ground was slippery and steep, and I had hedges to go over with my unconscious burden, which seemed to grow heavier at every step. The stars came out, the light from our window gleamed over the meadow, and soon I delivered him into my mother's arms. Warm blankets were procured, the fire replenished, and shortly my brother was himself again. By God's blessing I had saved his life. A few evenings afterwards we were to bear the punishment due to us for thus going a-fishing without leave, by retiring supperless to bed. But as we lay awake listening to the old clock at the top of the stairs, and sadly sobbing by turns, we heard the softest footfall on the chamber floor, and knew it was our mother stealing in with some thick slices of bread and butter. She could not bear to think of our going to sleep hungry.' The reference to saving William's life may contain a touch of exaggeration, but does not in any way belittle the good intentions and thoughtfulness of John (3) as a youngster of six years.

Some time before his eighth birthday, William accompanied his father and John (3) on a visit to the beach at Gwithian Towans on the North Cornwall coast, also described in his autobiography: 'Although our house was so situated that we could see the North and South Channels from the highest point of the hill, yet I was nearly ten years old before I was near the sea. Then, on a holiday, my father took me and my brother William to the sands at Gwithian, travelling on foot forth and back.[1] I shall never forget the impression made upon my mind when I first drew near the great ocean, beheld the huge cliffs and rocks, and heard the thunder of the billows upon the shore. I saw it afterwards in my dreams and heard its eternal roll among the daisies and lark-bursts of my mountain meads.' No doubt William was also impressed but totally oblivious to the fact that sixteen years later he would cross this great ocean!

Education

It is evident from John's (3) poems that when William was old enough, probably at about five years of age, he accompanied his brother to the cottage school at Forest Gate, and possibly spent from three to four years there.

William must also have availed himself of opportunities for self-improvement here in Cornwall and probably continued in America linked to the acquirement of knowledge through experience and travel. Although John (3) does not mention it, William could have joined the former in his efforts to broaden his knowledge. William certainly kept up a not insignificant correspondence with the writer's grandfather, Mark Smith Harris, for the whole of his life in America. In later years William served as a school clerk in Wisconsin. We will also see that he acquired an acumen for business in building up his land holdings on the prairie.

Working Life in Cornwall

It seems probable, although there is no available evidence, that William like John (3), commenced work on surface at Dolcoath at about nine years of age and went underground with his father and John (3) when thirteen. One thing is certain, that William was subjected to the deep descent over ladders into the mine and the much more exhausting climb out of the mine after a long shift in the poorly-ventilated, hot and dust-laden atmosphere. One speculates if initially during these climbs William would have been roped to his father or John (3) or both. He became a tributer working with his father and brother and in the Camborne Parish Census of June 1841 was designated a copper miner.

By the early 1840s Dolcoath was drawing to the end of its life as a copper mine and the underlying tin-bearing ground had yet to be discovered and developed. In any case, the prospect did not look good for the miner and especially the tributer. Coupled to this situation, the country had now entered the period historically termed 'The Hungry Forties' and so, not surprisingly, William's thoughts, like that of many other miners, turned to other possibilities in far-off countries.

The Decision to Emigrate and His Departure

No doubt William often talked about going overseas and discussed it with his parents and John (3), but it seems that they were completely taken aback when he announced his decision to go! Apparently they could not understand his desire to leave home and family. Of course his decision did herald the breaking up of this closely-knit family, as in due course five of William's brothers and a sister emigrated, none of whom ever came home again excepting Matthew (2), though only for a very short period to get married.

However, William did not go alone for James Sims, his sister Ann's fiancé, went with him. James Sims lived at Carwynnen, just over a mile west-north-west of Six Chimneys, and probably worked with William at Dolcoath. Certainly they would have been well acquainted in the Methodist circles of Troon and Plantation[2] chapels.

John (3) wrote upwards of fifteen poems about and to William, and those written around the time of the latter's departure range from unbelief and incomprehension at his going, to entreaty to stay.

To My Brother William When Leaving His Native Land for North America

My brother, companion of childhood adieu!
Too soon wilt thou haste o'er the waters so blue,
Too soon wilt thou turn from thy own happy hearth,
Too soon wilt thou leave the loved place of thy birth,
To contend with the world and thy sin-smitten kind;
While thy brothers and sisters are weeping behind.

Too soon must we part, Thou art here but to-day,
And tomorrow art posting away and away.

My brother, if Providence bless thee with lands,
And richly repay all the work of thy hands;
Ay, if thou shouldst prosper in basket and store,
Build houses, plant orchards, raise hillocks of ore;
O do not forget us in friendship's green wreath,
The scions of labour, the sons of the heath;
But often come forth at the eventide hour,
And muse on our mountain, my moss-mantled
  bower,
Our reed-cover'd cottage, thy mother, thy sire,
Thy brothers and sisters, beside the hall fire;
And surely this dream will sweet feelings inspire.
And if through the forest thy footsteps are borne,
When oak-leaves are dropping, and blossoms
  are torn,
When flowerets are drooping, and all things decay,
O think of thy brother, and muse on his lay;
For he then, perchance, may be moulding in clay.
But if from our crag-cover'd mountain you roam,
And poverty presses, O, brother, come home:
We'll stretch forth our hands to the prodigal son,
And greet with delight the poor rambling one;
We'll clothe you, and feed you, and solace your pain;
I weep at our parting, I cannot be gay;
For to-morrow thou'rt posting away and away.

My brother, well, go, and at evening's repose
Thy sisters shall gather the dew-dropping rose;
Thy brothers shall pluck from our favourite lea
A nosegay of wild flowers in memory of thee;
Thy mother shall call her loved younglings around,
And tell them with tears where their brother is found;
Thy father shall pace o'er the desolate wild,
Wiping off the salt tears for the thought of his child,
And wonder why thus in the spring-tide of bloom,
When the flowerets of hope shed their richest
  perfume,
His boy should be bounding away and away,
Like a spirit escaped from its prison of clay.
Go, brother, o'er mountains and woodlands to range.
I knew that this world was a sad scene of change;
And I knew, though thou ever hast twined round
  my heart,
That sooner or later we surely should part.
But I dreamt not so soon. Brother, why not delay?
No; to-morrow thou'rt posting away and away.

Long after William had departed and had settled in America, John (3) continued to entreat him to come home, always painting pictures in verse of the joys, beauties and sorrows of their native home:

Come leave cold Wisconsin, dear brother;
Let Fancy walk forth at your side,
And float on the pinions of thought
Across the Atlantic's blue tide;
And gaze for a moment or two
On the straw-cover'd home of your birth,
And weep, ay, in agony weep
Warm tears on the desolate hearth.

What a picture of sadness is here!
The spirit that Fill'd it is fled;
The voice once so pleasant and clear
Is silent - the Present is dead.
The Past like an echo is heard
Rolling over these desolate leas;
And tones which have long pass'd away
Come floating again on the breeze.

from The Deserted Home
(An Epistle to My Brother)

For we are on our mountain's head, watching the
  twilight grey,
And wondering why our brother thus so soon could
  haste away:
Ay, wondering why he thus could go from home's
  long cherished bowers,
And leave us here alone to cull the Summer's
  brightest flowers!

Thou canst not see my British home, with dusky
  twilight crowned;
Thou canst not see old England's hills and valleys lie
  around;
Thou canst not see the rising moon peer o'er our
  mountains brow,
How beautiful, how beautiful! But, brother, where
  art thou?

from An Epistle to My Brother

William and James had decided to go out to the lead mining region of south-west Wisconsin where there was already a substantial Cornish community; indeed, it was the earliest[3] region of America to attract Cornish miners in any numbers, especially from Camborne mining district. It has been stated that by the time of the 1850 census about 4,500 inhabitants[4] of Dodgeville, Mineral Point, Linden, Hazel Green and Shullsburg, together with Galena in Illinois, were Cornish!

And so the day of departure dawned. Picture the fare-wells of the family at Six Chimneys, the younger boys probably taking turns in carrying William's travelling chest down through Stony Lane and then, after wishing the youngsters farewell, William continuing along Chycairne Lane and down to Camborne Station via Troon, with his father and John (3), where they were probably joined by James Sims and members of the latter's family. Imagine this little group boarding the train[5] for the six-mile journey to the small port of Hayle.

From a poem *The Parting Scene* by John (3) it appears that having seen William and James Sims aboard the little schooner of anything from seventy to one hundred tons displacement[6] that would take its complement of emigrants to Bristol, from where they would proceed to Liverpool by rail, the two Johns set off across Hayle Towans in the direction of Gwithian and continued walking until they lost sight of the schooner.

> The parting knell was rung;
> A scene of tumult reigned;
> Hands clung to hands, and eyes of love
> Were on each other strained.
> These eyes which never wept
> For many, many years,
> Were shedding for departing friends,
> A gush of hallowing tears.
>
> The mighty[7] steamer moves
> Along its watery track
> And oft the weeping emigrant
> Turns round and gazes back.
> His friends are on the beach
> Within his misty view:
> He waves his hat, and silently
> Breathes forth a last adieu!
>
> A son is on that ship,
> A father on the shore:
> And silently he paced along
> Beside the breakers roar;
> And when the flying bark
> Out of his vision swept,
> He turned his furrowed face away,
> He turned away and wept.
>
> I saw him wipe the tear
> From off his cheek that day;
> The secret workings of his soul
> No poet can portray.
> He saw his son no more
> Beneath the spreading skies;
> And now the tears are wiped away
> For ever from his eyes.

The Journey to South-west Wisconsin

Arriving at Liverpool, William and James took passage on the barque Oronoco of 470 tons burthen of which Edward Butler was Master.[8] They set sail for America on 7 May 1845. Their choice of Liverpool as the port of departure from England was without doubt due to the fact that ships from this port carried the poorest emigrants, who of necessity had to travel by the cheapest means.[9]

As early as 1702 packet ships were established to ply from Falmouth to the east coast ports of America at infrequent intervals, but by 1807 there was a more regular service operating from certain small ports of south-west England by other ship owners. In these well-constructed small vessels passengers with sufficient financial means could enjoy a pleasant passage at, say, a cost of around fifty guineas,[10] but this cost would have been absolutely prohibitive to William and James.

After what must have been a harrowing voyage of over 3,000 miles that lasted for six and a half weeks, William and James finally arrived in New York on 20 June and disembarked the following day.

They then had to face another journey of considerable length, but whether or not they appreciated or understood the vast distances involved, especially where the routes were circuitous, is doubtful. However, one thing is certain, they had to decide which route to take. Interestingly, traveller's guides had been available as early as 1836[11] to those who could read and afford to purchase them. As the routes and means of travel were so numerous and varied it is difficult to ascertain how beneficial these guides were to immigrants who had no previous knowledge of the country. The means of travel also varied, with steam-boats on certain rivers and lakes, barges and flat-bottomed boats on canals, stagecoaches and wagons on roads and trails, together with limited travel on the few then existing railroads. In addition, any particular route could involve a combination of some or all of the foregoing means.[12]

After having travelled around 5,000 miles, involving experiences they were likely never to forget, William and James arrived at their destination - Dodgeville - where the lead mines had been operating for the past eighteen years.

The Promised Land

On the journey from New York, William and James had feasted their eyes on the spectacular scenery of their new country, but now before them was Dodgeville and the countryside round about. Despite the pitting and scars of mining operations, a scene very familiar to them, there was spread around Dodgeville, then just a village, the rural countryside. Areas of brushwood, patches of oaks, but most of all the wonderful grass-covered prairie. It was indeed a land of promise and exceptional beauty; and to William and James must have seemed limitless, as in reality it was. As yet they could not have fully appreciated the extent of this Badger State with its 5 million acres of forest, its mass of little hills and rolling plains, 15,000 crystal-clear lakes together with thousands of streams abounding in fish.[13] Where the land had been cultivated, the crops were bountiful compared to those grown on the cold Carnmenellis granite mass underlying Bolenowe Carn and Carwynnen, and there was game in profusion.

Some considerable time later when he was established in his new country, it seems that William wrote to John (3) extolling the benefits and virtues of this land of promise and suggesting that John (3) should come out and join him. It ill behoves John (3) that he replied in a somewhat petulant manner with a nine-verse poem called *My Cottage Home*:

You ask me why I do not come,
And share the stranger's feast;
And why I ever stay at home:
Think'st thou my joys are least?
Through England's flowery meads to trip,
Forgetting labour's life,
Charm'd with the melting voices of
A mother and a wife.

There may be woods around you spread,
With broad and glassy lakes;
Fire-flies may revel o'er your head,
And parrots in the brakes;
The mocking-bird's capricious note
May fall upon your ear,
And butterflies around you float
That never glitter here.

I care not for your woods of green,
Your Lakes and birds and flies:
You have not England's sunny stream,
You have not England's skies:
You have not England's holiday,[14]
When man and beast are free,
It is for these my boy, I stay;
They are enough for me.

Two sister-violets I've pluck'd
Beneath our hawthorn tree,
And wrapt them in this music sheet,
To send, my boy, to thee.
And brother, when they meet your eyes,
Far, far o'er ocean's foam,
Remember they were gems which clung
Around your Cornish home.

No doubt William and James selected Dodgeville rather than any other mining settlement in the region because an uncle of James, George Sims, was already living there with his family. Indeed, there were other cousins of James' and possibly of William already established there. The propensity of Cornish immigrants to seek out others born in the Delectable Duchy is well known and still continues; witness the Cornish Associations dotted over Britain and various parts of the world, even Cornish servicemen in Delhi during the Second World War.

Lead and zinc mining in south-west Wisconsin and north-west Illinois, the latter mineral in much smaller quantities than the former, was at this time totally different from the deep and complicated mining operations to which William and James had been accustomed in Cornwall. Although areas were pitted and scarred from working the lode outcrops, the shafts and levels were tiny, the former not more than one hundred feet deep and often much less. It must be admitted that the width of some of the underground stopes was of a size which must have necessitated considerable support of the hanging-wall when the ore was extracted. The lead mines around Dodgeville at that time when compared to Dolcoath were mere prospects, with little mechanisation, if any at all. The broken ore was hauled to surface by hand or horse-windlass through the shafts, and in wooden boxes on greased inclined planes from the open workings. Any accumulation of water being brought to surface in barrels.[15] At no time was there any requirement for massive pumping engines such as those in use in Cornish mines. The shallow shafts and open workings meant that there was no long and tiring twelve to fourteen hundred feet climb into and out of the mines such as William and James had been accustomed in Dolcoath.

It seems reasonable to assume that initially, and at least until the issue of mining leases was placed on a more legal basis by the Act of 1846,[16] that William and James found employment with one or the other of the little family-owned mines where there was plenty of opportunity to demonstrate their skills as experts in shaft sinking, driving levels, developing, breaking ore in the stopes and, where necessary, placing support timbers. It has not been possible to ascertain if they managed to obtain a mining lease, but if they did the arrangement would have been very similar to that to which they had been accustomed in Cornwall when working on tribute but on much superior terms.

From these small unmechanised mines there was never any prospect of making vast fortunes; and this no doubt was the reason for so many of their compatriots leaving the area in 1849 and 1850 in the hope of making quick fortunes in the Californian goldfields. William and James did not elect to go to California, they were content with Wisconsin, satisfied with the living they were making together with the prospect for the future. Wisconsin had been formed as a Territory in 1836 and in

1848 was admitted to the Union as an Independent State. William was determined to stay and become a part of his adopted country. In demonstrating his single-mindedness of purpose and perception he applied to become a citizen of the United States on 5 May 1848. His application was registered just two days prior to the third anniversary of his departure from Liverpool.

But what did the folk at home in Cornwall think of his action? It seems, that although large numbers of local people had gone out, and continued to go to the US, they could not appreciate why their relatives felt compelled to adopt the nationality of the country to which they had emigrated; a country which harboured such bright and enduring prospects for the future, not only for the immigrants, but for their descendants as well; prospects and opportunities which in Cornwall would never have come within their grasp. The objection was not engendered or fostered by any lingering sense of resentment of the outcome of the American War of Independence or the subsequent Treaty of Versailles; as the folk at home saw it, their relatives in America were selling their birthright, just as Esau had done, and this they would never accept. The opinion of the Harris family in Cornwall never changed despite the fact that later on four of William's brothers also emigrated to America. Seventy-five years after William's application the author remembers his mother Edith, née Harris, becoming most vehement on the subject! For a person to renounce his birthright was anathema to her. One must admit that the words of the declaration do appear drastic, especially as the statement develops into a crescendo of finality.

I do absolutely and entirely renounce and abjure forever, all allegiance and fidelity to any Foreign Prince, Potentate, State and Sovereignty whatsoever, and entirely renounce and abjure all allegiance and fidelity to the Queen of Great Britain whereof I was a subject.

But William was not to be dissuaded, his mind was made up, he was content to leave his decision to the test of time, and he was right.

The earlier reference to the war of 1775–81 reminds the writer of the occasion in 1983 when a great grandson of one of the Harris brothers, a third-generation American, visited Cornwall and while here attended a service in a village Methodist chapel. He was greatly surprised but fortunately saw the humorous side of the statement when he was welcomed from the pulpit as being 'A visitor from the Colonies'!

Initially William and James may have lodged with relatives of James, probably his uncle, George Sims, who had been resident in Dodgeville from at least 29 December 1843. It is recorded that circa 1842–43, Dodgeville only consisted of a few sod huts,[17] but it is possible that by 1845 there were families who, in order to supplement their earnings, took in lodgers. Certainly about 300 miles north of Dodgeville at Victoria in Upper Michigan there still exists a two-storey log house where, in the heyday of mining, a family lived downstairs and took in nine lodgers who slept in two shifts upstairs.[18] Similar arrangements may well have obtained in Dodgeville, but whichever mode of accommodation was adopted it would have been basic, even if William and James built a sod hut and batched for themselves.

Just over twelve months after William and James arrived in their new land, James purchased forty acres of prairie in the north-east of the north-west quarter of Section Thirty Six in nearby Linden Township. James

Reconstructed furnace for separating lead from the rock, sited alongside the pits and shafts

A reconstructed windlass over one of the shafts in the hill above Shake Rag Street, Mineral Point. The windlass is not of the normal design.

Iowa Series 31. Vol. 4. Page 7.

❖❖

To the Honorable CHARLES DUNN, Chief Justice of the Supreme Court of Wisconsin Territory, and presiding Judge of Iowa County District Court in said Territory.

I, *William Harris*, an alien born, free white person, of *twenty five* years and upwards, do hereby, in conformity with the first condition specified in the first section of the act of Congress, entitled "An act to establish an uniform rule of naturalization, and to repeal the acts heretofore passed on that subject," approved the 14th day of April, 1802, declare and make known to the said District Court in and for the county and Territory aforesaid, that my true and proper name is *William Harris* That I was born in the *Parish of Camborne* and County of *Cornwall* and in the *Kingdom* of *England* and that I am about *twenty five* years of age ; that I belonged to the *English* nation, and owed allegiance to the *Queen of Great Britain and Ireland* That I migrated from the port of *Liverpool* of *England* in the said *Kingdom* on the *7th* day of *May* A. D. 184*5*, and landed at *New York City* in the *State* of *New York* and in the United States of America, on the *21st* day of *June* A. D. 184*5*; that I have ever since my first arrival remained within the limits and jurisdiction of the United States; and that it is bona fide my intention to renounce forever all allegiance and fidelity to every foreign prince, power, potentate, state or sovereignty whatever, and more particularly such allegiance and fidelity as I may in any wise owe to the said *Queen of Great Britain and Ireland* either as a citizen or subject, and to become a Citizen of the United States, and to locate myself for the present in the county of *Iowa* and Territory of Wisconsin, whereof I am now an inhabitant, and that I do not now enjoy or possess, nor am I in any wise entitled to, any order of distinction or title of nobility, by virtue of the laws, customs, or regulations of the said *Kingdom of Great Britain and Ireland* or any other country ; and that I am sincerely attached to the principles contained in the Constitution of the United States, and well disposed to the good order, well being and happiness of the same, and desire that this my declaration and report may be accepted, filed and recorded, preparatory to my intended application to be admitted as a Naturalized Citizen of the United States, in conformity with the several acts of Congress heretofore passed on that subject.

Subscribed and sworn to before me, this *5th* day of *May* A. D. 184*8* } *Wm Harris*

Attest *William F. Henry*

CLERK,
District Court, Iowa County, Wisconsin Territory.

❖❖

Declaration of Intention by William to become an American Citizen

had asked Ann (2) Harris, William's sister, to come out and marry him, and prior to her arrival in the spring of 1847 one assumes that James and William had constructed a log house at some suitable location for her reception. Ann (2) and James were married in Dodgeville in June 1847.

William made his home with James and Ann until some time after the 1850 Iowa County census. In December 1848 James and Ann sold the forty acres together with all the hereditaments and appurtenances to William for the sum of $60. While the reason for selling by James and Ann is not clear, it suggests that William had decided to become a farmer, albeit in a small way, while continuing to follow his occupation as a miner. The dual occupation of miner and small farmer was consistent with that of his father and many others in Cornwall. William must have been very proud to be the owner of forty acres, the first land he had ever possessed, and prairie at that. Several times larger than his father's leasehold farm, it also had the certain prospect of being far more productive that the meadows on Bolenowe Carn.

By the time of the 1850 census, William had added the initial 'B' to his name, obviously to distinguish himself from two other William Harrises living in the locality. No doubt the 'B' emanated from the name Benjamin of both his grandfather and great grandfather.

At or about the time of his marriage to Agnes Jewel, William approached Joseph Lean, the legal guardian of Mary Agnes Jewel, a minor and daughter of Agnes Jewel above, with a proposition to purchase forty acres in the south-east of the north-west quarter of Section Seventeen in Dodgeville township. This particular real estate had been left to Mary Agnes on the death of her father. Joseph Lean made an application to Iowa County Probate

Court on 1 August 1854 requesting permission to sell the property. Having publicly advertised the sale and having received the highest bid of $160 from William, permission to sell was formally granted on 17 February 1855.[19]

Purchase of the property from his, or soon to be, step-daughter obviously removed from William any stigma attached to a person who upon marrying a widow of some means, was categorised as 'Walking in and hanging up his hat'! However, the main reason was that with a total of eighty acres, despite being in two parts three miles apart, William was now to give up mining and devote all his energies to farming. Certainly in the 1860 census William was designated a farmer, and by 1870 was listed as owning real estate to the value of $4,800 and personally of $2,950.[20] William did not forget his mother and the family in Cornwall, for at this time he commenced sending small drafts to them at roughly eighteen-month intervals, especially to his sister Kitty following the death of her husband twenty-two months after her marriage.

By 1876 the two surviving sons of William and Agnes had grown to manhood, and therefore in February of that year he acquired from Mary A. Lowry an additional eighty acres in the western half of the south-east quarter of Section Twenty-five in Linden Township. The purchase price was $2,000 to be paid in four instalments.[21]

In October 1883 William purchased yet another eighty acres, the vendor being J.T. Docker of Bournemouth, England, the purchase price of $1,600 being funded by a mortgage for the total sum. The land was con-

Jane Walters, née James,
second wife of William B. Harris

The two-storey loghouse at Victoria, Michigan, which housed a miner and his family and nine lodgers. Photographed 1985.

tained in the southern half of the south-west quarter of Section Twenty-five which linked up with his previous purchases in Sections Twenty-five and Thirty-six.[22] William had now reached a stage when he could reflect upon the fact that it was doubtful if any farmer within a thirty-mile east and west radius of Bolenowe Carn could claim to be the owner of 240 acres, and even if they did it would have been much less fertile. It must have been a source of satisfaction to William and confirmation of the soundness of his decision to stay and to become an American citizen.

In March 1886, within a month of his sixty-fourth birthday, William sold the whole of his holding to his two sons James John and Samuel who purchased it jointly. William could now sit back and enjoy the fruits of his labour. Between them the two sons paid $9,000 for the land, appurtenances and stock, and additionally agreed to accept responsibility for the $1,600 mortgage on eighty acres purchased by their father in 1883.

William had become interested in raising prize poultry, which locally earned him the nickname 'Chicken William'. In order to learn more of the genetics and rearing of poultry, William requested his brother Mark Smith Harris to obtain for him a copy of *The Game Laws of England*, which Mark despatched to him 16 October 1889. One of William's great-grandsons maintained that William (although he mistakenly called his great-grandfather John) was more interested in feather colour and other aesthetics rather than sound economics of egg or meat production, but it is obvious that it was in reality only a hobby.

Just prior to William selling the farm to his sons, an amusing incident occurred which was reported in the *Dodgeville Chronicle* of 1 May 1885 under the heading 'A Long Lost Brother Returns'. The following story was reported and is quoted verbatim:

As William B. Harris, the well known poultry man was working about his place, he espied a stranger approaching, and sizing him up, in his mind as a machine agent, book agent or some other of these philanthropic gentlemen who leave the comforts of home to go about conferring blessings upon the hard working granger and as he was quite busy and did not wish to buy anything just then, he made up his mind to cut the gentleman off rather short. Instead of talking machinery, or books or anything of that kind, the stranger said

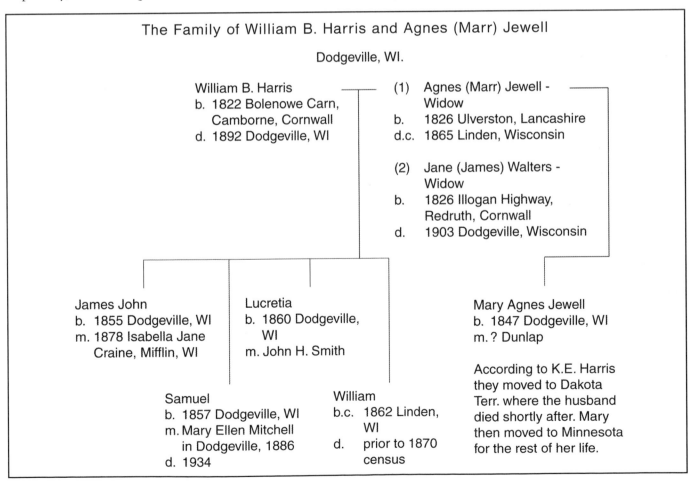

The Family of William B. Harris and Agnes (Marr) Jewell

Dodgeville, WI.

William B. Harris
b. 1822 Bolenowe Carn, Camborne, Cornwall
d. 1892 Dodgeville, WI

(1) Agnes (Marr) Jewell - Widow
b. 1826 Ulverston, Lancashire
d.c. 1865 Linden, Wisconsin

(2) Jane (James) Walters - Widow
b. 1826 Illogan Highway, Redruth, Cornwall
d. 1903 Dodgeville, Wisconsin

James John
b. 1855 Dodgeville, WI
m. 1878 Isabella Jane Craine, Mifflin, WI

Lucretia
b. 1860 Dodgeville, WI
m. John H. Smith

Mary Agnes Jewell
b. 1847 Dodgeville, WI
m. ? Dunlap

Samuel
b. 1857 Dodgeville, WI
m. Mary Ellen Mitchell in Dodgeville, 1886
d. 1934

William
b.c. 1862 Linden, WI
d. prior to 1870 census

According to K.E. Harris they moved to Dakota Terr. where the husband died shortly after. Mary then moved to Minnesota for the rest of her life.

that he had heard that Mr Harris did a little business in the chicken line, and as he was passing through the country he thought he would stop and see what he had. This struck Mr Harris in a soft spot, and accordingly he went to showing the stranger around, when after a few minutes the gentleman made himself known as Samuel Harris, Superintendent of the Quincy Copper Mines at Hancock, Michigan, William B's brother whom he had not seen in twenty-two years![23]

Marriages and Family

After having made his home with James and Ann for about six years, William married Agnes Jewell, widow of John Jewell. Agnes had been born at Ulverston, Lancashire,[24] England in 1826 and came out to Wisconsin with her parents. She was the seventh child of William Marr and Mary Higgins. Her father had been a timber merchant with a business in Canal Street, Ulverston.[25] When her first husband died, probably in California, Agnes was left with one child, Mary Agnes Jewell, who was three years old at the time of the 1850 Iowa County census.[26]

The record of William's marriage to Agnes has not been located, but a biographical sketch on William published in the *History of Iowa County* states that it took place in 1853. This date appears to be near the mark as their first child, James John, was born in July 1855. Their second child Samuel was born in 1857 and their daughter Lucretia on 14 November 1860. Their fourth and last child, William, was born circa 1862 and died prior to the 1870 census.

William perpetuated Harris family first names within his own family. James John seemingly in memory of the boy's uncle, James Harris, who had died in Melbourne, Australia twelve months previously, and the now familiar John; alternatively he could have been called after his young cousin James John Sims who had died when three years old in Dodgeville in 1851. Samuel was probably named after his uncle, Samuel Harris, later of Michigan but who at this time was also resident in Dodgeville. Lucretia was undoubtedly named after her cousin, the poet's daughter, who had died five years previously at six years old. All the children except William, who was probably born in Linden Township, were born in Dodgeville.

Around 1865 this little family were grief stricken when Agnes passed away. It seems that no death certificate exists for Agnes, or for that matter William junior who passed away a year or two later. Apparently, until 1897, there was no requirement to register a death unless a doctor had been in attendance![27] This situation raises questions: was the death sudden or was there no doctor immediately available? Whatever the cause, the trauma of the family is easy to imagine. Surprisingly, it has not

been possible to locate the graves of Agnes and William junior. Mary Agnes Jewell was around eighteen years old, and had now lost both her parents, but one imagines she was of considerable help in looking after her three half-brothers and half-sister.

Left in this situation, William married a second time on 1 August 1866. Again his bride was a widow, Jane Walters, whose maiden name had been James. Although she was then resident in Dodgeville, she was Cornish having been born in Illogan, an adjacent parish to Camborne, on 5 January 1824. The wedding ceremony took place in William's home on the farm in Linden Township and was a truly family affair because the religious ceremony was conducted by William's brother-in-law, Rev. James Sims, who had been ordained into the Methodist Episcopal Ministry and at that time was the pastor of Linden Methodist Episcopal Church. Jane was a wonderful mother to all her step-children and to Mary Agnes Jewell who, in reality, was no relation to her. The esteem in which Mary Agnes held her step-father and Jane, although she had married and left home, was proven by her making the long journey from Minnesota to attend their funerals in 1893 and 1903 respectively.

William served his community for a time as school clerk and also as a pathmaster. In the latter case he would have been responsible for organising and obtaining the assistance of his neighbours to carry out maintenance of the particular section of road allotted to his care. Brought up in and a member of the Wesleyan Methodist Church

James John Harris, eldest son of
William B. Harris and his first wife Agnes Marr Jewell

in Cornwall, William and his family attended, after taking up residence on the farm, the little white wood-framed Methodist Episcopal Church of Bloomfield Community which had been built circa 1846 by the pioneers and was located on the prairie. The church no longer stands and unlike the Primitive Methodist Church of the adjoining Laxey Community there is no marker or commemorative tablet on site, just a decorated iron arch at the entrance to the cemetery on which is inscribed the single word 'Bloomfield'.[28]

In politics William voted Republican like many other Cornish immigrants who exercised their rights as citizens of the United States.

James John Harris

James John, the eldest child of William and Agnes, was born July 1855 in Dodgeville. On the 1870 census he was listed as a farmhand although still attending school, and so was doubtless assisting his father on the two separate forty-acre farms.

On 24 November 1878, James John married Isabella Jane Craine of Mifflin.[29] Isabella was the daughter of John Craine and Ann Jane Skillicorn[30] and had been

born at Lonan in the Isle of Man in September 1856 prior to the family emigrating to America. By the 1885 special census for Linden, James J. and Isabella were living in their own house on the Harris farm in Linden Township.

In March 1886, as previously mentioned, James J. and his brother Samuel jointly purchased the whole of their father's holding in Linden and Dodgeville Townships. In April 1893 the brothers formally and equally divided the land between themselves, registering their action by Quit-Claim Deeds.[31] The deeds were signed by themselves and their wives and witnessed by the State of Wisconsin, County of Iowa Register - W.D. Prideaux and Richard Carter, Notary Public. There is, however, an exception to the division in that the southern half of forty acres in Section Seventeen, Dodgeville Township, is not mentioned on the deed signed by Samuel and his wife. Possibly this twenty acres had been retained by William for some specific purpose?

Additionally, there is a further Quit-Claim Deed of April 1893[32] signed by William's daughter Lucretia and her husband John Smith, whereby they relinquished for the sum of one dollar any claim to eighty acres situated in the west half of the south-east quarter of Section Twenty-five, Linden Township. Possibly a problem presented itself by the discovery of a will executed by William and dated prior to the sale of land to James J. and Samuel.

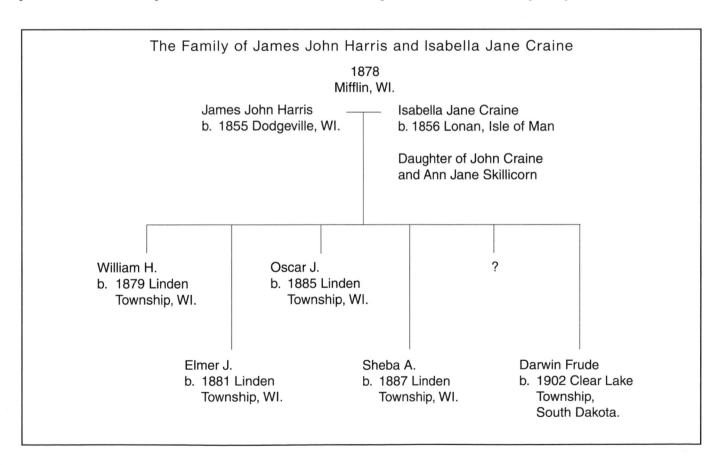

In March 1895, James J. and Isabella sold their interest in the 200-acre Linden Township farm to Samuel Harris for a consideration of $1,900. Whether or not James J. and his family immediately moved to South Dakota is not known, but the 1900 census for Minnehaha County shows them as being residents of Clear Lake Township. Then in November 1901 they purchased the north-east quarter of Section Thirty-five in Clear Lake Township from John and Jenny Mundt. They paid $12.5 an acre, amounting to $2,000 in all.[33]

By 1910 they had moved to Precinct Six, Stratton Township, Kit Carson County, Colorado, having sold their farm in Clear Lake Township to a Mr Black.[34] According to the census of that year, their youngest child Darwin Frude Harris was the only one of their children resident with them.

James J. and Isabella had at least six children. William H., Elmer J., Oscar J., Sheba A., another who passed away as a child and Darwin Frude. Excepting for the first child there was no attempt to perpetuate Harris family names; indeed, the remaining names were somewhat unusual, not to say strikingly innovative, although they may have been usual in the Craine or Skillicorn families.

Unfortunately it has not been possible to trace this particular family beyond the foregoing information.

Samuel Harris

Samuel, the second child and son of William and Agnes, was born in Dodgeville in 1857, but for some obscure

---

The Family of Samuel Harris and Mary Ellen Mitchell

1886
Dodgeville, WI.

Samuel Harris
b. 1857 Dodgeville, WI.
d. 1934 Linden
   Township, WI.
———
Mary Ellen Mitchell
b. 1865 Dodgeville, WI.
d. 1926 Linden Township, WI.

William James
b. 1887 Linden Township
d. 1970 Linden Township
   Farmer
m. 1909 Mabel Lorena
   Richardson a School
   Teacher of Wyoming
   Valley near Spring Green.
   Mabel b. 1888, d. 1965.

They farmed all their married lives on the Harris family farm, Bloomfield Community, Linden Township.

Ada
b. 1891 Linden Township
d. 1971 Dodgeville
m. 1911 John Roger Oxnem

John, a farmer, d. 1951. Their farm stood on the western edge of Dodgeville Town.

Ruth Ann
b. 1896 Linden Township
d. 1982 Dodgeville
m. 1917 Clyde Jones Thomas

Clyde, b. 1895, d. 1971. He worked for the Telephone Company for the whole of his life.

All above information received from Gerald and Delva Harris, Dodgeville, Wisconsin

---

reason his name did not appear on the 1860 Iowa County census transcript. On the 1870 census Samuel, like his brothers, was described as a farmhand but still attending school. To have been brought up from an early age to do his share of work on the farm, he was following the pattern of his father and uncles on Bolenowe Carn.

When he was twenty-nine years of age Samuel married Mary Ellen Mitchell in Dodgeville on 25 May 1886.[35] Mary Ellen had also been born in Dodgeville and was the daughter of James Mitchell and Elizabeth Ann Wedlake. The marriage ceremony was conducted by Samuel's uncle, Rev. James Sims, at that time resident in Fennimore, Grant County, Wisconsin, serving in the itinerant ministry of the Methodist Episcopal Church.

Mary Ellen (Nell) took up residence on the farm in Linden Township, and there the couple raised their family of a boy and two girls. William James was born at the farm 7 May 1887 and in due course became the third generation to own and work the land until he passed it on to his son Gerald Laverne Harris in 1950. Their elder daughter Ada was born in 1891 and the younger daughter Ruth in 1896.

Samuel was an ardent member of the Methodist Episcopal Church, and eventually became a lay preacher and instructor in Bible studies.[36] According to the disciplines of the Church, Samuel would not have been permitted to preach without a licence issued by the District Conference or where no District Conference existed by the Quarterly Conference. The process for obtaining a licence was fairly involved and was subject to the following provisions:[37]

(Continued on page 99.)

The house on the farm in Linden Township. It was built by Samuel and was the home of his children and grandchildren. The house was destroyed by fire in the early 1930s. In the picture are, from left to right, William J. Harris, his mother Mary Ellen and Samuel Harris.

The Samuel Harris Family
Samuel, his wife Mary Ellen and their children: William J.,
their elder daughter Ada and younger daughter Ruth holding a doll

The Family of William James Harris and Mabel Lorena Richardson

William James Harris
b. Linden Township 1887
Ran the family farm in
Bloomfield Community.
Introduced mechanisation
on the farm.
d. 1970

1909

Mabel Lorena Richardson
b. Wyoming Valley near
Spring Green 1888.
School Teacher.
d. 1965

Bernice Addanell
b. 1910 Linden Township
Stenographer
d. 1976
m. Norbert D Hipenbecker
b. 1914

Norbert farmed near
Muscoda, WI and later
worked for the Milwaukee
Railroad.

Kenneth Earl
b. 1915 Linden Township
Graduated from University of
Wisconsin at Madison and
also University of California.
m. 1938 Alice May Watson
graduate of University of
Tennessee at Dubuque, IA.

Served for 24 years in the
Foreign Service, US Dept. of
State. Served as Naval Officer in
the Pacific in World War II.
Following retirement he spent a
term in Africa as a volunteer
Missionary.
d. 1993 at San Diego, CA.

Dolores Jean
b. 1933 Madison, WI.
m. (1) ? Miller
   (2) William Eugene
       Beerkircher, a Farmer.

Gerald Laverne
b. 1913 Linden Township
m. 1938 Delva Christianson
of Cobb, WI.

Continued the mechanisation
of the home farm, becoming
the fourth generation to own
and work it. Sold the farm
in 1970 and 1972 took
full-time work with the
American Breeders Assoc.
as a genetic evaluator.
d. 1993 Bloomfield.

Joan Eliza
b. 1928 Linden Township
m. (1) Glen Stratman
   (2) Russel Gerard Gay

All information ex Gerald and Delva Harris,
Dodgeville, Wisconsin

Gerald Laverne and Delva Harris on the occasion
of their Golden Wedding, 10 September 1988

The Family of Ada Harris and John Roger Oxnem

Ada Harris —— 1911 —— John Roger Oxnem
b. 1891 Linden
   Township
d. 1951
   Dodgeville, WI.

Gwendolyn Marie
b. 1912 in Dodgeville
   Township
d. 1951
m. 1939 La Vern Hopps
   of Highland, WI.

Laverne Harris
b. 1915
m. 1942 Grace Elaine Dunn

They operated the Oxnem
Family Farm

The Family of Ruth Ann Harris and Clyde James Thomas

Ruth Ann Harris —— 1917 —— Clyde James Thomas
b. 1896 Linden
   Township
d. 1982

b. 1895
d. 1971

Worked for the Telephone
Company in Dogeville for
the whole of his life.

Florence Margery
b. 1920 in Dodgeville, WI.
d. 1970
m. 1941 Mason Tremelling
   in Missouri.

Robert Dean
b. 1923 in Dodgeville, WI.
   Founded the Thomas Oil
   Company in 1942.
m. 1948 Mary Jean Taylor.

Dean was named `Kiwanian of
the Year' in 1992.

Irene
b. 1927 in Dodgeville, WI.
m. 1949 Frank Filardo

Lives in Mineral Point, WI.

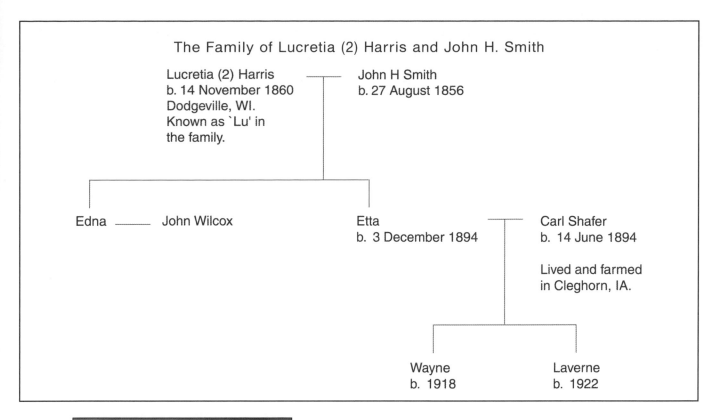

The Family of Lucretia (2) Harris and John H. Smith

Lucretia (2) Harris
b. 14 November 1860
Dodgeville, WI.
Known as `Lu' in
the family.

John H Smith
b. 27 August 1856

Edna ———— John Wilcox

Etta
b. 3 December 1894

Carl Shafer
b. 14 June 1894

Lived and farmed
in Cleghorn, IA.

Wayne
b. 1918

Laverne
b. 1922

Lucretia and John Smith circa 1926.

It has been something of a disappointment to have been unsuccessful in locating more information on Lucretia and her family.

It is known that John Smith was a farmer and that they were resident in Meriden, IA, in 1892 and in Cleghorn, IA in 1903.

(Continued from page 95.)

1. The candidate shall have been recommended by the Society of which they are members, or by the Leaders' and Stewards' Meeting, or the Official Board.

2. The candidate shall have been before the District Committee on Qualifications of Local Preachers, and shall have been recommended by them.

3. The candidate shall have passed a satisfactory examination in the studies prescribed for Candidates for Licence to Preach.

Having obtained his licence, Samuel was very active in his local church at Bloomfield and other churches round about. Samuel's uncle Mark Smith Harris received a letter from Samuel in April 1894, and on the basis that Mark's replies extended over several letters it is reasonable to assume that the topic was some profound interpretation of scripture on which Samuel was seeking another opinion.

As already stated, Samuel and his brother jointly purchased their father's land back in March 1886 and in April 1893 divided it equally and registered the division at the County Court. In March 1895 Samuel purchased his brother's share of 100 acres in Linden Township for $1,900 and so became the owner of a 200-acre spread. Samuel later sold eighty acres in the west half of the south-east quarter of Section Twenty-five thereby reducing his holding to 120 acres, the whole of which was retained in the family until 1970. In the final twenty years it was farmed by Gerald Laverne Harris, Samuel's grandson, a third-generation American and the fourth generation of the Harrises.

Nell died on 26 April 1926 and Samuel on 31 July 1934. They were both laid to rest in Eastside Cemetery, Dodgeville, in the same plot as Samuel's father, William B. Harris, and the latter's second wife Jane.

Eventide and Death

The fact that William B. was included in a biographical sketch in the *History of Iowa County*[38] is an indication of his stature among the folk of his community, especially so because the number of biographies was somewhat limited. Speaking of another Cornishman, Dr John Rowe in his book *The Hard-Rock Men* says, 'He found that honesty and industry were the qualities held in the highest esteem in the community in which he settled.' The description of being honest and industrious sums up the character of William B. Harris. The foregoing statement is paralleled by his obituary which read, 'Deceased was an exceptionally upright, honest and industrious citizen, and was held in the highest esteem among all his neighbours and friends.'

William B. died at his retirement home on Division Street, Dodgeville on 22 April 1892.[39] His brother Matthew travelled from Olivet, South Dakota to visit him before he died and stayed on to attend the funeral. Jane, the second wife of William B., lived on, although unwell for a considerable time, until 25 August 1903.[40] Both were laid to rest in Eastside Cemetery, Dodgeville, where their memorial still stands.

As previously noted, all ten of John (2) and Christian's children became members of the Christian Church, and it was a memorable occasion when the author paid a visit, in company with the Jay Harris family, to Gerald Laverne Harris and his wife Delva at their home in Rural Dodgeville in June 1985, to find that the faith and Christian charity of the Harrises of Bolenowe Carn had not dimmed. It was with a feeling of awe and humility that we stood beside the graves of William B., Jane, Samuel and Nell at Eastside.

The Graves - Eastside Cemetery, Dodgeville, WI, 1985

**right: William B. Harris and his second wife Jane
below: Samuel and Mary Harris**

5. Ann (2) Harris

Ann Harris and Rev. James Sims just prior
to their Diamond Wedding Anniversary in 1907

Early Life and Departure for America

Ann (2), the fourth child and second daughter of John (2) and Christian, was born at Six Chimneys, Bolenowe Carn on 1 March 1826 and was baptized at Camborne Parish Church on 11 April the same year.

Seemingly, as was the wont, Ann's parents did not deem it necessary for her to attend any educational establishment and so we find that at the age of twenty-two she could neither read nor write. In fact, when in December 1848 she and her husband sold forty acres of land in Linden Township, WI, to her brother William, she could only make her mark on the deed and this particular inability necessitated a special paragraph to be appended to the document. The addendum read as follows:

State of Wisconsin)
County of Iowa) Be it remembered that on the twelfth day of December AD 1848 personally came before me, the above named James Sims and Ann his wife, to us known to be persons who executed said Deed and acknowledged the same to be their free act and deed for the uses and purposes therein mentioned, and desired the same might be recorded according to law, the said Ann Sims being of full age, and by me

examined separate and apart from her said husband, and the contents thereof being first made known to her, declared that she did voluntarily and of her own free will and accord, seal as her act and deed, deliver the said indenture without any coercion, or compulsion of her said husband.

In testimony whereof I have hereunto set my hand and seal the day and year first above written. William James - Justice of the Peace.[1]

The foregoing apart, no doubt Ann from an early age was required to assist her mother in the home and to attend to the poultry and livestock on the small farm. However, the need for her to find full employment in order to support herself and her younger brothers and sister came all too soon, and by the 1841 Camborne census, when she was fifteen years old, she was listed as a mine girl, which means that she was employed on manual work most probably on the copper ore dressing floors at Dolcoath Mine.

That she was accustomed to hardship there is no doubt, but she was equal to the demands of her life which she demonstrated so clearly when she undertook alone the long and difficult journey from Bolenowe Carn to Dodgeville, WI. Additionally, Ann (2) was also a second mother to her younger brothers and sister which is so lovingly illustrated in the poem *The Burial* by John (3) when she made, at the request of the youngsters, a coffin for William's ferret which had died when left in their care:

> So Ann made a coffin so small,
> Of cast-off brown paper and thread
> This served for a shroud and a pall,
> False trappings unknown to the dead.

It seems that prior to the departure of James Sims in 1845 he and Ann (2) had reached an understanding. Just how they met is not known for certain; maybe within Methodist circles or probably through James being a friend of her brother William, but in any case their respective homes were only just over a mile apart as the crow flies. There can be no doubt that when James left for America the two made an agreement that if things went well with him Ann (2) would follow. And so it transpired that two years after his arrival in America, James asked her to come out and marry him. This she did in the spring of 1847.

Undoubtedly the family had been preparing themselves ever since James left for the time when Ann would announce her decision to go out and join him. No doubt either that William had written in some detail of the beauty and opportunities of his new land, and the reactions and feelings of the family had somewhat mellowed during the intervening two years. John (3) wrote a poem and presented it to her. The poem reflected her father's prayer at the moment of her departure. Picture the family at prayer, kneeling on the earthen floor of the living room, her father John (2) leading the prayers, unwell and as it happened having only fourteen more months to live, and knowing that he would never see her again. Her mother, the youngsters including the youngest, Jacob who was just four years old, and Mark who probably did not comprehend what was actually taking place but realising that in some way it was an occasion of some moment to the family.

To My Sister

The violet is dead in my bower,
The primrose hath long since decay'd;
Their being was only an hour:
Thus life is a vanishing shade.
And, sister, wherever we look,
Wherever we ramble and range,
We read in Nature's great book
That this is a region of change.

They say you've decided to roam
Away from the land of your birth,
From father and mother and home,
And loved ones that smile at the hearth.
O you cannot forget where we play'd,
Ere sorrow had shaded our brow,
Or time any havoc had made
On us with his scythe or his plough.

Methinks in the stillness of eve,
When years have flown by you so fleet,
You oft will your little ones leave,
To muse in some quiet retreat;
And the voice of your mother will float
Beside you wherever you stray,
And many a musical note
Attend you by night and by day.

Fair blossoms around you may blush,
By hedge-row and hamlet and stream;
But fairer are those on the bush
By the cottage of which you oft dream.
Your own English daisy so bright,
That welcomes the sunshine and shower,
Is dearer upon our hill's height
Than the strange clime's magnificent flowers.

Well, drop the last tear on the land,
The dearest you ever will love,
And haste to a far, foreign strand,
May He be your pilot above!

But when from the deck you descry
Its glimmer and fade from your view,
Gaze through the salt tear-drop and sigh,
'Sweet nook of my kindred, adieu!'

The entreaty never to forget them, and whatever might be her circumstances, never to relax her faith were admonitions which Ann (2) accepted and never failed to heed.

The Journey to Wisconsin

And now Ann had to face, to her, a momentous, hazardous and lonely journey to south-west Wisconsin, facing the same privations on the Atlantic crossing as had been experienced by William and James - perhaps more so because she was unaccompanied. Nevertheless she displayed determination so characteristic of the Harrises. There is no evidence that she was in any way fearful or daunted. She had made a positive decision, and with God's help she was certain that she would come through. When it is considered that she could neither read nor write, that she had never previously been more than, say, six miles from Bolenowe Carn and probably not further than Camborne and was now to attempt a lonely journey of not far short of 5,000 miles, unchaperoned and amongst strangers, some of whom could not possibly be described as genteel, the enormity of the prospect before her will be apparent to the reader. In the words of one of her great grand-daughters,[2] a third-generation American, 'I'm sure Ann Harris was one strong lady to have made that long voyage alone as well as the really strenuous trip to Wisconsin in those early days.'

It is reasonable to assume that James had sent Ann explicit instructions in respect of her route and means of travel, which no doubt followed those taken by William and himself two years earlier. It probably goes without saying that James sent Ann the necessary monies for her journey. The letters from James would have to be read to Ann by, say, her mother or John (3) and she would need to memorise whatever instructions James had written!

And now the moment came to leave. One can picture the tears of the parents, the youngsters clinging to her and probably being permitted to accompany her down over the Carn to the end of Stoney Lane to the point where it joined the Bolenowe to Chycairne road. Then, whoever of the older boys were not at work, possibly Matthew and James, carrying her luggage to Camborne Station with one of them travelling to Hayle to see her onto the boat which would take her to Bristol. No doubt the brother who accompanied her to Hayle walked back, the available money not extending to a return fare on the train.

Once aboard and among people who were comparative strangers, one wonders if at this moment of severance from her native Cornwall, some doubts as to her decision to leave home crossed her mind, but there was no turning back.

Arriving in Liverpool, Ann arranged a passage on the *Queen of the West*,[3] a vessel of 1,160 tons burthen which was two and a half times larger than that on which William and James had travelled. Most likely Ann's twenty-first birthday took place a day or two after she boarded the ocean-going vessel, but to Ann it would have passed, as usual, without celebration and unnoticed.

Ann arrived in New York on 12 April 1847 and it would be surprising if she did not feel lonely and bewildered, but perhaps with a feeling of nearing her journey's end despite that she still had 1,400 miles of strange territory and sights ahead of her. Having voyaged up the Hudson River, along the Erie Canal and through the Great Lakes, how marvellous it would have been if James Sims had been at Milwaukee to meet her, but it could not be so. In 1847 the system of communication was such that they would not meet until Ann arrived in Dodgeville. But what a joyous welcome James and William must have given her, delighted that she had arrived safe and sound and proud of her accomplishing such a very long journey alone under conditions of which James and William were only too well aware. The relief from anxiety on all sides must have been beyond words to express.

Marriage and Early Life in Wisconsin

Ann (2) and James Sims were married in Dodgeville on 24 June 1847, just over two months after her arrival. James had been born at Carwynnen, Troon, Camborne on 3 August 1823, the son and third child of James Sims, a copper miner, and his wife Mary Ann Toy. Both father and son were described as copper miners in the Camborne 1841 census. James senior also farmed a couple of not very productive tracts of land amounting to just over two acres. There can be no doubt that James junior received some sort of education as a juvenile, but probably the greater contribution in this respect was through self-improvement, initiated by his desire as a Christian to proclaim the gospel.

After his arrival in Wisconsin, James, surprisingly as it may appear in retrospect, purchased from the government under the Pre-emption Act of 4 September 1841, forty acres of prairie in the north-east of the north-west quarter of Section Thirty-six Linden Township. The entry patent was dated 8 August 1846.[4] We can assume that James was very much attracted to the productive possibilities of the prairie and intended to become a small farm-

er and to follow the time-honoured custom of the miner in Cornwall to combine his normal occupation with that of keeping a small amount of livestock and to cultivate the land. In order to qualify under the Pre-emption Law which permitted settlers to become owners of land at the extremely beneficial rate of $1.25 per acre, James had to be an American citizen or at least had officially declared his intention to become a citizen.

No doubt James and William had discussed and debated at great length the whole question of citizenship. However, it seems that the decision of James to apply for citizenship was very much influenced by his desire to become a farmer, but be that as it may both James and William submitted their applications to the Presiding Judge of the District Court of Iowa County on 5 May 1848.[5]

One wonders if the decision by James caused the same reaction from the Sims family in Cornwall as it had among the Harrises? It will be noted that whereas James obtained his land patent 6 August 1846, it was twenty-two months later that he submitted his application for citizenship. The question arises as to how he satisfied the Registrar at Mineral Point Land Office that he intended to become an American citizen. Was a verbal promise accepted coupled with a personal assessment by the Registrar of the character of James?

In the event James and Ann retained ownership of the forty acres for just over two years and then sold it to William Harris for sixty dollars in December 1848. Their reason for selling is not known.

From the very commencement of her married life Ann was kept busy, for she not only looked after her husband but also her brother William who lodged with her for six years; and when her next younger brother Matthew (2) came out to Wisconsin in early August 1850 he stayed with her until November of the same year while he took stock and assessed the possibilities of this little mining field. In addition Ann had a growing family of her own. Her first child James J. Sims was born in 1848, was listed on the 1850 census, but passed away as a child, possibly during the Dodgeville cholera epidemic of 1851 when there were 136 deaths among a population of 900.[6] So Ann in her blissful early years in her new country experienced sorrow. Her second son Jacob was born in 1850 and daughter Mary Ann in 1852.

We do not know if James had been a lay preacher prior to coming to America in 1845 but it seems probable. Be that as it may, he undoubtedly made considerable effort towards self-improvement during those early years in Dodgeville because in 1854 he passed the selection process set by Wisconsin Conference of the Methodist Episcopal Church and was granted a licence to preach, and became a member of that Conference. It was a pioneering time of evangelism in this new country and as the immigrants gathered together in settlements their desire to hear the word of God and to have their own places of worship became extremely important to them.

James accepted the call and, as we shall see, spent thirty-six years in the itinerant ministry. On becoming a member of the Annual Conference[7] James and Ann, now with a young and increasing family, set forth to endure the privations and hardships of a pioneer preacher. No doubt James could have made more money by continuing as a miner but the desire to proclaim the good news of the Gospel was uppermost and Ann was in total agreement. In her obituary in the Minutes of the 1911 West Wisconsin Annual Conference it stated that 'Mrs Sims shared with her husband the joys and sorrows, the sacrifices, labours and victories of the Pastorate... She was indeed a helpmeet to the man whose name she bore.' James later described some of the hardships attending pioneer pastors and their families: 'For many years there were no adequate railroad facilities in Wisconsin, and we had to move with horse and wagon, which was naturally quite a hardship when the distance was long. In three places to which we moved we found no house in which to live. In these cases we were dependent either upon our friends or upon own energy.'[8] The last phrase pictures the family living in the covered wagon until a log hut was hastily erected. In fact, it was not until 1880 that they travelled from one pastorate to another by railroad. But out of this hard life their children were nurtured, and those who survived grew up to become respected citizens of the land of their birth.

Ann and James, assumed to have been taken at the time of their marriage in 1847

The Pastorate and Family

In all James was to spend thirty-six years in the Methodist Episcopal Ministry. The first two years were under the Wisconsin Conference, after which the conference was restructured and renamed West Wisconsin Conference.

Their first appointment in 1854 was to Hazel Green in Grant County, and in 1855 they moved back to Iowa County to serve Wyoming Mission.

In 1856, now under West Wisconsin Conference, they moved to Platteville Mission, Grant County. They then spent two years in Fennimore also in Grant County, and in 1859 moved to Washburn for a short time and then to Fayette, both in La Fayette County. They remained in La Fayette County at Shullsburg for the next two years.

The following three years were spent in Montfort, Grant County, and in 1865 they moved to Linden and were stationed in Dodgeville during 1866 and 1867, spending three years in what may be described as their home territory. In 1868 they moved to Lancaster and Potosi in Grant County, remaining in Lancaster for a further two years.

During the foregoing period of service and movement within the itinerant ministry, seven more children were born to Ann and James. They also suffered the loss of another son, who was born and had passed away after the 1850 and before the 1860 census.

The years of 1871 and 1872 were spent at Mazomanie in Dane County and in 1873 they served Jamestown and British Hollow in Grant County.

Moving again in 1874 they returned to Shullsburg and in 1875 to Belmont both in La Fayette County; 1876 saw them back at Montfort and in 1877 they were given a double charge of Montfort and Washburn. They then spent three years at Benton in La Fayette County followed by a further three years in Patch Grove, Grant County. These longer periods in particular locations demonstrated the high esteem in which James was held, both by his congregations and the Conference that he served. They spent 1884 at Bloomington, Grant County, after which they moved back again to Fennimore for two years. The next three saw James serving at Prairie du Chien in Crawford County on the edge of the great Mississippi River.

In 1890 they moved back to Bloomington, where after thirty-six years in the travelling connection James was superannuated.[9] Talking in later life of his experiences in the Ministry, James said, 'When I began my work, Wisconsin was on the frontier, when I left the State was well settled, and a relatively high stage of culture had been reached. Particularly during the early years of my ministry conditions were often rather discouraging, but I generally had the pleasure of seeing the charges grow and improve while I was with them. There was always plenty for us to do. We arranged for the building of Churches and Parsonages, and to a large extent we supervised the financial affairs of our churches.' It is recorded that from the pioneering work of Rev. James Sims there resulted some of the best charges of West Wisconsin Conference.

There is something of a divergence of opinion amongst Methodist archival institutions in America as to whether or not James had a single church in each of his charges or if the named charge was a base from which he moved about on horseback between the various communities, sometimes being away from home for several days or even weeks. In the pioneer days, if the latter was the case, the description made several years later by his brother-in-law Mark Smith Harris about another circuit rider would seem appropriate to James: 'The horse and saddle was his studio, the Bible and hymn book his library.'

Jacob Sims

Jacob, the second child of James and Ann, was born in Dodgeville on 30 November 1850. It is not known where Jacob received his initial education and with the family moving from charge to charge within the itinerant ministry it would have been difficult to effect any sort of continuity in the matter. However, he graduated from Lawrence University at Appleton, WI, in 1874 with the highest honours in his class. He then entered the teaching profession and for one year acted as School Principal at Oconto, WI.

Jacob then went to Milwaukee to work with the editorial staff of the *Milwaukee Sentinel* and later became editor and publisher of *The Citizen* a weekly newspaper in Minneapolis, Minnesota, until 1878.

Following his experience in the newspaper industry Jacob moved to Council Bluffs, Iowa, and entered the office of Montgomery and Stone where he studied law and was admitted to the Bar in January 1879. He practised by himself for a time and then became associated with John M. Stone under the name of Stone and Sims. From 1890 to 1892 he was a partner of C.G. Saunders and practised as Sims and Saunders, which after 1892 became Sims and Bainbridge. Actually his partner W.E. Bainbridge married Jacob's sister, Mary Ann, in 1896 and the law partnership continued until some time after 1898 when William E. Bainbridge secured an appointment as Second Secretary at the American Legation in Peking.

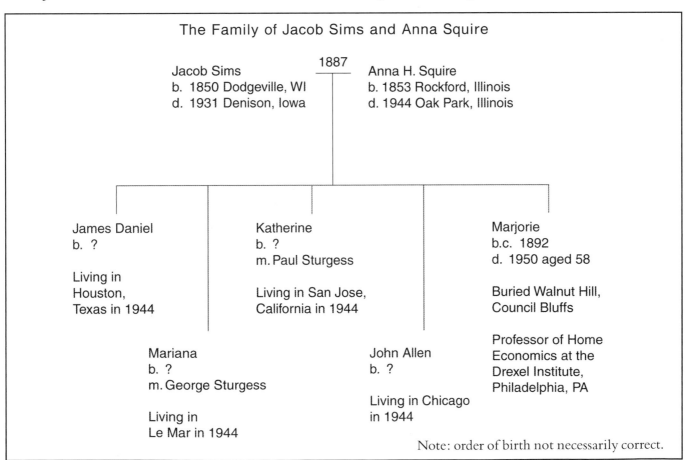

The Family of Jacob Sims and Anna Squire

Jacob Sims — 1887 — Anna H. Squire
b. 1850 Dodgeville, WI   b. 1853 Rockford, Illinois
d. 1931 Denison, Iowa   d. 1944 Oak Park, Illinois

James Daniel
b. ?

Living in
Houston,
Texas in 1944

Mariana
b. ?
m. George Sturgess

Living in
Le Mar in 1944

Katherine
b. ?
m. Paul Sturgess

Living in San Jose,
California in 1944

John Allen
b. ?

Living in Chicago
in 1944

Marjorie
b.c. 1892
d. 1950 aged 58

Buried Walnut Hill,
Council Bluffs

Professor of Home
Economics at the
Drexel Institute,
Philadelphia, PA

Note: order of birth not necessarily correct.

In 1900 Jacob moved to Denison which was just over sixty miles north, as the crow flies, from Council Bluffs, and formed a partnership there with Leslie A. Shaw and Carl F. Kuehnle, the firm being called Shaw, Sims and Kuehnle. In 1922 Floyd E. Page joined the firm which later became known as Sims and Page.[10]

Jacob married Miss Anna H. Squire on 11 January 1887 and to them were born five children. Anna had been born and educated at Rockford, Illinois, and had been a successful teacher for many years. She was the daughter of Daniel Squire of Ottumwa, Iowa. Jacob was a member of the Presbyterian Church in Denison and an ardent and faithful worker in all church affairs.

Like so many of the Cornish immigrants and their children, Jacob was a Republican but although taking an active part in politics never aspired to public office.

He was a member of Iowa State and American Bar Associations, by whom he was held in the highest esteem and recognised as one of the best lawyers in the State. He died at Denison on 19 January 1931 and was brought back for burial in Walnut Hill Cemetery, Council Bluffs. Three of his pall-bearers were judges. His obituary says that he was loved and respected by the citizens of his community, a leader in all movements for the betterment of the community, and gave much of his time and talents to help good morals and happiness of the community. Also as a forceful, entertaining and eloquent speaker he had frequently been the principal speaker on various community programmes. Loyal to his friends, devoted to his home and family, he was a kind and courteous gentleman.[11] What more can be said in praise of this son of humble Cornish parents?

Jacob's wife Anna passed away in December 1944 in Oak Park, Illinois, at the age of ninety-one and was brought back to Walnut Hill Cemetery to rest with him.

Mary Ann Sims

Mary Ann, the third child and eldest daughter of James and Ann, was born in Dodgeville, WI, in 1852. Nothing is known of where she received her education but it is certain that it was on sound principle. On the basis that her brother and at least two younger sisters became teachers, it does not seem unlikely that Mary Ann followed this profession, but no records have been found to prove this surmise. Nevertheless her later exploit as a diarist lends credence to the foregoing suggestion.

On 31 December 1873 Mary Ann married Thomas William McCarger in Plattville, Grant County, WI, where her parents were then stationed. Thomas William had been born on 31 May 1846 in Oxford Township, Grenville County, Ontario, Canada to Henry McCarger (1818-1900) and his wife Agnes Finlayson (1822-99) for-

merly of Glasgow, Scotland. Upon reaching manhood Thomas William left his native land for Wisconsin and became a representative for a firm who distributed farm machinery, a not unlikely occupation in that great agricultural State. Their elder son Hugh Albert (Bert) was born a year later.

In 1877 the little family moved to Council Bluffs, Iowa, when Thomas William obtained a position as managing agent for Nebraska with Aultman, Miller and Company agricultural machinery manufacturers, where by his untiring efforts the business grew to mammoth proportions. Indeed, as will be seen later, Thomas William completely wore himself out in the service of the company. A second son, James Finlayson, was born to the couple on 13 October 1881.

On 9 November 1885 Thomas William purchased a farm a few miles east of Council Bluffs, its location being described on the Sheriff's Deed[12] as Lot 1 of Block 1, Sub-division of Riddle Tract. The purchase was by public auction, duly advertised and authorised by the Circuit Court of Pottawattamie County because of an apparent dispute of ownership between a William Briz and D.G. and S.A. McLean. Thomas William secured the property with the highest bid of $1,091.03. Besides having the land farmed in the usual manner, Thomas William possibly utilised the farm to demonstrate agricultural machinery to prospective customers, and no doubt he and his family spent short breaks there enjoying the fresh air and peace of the rural landscape.

Thomas W. became a greatly respected citizen of Council Bluffs but his health began to suffer very ser-

Thomas William McCarger
1846-89

iously from overwork. He had a stroke in February 1888 and in July 1889 requested the company to relieve him from all duty whereupon he moved out to the farm in the hope that relaxation and the fresh air of the prairie would help him recover. But it was not to be. He moved back to his home in Council Bluffs where he died on 9 December 1889. When the news reached James and Ann they made the long journey right across the state of Iowa from Prairie du Chien, WI, to be with Mary Ann and her two sons. The obituary of Thomas W. stated that 'He had been loved and esteemed by everyone, faithful to his friendships and with a heart full of generous instincts; a man of sterling business qualities.'[13] The funeral took place under the auspices of the Masonic Fraternity of which he had been a member. The officiating Methodist Minister was Rev. Dewitt C. Franklyn of Broadway Church and interment was in Walnut Hill Cemetery. Among many floral tributes was one said to be of rare beauty and particular fitness, depicting a large sickle and sheaf of wheat mounted on a large base representing the land. In the present age it seems strange to read that the long and imposing cortege was headed by Dalby's Band playing sacred music.[14] Elderly Cornish folk will of course remember the walking funerals of yesteryear where the cortege proceeded along the road singing hymns, sometimes lustily! The author remembers one occasion in the early 1930s where the pall-bearers swung the coffin to the beat of the music!

Five years after the death of her first husband, Mary Ann married William E Bainbridge on 18 January 1894, the ceremony being conducted by her father Rev. James Sims. It will be remembered that W.E. Bainbridge joined the law practice of Jacob Sims at Council Bluffs in 1892, and doubtless he came to know Mary Ann through his association with her brother.

William Elmer Bainbridge had been born in Wisconsin circa 1861/62 and had graduated in classical subjects in 1886 and in law in 1889, both from the University of Wisconsin. In 1890 he decided to come to Council Bluffs where he practised in law. Within a couple of years of his joining Jacob Sims, William decided to make an application to enter either the Consular or Diplomatic Service of the United States. The procedure to obtain nomination

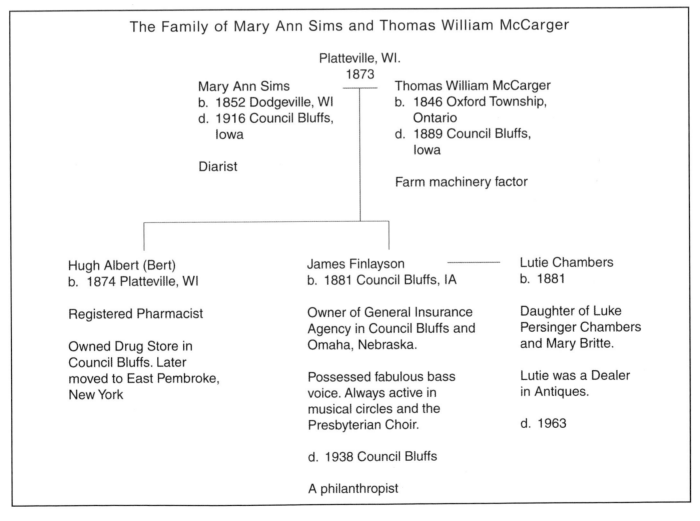

The Family of Mary Ann Sims and Thomas William McCarger

Platteville, WI.
1873

Mary Ann Sims
b. 1852 Dodgeville, WI
d. 1916 Council Bluffs, Iowa

Diarist

Thomas William McCarger
b. 1846 Oxford Township, Ontario
d. 1889 Council Bluffs, Iowa

Farm machinery factor

Hugh Albert (Bert)
b. 1874 Platteville, WI

Registered Pharmacist

Owned Drug Store in Council Bluffs. Later moved to East Pembroke, New York

James Finlayson —————— **Lutie Chambers**
b. 1881 Council Bluffs, IA   b. 1881

Owner of General Insurance Agency in Council Bluffs and Omaha, Nebraska.

Possessed fabulous bass voice. Always active in musical circles and the Presbyterian Choir.

d. 1938 Council Bluffs

A philanthropist

Daughter of Luke Persinger Chambers and Mary Britte.

Lutie was a Dealer in Antiques.

d. 1963

was quite involved. Initially a vacancy had to be located and then the applicant was required to be recommended by prominent members of the State, such as the State Governor, county officers, members of the judiciary and businessmen. Their recommendations were then forwarded to the State Delegation in Congress, who added their recommendations which, together with those from the other parties, were forwarded to the Secretary of State in Washington who advised the President. In William's case he obtained between 1 December 1896 and 1 February 1897 no less than thirty-eight recommendations for his appointment as Consul General at Kanagawa, Japan. In the event the entire Iowa State Delegation in Congress, Senators and Members in caucus assembled, endorsed the other thirty-seven recommendations along with their own. Following this procedure William made his own application to the President on 17 March 1897.

As a result of this process it transpired that he was nominated for a different post in early January 1898, namely that of Second Secretary at the American Legation in Peking. His appointment to this position was approved by the United States Senate on 25 April 1898 and in due course he and Mary Ann took up residence in the Peking Legation. In February 1899 they sailed from San Francisco to cross the Pacific to China, a voyage of about 7,000 miles, calling at Honolulu, Yokohama, Kobe, Nagasaki and Shanghai, arriving at Tientsin on19 March. They then had ninety miles of overland travel before reaching Peking.

Shortly after taking up duties at the Peking Legation William was recommended by Senator Allison for consideration for a Consular appointment in Canton. What prompted this recommendation is not known, other than possibly that William's eyes were set on a Consular rather than a Diplomatic appointment. Presumably it would have been a promotion for William. The recommendation was supported by Mr E.H. Conger, the American Envoy Extraordinary and Minister Plenipotentiary in Peking.[15] However, it was not to be, possibly due to murmurings of sinister happenings about to take place in China. On 1 January 1900 Sidney Brooks, an English missionary, was murdered in the village of Shantung in North China, and within the next few months amid mounting and increasing signs of horror what is known as the Boxer Rebellion burst upon the country and all the foreign Legations came under siege. Mary Ann and William were in Peking for the duration

The Diarist – Mary Ann Sims McCarger Bainbridge
at the time of her marriage to William E. Bainbridge

United States Legation, Peking, China in 1900.
L–R: F.O. Cheshire – Interpreter; H.G. Squires – First Secretary; Hon. E.H. Conger – US Minister; W.E. Bainbridge – Second Secretary

of the siege and Mary Ann felt prompted to record the events as she saw and experienced them day by day. And so this eldest daughter of Ann and James became the only domestic diarist of the grim, frightening and painful Siege of the Legations and some of the atrocities committed.

Mary Ann's diary is reproduced here in full with kind permission of the State Historical Society of Iowa.

A Siege in Peking of the Legations

May 6 1900

I had gone with Mrs R.K. Lowry up to Peng-Shik-Kou'vh to the afternoon service and on my return home I learned that during the afternoon the Boxers had been creating a disturbance up at Erbu-Piac-Hu-Tung and the Missionaries were greatly alarmed. Later in the evening a dust storm came up followed by heavy rain, which lasted until 4 o'clock the next afternoon. For a few days they were a little more quiet and then began again, going from one mission to another tearing bricks out of the walls and throwing them over into the compound.

May 28 1900

It was reported today that a railroad had been burned by the Boxers.

May 29 1900

Mr and Mrs Chamot went to Chang-Sing-Tien to rescue some French people, about sixty in all, and before they were half a mile from their homes they could see everything in flames. Things are becoming very alarming and the Ministers have telegraphed to Tientsin for help, very much against the wishes of the 'Old Lady' (Empress Dowager) and members of Tsung-Li-Tamen; their only desire being to murder every foreigner in Peking.

May 31 1900

Fifty Marines were sent to us and to the other Legations, not over 450 in all. It seems a very small number among tens of thousands of Chinese soldiers. Four sentinels parade the compound day and night, changing every hour. A Colts Automatic gun stands on the front walk which fires 400 shots per minute.

June 5 1900, 10.30 am

Mr Bainbridge with three of our Marines accompa-

nied Mr and Mrs Woodward to the station where they expected to take the train for Tientsin and sail shortly for home, but after waiting until 3 pm they all came back as no train was going. That night everything was destroyed and we were cut off from all communication with the outside world.

June 8 1900

Missionaries around Peking have all been ordered into the City and they with all those who live here are at Haiao-Shun-Hu-Tung (Methodist Mission).

June 11 1900

The Japanese Secretary was shot and killed.

June 13 1900

The Methodist street chapel, Tengo-hih-Kou'rh, (entrance to lantern market), and is the American Board. Erh-Tiao-Hu-Tung, (second valley) Presbyterian Hounaen, (back gate). Shih-I-Yuan (distribute healing court), London Mission Lu-Jou-Hu-Tung (donkey meat alley) were all destroyed.

Hsiao-Shun-Hu-Tung (filial piety) was not burned until the 23rd.

June 14 1900

The German Minister was walking down Legation Street when he saw two Boxers; he immediately gave the alarm and they were taken charge of. The women and children in our Legation came running up to my rooms, they thought an attack was being made upon us, for Dr Coltman came running into the compound with glaring eyes and calling to the top of his voice, 'An attack, an attack,' and they all thought their doom was sealed and wanted to get to a safe place, if one could be found. At seven in the evening the Captain told the ladies that when the alarm was given, no matter what hour of the day or night it might be, we were to fly across to the Russian Legation.

At 8 pm two marines were sent up to our quarters to watch for Boxers or soldiers who might fire on us from the wall. After two or three days, more were sent up and so far they have not had an opportunity of firing even one shot, and they seem quite disappointed. Some of them are very nice boys. They were the first to go to Cuba, and first to Manila. Many of them had met several of the boys belonging to the 31st Iowa. Bob Daily in particular they remembered. This forenoon 22 marines went out to rescue the inmates at the Nan-Fang. The Boxers had set fire to the building after tying some of the most helpless women and children to posts, trees or their beds, and torturing them in a most brutal manner. These barbarians are most wonderfully brave where there is no one but women and children. The boys shot 68 Boxers, and brought all the refugees back with them who were not dead or dying. An old Ahma of Mrs Squires who had gone out there on Sunday to Communion intending to return on Monday, but was unable to get back, came in with the others. Her youngest son was one of the Priests and was among the number who were burned to death. I went down to see the old lady and she told me that in, 'One hour more she be all finnee.'

I have a few things in a handbag, my umbrella and a hat near the door-way ready to fly at a moment's warning, since the 10th. This afternoon a number of German, English and Americans went out and shot 40 more of these brutes. I was out near the gateway when our boys came in, following behind at some distance were about a hundred or more refugees hobbling along as best they could, all bruised and bleeding from their wounds. One young girl who was being led by her companions was blind, her eyes had been dug out of her head; another had a wound on the back of her head and the brain exposed to view. They all sat down on the walk in the shade to rest and get a cool drink. The Army Surgeon dressed their wounds. I noticed one little boy whose hands were burned almost to a crisp and his poor little bare back was all bruised and blistered. And yet there was not a murmur. All was still at midnight except when the Surgeon asked for something.

Saturday morning the Marines were called to go to the outer gate, as Boxers were coming in great numbers to the inner city. So they hurriedly set out to greet them; in about an hour they came back saying they had killed 62 and the rest had gone home to tea. They also told us the outer city was in flames. One of our guards shot 10 Boxers and another killed 4. In the evening the Russians shot two Chinese soldiers who they caught setting fire near our Legations. At 10 pm we all went up on the wall to look over at the burning of the outer city and the once beautiful gateway. All the silk shops, curio shops and all manner of places were all going up in flames and smoke. They were not handsome to look at, little tumble down looking buildings, and nothing to show one whether you were entering a Joss house, Junk shop, silk shop, or opium den. Many thousand were homeless in less than 24 hours.

June 16 1900

The Captain took our guards and put them on the wall last night.

June 17 1900

At 3.30 am we were aroused from our peaceful slumbers, by quick rifle shots on or near the wall, and hastily dressing went downstairs to see what was going on. By the time we got down, Captain Myers came to tell us what it meant. Some Chinese Soldiers were seen sneaking along the wall and our boys fired on them. The Chinese very quickly gathered themselves together and took to their heels, did not wait for a second salute so early in the morning. We went to bed again, but did not undress, had no further occasion to be further alarmed, until during the forenoon the Germans and Austrian Soldiers had a small battle with Chinese Soldiers, killing 30 or more of them.

At 10 pm Sunday evening three officials from the Tsung-Li-Yamen came for an interview with Mr Conger and also to present him with the Empress Dowager's compliments saying she was very anxious for the safety of the Foreign Ministers and all connected with the Legations especially Americans. They were not however anxious we should have any more troops here, and very reluctantly gave their consent. They were served with tea, after which they went home, seemingly in a very peaceful frame of mind.

June 18 1900

We all went to bed and slept quite peacefully until 7.30 the officials having assured us the Chinese Soldiers should not interfere with us. The night was very quiet, a number of our guards seeing them safely outside the picket line. Everything is quiet and all we can hear is the click of typewriters and the tread of Marines. (Children's voices thrown in.)

June 19 1900

At 4 pm a messenger came from the Tsung-Li-Yamen saying we had been given 24 hours to leave the city. It was not a very happy night, for any of us, for it was utterly impossible to get away. The train had been destroyed, the carts all taken to the outer city and we saw nothing but death staring us in the face. The next day the Ministers decided to call all foreigners together and to go to the British Legation (it being the largest of all) and try to fight it out until relief came.

June 20 1900

Baron Von Kettler - German Minister - was shot while on his way to Yamen, his interpreter was wounded but did not die. The Minister's body was not recovered. At noon all the Missionaries came pouring into our compound, bringing nothing with them only what each one could carry in their hands. There were nearly one hundred men, women and children. It was a pitiable sight to look upon them as they came marching in homeless and forlorn, their possessions all gone. As I stood in the doorway of the office building watching them as they came along, my heart seemed to almost stop beating. I never had witnessed such a scene before. I shook hands with each as they drew near, those I had not seen before as well as the ones I had become acquainted with. I could not speak, my heart was too full for utterance. As Mrs Lowry came along alone (her husband was caught in Tientsin and could not get back) my heart went out to her, she looked so forlorn, she pressed my hand warmly and neither or us spoke a word, but walked away silently to a quiet corner in the compound where we were alone. The last time I had seen her was the day before I went to Tientsin when she came down and spent the afternoon with me. Everything had changed during these few weeks. I had gone with Mrs Hoover[16] to Tientsin, had very suddenly been called home, Mr Bainbridge was dangerously ill; we were in quarantine ten days, and when she and I met again, she was a homeless wanderer in the streets of Peking, and alone. After everyone had a lunch we gathered up a few things and all came over to the British Legation. The British Minister and his wife (Sir Claude and Lady McDonald) had everything all arranged and we are much more comfortable than we had anticipated. The Missionaries are quartered in the English Chapel which is not very large, so a number of the ladies sleep in Lady McDonald's ball room. The two foreign merchants gave over their store to be used for all, and as soon as things could be brought in, it was done.

June 22 1900

The fire alarm sounded at 5 pm. A fire was discovered outside the wall of this Legation, and for some hours we almost gave up in despair, but after heroic work on the part of the men, women and children, carrying water, it was finally subdued. Considerable firing was done on both sides of the wall. One English and one German Marine were shot. Our American boys are still holding our Legation, and will do so just as long as it is possible for them to do so.

We had rather a quiet night after the fires died out and the firing ceased. These Boxers are said to be spiritualists. A man of the 'American Board' says the origin of the Boxers is made up of 64 different religions. They are working with the belief that what they are doing does not come from themselves, but from dead spirits and they believe they cannot be killed. This however, has been proven to be false. They are an immense army, and have been accumulating for years to make this bold stroke. They do not come in large numbers, but small groups. They think foreign people are to blame for much of their poverty, that is in taking away their employment in building railroads, steamboats and many other things which is causing so much of their work to be of no value to them so far as money is concerned. A Chinese can only do one kind of work. If he is a cook and has lost his job, he knows nothing but to starve, and all other workmen likewise. It has been so for generations back, and no doubt will be to the end of time. There are two elements, none between. The hostile and the friendly. Those who have lived here 30 or 40 years cannot say they are sure which class they are running up against. Dr Martin, President of the Tung-Wen College, who has lived in China 50 years, said he did not know of one friend he could rely upon among any of them.

11 am. A terrific fire broke out at the back of this compound but as before, was subdued by a great effort on the part of all.

At 2 pm fires were discovered at the front, on the left and it seemed that we were to be soon in a sea of fire, again it was quieted down. Heavy firing was kept up all afternoon, and all night; a very large number of Boxers were killed and several hundred Chinese Soldiers. One American Marine was shot and one Italian. One English and one Russian wounded. An American flag was wrapped around the dead body of our Marine and he was laid to rest in the Russian Legation Compound. The Russian bank and the Customs were burned last night.

June 24 1900 - Sunday

Our foreign Soldiers have been trying to capture the Chinese gun which is stationed near us, but after making three attempts with no success they gave it up.

June 25 1900

At 1 am we were awakened by heavy firing and as we have done for many nights past, got up and put on our clothes. After an hour or so the ladies retired without undressing and slept until daylight. All the men being on guard in different places. At 9 am firing began again and has been somewhat lively ever since. Bullets are whizzing through the air from all quarters. 5 o'clock pm a proclamation was posted up at the bell tower saying Chinese had been ordered to stop firing on foreigners. The officials had sent a messenger from the Tsung-Li-Yamen, saying the Empress Dowager had given the order, but as we had lost all faith in Chinese Powers no one believed it to be anything but false and went to work harder than before, making sandbags, building more barricades, digging trenches and all manner of things so that should the Chinese make an attack that night everything would be ready for their reception.

One German and one Japanese were shot, and two Americans wounded during the day.

Most of us went to bed rather earlier in order to get a few hours sleep if possible. At 12.30 we got up in a great hurry, as the heaviest firing we had ever heard was close around us. They came upon us like a thunder clap. The shots were quick and it seemed as though there were thousands of soldiers outside the compound. I did not go to bed it seemed too awful. Mr Bainbridge went out on his watch a 1 o'clock, and I thought I would sit here and write while he was out. 3 am we tried to sleep after the firing ceased, but very shortly they began on us again and no one got any more rest all night. Sergeant Fanning of our Marines was killed early this morning and one wounded.

June 26 1900

Considerable shooting was done all afternoon, but no accidents to our men. At 7 pm very severe fighting began and for a time we thought our American boys must give up their position on the wall, but the brave fellows held their place amidst shot and shell and drove the Chinese back.

3 am June 27 1900

Another attack which lasted until daylight. I do not know that even one foreign soldier was scratched.

11 am. Another attack which lasted all day long. We felt quite sure that we should have a quiet night after the anxious day, but we had no sooner closed our eyes than there was the sound of general alarm 'All civilians to Arms'. None of us went to bed again that night.

June 28 1900

Shells were being fired at us from the Imperial Palace wall, but all the damage done was a horse killed.

10 pm. Shots were heard not far away which be-

came louder and nearer and we had no rest all night. Chinese were killed in great numbers, but not one foreign soldier was hurt.

June 29 1900

Shells were fired into the Foo where the refugees are living, but no one was hurt. The Italians turned their big gun on them and they quickly retreated. This afternoon our Navy Surgeon was wounded by a stray bullet and was brought into the hospital. It is feared he may lose his limb.

7.15 pm. The noise has begun again and we are keeping in the shade. Trenches are being dug in many places where we are to run into in case of necessity. We thought to have a quiet night, but by the time we were settled comfortably in our beds the noise began and we got no more sleep until 5 am the 30th.

10 am. Bullets are flying through the air thick and fast, it is not safe to be outside.

June 30 1900 1 pm

Rather more quiet after the terrible night we passed through. One of our boys was shot this evening and another wounded. Mr Conger, Mr Knoble (Dutch Minister), Mr Bainbridge, Dr Wherry, a Russian Soldier, and our little hospital Steward, who at all times has a smile on his boyish face, buried the Marine at 9 pm by the side of his two comrades in the Russian compound.

July 1 1900

Last night was quiet and no shots have been heard up to 11.30 when things became suddenly more exciting. Three Italians were shot and two of the customs boys wounded. Later in the day one of the customs boys was killed. 5.30 pm another of our Marines was shot. Mr Bainbridge with the little sailor lad have gone to see about digging the grave, then when it is dark, the body will be brought down from the wall and buried. Dr Wherry will read a service at the grave. This has been a very sad Sunday for us all and a very busy one. The ladies have made 2,000 sandbags today to use on the wall for barricading. Our little handful of Marines are still holding it and we must help save their lives by sewing as fast as we can. A certain lady who claims to be a faith cure and a fanatic on religion came along when several of us were sitting outside the chapel busy as bees, and said, 'Now ladies let us lay aside our work and go inside to have a few prayers, I think it will strengthen the courage of our boys on the wall.' Some of them put down their work, but Mrs Lowry, Mrs Killey and myself sat there. I did not know their thoughts, neither did they know mine. Mrs Smith looked at us, then said, 'Come, aren't you going in?' I finally said to her that I could pray and sew at the same time and I would not give much for a person who could not, and that while bullets were flying over our heads by the thousand, that sandbags would be of much more use just now in saving the lives of our boys on the wall in their awful position than prayers. So we three sat and sewed while the rest held a prayer meeting. Shells were exploding about us, cannons booming and shots could be heard on all sides. It seemed to me that it was wicked to waste one minute in anything that was not to help save the lives of the 20 or 30 brave Marines who were holding the wall and driving back thousands of Chinese Soldiers. We have been expecting a relief from Tientsin for many weeks, but so far have heard nothing. If they do not come soon it seems as if we must give up.

July 2 1900

Loud firing and heavy shelling all afternoon.

July 3 1900

Early this evening we were heavily attacked and the firing was kept up all night, then a heavy rain set in and all was quiet. During the night two of our Marines and one Russian were killed. Our Marines had made a charge on the Chinese and took one barricade. Captain Myers who was leading the men was wounded in the right leg. Mr Bainbridge is now at the Russian Legation attending to the burying of the Marine. It is very dark and gloomy and the rain steadily falling. Our boys have all now been buried after dark, or, when it was raining. Some of the Missionaries have been going around barefooted in order to save their one pair of shoes. Many of them have been burned out of house and home, many have nothing left only what they have on their backs. Retired at 9.30 thinking all was peaceful, but at 9.40 we bounded out and hustled into our clothes, as we have done almost every night for five weeks, and when I undressed again it was 7 am July 4. It seemed as though all the powers of hell had been let loose. Chinese were killed in great numbers and are lying all around us. Only one foreign soldier wounded and one Italian shot. 36 Marines have been killed and 53 wounded.

July 4 1900

Capt. Perry Smith commanded our Marines on the wall today. He is an Englishman and our boys think a great deal of him. This day is one none of us shall forget so long as we have our reason left us. The noise is something terrible. We have made sandbags all day long. Not a curtain of any description has been left in our homes, no matter of what material they were; all have been used, also table cloths, sheets, and everything which would hold sand has been cut up and made use of. When we had used everything we had the soldiers loot Chinese shops and we have cut up some very beautiful silks, velvets, and all sorts of lovely goods.

July 5 1900

Last night was rather quiet, most of us slept the greater part of the night. Occasionally we heard shots, but not noise enough to get us out of our beds. About daylight the Chinese began shelling us again, but did no particular damage.

12 am. Mr Olifant was wounded very seriously and died at 2 pm. The Chinese had their big gun mounted inside the palace grounds, and we understood they expected to put us out of existence before morning.

10 pm. The racket began and lasted all night, early in the morning the Chinese got worn out and retired to drink their tea and cool off, and we are still on deck. It is said they always carry with them a teapot and fan no matter where they may be going, or on what business they are to attend to.

July 6 1900

The shells are still falling over and around us, but no one hurt.

July 7 1900

A quiet night, but early this morning the serenading began, and is being kept up rather lively. At noon a shell came through the roof into Sir Claude's dining room, and fell in the center of the table which was all set for dinner; cut glass and china were scattered all over, but no one was hurt.

The Chinese made another attack on the French Legation during the forenoon, two French Marines were wounded, and the French Minister slightly. For a few hours in the evening it was quiet, but at 10 the noise began and we were kept awake all night.

July 8 1900

There was a report last night that Russian troops were nearing us, but no one could prove it. This afternoon some coolies saw the American gunner trying to rig up a big gun out of some old things which had been found, and after watching him for some time two of them started away and in a short time they returned bringing with them an old English gun which they found in a Chinese shop not far off. It was brought here in 1860. Our gunner looked at it with a smile, laid aside his other work and set himself to work fixing up the one which the coolies had brought in. He had it mounted on an Italian carriage and with Russian shells which the Russians could not use. The American gunner fired it over into the Imperial City about 5 pm and it proved a great success, as the Chinese got up to 'look see' what had happened they were picked off in great numbers and we all rejoiced at their loss.

July 9 1900

Very noisy all night. In the early part of the evening it was rather quiet and I went to my room thinking I might be able to take a sponge bath, but by the time I was undressed they began with such a racket that I hustled into my clothes and concluded to wait until a more convenient season in which to bathe.

July 10 1900

We got very little sleep last night because of the noise.

July 11 1900

At eleven am the Chinese began shelling on us from the Imperial grounds, which is not far from us. Three shells came inside the compound, one going through the gate house, making quite a hole, but killing no one. They all landed in the tennis court, which is in the center. Every one sitting outside were ordered indoors, (after the bombs had exploded). We had a quiet afternoon and were greatly surprised at not having to get up after going to bed.

July 12 1900

A German Soldier was killed this afternoon and two others wounded.

July 13 1900

Last night was more quiet than usual, so quiet in fact that we could not sleep. The change was too great. Early this morning the Chinese have been blazing away at us with their big gun, but no one has been hurt. Yesterday 18 Chinese soldiers were caught setting fire in the French Legation and they were every one shot.

Later in the day fourteen Boxers were found doing the same thing and (like the soldiers) were shot. This morning a Boxer walked into the French Legation and gave himself up. He was taken to the American Legation to be interviewed by Mr Pethye. He said all the foreign portion of Tientsin was burned and that foreign troops had taken the forts at Taku, that 48 thousand troops were on there way here, also that 3,000 Chinese soldiers had drawn their pay and left the City. They locked him up over night and will see what more he has to say in the morning and whether his stories hang together.

July 14 1900

At 9.30 last evening shots began to fly thick and fast and it seemed for a time that the Chinese would overpower us, but as before our boys got the best of them. The noise was kept up all night and we got very little rest. Shells have been falling in our midst and still we are alive. Two French Marines were wounded during the night. Our men captured two Chinese flags this afternoon. A few minutes ago an Italian Marine was shot. His head was shot off. Two Germans and one French were wounded. It has been a very anxious day. At 6.60 pm 500 Chinese Soldiers came down the back street and our boys on the wall did not miss an opportunity to fire into their midst and in less than 10 minutes 45 of them were shot, the rest took to their heels and fled much quicker than they came. Another crowd of them attacked the French Legation also the German, and the noise was something never to be forgotten. They did not cease firing until daylight. Both Legations are badly damaged. Three French Marines were shot, two could not be taken out from under the ruins. Three were wounded.

3.30 pm. An Italian and one of the French Marines were buried this afternoon. A messenger came in from the Yamen with a letter to the Minister in which it said 'Minister and their Staffs were to come to the Yamen for protection and must come without guards and unarmed', the Ministers however, took no stock in what the man said. Everyone who wished to enter our gates must have a pass (Chinese I mean). All the servants have a card pinned in their sleeves, and if they go out without it they cannot get back.

The canons have been booming the greater part of the day, and two or three attacks have been made. One of the customs young men had his jaw broken by a shot.

July 15 1900

Last night we had quite a heavy attack and at 1 pm on 16 July one of our Marines was killed on the wall. There had been a battle and the night was one long to be remembered by everyone. The Captain of the British Marines was killed and one of the French[17] Students.

At 2.30 pm we buried our American boy by the side of his six companions in the Russian compound. All of the Legation ladies and many of the missionaries went over to the funeral. Mr Bainbridge had already gone over to superintend the digging of the grave and we went over with Mr Conger. We gathered what flowers there were to be found and some green leaves to strew over the graves of all. It was the first one of our boys who had been buried when the ladies could go. The rain was falling softly down on our umbrellas and the tears silently rolling down most of our faces. I stood at the foot of the grave and as I looked down upon the form of the poor boy lying in the cold ground dressed in his blue clothes and an American flag wrapped around his lifeless body, I thought of the poor mother at home whose heart would be sadly grieved did she but know her boy had fallen in trying to save others. He gave his life for all the nations represented in Peking and his work was done. Dr Wherry took charge of the service after Mr Conger had made a few remarks. Three of his comrades were there to help Mr Bainbridge, Mitchell (the gunner), Young and Stanley the Sailor lad. As I was putting the flowers on all the graves and was coming out I shook hands with the three boys and they could not speak, they were almost heart broken. I have tried to imagine a Soldier's funeral in a foreign land, but never dreamed it would ever be my lot to be in the midst of a battle, or drop a tear over an American Marine's grave in far off China.

At 5.30 pm the Captain and Mr Warren, the British Student, were buried in this Legation. Mr Harris, Rector of the little English Chapel here in the compound officiated. Both bodies were laid in the same grave. The British flag was wrapped around their bodies and quantities of flowers were strewn over them. The rain had ceased so that it did not seem quite so sad as when two hours and a half previous we laid our American boy to rest.

July 17 1900

It was not such a bad night as the past three, only one attack was made, and so far as I can learn, only one British Marine wounded. We have used up what goods we had for sandbags, and I am going to find something to make a doz. handkerchiefs for our Marines, the poor fellows have very little of the necessities of life. Their clothes were all lost excepting what they had on their backs.

Five or six Chinese soldiers gave themselves up today at the French and German Legations and were brought here to be interviewed. One of them had been slashed over the ear by his commander because he did not blow his horn loud enough to suit him. When they wish to get their troops together they begin blowing horns and you never heard such awful sounds in your life.

At six o'clock a messenger came with a telegram for Mr Conger. The Chinese Minister is supposed to have sent it. He enquired after the health of Mr Conger and that is about all we could make out of the message. The Yamen sent word that their troops had been ordered to quit firing on us, but we are inclined to think they only mean to work out some plan to destroy us. Mr Conger had a notice posted up on Legation Street saying if the Chinese built any more barricades on the street they would be fired on, but they paid no attention to it and went right on with their work and consequently our boys turned the gun on them and blew the barricade down, killing a few Chinese. It was quiet the rest of the night.

July 18 1900

Very quiet. We walked over to our Legation to see how things looked and see what had happened since we left it. Four weeks had passed since we all fled to the British Legation, and desolation was on every side. The gate house was badly shelled, trees cut down and lying in all directions, bullet holes everywhere. In our rooms I counted 66 bullet holes. The windows all broken, blinds hanging by one hinge, and one place in our bedroom where a shell came through large enough for a man's body to get in, carpets and furniture ruined. At 2.30 pm a Japanese messenger who had been sent out on the 30th of June returned from Tientsin with a message saying foreign troops had taken Tientsin and the Chinese General had committed suicide, so that on the 20th, 30 thousand soldiers would start for Peking.

July 19 1900

More quiet last night and continued so all through the day.

July 20 1900

Nothing unusual transpired during the day, excepting two loads of melons were sent down from the Yamen with compliments. Melons will do very well after a substantial meal of fried chicken, mashed potatoes, and all sorts of good things, but when one has been living for six weeks on rice and horse meat three times a day with shot and shell booming all around you, melons are not very palatable. I presume they thought if they could not kill us with powder and shells they might succeed with choleramorbus. A few people ate some, but I did not care for any. The days and nights are excessively hot and many children are very sick. The past four days I have been with Dr and Mrs Inglis helping take care of the little baby who is dangerously ill. Three babies have died since we came in here. The German merchant where we used to take our meals when we first came to Peking, buried two within 10 days. The poor little things were simply wrapped up in a sheet and taken by one or two men to the German Legation to be buried. A few days later another little child died and was buried in a rough box.

July 21 1900

Shooting all night.

July 22 1900

I came to my room at 5 minutes to 12 o'clock last night thinking the baby was better. The Dr said, 'I think the baby is some better, so get a good nap tomorrow morning. Don't come over so early.' Just as I was finishing my breakfast a messenger came saying, 'Can you come quickly? The baby is sinking rapidly.' I hastened away and found the father and mother almost heart broken. Their home and possessions all burned and now the baby was soon to be taken from them. It was a sad Sabbath morning, we watched by her little bed quietly and just as the clock finished striking the noon hour, her little spirit took its flight. One of the missionary men made a little casket of pine boards and the ladies covered it with white flannel and lined it with some white silk which the ladies found. We found some little white flowers and with a few green leaves tied them with some satin ribbon Mrs Conger sent over. I put a little pink rose in her left hand and as we looked at the little form lying there so quietly,

while bullets were flying over our heads outside, we could not but feel that it was all for the best. Just as the sun went down we laid the little lamb beside the brave soldier boys who had given their lives in trying to defend us here.

July 24 1900

The Japanese interpreter who was wounded some time ago, died this morning and an Italian shot.

July 25 1900

At 1 am we were suddenly aroused from our slumbers by the familiar sounds of shots and for half an hour or more the noise was something terrible. One of our Marines was shot. Yesterday was the Emperor's birthday and it was being celebrated in the usual way and I presume that they thought they would give us an early morning serenade.

July 26 1900

The report last evening was that our troops were halfway between here and Tientsin, that they had fought a battle and driven Chinese back some distance which we hope is true.

July 28 1900

For two days it has been very quiet until 2 am when they fired a few shots at us and retired. It is reported that 40 thousand Chinese soldiers have gone out to meet our troops, taking with them 24 big guns and that a battle will be fought at Tung-Chou, 12 miles from here. We are still very anxious to know what will be the result of the battle. It took our troops 24 days to take possession of Tientsin.

Last evening three or four cart loads of vegetables, flour and rice were sent here, whether to poison us or what, is the question in our minds. We understand the 'Old Lady' and her crowd are preparing to leave the city. She might not have an opportunity to go if she waited until foreign troops arrived.

July 29 1900

Last night soldiers and boxers attacked the Pei Fang killing 100 of the inmates. An Italian was wounded by their gun this afternoon in trying to knock down a Chinese barricade, which had been put up against orders. They are blazing away at each other through look holes in their barricades and the Chinese.

July 30 1900

Very noisy all night and still continues.

Saturday afternoon I chaperoned Miss Pierce and Mr Daysberg over to look at the Japanese, French and German Legations. They are all very much damaged. We went down through the canal and came back on Legation Street as it was quiet.

July 31 1900

Last night two Chinese were beheaded as they were trying to enter the Chien-men (gateway). It is supposed they were messengers sent to us from Tientsin. Two others who managed to get through brought word that the troops were only 18 miles from here, that they had fought a battle on Sunday and had taken every village as they came along. We have heard so many rumors of relief being near that we shall not believe it until we see them. I feel as though I had seen quite enough of China and heathenism and am ready to go back to the land of my birth and civilisation.

August 2 1900

Was very sick in bed eight days, but Mrs Lowry has told me of all that has transpired during that time. I got so that I could not eat the horse meat any longer and it was that or starve, so I concluded starvation was as good as horsemeat. I found a little corn starch and with a little water and sugar (no eggs) the boy fixed it up and once or twice a day I had that. Chinese soldiers shot every one who went outside to look for eatables and no one was allowed to bring anything to us and here we are behind these walls like prisoners. I heard a great hurrahing at the bell tower just at sundown and Miss Pierce came to tell us the good news. A messenger who had been sent from here some time ago and who was one of Mr Lowry's converts at Hsiao-Shun-Ha-Tung, came from Tientsin with a number of messages. One letter from Mr. Bagsdale saying they never expected to see us again until they got Mr Conger's telegram in July saying we were alive. There was a telegram from London they had seen Mr Conger's message to the Department. It was the only thing they had been able to learn of any one in Peking, only what the Chinese Minister had informed them. They had been led to believe that we were being well cared for by Chinese officials, that we were all comfortable and happy. Here we have been since the early part of June with no communication whatever with the outside world. The messenger had his letters sewed between two old Chinese straw hats and no one suspected he had but one hat on. One of the letters

said that on 31st of July ten thousand troops would leave Tientsin for Peking, and that by the middle of August 50 thousand would reach us if we could only keep up our courage a little longer.

August 10 1900

We have not had one quiet night since Aug. 2. The Chinese seem to be getting more desperate every hour. The 'Old Lady' has ordered two of the members of the Tsung-Li-Yamen beheaded, because they were inclined to be friendly to foreigners. We have had two and three attacks every night. Last night at dinner time they began at a furious rate and the British gave them a few greetings with 'Betsey' the International, and they very shortly retired for refreshments, tea and a smoke, and to cool their heated brows.

At 4 am they seemed to be rested and began again more furious than before, but thank God none were killed but Chinese.

A messenger brought letters from the British and Japanese Generals saying the troops were half way here, and they had defeated the Chinese in two battles on the way up and for us to keep up our courage yet a little longer, five or six days at the most and they would be here. We had not finished our supper until they began popping away at us quite lively. 9.30 pm. A heavy shower came down upon us and at the first clap of thunder the Chinese began to fire furiously and for half an hour or more it made us feel as though we were not out of the woods yet, if the troops were nearing.

I was told today that the chapel at Hsiar-Shun-Hu-Tung had not been burned as the Boxers said a spook was on the roof and they were afraid to go near it. During the time the Missionaries were quartered there, Dr Reed, a very tall slender man, had that as a place he was to watch at night, and they were frightened away by his long legs.

August 11 1900

Rather quiet last night, but considerable mêlée all forenoon.

August 12 1900

A terrible racket all night and the greater part of the day. The heavy guns have fired more shots than ever before (our guns I mean). Three attacks have been made since 2 o'clock. We begin to feel that our troops are nearing and the Chinese think they must make the most of what little time they have, so they keep blazing away at us from every side. A German was wounded and a French Marine killed.

Prince Ching sent word today that the members of the Yamen were coming to the Ministers tomorrow at eleven am. If I were in their place I would lock them up as soon as they entered the gates and treat them exactly as they have been doing by us, then seize the Old Lady and give her a dose of her own medicine.

August 13 1900

The attack was very heavy last night. It seemed as if the walls around us would surely be blown down and we should all be killed before morning, but we are still alive.

August 14 1900

Last night was the worst of all. One German Marine was killed, our gunner wounded, and one Frenchman, one Russian, one Japanese Dr was wounded also. A Russian was buried this forenoon who died in the hospital, during the night. Just after Mr Bainbridge had come in from his watch and gotten to sleep I heard away off in the distance heavy cannonading and firing which I knew was something I had never heard before, and the more I listened the more I was convinced that relief was very near. Shortly I heard Mr Conger's voice outside, then all the ladies were out talking and laughing as I had not heard before in many long weeks. After an hour or so they all retired again and at 7 am big guns were heard very near and we knew our troops were blowing down the wall to get into the city.

August 15 1900

2.30 pm. Shouts went up on all sides 'Soldiers are coming by the thousand.' There was great rejoicing by every man, woman and child. Some were shouting, others waving their handkerchiefs and others standing quietly with tears silently falling down their thin cheeks. 22 thousand came to our rescue on the first day. They had not been in over an hour before they began work on the Chinese. A company of Sikhs (Indians) were sent out near our quarters to take a barricade and when they got over the wall there was not a Chinese to be found anywhere. So they settled themselves in the Imperial carriage grounds and had everything their own way. Troops were sent all around blowing down barricades with great success.

August 16 1900

The Americans fired on the Imperial City and captured it. We lost seven men in the fight, Captain of the Artillery and six privates were killed. The privates were buried in the American compound at 6 pm. The Captain was buried at nine the next morning. All were put in one grave.

August 17 1900

We were asked to give up our front room this morning as a hospital. There are only ten rooms in the Minister's house, and thirteen which the 1st Secretary occupies, which we only had two. The one we are in has no window lights, and the outside blinds hang in all directions, bullet holes everywhere and just over my head is where a shell came through the roof and when it rains, we usually know that it is damp inside as well as out.

August 18 1900

Baron Von Kettler's body was found yesterday at the Yamen and was buried in the German Legation this morning at 9 o'clock.

This evening Mr Bainbridge and myself went down to see our Marines who had been removed from here to the Chien-men gate. I found two of them sick and they seemed quite pleased to see me. Before they left here some of them gave me some very nice little presents which I shall prize very highly, coming from the boys who fought so bravely for our lives for eight long weeks. I asked why they have given me such lovely things, and one, with tears in his eyes said, 'Because you have treated us all like white folks, and what you did for one was done for all.' It has made my heart ache many times to see how worn and weary these poor boys look, after such a siege. One of the sick ones held up his hand to show me how thin he was getting and remarked that the ring on his finger belonged to his mother, but she was dead, and he said, 'I am afraid I shall lose it.'

Captain Myers and Dr Lippet are improving slowly. [Signatures of the above two are in original copy.]

Of the whole eight weeks of terrible anxiety and dread, three nights stand out with special prominence. They are spoken of by the besieged as 'The three terrible nights.' The first was a few nights before we fled from our Legation. All night long went up terrible cries, howls and shouts of thousands upon thousands of Chinese crying for the blood of foreigners. The second was about the middle of the siege, when one of the most violent thunder storms I have ever experienced broke over the City. Everybody had predicted the Chinese would cease firing, but the effect of the storm was just the opposite. It was a night of bellowing thunder, roaring artillery, incessant lightning and pouring rain. The third and last night of horrors was that of August 13 the day before the relief came. The Chinese were a howling, frenzied mob and moved Heaven and Earth to break in and kill us. Firing that had seemed furious was tame compared with the hail of shot and shell that poured in upon us that night, long to be remembered by all. We expected that any moment might be our last, as many breaches were made by shells and a determined assault at any one place would have opened the way for the hordes outside, when at 2 am on the 14th, faint sounds were heard away in the distance, of what seemed to us like heavenly music. Nearer and nearer came the sounds of cannonading and artillery, until every foreigner said in their hearts, 'Thank God they are coming.' There was no mistake in that sound. All were listening eagerly, rejoicing deep down in their hearts. 'The troops are outside the city and we are saved'. At eleven they reached the City wall and blew open places to come through. Some however, scaled the wall, and the first man up was an Iowa boy. Hurrah for Iowa.

The Siege of Peking was ended.

Mary Ann (Sims, McCarger) Bainbridge[18]

How solid, dependable, undaunted and caring were the actions, during the Siege, of this first-generation American of Cornish descent - Mary Ann Sims McCarger Bainbridge. She rose to the occasion, held her head high for her husband and her country. She understood and accepted that duty was a task not to be delegated but to be performed by oneself. Her daughter-in-law Lutie was wont to describe her as a 'take charge person', and this description sums up the character and attributes of Mary Ann.

Mary Ann's day-to-day account of the Siege of the Peking Legations is further enhanced by a letter which she wrote to her friend Mrs Wheeler, extracts of which are here presented:

Legation of the United States of America
Peking, China   December 16 1900

My Dear Mrs Wheeler,

When one is in very great trouble it is not a hard matter to find out who are your friends. You, I shall always have on my list. Mrs Smith, Mrs Brown, Mrs

Caldwell and yourself are the only ones outside the family who have written to me.

It was a close call I tell you, and but few ever expected to get out of it alive. We were not a very presentable lot after being fired on for over two months, and dining on mule meat, curried horse and rice; those who could eat it got along better than a few who could not. I was one of the latter. Occasionally I'd try a little horse soup, but even that would not stay down. I lost all my flesh and all my hair, but I had plenty of company. It is all like a horrible nightmare. The siege of Peking will never be forgotten, it will live forever in the hearts and minds of those who were here.

On the 19th June we were given just twenty-four hours in which to leave the city, but where were we to go, and how, was the question; train burned, carts taken away, rickshaws and donkeys all gone and the city surrounded by a howling mob of Chinese soldiers and Boxers. That was a night to be remembered among a number of others later on. I had for several days a few traps in a handbag, my hat and umbrella all near the doorway ready in case we were attacked and an order given for us to fly. It had been decided some days before that if they made a rush we ladies were to fly across the road to the Russian Legation for safety, there American and Russian Marines could probably keep the mob back; but as you know we were obliged to gather in the missionaries on the 20th of June and all fly to the British Legation where we spent the summer. No one had time to get lonely for there were sandbags to be made for barricading, serving for the hospital, the sick and wounded to be taken care of and any number of things to keep one's fingers and mind occupied.

We got used to the sound of bullets whizzing over our heads, and did not pay much attention to them. The most we feared was that our brave boys over the wall and elsewhere should or would be shot. Our lives depended on what might happen to them.

There was lots of sickness amongst us but only one death among the Americans in the Legation, that was the only child of Dr and Mrs Inglis. Three German babies died and one Swede, and a great many children belonging to the native Christians.

We were all on equal footing, just like one family, one looked just as clean as the other, for we had no washmen. In the six-roomed house we occupied there were thirty-one people, and nearly all the time one was sick and could hardly drag around. The last eight days I had to give up, if the Boxers got me I did not care, but when I heard the welcome sounds away off in the distance at 2 am on 14th of August, I was able to stagger to the door in the afternoon when the troops got in and shake the hand of dear old General Chaffee and hand him a drink of cool water, for he looked very much worn and tired out, as they all were. I could not say much my heart was overflowing as well as my poor old eyes, we were saved.

The next morning the captain of the artillery was shot and his men were so indignant over it they shot everything in sight with a pig-tail hanging down its back.

Seven American soldiers were killed the same day and are buried in this compound, all in one long grave lying side by side. I can see where they are from my bedroom window. It is a sad sight to see a poor soldier laid away in clothes and boots just as he fell. Not long before the relief party came one of our Marines was shot and the ladies went to the funeral, it was the first one we had been able to attend as the others had been at night. Miss Pierce and I got a few flowers and after the sad ceremony we placed some on each grave. As I stood at the foot looking down upon the lifeless form of *somebody's* son my heart was almost bursting, he had given his life to save ours, and as Mr Conger tried to tell us why we had there assembled the tears were falling down our cheeks like rain, he too was all broken up, and as the rain fell softly on our umbrellas while the faithful white-haired missionary read the service (for he had been the one who was always ready, no matter at what hour of the night or day it might be) our hearts were overflowing. The same day two British Marines were buried and in the midst of the service a shell exploded not far from where the Rector stood.

Since the siege we have been to see all the sacred temples and everything, 'The old lady' you know is away at present. The summer palace is about 12 miles from here. I have been there twice, once with the Congers and some military officers to a picnic, and once General Chaffee gave the missionaries permission to go and sent his own ambulance for me to accompany them.

There are two Council Bluffs boys here. Major Hugh Gallagher and Phil Paschel, yes and a young man Mr Nolan who said he lived near us on 4th Street. He said, 'of course I know you, all the boys liked Bert's[19] mother, she used to always have apples or something for us when we were kids', but he has been in Omaha for five years so I had forgotten him. They all come to see me quite often. The major is at the head of the Commissary Department. Phil and John are clerks. Phil is chief clerk and a fine singer. I have a *kind* of a piano for the *winter*, so we have music occasionally.

My best wishes to all enquiring friends and much love to you all, and a kiss for each of the little girls.

Yours sincerely,
Mary Bainbridge

Party which attended General Chaffee's 'Tiffin' on 22 February 1901
L-R back row: second, William E. Bainbridge
L-R front row: second, Mary Ann Bainbridge; Centre: General Chaffee
sixth, Hon. E.H. Conger, United States Minister

The Americans returned to their Legation on 16 August 1900. It was in quite a state and repair work was still in progress sixteen months later. Mary Ann records that it was hard-tack and water during the first two days they were back in their Legation.

However, great efforts were being made both by the foreign Legations and the Chinese to effect a return to a normal way of life. Mary Ann records that on 13 and 14 September she, William Elmer Bainbridge and others dined with the Congers when the band of the 14th Infantry were posted on the porch and played some lovely music. It was, she said, 'Quite a change from what we had listened to all summer.'

William had been highly praised by the American Minister for his conduct during the Siege. When the First Secretary at the Legation, Mr H. G. Squires, indicated a desire to move on, Walter H. Smith of the House of Representatives, Washington, recommended to the Secretary of State that William be promoted to the position, in the event of a vacancy occurring, but apparently nothing came of this suggestion.

On 1 February 1902 the Empress Dowager gave an Audience to the ladies of all Foreign Legations. After Mrs Conger had received some magnificent presents from the Empress Dowager, Mary Ann and the others were also recipients of gifts. Mary Ann received a handsome pearl ring and bracelets with jewels. The following day each of those who had attended the Audience received six rolls of beautiful silk in a glass case, four from the Empress Dowager and two from the Emperor, together with a box of ten different Chinese combs as used by the Empress Dowager.[20]

At some stage William became a Member of the Chinese Indemnity Commission, and it was said later that in this capacity he displayed the attributes of a keen logical and incisive mind so necessary in this type of negotiation.

In early summer 1902 Mary Ann and William were preparing to return to the United States, either on leave or at the end of William's tour of duty. Certainly William resigned his position as Second Secretary on 25 March 1903.[21] For some reason which is not understood, it has not been possible to ascertain from American archival institutions details of William's further career, but information and photographs from the family,[22] together with his obituary[23] have provided some insight. We know that for a period he became one of the Judges of the Venezuelan Claims Commission in Caracas, for which he was commended with a personal letter from the President.

From a photograph taken with four other persons in Berlin on 4 April 1907 it is obvious that William was there on

The Party who attended the first Audience after the Court returned to Peking. Mary Ann Bainbridge below the arrow.

Caracas – William E. Bainbridge seated fourth from left.
Note the spittoons under the table!

Paris – Notice on the door reads Special Agent United States Treasury.
William E. Bainbridge is first on left.

official business, and it is known that from that year at least, he became the Special Agent United States Treasury, working from the Paris Consulate in charge of the Customs Bureau, where he rendered the Government very valuable service in overcoming smuggling. It seems, however, that the cruel nervous strain to which he had been subjected during the Siege of the Peking Legations had taken its toll, and on 17 April 1909 he died tragically in his office at the Consulate, additionally, and presumably due to the same cause Mary Ann had been far from well during much of her time in Paris. As soon as the news was broken to Lou Hoover she immediately cabled Mary Ann to say that she would leave Monterey, California, the following day in order to be with Mary Ann in her bereavement.[24]

The Pastor of the American Church in Paris confirmed to Rev. J.M. Williams of Broadway Methodist Church, Council Bluffs, that Mary Ann sustained herself with remarkable courage and strength in going quietly about the trying work and packing and setting all in order for her journey home with the body of her husband. A short service was held at the mortuary chapel of the American Church before Mary Ann set out on her lonely and heart-breaking journey to Council Bluffs. Her younger son James F McCarger travelled to New York to meet her. They then continued by railroad for the final stage of Mary Ann's journey, where they arrived on 7 May. The public funeral service took place at the Bainbridge home, 315 Glen Avenue, on the following Thursday afternoon followed by private interment in Walnut Hill Cemetery. There were many expressions of sympathy and condolence to Mary Ann and eulogies to the deceased. Among the latter was one from the Pottawattamie Bar Association which with other tributes said that William 'by education, natural ability and high character, was fitted to and exemplified the ideals of his chosen profession, and that in the long dreary weeks of the Siege in Peking he displayed courage and devotion to duty unsurpassed by any soldier of the Republic.'[25]

Mary Ann continued to reside at Council Bluffs, but at some stage moved to 621 Harrison Street. She was an active member of Broadway Methodist Episcopal Church and found much pleasure and delight in her grandchildren. For the last few years of her life she was in failing health and passed away in April 1916 aged sixty-five. Not a great age, but no doubt the traumas through which she had passed had shortened her life. Three ministers officiated at her funeral service and interment took place in Walnut Hill Cemetery, where she was laid to rest beside her two husbands, both parents and her sister Sarah. Her obituary described her as a brilliant and interesting woman.

Jane Sims

Jane (Jennie), the fifth child of Ann and James, was born at Dodgeville, WI, in 1856. Jennie became a schoolteacher and an accomplished painter in watercolours, who embellished her greeting cards with her own paintings. The author and his mother's family were recipients of these cards, some of which still exist.

Jennie commenced her teaching career in Wisconsin and then from 1898 spent several years in Council Bluffs. She then moved to Connecticut, returning again to Wisconsin in 1918 and remained there until she was taken ill in 1933. At this point her nephew James F. McCarger and his wife motored to Wisconsin and brought her back to their home at 738 Perrin Avenue, Council Bluffs. Jennie died in July the same year and was laid to rest in Walnut Hill Cemetery.

Cora Sims

Cora, the seventh child, was born circa 1860, probably in Fayette, WI.

On 5 September 1882, Cora married George Snowden Bell of Montfort, WI, who had been born in that town on 30 October 1855. He was the son of Edward Bell, who had operated one of the first stores in the town. Following the death of his father, George continued with the store until he was persuaded by his family to move to Council Bluffs. This Iowan town appears to have acted like a magnet to the Ann and James Sims family, but after spending only a few months there George became so homesick for his native town that he and his immediate family returned to Montfort. George opened his own store, which he operated until 1907. He then became Station Agent at Preston but around 1916 became unwell and was never to regain a full measure of health again. George loved nature and enjoyed taking long walks through the woods and along the streams, and was especially interested in birds. He held several public offices and was town treasurer for many years.

Two children were born of this marriage. Nina, who died in 1887, and Grace, who married Richard Goodlad and was living at Madison, WI, in 1931.

George died at his home in Montfort on 3 February 1931. His obituary records, 'He was a good citizen and a good neighbour, faithful in all trusts he assumed, and a man well thought of and highly honoured in the community. He was unassuming and avoided display of any kind. The entire community will miss George Bell.'

Unfortunately it has not been possible to obtain any further information on Cora and her family.

May E Sims

May, the ninth child, was born in 1864 probably in Montfort, Grant County, WI. She graduated from High School in 1884 and in 1886 commenced her career in teaching. May never married and when her parents retired to Council Bluffs in 1890 she joined them and became Principal of Bloomer, The Old Hill and Madison Avenue Schools. It was while Principal of the latter school that she was taken ill in November 1913 and underwent a serious operation at the Jennie Edmundson Memorial Hospital from which she never recovered, passing away at the early age of forty-nine. An indication of her life of service is contained in the *Council Bluffs Nonpareil* of 18 November 1913, which is here quoted verbatim:

To her was given an opportunity for a life of wider

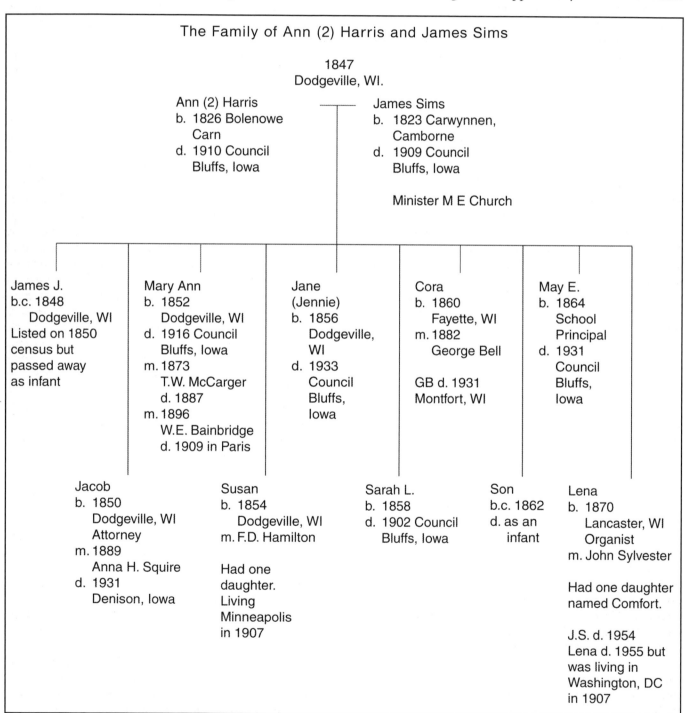

The Family of Ann (2) Harris and James Sims

1847
Dodgeville, WI.

Ann (2) Harris
b. 1826 Bolenowe Carn
d. 1910 Council Bluffs, Iowa

James Sims
b. 1823 Carwynnen, Camborne
d. 1909 Council Bluffs, Iowa

Minister M E Church

James J.
b.c. 1848 Dodgeville, WI
Listed on 1850 census but passed away as infant

Mary Ann
b. 1852 Dodgeville, WI
d. 1916 Council Bluffs, Iowa
m. 1873 T.W. McCarger
d. 1887
m. 1896 W.E. Bainbridge
d. 1909 in Paris

Jane (Jennie)
b. 1856 Dodgeville, WI
d. 1933 Council Bluffs, Iowa

Cora
b. 1860 Fayette, WI
m. 1882 George Bell
GB d. 1931 Montfort, WI

May E.
b. 1864 School Principal
d. 1931 Council Bluffs, Iowa

Jacob
b. 1850 Dodgeville, WI
Attorney
m. 1889 Anna H. Squire
d. 1931 Denison, Iowa

Susan
b. 1854 Dodgeville, WI
m. F.D. Hamilton
Had one daughter. Living Minneapolis in 1907

Sarah L.
b. 1858
d. 1902 Council Bluffs, Iowa

Son
b.c. 1862
d. as an infant

Lena
b. 1870 Lancaster, WI
Organist
m. John Sylvester
Had one daughter named Comfort.
J.S. d. 1954 Lena d. 1955 but was living in Washington, DC in 1907

service than comes to most people, and many a young man or woman of today has owed his impulse towards better things to a kindly word of help at the right moment. One of the gentlest of women, her kindly influence was felt throughout her school, and yet beneath the gentleness was a force of character that made her equal to the most difficult situation.

A member of the Broadway Methodist Episcopal Church since her girlhood, she was active in church work, and will be greatly missed in both church and Sunday School.

In her work as a teacher she was most professional and took great interest in all movements to advance the standard of schoolwork, and extend the efficiency of the instructor. She was an enthusiastic member of the Council Bluffs Teachers' Club, having assisted in its organisation, and served ably as a member of the general committee.

May was ill for only two weeks and died as she had wished in the midst of her work, and in the event painlessly in her sleep. Prior to burial in Walnut Hill Cemetery her body was rested at the home of her sister, Mary Ann Bainbridge, and here a custom which to some folk may seem unusual took place when the children of her school were given an opportunity to call for a last look at their Principal.

The funeral service was held at Mary Ann's house and was conducted by Rev. G.W.I. Brown minister, of Broadway Church, assisted by Rev. J.H. Senseny of Denison and former Pastor in Council Bluffs.

Retirement and Death

When James was superannuated in 1890, he and Ann moved in the fall of the year to Council Bluffs, Iowa. His last charge under the West Wisconsin Conference had been at Bloomington, Grant County, WI. In Council Bluffs they took up residence in Platner Street, later moving to Park Avenue. The move to Council Bluffs was obviously due to the fact that their son Jacob and daughter Mary Ann were already resident there, and possibly other of their children.

Where there was an opportunity and a call to serve God, James, even at sixty-nine years of age, did not stand aloof; in 1892 he became Pastor of Epworth United Methodist Church at Council Bluffs. The appointment was under the Iowa Conference and in this initial term he faithfully served the charge until 1896.

The little timber-framed Epworth Church had only been built three years previously and originated from a non-denominational Sunday School which had met in the Streetsville Day School, just across the street from the new church. The church had been built in sixty days at a cost of $1,500, but there was no parsonage. At the time James became Pastor, the church Sunday School had 12 officers and 125 pupils. The church comprised thirty-five full members and eleven probationers. In the event James served here as Pastor for a second term from 1897 to 1899. It was indeed a growing church and in 1909, about the time that James passed away, the original church was sold and it was moved to the business area of West Council Bluffs, where it served as a food store for a number of years until it unfortunately burned down. Following erection of a new church in 1909, an educational unit was added some years later and in 1965 a new sanctuary was built.[26] The foregoing demonstrates the sure foundation on which this particular Society was nurtured.

In 1896 James accepted Pastorship of Silver City Methodist Episcopal Church. Silver City lies about twenty-five miles from Council Bluffs, and the available information suggests that James would have had to revert to some form of horse transport to carry out his duties as means of travel were still difficult in this area. The church at Silver City had been dedicated in January 1883, although planning had started in 1881 when the first three meetings were held in the street! After James had been Pastor for two years it was decided by the Methodist Episcopal and Baptist Churches to hold a joint evangelistic mission. As neither of the two churches were large enough to accommodate the crowds who attended, the meetings were held in the Opera House in Main Street. The mission lasted from 24 February to 9 March 1897 and there were seventy conversions. The meetings were conducted by the Baptist Minister, James Sims, a Mr Oliver from Chicago and Billy Sunday.[27] This Iowa-born evangelist, Billy Sunday (1862-1935), had in a magazine popularity poll of 1914 tied for eighth place as 'The Greatest Man in America'. Unorthodox by any standards - Jim Holston in his article on Billy Sunday in 1985 said , 'Even today, fifty years after his death, his name - Billy Sunday - conjures up an image of spellbinding shirt-sleeved evangelism, the type of religious oratory meant to serve the Lord and save souls that survives today in the more buttoned-down version of Billy Graham.'[28] Sunday admitted to knowing 'Less about theology than a jack-rabbit knows about ping-pong.' It would have been very interesting to have had an assessment by James of this extraordinary evangelist!

In 1899 at the end of his second term as Pastor of Epworth Church, and at seventy-six years of age, James at last laid down the full-time duties of the Pastorate but still continued to preach as a supply to the pastors of Des Moines Conference. It is recorded that he was a forceful and effective preacher, and as having an unusual knowledge of the Scriptures together with

The Diamond Wedding Group 24 June 1907
Photograph taken in the garden of the home of James and Ann, 312 Park Avenue, Council Bluffs, Iowa.

Standing L–R: James Daniel Sims – Jacob's Son; Mary Ann Sims McCarger Bainbridge; Cora Sims Bell;
Jennie Sims; Lena Sims Sylvester; May E. Sims; Marianna Sims Sturges, Jacob's Daughter;
Susan Squire Sims, Jacob's Wife; Jacob Sims; James Finlayson McCarger, Mary Ann's Son.

Middle Row L–R: Rev. James Sims; Comfort Sylvester, Lena's Daughter; Ann Harris Sims;
John Alan Sims, Jacob's Son.

Front Row L–R: Grace Bell Goodlad, Cora's Daughter; Marjorie Sims, Jacob's Daughter;
? Hamilton, Susan's Daughter; Catherine Sims Sturges, Jacob's Daughter.

clearly-defined conceptions of the fundamental doctrines of the Christian religion.[29]

In 1894 James managed to pay a visit to the parish in which he was born. Mark Smith Harris' diary records for 20 May 'Rev. James Sims paid us a visit' and on 6 July 'James Sims left for America'. During this vacation the Camborne Wesleyan Circuit made considerable use of his services. On 27 June he assisted in chairing the Circuit Quarterly Meeting, held at Pool. He preached a farewell service at Troon Chapel on the evening of Monday, 2 July, having taken the Sunday School Anniversary service at Bolenowe the previous morning. Finally, on Tuesday, 3 July, he shared the platform at a public meeting at Bolenowe with his brother-in-law, Mark Smith Harris.[30] The transport system both in America and England had undergone very considerable change and improvement since James had emigrated forty-nine years previously and what a contrast the conditions would have appeared to him. At Carwynnen both of his parents had passed away, his father two years after James had emigrated and his mother who lived on until 1883 reaching the great age of eighty-three.

As the years passed Ann became an invalid and in 1908, when James had accepted an invitation to preach at the twenty-fifth anniversary of the Silver City Society, he had to disappoint them owing to Ann's state of health, but in reality he himself was failing in health; in fact, two years previously - 1906 - he had been due to deliver a paper at the fiftieth anniversary of the West Wisconsin Conference but had been too unwell to travel. However, in the event he arranged for the Conference Treasurer, Rev. Thomlinson, to read it for him. It has not been possible to find the paper and neither was it included in the Conference Minutes. It was entitled *Some Preachers of the Early Days*.[31]

Despite their poor state of health they were able to celebrate on 24 June 1907 that relatively rare and unique anniversary, their Diamond Wedding. The celebration was held at their 312 Park Avenue home and was an exclusively family affair. The love and respect of their family was demonstrated by the presence of all their seven surviving children, ten grandchildren and their only daughter-in-law, Jacob's wife; they all sat down to a special lunch at 1.30 pm.[32]

Just thirteen months later, on 30 July 1909, James was called to higher service and by now Ann was a helpless invalid. The funeral service was held at their home and burial took place at Walnut Hill Cemetery. That there were four officiating ministers - Rev. J.M. Williams, Broadway Methodist Church; Rev. M.P. McClure, Presbyterian Church; Rev. F.A. Case, Baptist Church and Rev. J. O'May of Wilmette, Illinois - serves to confirm the statement in the Conference obituary of James which stated: 'He was a friend of every minister in the city regardless of denominational lines.' The minute goes on to say, 'His faith in Christ was absolute. During the long months of his physical helplessness his spirit was buoyant and happy. To the writer who frequently called, he would say, "I am still waiting. The best of all is, God is with me". His last days were spent in continuous prayer. Brother Sims was one of the most genial men of our Conference, none of us can ever forget that happy, hopeful face. In business or politics or in any calling of life it would have won him friends and patrons. It was not put on for the occasion, but was the result of the possession of the union with the Saviour which was like a well of water springing up unto everlasting life'.[33] At least two of the pall-bearers were Cornish or of Cornish extraction: J.H. Arthur (possibly a relative of James) and W.S. Mayne. Another pall-bearer was Senator C.G. Saunders.

Fourteen and a half months later Ann passed away on 15 October 1910. She also merited a Conference obituary,[34] some of which has already been quoted but additionally it stated: 'Very early in life Mrs Sims gladly recognised the voice of the Master calling her to a life of communion and service, and in that fellowship she walked unto the journey's end. Her sufferings were borne with Christian fortitude and confidence. We will not say she is dead for:

There is no death, the stars go down,
To rise upon some fairer shore,
And bright in Heaven's jewelled crown
They shine forever more.

There is no death! altho we grieve
When beautiful familiar forms
That we have learned to love are torn
From our embracing arms.

They are not dead! they have but passed
Beyond the mists that blind us here,
Into the new and larger life
Of that serener sphere.

Again four ministers officiated at the funeral and in addition to the pall-bearers who attended the funeral of James there was another Cornish person, J.C. Pryor. Interment was with James at Walnut Hill Cemetery.

6. Matthew (2) Harris

Nanny Toy (Sims) Harris 1828–86,
wife of Matthew (2) Harris

Early Life and Reconnaissance of Mining Fields in Various Parts of the World

Matthew (2), the fifth child and third son of John (2) and Christian, was born at Six Chimneys, Bolenowe Carn on 20 July 1826 and baptized at Camborne Parish Church on 16 August the same year.

Apparently like his sister Ann (2), Matthew (2) did not attend school. The reason for this omission may have been due to closure of the school at Forest Gate which John (3) and William had attended. Possibly the one-legged miner/teacher had become physically incapacitated or had passed away. The other available school at this time was Mrs Percival's Endowed School at Penponds, a walk of over three miles. At the 1841 census Matthew (2) was listed as a copper miner, which suggests that he had long since joined his father and elder brothers underground at Dolcoath Mine.

Actually little is known about the working life of Matthew (2) prior to his departure overseas, but seemingly he was not in a position to help the family financially when his father died in 1848, and this suggests that by this time he had decided to leave Dolcoath and the family home at Six Chimneys to assess the possibilities of other mines in Cornwall. He would have been aware that the days of Dolcoath as a copper mine were drawing to a

close and either did not realise or at least did not believe that its future lay in tin; whichever way his assumption, as it turned out, was mistaken. Matthew (2) was not a person to let the grass grow under his feet! By leaving Dolcoath he was demonstrating a desire, which was to gain impetus over the ensuing years, to locate a mine or mining field which showed promise of a continued profitable working to the mutual benefit of himself and other miners who were and are the backbone of any mining operation. As we shall see later, he eventually realised his ideal if not his Eldorado at the Minesota Mine in Upper Michigan.

By 1850 Matthew (2) was courting Nanny Toy Sims of Carwynnen, a sister of his brother-in-law James Sims. There can be no doubt of his desire to do the best he could for his future wife, and not being satisfied with prospects in Cornwall he made the decision to go out to America, from where his search took him around the world. How better than to start in the lead-mining region of south-west Wisconsin, and to observe how William and James were progressing. He said farewell to Nanny, his family and friends and set off on 15 May 1850 on what was to be a not inconsiderable tour and adventure. Matthew (2) may not have received a formal education but he possessed an astonishing memory, especially for dates which he subsequently recorded in a précis and which research has proven to be absolutely correct.

It has not been possible to obtain details of Matthew's (2) initial voyage to America but on the basis that it took seven weeks and six days from the time of leaving home to his arrival in New York it suggests that the vessel, and for that matter the conditions, were identical to those experienced by William, James A.nd Ann. No doubt he had received detailed instructions from William and with his ability to memorise would have found little difficulty in making the journey. In any case, he arrived in New York the following 9 July.

Imagine the meeting with William, Ann and James and probably other Camborne folk whom he had known back home. What stories would have been exchanged, not least the account of the death of their father. No doubt they talked far into the night and perhaps Matthew (2) had brought out some little memento for Ann from the family at home.

Matthew (2), like William, lodged with Ann and James during his stay in Dodgeville, and although he may have visited other mines at Mineral Point, Linden or even Platteville and Shullsburg, he makes no mention of this in his précis. Be that as it may, it seems more likely that he worked along with William and James. By this means he could experience and assess the possibilities of lead mining in these very shallow lodes. It seems that

Matthew (2) was not over impressed by the prospects of this particular region, and about three months after his arrival he left in November 1850 and went up to the Bruce Mines in Ontario. Despite his disappointment with prospects in the lead mines he had obviously accumulated sufficient money to make it possible to move on.

Canada

Matthew (2) would probably have travelled across southern Wisconsin to the western shore of Lake Michigan to find a steamboat to take him up and through the Mackinaw Straits, where he may have had to tranship to reach the Bruce Mines on the northern shore of Lake Huron.

The Bruce Mines had been opened up by a certain William Harris who in 1850 became Captain of the Minesota Mine with which he was associated for twenty-two years. This William Harris served two terms from 1871 to 1875 on the Michigan Legislature, had been born at Carn Brea, Cornwall in 1818, and had come out to Canada in 1846. Spending his first four months on Michipicoten Island in Lake Superior, he then prospected along the Canadian shore of Lake Huron, sleeping under an Indian canoe until he was able to obtain more favourable accommodation.[1] No doubt William Harris had been attracted by the purple sulphide of copper ore which occurred near the surface. Below the outcrops the ore was mainly copper pyrites.[2]

As far as can be ascertained William Harris was not related to the Harrises of Bolenowe Carn, but no doubt his exploits appealed to Matthew (2), news of which had doubtless filtered south to the lead-mining region. One may speculate as to why Matthew (2) elected to go to Canada rather than the Keweenaw Peninsula, but the mines in the latter location were only in an embryonic stage and the eventual large mines were not in evidence excepting perhaps the Minesota in Ontonagon County which had been initiated in 1847. In 1848 it had only sold 13,000 pounds of copper (six and a half short tons) and did not reach the rich copper deposits until 1851. The first profit was made in 1852.[3] It is doubtful if Matthew (2) actually worked under William Harris and if their paths crossed it could only have been of a few weeks' duration at the Bruce Mine. Later, Matthew (2) did work under him at the Minesota Mine and Matthew's brother, Samuel B. Harris, became a friend of William and was a pall-bearer at his funeral.

Matthew (2) spent five to six months at the Bruce Mines and then made an almost inexplicable decision to move to the Isle Royale. Maybe he was unable to accumulate funds as readily as he wished. Certainly the impression left with one of his descendants, a third-generation American, was summed up with the words: 'That Matthew just could not make money fast enough.' On the basis that the Bruce Mines had only been opened a short time previously it could well be that Matthew (2) felt they held for him no better prospect than the mines in south-west Wisconsin, although in the event the workings extended for nearly two miles across the Bruce, Wellington and Huron Bay locations; the mines operated for thirty years from 1846 to 1876 and produced $3,300,000 worth of copper.[4]

Isle Royale

Matthew (2) was now faced with the journey to his new destination, which was not without its perils. Indeed, for the first three months of a year navigation on Lake Superior was closed due to storms and ice floes and could well be similarly affected in December and April, so Matthew bided his time and made the journey in May. From Bruce Mines he would have proceeded by boat up St Mary's River until he arrived at Sault Ste Marie and the rapids, where from as early as 1791, on the Canadian side, a small lock and canal had been constructed but it was only sufficient to accommodate canoes. On the American side rolling logs and a little railroad were used to carry small vessels, all being necessary to overcome some twenty feet of differential level between Lake Huron and Lake Superior. In 1851 construction on the great 'Soo' canal and locks was under way, but it is probable that Matthew (2) passed through on the Canadian canal and locks. Eventually arriving on the vast expanse of Lake Superior he would then have taken passage on a somewhat larger vessel for the crossing of about 235 miles to the Isle Royale. Providing the weather conditions were good it would have been quite a pleasant trip, but even in summer the lake is subject to sudden storms, fogs and squalls which can be hazardous, coupled to the possibility that the skills and competency of the skippers and crews might be no better than those mentioned earlier on the Atlantic crossings. There is no mention in Matthew's précis of the voyage being eventful or, for that matter, on which copper mine on the Isle Royale he found employment. By now, in respect of the latter, his choice was somewhat limited in that mining on the Isle was in the evening of its life. It was possibly the Siskowit, which had been operating for the previous five years.

It was on the Isle Royale as well as the Keweenaw Peninsula that the ancient copper miners extracted surface deposits and where their pits can still be seen.

Apparently Matthew's move to the Isle must have benefited him financially for he remained there for twelve months, his longest sojourn in any of the three areas visited to date. Then it seems that he was gripped once again with the urge to move on. Whether he felt that he had seen the best of Siskowit - it closed down in 1855 - or whether his seemingly transcending desire to sample other possibilities was uppermost in his mind it is difficult to say, but on balance it seems most probable that it was the lure of gold which had been discovered in 1848 in the Sacramento Valley in California. It is true to say that some of Matthew's (2) descendants maintain that his real intention was to go to Alaska but in the event stopped off in California. Why he should have intended to go to Alaska is difficult to understand because gold was not discovered there until nine years later in 1861 and it was Russian territory until 1867.[5]

In May 1852, Matthew (2) retraced his journey across Lake Superior to Sault Ste Marie, down the Canadian canal and locks and St Mary's River, at the mouth of which he boarded a steamer on Lake Huron to take him via St Clair River and Lake, Detroit River and Lake Erie to Buffalo, then along the Erie Canal by canal boat to Albany and thence by steamer to New York.

California

Arriving in New York it was now necessary to arrange passage to San Francisco. The voyage around Cape Horn was over 14,000 miles, whereas by crossing the Panamanian Isthmus it was just over 5,000 miles, but crossing the tropical rain-forest of the isthmus with its mud, swamp and mosquitoes was an experience so fraught with the almost certain possibility of contracting fever that few would contemplate it by design.[6] Most probably all of this meant nothing to Matthew (2) and hundreds of others who wished to cross over to the Pacific Coast. Knowledge of the geography and climatic conditions were to the vast majority of these folk only obtained by experience, not by scholastic attainment. It is almost beyond comprehension how these untaught and unlearned Cornish miners with no pre-realisation of the distances, climatic conditions, hazards and duration of the journeys made their way around the world and from continent to continent.

However, by 1848 another person, the extraordinary entrepreneur Cornelius Vanderbilt,[7] was studying the possibilities of easier and quicker travel between New York and San Francisco. Perusing the map of Central America he saw that right in the middle of Nicaragua was the lake of the same name which was 100 miles long and 50 miles wide. From San Juan del Norte on the east coast the San Juan River, the boundary between Nicaragua and Costa Rica, meandered for 119 miles to the lake. By crossing the lake for approximately sixty-five miles on a north-westerly bearing it was possible to get within twelve miles of San Juan del Sur on the Pacific coast. Admittedly this twelve mile stretch was through jungle, but Cornelius Vanderbilt saw that if this route could be opened up it would reduce the total journey by 500

miles and avoid the disease-ridden isthmus of Panama. Additionally it would take less time and this latter advantage would no doubt be the main incentive, and probably the only one that could be readily understood by the miners in their race to the goldfields. Cornelius Vanderbilt was convinced of the possibilities and in 1851 set up the Accessory Transport Company and secured a charter to cross Nicaragua by river, lake and stage. Thereafter, every two weeks his large steamships left New York, travelled down the Atlantic coast, through the Gulf of Mexico to San Juan del Norte at the mouth of the San Juan River. From this point smaller iron-hulled steamboats took the passengers up-river to the lake where they transferred to a steamboat. Arriving on the western shore of the lake they were then taken by stagecoach, drawn by mule teams, through the jungle to San Juan del Sur where Cornelius Vanderbilt had constructed a small port. Another steamer then took them to San Francisco, completing a journey of 4,531 miles. The company carried 2,000 passengers per month for nine years from 1851 to 1860. Originally the fare was $100 but with the eventual volume of payload Vanderbilt reduced it to $50.

On the basis that this was the shortest and now the most direct route, it seems highly probable that this was the particular route taken by Matthew (2) and indeed his timetable as recorded in the précis certainly correlates this assumption. Upon arrival in San Francisco in July 1852, Matthew (2) spent four weeks in hospital. While first impressions might suggest that he contracted fever on the journey, his descendants are adamant that it was a severe attack of influenza. From the description by Cornelius Vanderbilt's biographer of these particular journeys, credence must certainly be given to the probability of a severe attack of influenza. In fact, about one third of the passengers were provided with bunks, the remainder having to sleep on deck without any covering but their blanket. Arthur Vanderbilt labelled conditions on the ships as agonising and the journey as horrendous! Recovering after his spell in hospital, Matthew (2) visited the goldfields and recorded that he worked some claims.

It would seem from this statement that he ventured to Grass Valley where in 1850 a certain George McKnight stubbed his foot against a chunk of gold-bearing quartz[8] and this incident gave birth to winning gold from the rock of this area. On his journey Matthew (2) would have noted the washing of gold-bearing alluvial gravels at Rough and Ready but seemingly this method of working did not appeal to him. To get to Grass Valley, Matthew (2) would have taken a steamboat from San Francisco to Sacramento and then proceeded by stagecoach to his destination.

Then, very surprisingly, six weeks after leaving San

Francisco, Matthew (2) was back there again arranging a passage to Australia! What had happened for him to terminate so abruptly his stay in California? Maybe he was not impressed with the prospects, or maybe the then method of working the outcrops did not appeal to this underground miner; or could it be that he had witnessed or had even been subjected to some of the lawlessness of the Californian early mining camps? One thing is certain, if the latter reason is correct, and that is that Matthew (2) having been born and nurtured within the gentle and peace-loving Harris family would have been very disturbed and would have wished to distance himself from any form of lawlessness.

But now, for whatever reason, his destination was Australia.

Australia

In selecting Australia for his next area to be sampled, the question is, was Matthew (2) following the crowd in joining another rush to goldfields, or did he decide to visit Australia without any preconceived intention of what he would do when he got there? As far as the Victorian goldfields were concerned, these proved to be the third and final territory which he visited, albeit the one in which he remained for the longest period.

And now, as he left San Francisco on 26 September 1852, Matthew (2) was to take his longest sea voyage to date, that via Honolulu and Suva that would bring him to Sydney where he arrived on 17 November after a voyage of just over 6,500 miles which had taken seven weeks and two days.

New South Wales

Before proceeding to any other territory, Matthew (2) decided to take a look at the mining prospects in New South Wales. By this time gold, copper and lead were being worked, but no single large mines were in evidence, although there had been a considerable goldrush from as early as 1851. The massive silver/lead orebodies of Broken Hill were not discovered until 1883.[9]

The area being worked extended from Gulgong south-south-west to Bathurst and on down to Yass, a distance as the crow flies of about 175 miles. Bathurst as the central point was only about 110 miles west-south-west of Sydney.

Copper was being worked at Cornish Settlement, later known as Byng, twenty miles from Bathurst and copper and lead in other districts of Bathurst and at Yass. The goldfields extended from around Bathurst up to Gulgong. The Government had introduced a $3 licence fee in 1851[10] so that it was relatively simple for incoming hopefuls to obtain a licence to work a designated area. Obviously it would have taken Matthew (2) some little time to travel through the whole area and to try to assess if there was a future here for himself. Apparently he decided this was not what he was looking for and after four and a half months he moved on.

South Australia

Leaving Sydney on or about 24 March 1853, Matthew (2) took ship for Adelaide, South Australia, where he arrived during the first week of April. There was little gold to be found in South Australia but no doubt Matthew (2) was attracted by the copper discovery at Kapunda which had taken place in 1843 and lay about fifty miles north of Adelaide. Additionally there was the great Burra Burra Mine which had been discovered in 1845 and lay another fifty miles or so north of Kapunda. The subsequently greater mines of the Yorke Peninsula, Wallaroo, Moonta and Kadina were not discovered or operated until several years after Matthew (2) had visited. The carbonate of copper ore at Burra Burra consisted of the marvellous dark and light-green malachite and deep-blue azurite, but from the start of the Victorian goldrush in the early 1850s there had ensued an almost crippling shortage of miners in South Australia and especially at Burra Burra and Kapunda. No doubt the lure of gold had outstripped that of copper. Great efforts were made by the owners and management of Burra Burra and Kapunda to attract labour and this shortage, coupled to the fact that at Burra Burra the Captain was Henry Roach, a Cornishman from Redruth who held this position from 1847 to 1868,[11] must surely have been sufficient reason for Matthew (2) to head in the direction of this mine. Indeed, it would seem to be an almost heaven-sent opportunity for him to demonstrate his expertise learned in the copper mines at home in Cornwall and thereby benefit himself financially. But he did not remain long in South Australia, just two months in fact. Why did he decide to move on once again, and after such a short stay? What a pity that he did not pass on his reasons to his descendants. Was it because he felt that sufficient miners would never be available to adequately exploit and develop these large orebodies, or was he somewhat confounded by the carbonate ores of this district as against his experience in mining the sulphide ores of Cornwall? In the event, for whatever reason, we can only assume that Matthew (2) felt that there must be greater opportunity in one way or another in the Victorian Goldfields and so retraced his steps to Adelaide and obtained passage to Melbourne where he arrived on 8 June 1853.

Victoria

Gold had been discovered at Clunes in March 1850 and the great discoveries in Mount Alexander district took place in July 1851, while those at Ballarat followed during August 1851. When the news of these discoveries became public knowledge in late 1851 it resulted in an enormous goldrush. It is reported that by February 1852 there were 30,000 gold-seekers around Castlemaine and by June the same year 40,000 at Bendigo.[12]

All of this tremendous activity was taking place in a radius of about ninety miles and within a north-west quadrant whose axis subtended at Melbourne. So when Matthew (2) docked in Melbourne he did not have to travel any great distance to reach the goldfields. Most probably he accomplished this on foot, and certainly the movement from digging to digging was accomplished in this manner. It is apparent, as was the practice, that Matthew (2) moved from digging to digging because his précis states that he 'worked on nearly every gold-digging in the country' (sic). The movement from place to place was dictated by at least two reasons: first and foremost, the paucity of gold in a particular site and the news or prospect of richer finds somewhere else; and secondly, to obtain sustenance for the body. Food was sometimes very scarce, resulting in exorbitant prices. Water for separating the gold was sometimes some distance from the digging and good drinking water was a precious commodity. James Skewis, a Camborne miner who had also arrived in Victoria from California in the same year as Matthew (2), and were probably known to each other, has recorded: 'Good water was not always easy to find, often we would dip water from a wheel track by using a small cup, and careful not to stir the mud!'[13] In these circumstances it is not surprising that typhoid and dysentery were ever present dangers. It was indeed a hard and tough life. Some gold-seekers constructed crude huts in which to live but the majority made do with tents, which also facilitated moving from place to place. Additionally there was the problem of hold-ups and robberies, which were seemingly endemic where gold is concerned, but apparently the authorities in Australia made greater efforts to control the situation than those in California.

During Matthew's (2) sojourn in Victoria, the methods for winning gold were still by washing the alluvial gravels and also by normal mining methods in the quartz rock, even if the latter method was somewhat Heath Robinson. It was not until after 1855, when Matthew (2) had left, that the Victorian goldfields were organised and worked in an effective engineering manner.

Whether or not Matthew (2) suggested, through a third party, that his next younger brother James should join him in Victoria is not known, but as will be seen later in the narrative on James, that was not to be. James started out for the goldfields, was taken ill on board ship, was admitted to hospital immediately on arrival in Melbourne and died two weeks later.

Matthew (2) must have done reasonably well in Victoria because he remained there for nineteen months, after which he decided to go back to Cornwall to see the family and to marry Nanny Toy Sims. With the inability of both Nanny and Matthew (2) to read or write and having to rely for contact and correspondence via a third person with whom they may not have wished to divulge their innermost feelings, one wonders if Matthew had any doubts about Nanny still being at Carwynnen and still unattached. For that matter did Nanny wonder if Matthew (2) would ever return? After all, he had been absent for a full five years by the time she saw him again.

Whatever may have been their thoughts and concerns, Matthew (2) boarded a vessel at Melbourne on 15 January 1955 for a voyage of thirteen weeks, which as will be seen was of the same duration as that for James on his outward voyage. Matthew (2) arrived in London on 16 April following. It was a voyage of almost 12,000 miles via the Cape of Good Hope. Conditions on board were shocking and such as that in which his brother James did not survive. It was as bad or even worse than the horrendous voyage from New York to San Francisco but for a much longer period.

Marriage and Decision to go to the Upper Peninsula of Michigan

Arriving in London, Matthew (2) travelled to Bristol by rail and then by boat to Hayle,[14] then on the Redruth-Hayle Railway from Hayle to Camborne. The probability is that the family was totally unaware of his coming, and what a reunion it must have been after an absence of five years. Matthew (2) was the only one of Christian's children who came home for a visit. What stories must have been told of the experiences of Matthew (2). Imagine the avid attention of the younger members of the family. John (3) summed up the scene in some lines from his poem *The Mine*:

> Then tales were told and loving questions ask'd,
> And lengthy queries answer'd, till the moon
> Slid into midnight with her suite of stars.

And Nanny was waiting. They were married at Treslothan Church 26 May 1855. It was the only wedding of this generation of the Harris family to take place in this church. The ceremony was performed by Rev. George T. Bull the Perpetual Curate who had befriended and encouraged John (3) into a wider sphere of reading. The bride and groom could only make their marks in the register and both were twenty-six years of age. It seems doubtful if anyone other than the Rev. Bull and the witnesses were present. The latter were Henry Arthur, Nanny's brother-in-law and husband of her eldest sister Mary Ann Sims, and Charley Whear, the Master of Mrs Percival's Endowed School that stood adjacent to the church. Charley may have been a family friend but it is more likely that he was readily available to act as a witness at that particular moment.[15]

The couple left soon after for Liverpool, arriving in New York on 14 July. Following by now the almost time-honoured route of the Harrises from Camborne to Hayle, to Bristol, to Liverpool, they obtained passage on the *John Cottle* of 1,747 tons burthen. What an experience it was for Nanny, the first time on a train and the first time on the ocean. If only she could have recorded her thoughts and experiences. Conditions on the *John Cottle* would have changed very little since Matthew (2) made his previous crossing in 1850, although the vessel was somewhat larger.

News of the copper-rich Minesota Mine in Ontonagon County, Upper Michigan, had by some means become known to Matthew (2), and also the news that William Harris, previously of the Bruce Mines, was now Captain of this Copper Country mine, made him decide to take Nanny to the southern shores of Lake Superior to set up home and raise a family. The Minesota Mine, in 1852, had raised one million pounds of copper and the eventual total production between 1848 and 1885 amounted to 34,800,000 pounds of copper.[16]

But first Matthew (2) decided to take Nanny down to south-west Wisconsin to visit what had become by now a growing number of relatives. In fact, there were at least the following Simses: Nanny's uncle George and his family, her first cousin John, and her brother James A.nd Ann Harris with their four children; on the Harris side there was William and his younger brother Samuel B. with his wife Mary and their seven-month-old son James A.

Since Matthew's previous journey to Wisconsin from New York in 1850 considerable progress had been made in provision of railroad travel, a number of different companies being involved. Indeed, when Matthew's younger brother Samuel and his wife Mary made the journey twelve months earlier in 1854 they had been able to travel by railroad virtually to the Mississippi. However, at the time travel by railroad from New York to Galena, Illinois, would have involved many changes of train as there was no consolidated ownership of the railroads. Additionally, having reached East Chicago it was necessary to transfer to a stagecoach to get to West Chicago to join the Illinois Central Railroad to Galena as there was no continuous railroad across Chicago. Having arrived at Galena, Matthew (2) and Nanny would have taken the stage for the final sixty miles or so to Dodgeville.

For Matthew (2), who had already decided that his ultimate destination was the Minesota Mine in Ontonagon County, MI, the journey to south-west Wisconsin was a considerable diversion. Possibly he wanted to give Nanny a preview of the new country and way of life now being enjoyed by those members of their families who had earlier made the decision to emigrate. What a joy it must have been for Matthew (2) and Nanny to be with

Interior of Treslothan Church where Matthew (2) Harris and Nanny Toy Sims were married 26 May 1855. It was the Pendarves Family Church and was consecrated 25 July 1842. The Parish Registers date from the same year.

The Pendarves Family Hatchment in the church. Both photographs were taken on 18 July 1993 by Jay A. Harris of Plymouth, Michigan, great-grandson of Matthew (2) and Nanny.

family and friends once again and to see their young nephews and nieces for the first time. Again Matthew (2) would have related the experiences of his around-the-world journey to eager audiences.

After spending a few weeks with the family, Matthew (2) and Nanny left for Minesota Mine. Taking the overland route was a possibility in late August but in 1855 the road was little more than a trail and was fraught with many hazards in the form of natural obstacles to which Matthew (2) would not wish to subject Nanny. So they made their way to Milwaukee and thence by steamer to Lake Huron and the St Mary's River. In contrast to Matthew's (2) previous experience at this stage of the voyage, the great 'Soo' Locks at Sault Ste Marie had just come into operation and so they passed into Lake Superior without difficulty. Then proceeding along the southern shore of the lake they arrived at the mouth of the Onto-nagon River, which is the largest on the south shore of Lake Superior and navigable for some miles upstream from its mouth. Having reached the Minesota landing pier, a very primitive road brought them to the Minesota Mine, a distance of only about two miles. This would not have presented them with any great problem, although the Copper Country at this time was just a vast wilderness and before 1843 had belonged to the Chippewa Indians. And so Matthew (2) and Nanny arrived at their final destination, probably with a sigh of relief from Nanny.

Life and Family in Upper Michigan

It was not difficult for Matthew (2) to obtain employment at the Minesota Mine because it was expanding having reached the rich copper deposits in 1851 under the able direction of the mine captain, William Harris, who Matthew (2) had possibly briefly met at the Bruce Mines in 1850. It was in 1851 that the largest mass of native copper in any of the Upper Peninsula mines was exposed in the Minesota Mine which was estimated to be at least 500 tons in weight.[17] In course of time other large masses were exposed. With these extraordinary discoveries the Minesota Mine became one of the wonders of the mining world.[18] Matthew (2) had chosen well - a well-managed and truly productive mine. His travels had not been in vain. Indeed, from 1856 to 1858 two-thirds of the copper raised in Upper Michigan came from the Minesota Mine,[19] and in 1858 it raised over 1.900 tons of copper. In 1856 Matthew (2) was joined by his younger brother Samuel B. Harris, who came up from south-west Wisconsin and stayed until 1858. It was Samuel's first sight of the incredible copper deposits of the Upper Peninsula. He would have been most impressed and would have studied the formation with the keen eye of an assayer, doubtless making mental note for future reference. Despite the prospects that this incredible orebody offered, Samuel B. sometime after acquiesced to the lure of gold in Nova Scotia which, as we shall see later, was a false move.

Alongside the excellent mining prospects on the southern shore of Lake Superior there were the physical hardships with which these pioneers had to contend. Some folk were convinced that one winter was more than sufficient and left to find a more hospitable climate. Actually this was the case with Matthew's (2) youngest brother, Jacob S. Harris, who came out to the Upper Peninsula in 1865 but soon managed to get transferred southwards to a more agreeable climate. The courage and single-mindedness of pioneers such as Matthew (2) and Nanny are almost beyond belief. However, beyond the harshness of winter there was, and is, the striking beauty of this particular area with its hills, pines, rivers and streams. The scars of mining were all familiar to Matthew (2) and Nanny, but how wonderful that nature is again in control and slowly healing these scars.

But what of Nanny in this environment? At the age of twelve years she had been a dressmaker and at twenty-two had progressed to millinery and thus was well experienced in all matters and skills of the drapery profession. Beyond doubt these skills became of immense benefit to her and her eventual family, but the harsh living conditions in this strange country may have presented some problems to her. One could postulate that if Nanny, like many other Cornish girls and women, had worked on a mine as a 'bal maiden' she might have been better equipped for the pioneer life. It did not matter; Nanny proved equal to the situation. She had been accustomed to do her share of housework at home at Carwynnen and to help look after the large family of which she had been the sixth of twelve children.

Site of the Minesota Mine, photographed in 1985

Matthew (2) and Nanny set up house and their first child, Elizabeth Jane, was born in 1857 followed by Matthew (3) in 1859. By this time Nanny not only had two young children but also six lodgers to care and provide for. Five of these lodgers were miners and the sixth a fireman. From their names on the census return it is reasonable to assume that they were Cornish, possibly from Camborne parish.

There is a story which emanates from the descendants of Matthew (2) and therefore suggests that he was the progenitor of the incident. That being the case it proves that Matthew (2) was not unlike his uncle Matthew (1) in his regard and treatment of explosives. Apparently their stock of firewood, stored outside the cabin, was diminishing somewhat faster than the usage by the occupants. The question was, who was stealing the firewood? In order to find the thief a hole was bored in a particular block, some explosive inserted, the hole being finally closed with a wooden plug. Result: in due course a neighbour's fireplace was destroyed in an explosion! Fortunately there were no casualties. Great laughter, no further action taken, it was sufficient just to know the identity of the thief.

In 1869 Matthew (2) followed the example of his brother William and on 8 June filed his declaration of intent to become an American citizen. This suggests that he had given up all thought of again roaming to other parts of the world. The life he had found in the States had now met with his full approval. It was here that he would put down new roots. Strangely, however, Matthew (2) did not seek to take the oath of allegiance until twenty-eight years later in 1887. At this point it was conditional in 'proving up' his Homestead Claim in South Dakota. Was it a case where after making his original application he had second thoughts about relinquishing his allegiance to his mother country? Possibly he remembered the opposition of the family in Cornwall to William's decision and kept putting off an act by which he would forego his birthright.

Another aspect of pioneer life in this new country was the abundant wildlife. Deer, rabbits and food on the wing were available to all without let or hindrance. To benefit his family, Matthew (2) invested in two muzzle-loading shotguns, both of which have been reconditioned by his great-grandson, Jay A. Harris, who still uses them. The first gun, a field piece, double barrel, eleven-gauge Belgian Reeltwist originally cost about $35 as against the more common shotguns costing about $10. Matthew (2) then progressed to a Rubin Finn fourteen-gauge saddle gun of deluxe quality. It is estimated to have cost $100, a considerable outlay in those times for a miner. Matthew (2) in this context was undoubtedly the most sporting of the Harris brothers. On the

basis that he would never waste money, he must have considered the investment well worth while.

In 1864 a second daughter, Nannie, was born to Nanny and Matthew (2) and their second son John James followed in 1867. This completed their family. Despite their own lack of education, they ensured that their children would not be subjected to this omission and sent the youngsters to school in Rockland Township and later in Greenland Township. At his marriage in 1855 and at the time of his original application for citizenship in 1859, and also on a Minesota Mine pay deduction slip of 1860, Matthew (2) was unable to write his name. This situation was about to change, for at the time the eldest daughter started school in 1862 Matthew (2) commenced learning to read and write. In reality it was equally important for him to be able to read and write as for his children to be educated. His efforts in this direction could well have taken place during his convalescence from a serious accident in 1861, an account of which is detailed later. As a result of his studies, on 5 December 1867 his brother Mark Smith Harris back in Cornwall received a letter from him! The correspondence between the brothers never amounted to any great volume but was significant and continued until Matthew's (2) death in 1895. Additionally, his signatures are to be found on his homesteading documents of 1881 and 1888. It is of interest that Matthew (2) and Nanny obtained a family Bible in which the names, births and marriages of their family are recorded. Both their names are engraved on the cover. [The bible is in the possession of their great-grandson Jay Harris.]

Early in April 1861 there were three separate accidents at Minesota Mine, two of them fatal. The third, and in its way the most remarkable, happened to Matthew (2). He had been carrying out some repairs, probably setting timbers, in one of the upper levels at its junction with one of the shafts when he lost his hold and fell 320 feet down the shaft. When his comrades reached him they assumed he was dead. The shaft was inclined at something of the order of forty-five degrees so it would be more correct to say that he tumbled from stage to stage. His body was brought to surface and placed in the 'Dead House'. Nanny was notified; she went to the mine and demanded to see him. After some reluctance on the part of the officials they agreed. Admitted to the mortuary Nanny found him alive and in terrific pain. She detailed the persons with her to take him home and she nursed him back to health. He had been very seriously bruised and had broken both arms and a thigh-bone. The thigh was never properly set but overlapped and grew together in that manner, resulting in one leg being shorter than the other. At the time a local newspaper, the *Lake Superior*

Miner, reported: 'Strange as it may seem, he was living at latest accounts, and hopes are even entertained of his recovery.'[20] His convalescence must have extended over a considerable period. Whether or not the mining company made any contribution to the family finances during Matthew's (2) incapacity is not known, but in general the paternalism of mining companies in the Copper Country, certainly in later times, is well known. Additionally, the company may subsequently have employed Matthew (2) on less arduous work. In 1870 the mine pumps were closed down and shortly after the mine was put on tribute; by this latter arrangement of operating the mine Matthew (2) could, at this stage, have continued mining above adit level in a more relaxed mode conducive to his disability.

But what of Nanny at the time of the accident and during the period when Matthew (2) was unable to work? In addition to nursing her husband she had two infant children to care for, one just under four years and the other just under two years, together with her lodgers. The income from the latter would no doubt have been essential and very welcome at this time. It also seems likely that she would have carried out some dressmaking for folk in the community in order to supplement the family income. What strength of character this thirty-three-year-old Cornish woman exhibited during these trying times and in harsh surroundings. But she was one of many pioneers who braved circumstances and elements in expanding these new frontiers. She was a very determined, hardworking and committed lady.

The 1880 census shows the family had by that time moved from Rockland to Greenland Township. From 1871 to 1883, Samuel B. Harris was Agent for an Ontonagon Group of Mines which included Adventure, Ridge and Hilton Mines in Greenland Township, and so it may well be that Matthew found employment under his brother.

There were instances of lawlessness, feud, riot and even murder in the district during the sojourn of Matthew (2), but as earlier in Australia he kept well clear of such occurrences. He and Nanny were solid members of this new and growing community. He joined the Rockland Lodge of the Independent Order of Oddfellows at or about 1865. He was a member of the Methodist Church, as are many of his descendants.

Early in 1881, Matthew (2) and his elder son Matthew (3) succumbed to the American urge to move on and to try something different. They decided to go farming in Dakota Territory where the land boom had commenced in 1875. As early as 1871 the first Immigration Commissioner for Dakota Territory had arranged for newspapers to publish, and for literature to be distributed in likely areas of different States, to spotlight the availability and benefits of homesteading in the Territory.[21]

The possibility of moving down could well have been discussed by the Harris family in Ontonagon over many months prior to making the final decision, and so it was agreed that Matthew (3) should carry out a reconnaissance in Dakota Territory and in effect become a one-man advance party to view and assess the prospects. Additionally, it seems that an agreement was made whereby Matthew (3) would become independent of his father in the matter of homesteading. His subsequent report to his father was sufficiently convincing for Matthew (2) and the rest of the family to leave Greenland Township the following September to homestead a quarter section half a mile distant from his son.

Homesteading and Farming in Dakota Territory

Moving down to Dakota Territory, and specifically to Yankton, from Ontonagon County was, by 1881, a relatively simple journey and could be accomplished entirely by railroad. Initially Matthew (3) and later Matthew (2) and the family travelled from Ontonagon Township to L'Anse by the Copper Range Railroad, which had been opened in 1877, and then by the Ohio and Nor-West Railroad south to Chicago. From Chicago they changed to the Chicago and North Western Railroad westward to the Missouri River and then changed to the northern branch through Sioux City to Yankton. It was necessary to go first to Yankton because it was here that the District Land Office, which dealt with homesteading matters, was located. As it happened, the land at Olivet that the Harrises selected lay some thirty miles north-north-east of Yankton.

The Homestead Act of 20 May 1862, which was signed by President Lincoln, was not completely repealed until 1986. The Act permitted any person over twenty-one years of age, who was or intended to become an American citizen to file an application for 160 acres of public land, the area of 160 acres being a quarter of a section of land which was one square mile in area. This particular acreage had been decided on by the Government as being large enough to support a family, but not large enough to support a social class based on slavery.[22] Considering the briefly-mentioned procedures for obtaining land, a quarter section was half a mile long by half a mile wide. It is reminiscent of, and somewhat similar to, the 'bounding' of mining claims in Cornwall and Devon, where under the Stannaries Charter of 1201 a tinner could bound an area of his choice and was then entitled to work for tin without let or hindrance. However, the surveys by the American Government surveyors for allocation of land to the homesteaders were rather more scientific and accurate procedures than earlier times in Cornwall and Devon where the uncontrolled system led to numerous disputes between tinners on adjacent bounds.

There were two methods of obtaining land for farming at nominal cost by pre-emption or by homesteading. Pre-emption had been introduced as early as 1841 and continued until 1891. It applied not only to those who intended to farm the land but also to those who intended to abstract minerals, and was very much the method by which leases were originally acquired in the Copper Country of Upper Michigan, where in some cases individuals became front men for the mining companies. It permitted any American or person intending to become an American citizen to file for 160 acres, build some sort of dwelling, make some improvement to the land, then after six months he could purchase the land outright for $1.25 per acre amounting in total to $200.

Homesteading was a method for obtaining ownership of 160 acres at a very minimal cost but was a much longer and labour-demanding process which extended over five years. However, upon providing proof of his total compliance with the requirements of the Homestead Act, the homesteader became the outright owner for only $10 plus a slightly-less amount for fees to the Receiver at the Land Office for producing the necessary documentation and so on. Conversely, if the homesteader so wished he could, under the Pre-emption Act, purchase outright at the end of six months by paying the full $1.25 per acre.

For the homesteader adopting the first option, over and above the age and citizenship requirements, and after filing his application for the land, he became an 'Entryman' and had to fulfil further conditions under Homesteading Law. Firstly, he had to move onto the land within six months and to reside there during the five-year qualifying period for at least seven months in each year. These permitted times of absence had to be notified to and approved by the Registrar at the Land Office. Additionally, he had to build a habitable house and to cultivate at least one-eighth of the land (twenty acres) by the end of the five-year period, although strangely it was not absolutely necessary to have produced a crop! Irrespective of this latter statement, he had to break the sod to obtain his patent to the land. To use the total area as pasture did not qualify.

The land mass of Dakota Territory, which was originally attached to Minnesota, had been the homeland of the Sioux Nation and the summer range of buffalo herds.[23] It was estimated that at the time of the discovery of America by Columbus in 1498, sixty million buffalo[24] roamed over parts of the North American sub-continent. In the 1870s the buffalo had been slaughtered on a gigantic scale by the white man, resulting in almost the total extinction of the breed. According to an 1894 survey, only eighty-five buffalo survived in the wild. Wiping out the buffalo was seen by some as a means of denying the Indians their birthright, their way of living and food source, and in turn destroying the Indian Nations. Little wonder the Indians were in ferment, which resulted in terrible slaughters on both sides. It was in 1876 only five years prior to the Harris family migration to Dakota Territory that the Sioux under their Chief, Crazy Horse, had defeated and killed General George Custer and the 7th Cavalry at the battle of Little Big Horn in Montana, some 160 miles beyond the western border of Dakota. President Buchanan created Dakota Territory in 1864, which was later divided into the States of North and South Dakota. When these two States became a part of the Union in 1889 South Dakota, where the Harrises were, became the fortieth State of the great alliance, but it was still a rough and ready frontier.

Homesteading was a hard and relentless life. Those who persevered and stuck it out reaped the benefit, those who did not persevere, lost and moved on. From the time of filing his application to 'proving up' and receiving his Patent from the General Land Office in Washington, DC, the land remained the property of the Federal Government. However, once the homesteader had obtained his patent he was at liberty, if he so wished, to move away or sell the land at obviously a considerably higher price.

Matthew (3) complied with the initial requirements of the Act in that he had reached the age of twenty-two years the month prior to filing and was a first-generation American. It was also necessary for a prospective homesteader to make a personal inspection of the particular quarter section before filing his application in order to satisfy himself that it would be satisfactory to his intended use. Having called at the Land Office and ascertained what land was available, Matthew (3) decided to look at a quarter section which had been relinquished by a pre-emption claimant, and on which the latter had made no improvements whatsoever. He could if he wished avail himself of the services of a local person who knew the area and particularly the boundaries of a nominated quarter section, who, for a fee would give of his knowledge and probably convey him to the site. Matthew (3), having been born in a family who by nature and circumstance were careful, it can be assumed, went by himself in the same spirit of adventure as his father had visited mining camps from Wisconsin to the Great Lakes, California and Australia. On this visit he would also wish to ascertain the kind of people he would have as neighbours, irrespective of the fact that these neighbours would have lived at some little distance from him, not least because he was to settle among them but also that initially for a short period he might well obtain lodgings with them whilst he constructed his own accommodation; otherwise he would have to be satisfied with a makeshift structure on his own land.

The arrival of Matthew (3) in Dakota Territory no doubt fixed in his mind the vastness of the country of his birth. Now he was virtually in the centre of the huge American Prairie - The Great Prairie - and to him this great expanse of land must also have seemed limitless. It has been described as, 'A raw sprawling country, where waving prairie grass raced against an endless blue sky, and thick black soil promised abundant harvests.'[25] Douglass H. Chadwick in his article *Roots of the Sky* published in the October 1993 issue of *National Geographic* mentions in respect of the formation of the Great Plains, 'They are built from sediment washed out of the Rockies over millions of years, mixed with rubble from continental glaciers and windblown deposits of silt, sand and clay known as loess. Resting on the former bed of a shallow sea, the Great Plains slope gradually downward for eight hundred miles from the feet of the mountains to the Mississippi Valley. The Rockies helped form the prairies in another sense as well. Ever since the mountains began rising some sixty million years ago, they inter-

cepted the flow of moist air from the Pacific and dried out the interior, favouring the dominion of grass over trees.'

Matthew (3) was impressed and hastened back to Yankton and filed his application No. 5091 on 17 June to homestead 160 acres in the north-east quarter of Section Twenty-five, Township ninety-eight north, Range fifty-nine west of the Principal Meridian. It cost him $14, which included a $4 documentation fee.

Now a tremendous amount of hard work lay before him and he would have needed tools and implements. It should not be considered that he came down to Dakota penniless, far from it. It can be seen that he had accumulated some sort of 'nest egg' from his labours in the Ontonagon mines because in his 'proving up' testimony in 1887 he declared that he owned the following implements and tools and moreover stated that he owned most of them in 1881: two ploughs, one harrow, one corn cultivator, one farm wagon, one hay rake, a spade, shovels, hoes, pickaxe and other tools. Additionally, he had a horse and yoke of oxen.

But first he had to select a site for his sod house or

Initial and final Homestead receipts from Yankton Land Office to Matthew (3) for the north-east quarter, Section 25, Township 98, Range 58 west of the Principal Meridian.

'soddy' and then to build it with the abundant material which was at hand: natural sod matted in buffalo grass with long roots. Though it remained stable during the process of excavating with a plough and building into position in the walls, the stability did depend to some extent on the nature of the soil. Timber was a scarce and expensive commodity on the prairie.

The sod house was not exactly an architectural gem, but its thick walls moderated the extremes of temperature, being warm in winter and cool in summer. Its construction required a basic knowledge of setting out and of bonding the sods or turves. In this respect Matthew (3) was advised by his neighbours, who also probably helped in the actual construction. The very remoteness from the normal services of civilization made it imperative that the pioneer homesteader improvised and became a 'do-it-yourself' expert, acquiring a certain degree of knowledge of various trades.

Homestead Law required the structure to be at least ten feet by twelve feet. One assumes that for a soddy these would be the inside measurements. Having ploughed the sod strips of about twelve inches wide they were then cut with a spade into pieces two to three feet long so they could be handled with relative ease. They were then transported by wagon to the selected site. Having pegged out on the ground the actual shape and size, Matthew (3) may have included a division wall for one purpose or another, not least to help support the roof. He was now ready to place the sods. The first course was placed longitudinally with at least two runs side by side to form a two to three-feet-wide base. The walls would taper in vertical section to one foot wide at roof level. The second layer of sod strips was then laid transversely overlapping the joints of the first layer. Subsequent layers were added in much the same principle as a bricklayer would build in English Bond. Matthew (3) would have built in a couple of small windows, each with four small panes of glass, together with a door. The windows would have had a wide cill internally, due to the considerable thickness of the walls, and this provided a couple of very convenient shelves for the occupants. The windows and door, of very basic construction, having been purchased most likely in Yankton, were no doubt the product of some enterprising handyman. Once the wall reached roof elevation a wall-plate was placed on top to which rafters were secured, the rough timber being purchased at the same time as the windows and door. The roof covering consisted of slough grass or willows covered with a layer of soil to hold the covering down. Seemingly it would have required frequent maintenance, much more so than the thatch on the cottage at Six Chimneys! Internally the earth floor was packed so tight that it could be swept with a broom. Finally, with the installation of a cook stove the soddy was complete.

Because of the lack of wood the fuel consisted of buffalo chips, turf and twisted bunches of wild hay and straw.

The next job of work for Matthew (3) was to provide a supply of drinking water, and to this end he sank a well twenty-two feet deep. This task was very much in line with his previous occupation as a miner, the sinking and timbering being second nature to him. Also in his first year he built a sod stable measuring seventeen feet by seventeen feet in plan.

These tasks being complete, after two months of solid labour, Matthew (3) took up residence on his quarter section on 15 August 1881. At this point he was now ready to consider commencing work on the land in order to convert some of the prairie sod to pasture and to produce crops. First it was necessary to burn off the tangled prairie grass in order to promote and encourage a fresh and stronger growth of grass for pasture and also to make ploughing much easier. In fact, he ploughed fifteen acres during the first year. The foregoing stresses the hard work and privation endured by the pioneers.

Now we leave Matthew (3) for a time because his parents, sisters and younger brother had arrived from Ontonagon, having left Greenland Township on 11 September.

Matthew (2) filed his application No. 5242 for a quarter section in the north-west Quarter of Section Nineteen, Township ninety-eight north, Range fifty-eight west of the Principal Meridian on 27 September 1881. This particular quarter section was half a mile north-north-east of that homesteaded by Matthew (3). It was here that Matthew (2) and Nanny would remain for the rest of their lives, and here on the prairie they would be buried.

It is of interest that between 17 June 1881 when Matthew (3) filed his application and 27 September the same year when Matthew (2) filed his, no less than 151 applications were filed at Yankton Land Office, not to mention all those applications filed in other land offices within the United States.[26] Indeed, the Homestead Act was one of the extraordinary actions which changed the course of American History.

Matthew (2) wasted no time in constructing his sod house, no doubt benefiting from the experience of Matthew (3) together with the help of his younger son, John James, who at this time was about fourteen and a half years old. The family took up residence in the sod house on 15 October 1881, just two and a half weeks after filing the homestead application. Possibly the family had shared the soddy of Matthew (3) during construction of their own. Once the sod house was built, Matthew (2) valued it at $50. Other work carried out on the homestead by Matthew (2) followed much the same pattern as Matthew (3), including ploughing fifteen acres in the first year. In July the following year the family vacated the sod house, having built themselves a timber-frame house which was much more comfortable and shows that Matthew (2) was not without funds.

Records show that the elements also played their part in creating difficulties for the homesteaders. There were bad blizzards in 1881, 1886, 1887 and 1888. In 1889 occurred the first dust storm caused by a dry season. There was a severe drought in 1886, which was followed by a disastrous winter.

At the end of the fifth year of occupation it was the responsibility of the Local Land Office to ascertain if the homesteader had met all the requirements of the Homestead Act. Providing the homesteader had complied he was then entitled to receive the Land Patent from the Federal Government. However, this action was permitted to take place at any time between the fifth and seventh year of occupation. As it happened, Matthew (2) did not notify his intention to 'prove up' until 12 May 1888, some twenty-two months beyond the qualifying date. The procedure for 'proving up' was very thorough. At the same time as Matthew (2) notified his intention to the Land Office at Yankton, he had to submit the names of four witnesses, two of whom would be selected to testify before the Judge, or in his absence the Clerk of the District Court, Hutchinson County, Dakota Territory. Furthermore, the Land Office had to issue a public notice in a local newspaper detailing the intention of the homesteader and listing the names of the four witnesses. In the case of Matthew (2), the notice appeared in the *Hutchinson County Herald* and an official of the newspaper had to produce proof to the Clerk of the District Court that publication had taken place. Also the Registrar at the Land Office had to display a copy of the notice in a public part of his office for a period of thirty days. Once these formalities had been completed, two witnesses selected by the officials from the four names submitted were called to testify. Matthew's (2) witnesses were Truman S. Patten, who farmed the adjacent quarter sectioned to the west of Matthew (2), and Lauren W. Porter, who farmed the quarter section immediately to the north. The testimonies of both witnesses and that of the claimant were all taken separately at the same time and place. The witnesses were expected to be in a position to testify in their four-page statement that they had intimate knowledge of precisely what Matthew (2) had done to meet all requirements under the Act. With reference to United States citizenship, Matthew (2) had obtained this just over twelve months previously in 1887.

Matthew's (2) testimony, in which he had to answer forty-four questions, contains interesting information especially in respect of the progress made in living accommodation, farm equipment, stock and agriculture:

1. The timber-frame house built in 1882 was eighteen feet by twenty-four feet in plan with a lean-to measuring ten feet by twenty-four feet. The house was twelve feet to eaves and had a shingle roof. It was valued at $500.
2. A timber-frame stable sixteen feet by thirty-two feet also with a shingle roof, valued at $150.
3. A dugout stable twelve feet by forty-eight feet, value $50.
4. A granary worth $50.
5. Fifty-five acres of land had been fenced, the fencing being valued at $175
6. Well and pumping equipment, value $30
7. Eight acres of land ploughed and valued at $240.

The farm implements of Matthew (2) consisted of a self-binder, mower, seeder, cultivators, farming mill, ploughs, wagons and harrows.

To the question 'What domestic animals and livestock do you own and keep?' he listed twelve horses, two cows, four head of young cattle, a yoke of oxen, eight hogs, poultry and two cats.

Enumerating the articles of furniture, he listed one heating stove, one cook stove and cooking utensils, tables, chairs, dishes, cupboard and a sewing machine, the latter obviously had been essential to Nanny. Finally, four beds and bedding.

Matthew (2) also noted that he had raised crops of wheat, oats, corn, flax, potatoes and barley.

He ploughed fifteen acres in 1882, thirty-five in 1883, fifty-five in 1884, seventy in 1886, seventy-five in 1887 and eighty in the current year of 1888. Matthew (2) accomplished all the necessary work to qualify under the Act despite his disability resulting from his accident at Minesota Mine.

It was also necessary for Matthew (2) to complete an affidavit to the effect that the land to his knowledge contained no vein of quartz or other rock in place bearing gold, silver, cinnabar, lead, tin or copper or any deposit of coal. A second and final affidavit confirmed his complete compliance with the requirements of the Homestead Act.

Having paid $13.99 (the odd amount of money was relative to the area of the quarter section which happened to be thirteen twenty-fifths of an acre less than 160 acres) when he made application to homestead, then paid, 28 July 1888, a further $4 for the filing fee. So with much hard work and for a total of $17.99 he became the undisputed owner of a Quarter Section, which with the improvements he had effected was then worth, according to the witnesses, $2,000.

It only remained for the Land Office Officials to send the claim to General Land Office Headquarters in Washington, DC, who being satisfied issued the Patent under the signature of the President of the United States.

United States of America.

District Court, Hutchinson County, Second Judicial District of Dakota Territory, ss.

BE IT REMEMBERED That on the ____ 1st ____ day of ____ June ____ ____ In the year of our Lord one thousand eight hundred and ____ eighty-seven ____ personally appeared before the Honorable ____ Bartlett Tripp ____ Presiding Judge of the District Court of Hutchinson County for the District aforesaid ____ Matthew Harris ____ an alien born, above the age of twenty-one years, and applied in open Court to be admitted to become a naturalized citizen of the United States of America, pursuant to the sever l acts of Congress, heretofore passed on that subject. And the said ____ Matthew Harris ____ having there upon produced to the Court record testimony, showing that he had heretofore reported himself and filed his declaration of his Intention to become a citizen of the United States, according to the provisions of said several acts of Congress, and the Court being satisfied, as well from the oath of the said ____ Matthew Harris ____ as from the testimony of ____ Samuel Gange ____ and ____ Johns Nagner ____ who are known to be citizens of the United States, that the said ____ Matthew Harris ____ has resided within the limits and under the jurisdiction of the United States for at least five years last past, and at least one year last past, within the Territory of Dakota, and that during the whole of that time he has behaved himself as a man of good moral character, attached to the principles contained in the Constitution of the United States, and well disposed to the good order, well being and happiness of the same ; and two years and upward having elapsed since the said ____ Matthew Harris ____ reported himself, and filed his declaration of Intention as aforesaid, ____

IT WAS ORDERED, That the said ____ Matthew Harris ____ be permitted to take the oath to support the Constitution of the United States, and the usual oath whereby he renounced all allegiance and fidelity to every Foreign Prince, Potentate, State or Sovereignty whatever ; and more particularly to ____ Victoria Queen ____ whereof he was heretofore a subject, which said oath having been administered to the said ____ J. G. ot Brian Axel Deland ____ by the Clerk of said Court, it was ordered by the Court that the said ____ Matthew Harris ____ ____ Matthew Harris ____ be admitted to all and singular the rights, privileges and Immunities of a naturalized citizen of the United States, and that the same be certified by the Clerk of this Court, under

In Testimony that the foregoing is a true copy of the proceedings taken from the record of the Court aforesaid I subscribe my name hereunto and affix the Seal of the Court this ____ 1st ____ day of ____ June ____ In the year of our Lord one thousand eight hundred and ____ eighty ____
____ Several ____

Bartlett Tripp ____ Judge.

James C Bayliss ____ Clerk.

**"the Seal of said Court, which is done accordingly.

The Final Naturalization Record of Matthew (2) Harris
Per courtesy Ms Marveve Riis, Archivist, South Dakota Historical Society

UNITED STATES OF AMERICA

Filed for Record this 13th day of February
A.D. 189[6] at 8 o'clock P.M.
J. Powell Register of Deeds.
Deputy.

Matthew Harris
—TO—

THE UNITED STATES OF AMERICA.

To all to Whom these Presents shall Come, Greeting:

APPLICATION 5212

HOMESTEAD CERTIFICATE NO. 5308

Whereas, There has been deposited in the General Land Office of the United States a Certificate of the Register of the Land Office at Yankton Dakota Territory whereby it appears that, pursuant to the Act of Congress, approved 20th May, 1862, "To secure Homesteads to Actual Settlers on the Public Domain," and the acts supplemental thereto, the claim of Matthew Harris has been established and duly consummated, in conformity to law, for the Lot numbered one and two and the East half of the North West quarter of Section Nineteen in Township Ninety Nine North of Range fifty eight West of the Fifth Principal Meridian in Dakota Territory in Township

containing two hundred and fifty nine acres and forty eight hundredths of an acre according to the Official Plat of the Survey of the said land returned to the General Land Office by the Surveyor General.

NOW, KNOW YE, That there is, therefore, granted by the United States, unto the said Matthew Harris the tract of land above described, to have and to hold the said tract of land, with the appurtenances thereof unto the said Matthew Harris and to his heirs and assigns forever; subject to any vested and accrued water rights for mining, agricultural, manufacturing or other purposes, and rights to ditches and reservoirs used in connection with such water rights as may be recognized and acknowledged by the local customs, laws and decisions of courts, and also subject to the right of the proprietor of a vein or lode to extract and remove his ore therefrom, should the same be found to penetrate or intersect the premises hereby granted as provided by law.

IN TESTIMONY WHEREOF, I Benjamin Harrison President of the United States of America, have caused these letters to be made patent, and the seal of the General Land Office to be hereunto affixed.

Given under my hand at the City of Washington the Eleventh day of October , in the year of our Lord, one thousand eight hundred and Eighty-Nine fourteenth and of the Independence of the United States the one hundred and

By the President: Benjamin Harrison
By Geo. Macfarland Asst Secretary.
K. M. Bronson Recorder of the General Land Office.

Recorded, Vol. 11 Page 377

PATENT RECORD

Matthew (2)

This particular document was obviously requested by the Executor following Matthew's death in 1895

Matthew (2) now had full possession of the land. He was now at liberty to move out, sell the land or continue to farm it, which he did until his death when it was farmed by his younger son and, eventually, his grandson.

The land was irrevocably his.[27]

The Family of Matthew (2) Harris and Nanny Toy Sims

Elizabeth Jane Harris

The eldest child of Matthew (2) and Nanny, Elizabeth Jane, was born in Rockland Township, Ontonagon County, Michigan on 27 July 1857. Within the family she was known as Libby,

Libby was attending school at the time of the 1870 Rockland Township census, and we know that she received both Grade and High School Education. Upon leaving school she helped her mother keep house and also assisted her in making clothes for the young family.

In 1881 she moved down to Olivet, South Dakota with the rest of the family and on the 1885 census for Hutchinson County was described as Housekeeper, which meant that by that time she had taken over full responsibility for the household because of her mother's state of health. In fact, Nanny passed away a year later.

In early 1889, Libby married John H. Piper, a son of John G. Piper and Lucinda (Gilbert) Piper who had homesteaded the north-east quarter of Section Twenty-eight which lay about two miles east-south-east of her father's farm. John G. Piper's initial application to homestead, No. 1377, was dated 30 October 1878 and he had taken up residence on his quarter section with his wife and five children on 15 November the same year. There is a very interesting story about John G. which came to light when he announced his intention to 'prove up' towards the end of 1883. Apparently when he made his initial application he declared himself, in good faith, to be an American citizen. He was then forty-eight years of age and had come to America from England with his parents when he was fourteen. However, when required to produce his naturalization papers he truthfully explained to the authorities that the papers had been destroyed in the Great Fire of Chicago in 1871.

In reality it must have been his father's papers on the basis that children of settlers received derivative citizenship through the parent, even if they were not themselves born in the United States. The loss of the relevant papers suggests that, along with all the others, their house in Chicago had been completely destroyed. In the event, after making a written deposition of the foregoing events, John G. was granted United States citizenship on 21 December 1883. He had been a carriage maker and blacksmith in Chicago and his son John H. followed him in the craft.

There were three sons born to Libby and John H. Piper. John G. (2), Roland G. and Harold M. Piper. At some point the family moved to Wessington Springs, Jerauld County, South Dakota, and it was here that Libby died in 1921 and her husband in 1942. A year or two prior to her death, Libby commenced corresponding with her uncle Mark Smith Harris in Cornwall.

Elizabeth Jane Harris 1857–1921,
as a young woman

The Family of Elizabeth Jane Harris and John H. Piper

Elizabeth Jane Harris   1889   John H. Piper
1857 - 1921   —————   1867 - 1942

John G. (2)
b. 1890
d. 1965
m. Bertha M.
   Waldschmidt

Living Fort Wayne,
Allen County,
Indiana in 1930

Roland G.
b. 1 January 1894
d. 4 April 1973

RG was a Toolmaker for
Dello Remy Division of
General Motors in
Anderson, Indiana. He
worked in the
Experimental Department
with the job title of
Special Machine Builder.

m. 1 January 1920
   Mary J. Stohler in
   Anderson, Indiana.
   Mary J. was born
   25 Nov 1894.

The Stohler family were
what is known as
Pennsylvania/Dutch and
originally came from
Germany. Mary J.'s
mother was Flora Bray
of English extraction.

Roland G. and Mary J.
had two children.

Harold M. (1)
b. 10 April 1895
d. 24 February 1980

A veteran of First World War,
he served in 36 Coy 12th
Regiment of Infantry.

m. 27 June 1921 Evelyn Downs
   at Mount Vernon.

Evelyn was the daughter of
George Downs and Olive
Onderdonk. She was born
4 March 1901 and died
31 January 1991.

Harold M. and Evelyn had
four children. Harold M. (1)
owned and operated a
Luandry/Drycleaners in
Madison, SD, from 1925
to 1962.

He was Mayor of Madison
from 1962 to 1967. He had
received High School and
College education. Was
a musician devoted to
the trumpet.

The Family of Harold M. (1) Piper and Evelyn Downs

Harold M. (1) Piper
1895 - 1980

1921

Evelyn Downs
1901 - 1991

Joan
b. 8 April 1922,
    Wessington, SD
College Graduate
m. 30 May 1947
    Frank Williams.
    Frank born 1927
Resides Nebraska

Patricia
b. 9 February 1927
    High School and College education.
m. 27 December 1946 John W. Erickson.
    John W. born 17 May 1924

Resident in Huntington Beach,
California 1980

Harold M. (2)
b. 24 August 1923,
    Sleepy Eye, MN
d. 4 December 1967

High School and College
educated. Served in US Army
Second World War in 86th
Infantry Div.
Actor and Singer, Bass/Baritone.
Stage Name: Hal Hackett
Repertoire:

Shirley
b. 17 July 1930,
    Madison, SD

Television:
Schlitz Playhouse			Racket Squad
Private Secretary	...	... with Ann Sothern	Odessey
I Am the Law	...	... with George Raft	Jackie Gleason
Modern Romances		... with Martha Scott	Look Up and Live
Robert Montgomery Show			Edge of Night
Suspense			Accent
Medic			

Screen:
Train to Auburn	...	... (Lead with George Raft)	
Summer Holiday	...	... (Second lead) (MGM)	Musical Version Ah! Wilderness
Love Laughs at Andy Hardy		(MGM) (Second Lead)	
Campus Honeymoon		... (Lead) Republic	
The Show-off	...	... (MGM)	

Stock:
Picnic	...	... (Lead)	Carousel	...	... ...	(West Coast Company)
The Rainmaker	...	... (Lead)	Gentlemen Prefer Blondes	...		(Lead Opposite Marie Wilson)
Tender Trap	...	... (Lead)	Bells Are Ringing	...	...	(Lead)
Seven-year Itch	...	... (Lead)	Brigadoon	...	... ...	(Jeff)
Wonderful Town	...	... (Lead)	Born Yesterday	...	...	(Lead)
Solid Gold Cadillac	...	... (Blessington)				

Stage: (On Broadway)
Kismet	...	... (Principal - also on Columbia Record)	Book of Job	
Bonanza Bound	...	... (Juvenile Lead)	To Broadway With Love (World's Fair)	
Lend An Ear	...	... (Principal)		
The Lady's Not For Burning		(Role: Humphrey)		

Radio:
    Actor-Singer on all major networks

Matthew (3) Harris

Matthew (3), the second child and first son of Matthew (2) and Nanny, was born 30 May 1859 in Rockland Township. At the time of the 1870 census he was still at school.

By the 1880 census he was listed as a miner which would be a correct general description as there is a possibility that he was also a skilled timberman. This latter is partly substantiated by his later proven expertise in the construction of two frame-houses and other timber structures on his farm at Olivet, SD.

We previously left the narrative about Matthew (3) when he had completed his first year as a homesteader, having constructed a timber-frame house in July 1882 in order to improve his living accommodation. However, in the fall of 1884 he constructed yet another timber-frame house, possibly because he was in love with his neighbour's daughter and was contemplating asking her to marry him. This particular frame-house was fourteen feet by twenty feet and twelve feet to eaves, set on stone foundations. It had a shingle roof and pine floors complete with a cellar. At the date of 'proving up' in 1887 it was valued at $350.

Despite the better accommodation than that of his soddy, Matthew (3) was struck down with typhoid fever during the summer of 1885. Although under medical attention, he was moved across to his parents' home where Nanny and his sisters nursed him back to health, just as Nanny had done for his father following his accident at Minesota Mine. Matthew (3) was in his parents' home for a month, was the only prolonged occasion he was absent from his land during the whole six-year period of his time as an entryman.

His sickness behind him, Matthew (3) was married on Christmas Day 1885 to Alice A. Porter. Alice was the daughter of Lauren W. Porter a neighbour who became a witness for Matthew (2) when he 'proved up' in 1888. Two sons, Ralph and Mark, were born to Matthew (3) and Alice in September 1887 and September 1889 respectively. Unfortunately it has not been possible to trace the individual progression of these two sons.

The formalities and conditions for 'proving up' were as previously detailed in the narrative of Matthew (2) but information contained in the documents of Matthew (3) is also interesting. He submitted his declaration of intent to 'prove up' in the spring of 1887. Subsequently two neighbours, John F. Patten and Henry Riedemann, were called as witnesses. From the answers of both witnesses it is clear that neighbouring homesteaders helped each other during harvest, visited each other in their homes and attended church together.

The list of improvements carried out on his quarter section by Matthew (3) included the frame-house, a frame barn sixteen feet by sixteen feet, a frame granary

John G. (1) Piper
Born England 1836
Died South Dakota 1933

Lucinda A Gilbert
Born Pennsylvania 1837
Died South Dakota 1916

Parents of John H. and Cora Mae Piper

seven feet by twelve feet and a sod stable seventeen feet by seventeen feet. Also a twenty-two feet deep well complete with pump, a cattle corral, a hog pen, three acres of forest trees planted in 1886 and 1887 (was he missing the pines of Ontonagon?) and one acre of fruit trees. He had dug and hauled fifty loads of stone and had broken seventy-four acres of prairie, the agreed value of the foregoing being $1,070.

Additionally, he had raised the following crops:

1882   Nineteen acres cropped to flax, oats and potatoes.
1883   Twenty-six acres cropped to wheat, corn, flax and potatoes.
1884   Forty-six acres cropped to flax, corn and potatoes.
1885   Sixty acres cropped, producing eighty bushels of wheat, one hundred and fifty bushels of flax, seventy-five bushels of corn and eighty bushels of potatoes.
1886   Sixty-four acres cropped, producing one hundred and twelve bushels of wheat, three hundred and sixty-five bushels of oats, one hundred and four bushels of flax and twenty bushels of potatoes.
1887   All cropped to small grain, corn and potatoes.

The value of the crops raised amounted to $1,200.

In addition to the horse and yoke of oxen previously mentioned, Matthew (3) now owned three more horses, five head of cattle, two hogs, seventy chickens, six ducks, three cats and a canary!

In answer to the question as to what furniture he owned he declared: two bedsteads and bedding, one table, seven chairs, a bookcase, a bureau, trunks, a sewing machine, two clocks, a looking glass, cooking utensils, carpet and pictures. He also stated that he had had some of these items when he first moved in and had purchased the remainder since his marriage.

Like his father, Matthew (3) was required to sign an affidavit in respect of there being no minerals on the land. Having now fully complied with all conditions and requirements of the Homestead Act, he was granted outright ownership on his quarter section on 16 June 1887. This was precisely six years after filing his original claim. His filing fee was $4 making a total payment of $18.

It seems that at this point in time Matthew (3) was extremely happy with his progress and the opportunities which farming provided, because on 24 September 1888 he purchased the south-west quarter of Section Eighteen, Range fifty-eight west from his father-in-law, Lauren W. Porter, for the sum of $1,100. He was now the owner of 320 acres, albeit in two quarters one mile apart. Having made this acquisition it is difficult to understand why he sold it again in 1890. Maybe it was because of financial losses incurred by the severe drought experienced in the late 1880s, which culminated in the great dust storm of 1889. But sell he did on 10 February for the same amount as he gave for it and to his father-in-law! It should be mentioned that both parties to the transactions had the full agreement of their wives. It can only be assumed that something, perhaps traumatic, even greater than the drought and dust storm, happened to one or the other of the families for shortly after Matthew (3) and his family moved to Michigan, where in *Polk's Directory* we find Matthew (3) employed as a timberman at Tamarack Mine, Houghton County and in the

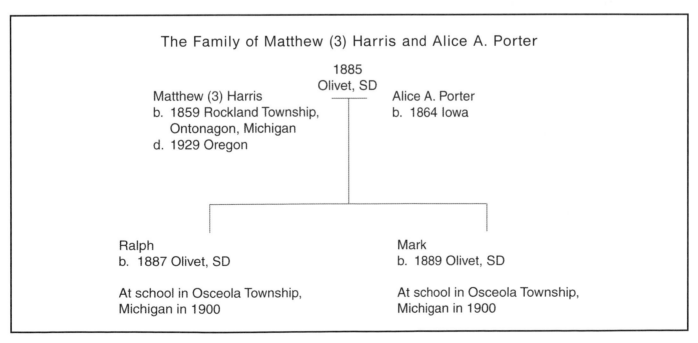

The Family of Matthew (3) Harris and Alice A. Porter

1885
Olivet, SD

Matthew (3) Harris
b. 1859 Rockland Township, Ontonagon, Michigan
d. 1929 Oregon

Alice A. Porter
b. 1864 Iowa

Ralph
b. 1887 Olivet, SD

At school in Osceola Township, Michigan in 1900

Mark
b. 1889 Olivet, SD

At school in Osceola Township, Michigan in 1900

1900 census for Osceola Township he was described as a carpenter, which is in line with his proven ability in erecting his frame-houses. Tamarack Mine had opened in 1885 and in 1890 a Cornishman, Captain William Parnell, became assistant superintendent and later superintendent.[28] With his undoubted skill as a miner and timberman and with a Cornish Captain, Matthew (3) would have had little difficulty in obtaining employment.

Matthew (3) retained ownership of his original quarter section, probably letting it to some other person until 1911. At this point he sold the east half of eighty acres to his younger brother, John James Harris, for $3,360, together with the western half to John Bartikoski $3,840. Following the death of his father in 1895, he sold his forty-acre share of Matthew's (2) quarter section for the

very reasonable sum of $300, also to his brother John James. It seems that Matthew decided in the final analysis that there was less financial risk for him in mining rather than farming.

Tamarack Mine closed in 1917 and from that year the movements of Matthew (3) have not been ascertained, although it is understood that he moved to Oregon where he died in 1929.

Nannie Harris

Nannie, the second daughter and third child of Matthew (2) Harris and Nanny Toy Sims, was born in Rockland Township, Ontonagon, MI, on 4 June 1864.

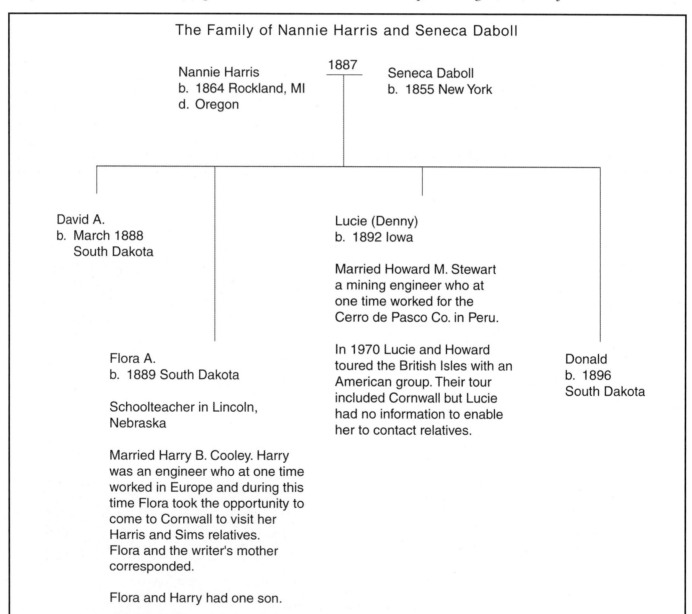

The Family of Nannie Harris and Seneca Daboll

Nannie Harris
b. 1864 Rockland, MI
d. Oregon

1887

Seneca Daboll
b. 1855 New York

David A.
b. March 1888
South Dakota

Flora A.
b. 1889 South Dakota

Schoolteacher in Lincoln, Nebraska

Married Harry B. Cooley. Harry was an engineer who at one time worked in Europe and during this time Flora took the opportunity to come to Cornwall to visit her Harris and Sims relatives. Flora and the writer's mother corresponded.

Flora and Harry had one son.

Lucie (Denny)
b. 1892 Iowa

Married Howard M. Stewart a mining engineer who at one time worked for the Cerro de Pasco Co. in Peru.

In 1970 Lucie and Howard toured the British Isles with an American group. Their tour included Cornwall but Lucie had no information to enable her to contact relatives.

Donald
b. 1896
South Dakota

By the time she was six years old, Nannie was attending school in Rockland and proceeded from Grade to High School, and was still at the latter on her sixteenth birthday. She moved down to South Dakota with the family in 1881 and according to the 1885 census for Hutchinson County was housekeeping for the family.

Around 1887 Nannie married Seneca Daboll who was a railroad mail clerk. A Flora Daboll farmed the north-east quarter of Section Thirty-three, which lay about two miles south-east of the Harris farm. The south-west quarter of the same Section together with the east half of the south-east quarter of the adjacent Section Thirty-two was farmed by a Solon Daboll. No doubt these folk were relatives of Seneca, especially so because in the case of the first mentioned, Nannie and Seneca named one of their daughters Flora.

In 1895 Nannie and Seneca were living at Running Water, Bon Homme County, SD, and at this time Nannie wrote to the author's grandfather to acquaint him with the news of her father's death.

In 1897 Nannie sold her forty-acre share of her late father's farm to her younger brother John James for $300. In 1898 Nannie and her immediate family moved to Chadron, Nebraska. While one is not certain of the reason for the move, maybe Seneca had to move in connection with his occupation.

John James Harris

John James, the youngest of the family of Matthew (2) and Nanny, was born at Rockland Township, Ontonagon, 8 April 1867. 'JJ' as he is called within the family, attended school in Rockland but it seems doubtful that he continued at school after the family arrived in South Dakota in September 1881.

JJ was then fourteen and a half years old and this was the beginning of a whole new life for him where he would be subject to all aspects of pioneer life on the prairie. It is evident that he enjoyed it to the full, spending his whole working life in this rural expanse. In due course he displayed a distinctive entrepreneurial flair and ingenuity by extending his father's original homestead of 160 acres to a 480-acre farm. He enjoyed the pleasures and overcame the problems of breaking in the prairie and producing crops. Imagine this young lad helping to build the sod house, working the horses, witnessing the transformation of the land, seeing the crops grow and being keen to help his crippled father in all these activities, and all within the bosom of his family but with a feeling of absolute freedom. Perhaps JJ did not realise it at this young age but his contentment must have amounted to a constant feast. It is also easy to picture young JJ helping to construct the frame-house that replaced their soddy in the summer of 1882.

John James Harris (1867 - 1952) and his wife Cora Mae Piper Harris (1870 - 1946)
Photographs taken 1940

By his late teens JJ was undoubtedly the farmer, and with the death of his mother in 1886 and with his sisters either married or about to be married, he turned his attention to finding a partner. He chose Cora Mae Piper, a younger sister of John H. Piper and daughter of John G. (1) Piper and Lucinda Gilbert. Cora Mae had been born in Chicago 24 July 1870 and at the age of eight years had travelled with her parents by covered wagon to homestead in South Dakota. The family had taken up residence in 1878, three years prior to the arrival of the Harrises. JJ and Cora Mae were married on 24 July 1889 and Cora Mae came to the Harris household where in addition to looking after JJ she cared for Matthew (2) for the remainder of his life. JJ and Cora Mae had five children, three boys and two girls.

On 20 September 1893, JJ doubled the size of the farm by purchasing the south-east quarter of Section Twenty-four from the Mansfield family for $1,250. Possibly the working of these two quarter sections was a little inconvenient in that they were not in line but connected diagonally, the south-west corner of the original holding being adjacent to the north-east corner of the new holding. However, the latter was immediately adjacent on its south side to the quarter section homesteaded by Matthew (3) in Section Twenty-five.

When Matthew (2) died in 1895 the quarter section he had homesteaded was divided equally between his four children, although farmed by JJ. At this time, 28 December 1895, Matthew (3) sold his forty-acre share to JJ for $300. Likewise Nannie (Harris) Daboll sold her share to JJ in February 1897 for $200. JJ was now farming 320 acres, of which he owned 280. He continued to

increase his holding by buying in 1911 the east half, eighty acres, in the north-east quarter of Section Twenty-five from Matthew (3) for $3,360. On 24 August 1917, JJ purchased the remaining eighty acres of this quarter section from Nathaniel Grosz for $5,200. It is assumed that JJ continued to rent the forty acres which Matthew (2) left to his eldest daughter Elizabeth Jane, who had passed away in 1921. However, her husband John H. Piper made over her share to JJ in 1936 for the sum of only $1! Thus JJ was now the owner 480 acres, all of which he had been farming since 1917 and continued to do so until 1929 when he retired, a status never enjoyed by his forebears. Around 1923, JJ purchased a further 240 acres from the Piper family, making his total holding 720 acres, although he never himself farmed this particular acquisition.

For their retirement, JJ bought a house in Humboldt, SD, to be near their eldest son, Jennings Howard, and it was here that Cora Mae passed away 19 December 1946.

At the time of JJ's retirement, John Matthew Harris, his second son, gave up his career as a civil engineer and came back to Olivet and took over the farm. For John Matthew it must have a circumstance as outlined in an article by Eunice Jewell on the Jewell family in Wisconsin,[29] which stated, 'You can take the boy out of the farm, but you can't take the farm out of the boy.' John Matthew confirmed this statement in more basic terms during a conversation with his son-in-law Richard Buechler and the author in June 1985 when he said, 'I left the farm as a young man because I could not bear the smell of horse manure, but after a time realised that I could not live without the smell of it.'

Around 1949, JJ decided to move from Humboldt

The house on Section 19 of the farm at Olivet, circa 1913 Standing in the doorway: Florence Nanny Harris; sitting on the South Porch: (left to right), Lula Maud and J. Arthur Harris

The barn which stabled fifteen horses together with storage for thirty to forty tons of hay, twelve hundred bushels of oats plus a number of cattle. The original barn was ten feet longer but burnt down between 1916 and 1920

The Family of John James Harris and Cora Mae Piper

John James Harris
b. 1867 Rockland
Township, MI
d. 1952 Clarinda, Iowa

1889

Cora Mae Piper
b. 1870 Chicago,
Illinois
d. 1946 Humboldt, SD

Jennings Howard
b. 1890 Olivet, SD
d. 1973 Humboldt, SD
m. 1916 Marguerite
Surface

Marguerite born 1892,
died 1984 Little Rock
Arkansas. J. Howard
was a Superintendent of
Schools. The couple
had one son, Mark Dwayne

John Matthew
b. 1897 Olivet, SD
d. 1986 Scotland, SD

JM was a 1922 graduate in Civil
Engineering of Ames University,
Iowa, where he was a member of
the Tau Kappa Epsilon Fraternity.
An active Mason he was a member
for over sixty years and became a
thirty-three degree Mason in 1949,
the highest honour that can be
obtained. He was a member of the
UM Church in Scotland. JM, a
Chartered CE who was employed by
consulting engineers, was a
specialist in the Plenum Process
(compressed air working in tunnel
excavation). He worked in Illinois
and Indiana. JM married Jessie Jones
of Chicago in 1926. Jessie was born
1896, Easton, PA died 1990 Scotland.
She was the daughter of David Jones
and Kate Harrington. She graduated
from Chicago Business School, was
a life member of the Eastern Star for
sixty-five years, a past Matron of
Augusta Chapter in Scotland and
Member of Keystone Chapter, Yankton
and the UM Church. They farmed at
Olivet from 1929 until 1963.
They had two children, John James (2)
b. 1928 and Kathryn Mae, Mrs Richard
Buechler, b. 1932.

J. Arthur
b. 1905 Olivet, SD
[d. 2000]

Graduate of University
of SD at Vermillion. BA
in Biology and Chemistry
1926. MA Bacteriology
1928. Superintendent of
Schools in various
locations.
m. 1934 Ester Kathryn
Koch.

Ester b. 1903 was the
daughter of Henry E.
Koch 1867 - 1941 and
his wife Susan 1869
- 1950. Ester died 1998.
J. Arthur and Ester had
two sons, Jay A. born
1941 and Daun Harlyn
born 1945.

Lula Maud
b. 1892 Olivet, SD
d. 1948 Sioux Falls, SD
m. 1916 Ray E. Bohner

REB, Minnehaha County
employee, born 1888 Cherry
County, Nebraska. He was
also a professional baseball
player. No children of this
marriage. He died 1977
Penny Farms, Florida.

Florence Nanny
b. 1901 Olivet, SD
d. 1953 Montrose, SD
m. 1933 Theodore (Ted) Cross

Ted a J. S.. Penny Employee. He
was born 1908, died 1974 Tucson,
Arizona. They had one daughter,
Sally Jane born 1937.

and took up residence with his daughter Florence Nanny (Harris) Cross in Clarinda, Iowa, where he passed away 7 May 1952, closing a life of pioneer farming, hard work, piety and happy family life.

Following the death of JJ, each of his three sons inherited a quarter section effective from 24 February 1953. The division was as follows: John Matthew the home quarter, Jennings Howard the pasture quarter and J. Arthur the hay quarter. Additionally, Florence Nanny received bonds to the value of $16,000. JJ's eldest daughter Lula Maud had passed away in 1948. In the event, John Matthew purchased the pasture quarter from Jennings Howard and continued to work the farm until 1963 when he and his wife Jessie moved into Scotland, SD. On 11 December 1962 they had drawn up a rental agreement to let the farm to Ruben O. and Irene E. Grosz.

Demise of Nanny and Matthew (2)

It is painful to reflect that after all her efforts and struggles with and for her family Nanny was not destined to live to see the land transferred by the Federal Government to Matthew (2). She passed away on 23 October 1886, just three months before her fifty-eighth birthday and twenty-two months before the 'prove up' date. She was laid to rest in Pleasant Hill cemetery, which lay about five miles south-east of the farm.

We can assume that despite his loss Matthew (2) could look back with a degree of pride about his travels, accomplishments and progress since leaving his native Cornwall. To now own and 160 acres of very productive land far excelled what would have been remotely possible for him in Cornwall; but one wonders if he saw this acquisition of land as the manifest destiny of the immigrants over the native Indians, where the white Americans had taken and created an empire from the Indians. What were his thoughts and those of his family when, on 27 December 1890, United States troops carried out the brutal massacre of the Indians at Wounded Knee Creek? The site of the Massacre was only 230 miles west-south-west of their farm.

Matthew (2) lived on for another nine years after Nanny's death but passed away 17 June 1895 aged sixty-seven years and was laid to rest with Nanny. Subsequently JJ decided that all the family should be buried in the same spot and so around 1923 JJ, J. Arthur and other members of the family exhumed the remains of Matthew (2) and Nanny and re-interred them in Rose Hill cemetery, Scotland, South Dakota. Up to the present, additional members of the family, together with members of associated families interred there, include JJ's wife's parents, John G. and Lucinda Piper, his sister Lula M. Bohner, his son John Matthew and his wife Jessie, relatives of his son-in-law Richard Buechler, himself and Cora Mae. Also other members of the family have their plots reserved. 'In Life United in Death Not Divided.'[30]

The family on the farm at Olivet circa 1917
Standing (L – R): Ray Bohner; Lula Bohner; Cora Mae Harris; J. Arthur Harris;
John James Harris; John M. Harris; Marguerite Surface Harris;
Squatting: Jennings Howard Harris; Florence Nanny Harris

Ester Kathryn (Koch) 1903 – 1998 and
J. Arthur Harris 1905 – [2000]
Photograph taken on their Golden Wedding in 1984

Jessie (Jones) Harris 1896 – 1990 and
John Matthew Harris 1897 – 1988
Photograph taken in 1971

The Family of Matthew (2) Harris and Nanny Toy Sims

Treslothan
1887

Matthew (2) Harris
b. 1828 Six Chimneys
d. 1895 Olivet, SD

Nanny Toy Sims
b. 1828 Carwynnen
d. 1886 Olivet, SD

Elizabeth Jane
b. 1857 Rockland Township,
   Upper Michigan
d. 1921 Wessington Springs,
   SD
m. 1889 John H. Piper

John born 1867 Chicago
died 1942 Wessington Springs

Nannie
b. 1864 Rockland Township,
   Upper Michigan
d. Oregon
m. 1887 Seneca Daboll

Seneca born 1855 New York

Matthew (3)
b. 1859 Rockland Township,
   Upper Michigan
d. Oregon
m. 1885 Alice A. Porter

Alice born 1864 Iowa

John James
b. 1867 Rockland Township,
   Upper Michigan
d. 1952 Clarinda, Iowa
m. 1889 Cora Mae Piper

Cora Mae born 1870 Illinois
died 1946 Humboldt, SD

7. James Harris

James, the sixth child and fourth son of John (2) and Christian, was born at Six Chimneys on 28 September 1831 and baptized at Camborne Parish Church on 29 October the same year.

Following the interval when Ann (2) and Matthew (2) were unable for one reason or another to attend school, it seems that John (2) and Christian made arrangements for James to attend the National School at Camborne. Initially he was probably escorted, at least part of the way, by Ann (2), but in his final two years James would have escorted his younger brother Samuel. James obviously developed an interest in reading poetry because in John's (3) autobiography is the following statement: 'My younger brother James possessed an eighteen penny copy of Burns' poems, to which I had access.'

As a boy in his early teens, James was taken down into Dolcoath Mine with his father and older brothers to learn the rudiments of copper mining. Initially James did not enjoy working underground and would have welcomed the opportunity to enjoy a more healthy form of work, but this was not to be. John (3), in humorous tone, wrote the following lines for the amusement of the younger members of the family under the title *A Domestic Scene*. It was centred on the occasion when James contrived to make himself too late to join the shift underground, and in fact succeeded!

Jem rose this morn at seven o'clock,
Put on his waistcoat and his frock;
With appetite both quick and keen,
He ate his breakfast by the screen;
And mother thought, and so did I,
That he to work would shortly hie;
But no, he had a button lost,
And Jem sat down to count the cost.
'Twas late when he began to whine,
And Dad and Will had reach'd the mine;
So he concluded in his ire,
To spend the morning by the fire.
When I came in surprised to see
Poor Jemmy lift his eyes to me,
'Why don't you go to work, d'ye hear?'
'Twas late,' said Jem, 'and I sat here.'
And soon we both went out to plough.
Poor boy! methinks I see him now
With tearful eyes and trembling limb;
For work will not agree with him.
Bleak Boreas roar'd with might and main,
And shook poor Jem through every vein;
His cap was pull'd down in his eyes,

And his thick frock was such a prize.
With staggering step, and reft of glee,
He drove the red horse o'er the lea.
He watch'd the birds that flutter'd near,
Touch'd up his cap, distinct to peer,
And counted clods and bits of clay,
And drove by fits and starts away;
So that 'twas hard the plough to guide,
And let it in the furrow slide.
When evening came we finish'd all,
And led the red horse to his stall;
And Jem, within the faggot's gleam,
Ate up his brown bread, milk, and cream.

The family had left Six Chimneys for a cottage at Troon by early 1850 and in May of that year Matthew (2), the next older brother of James, had left for America. In this situation James was now the main wage earner of the family. It was beyond doubt a very difficult time for the family, and so like William and Matthew (2) before him, James was considering the possibility of emigration. Two other Troon miners, William Carter and William Evans, who probably worked with James in Dolcoath, were thinking along the same lines. What finally decided them to go to the gold diggings in Victoria, Australia is not known. Possibly some word had got back to them from Matthew (2) who had been in Victoria since June 1853. It is known that some Cornishmen had returned from Victoria with quantities of gold and perhaps this positive proof of the opportunities in that far-off land became the deciding factor. Philip J. Payton in *The Cornish Miner in Australia* records a letter from the Victorian Goldfields that said, 'Tell Mr Stephens of Troon, that the best thing for his sons is to send them to Australia.'

And so the die was cast. James, William Carter and William Evans left Troon, going by train from Camborne to Hayle and then by boat to Bristol and train to Liverpool. On arrival in Liverpool they obtained passage on the sailing ship *Saldanha*. The *Saldanha* had been launched in Quebec in 1853 and this was her maiden voyage to the Antipodes. She had a displacement of 1,568 tons, was almost 193 long with thirty-three and a half feet beam, and just over twenty-nine feet depth of hold. Seemingly she had been built speculatively by J. Nesbitt and sold immediately to Gibbs, Bright and Co., who in turn sold her to James Baines and Thomas Mackay on 16 March 1854. It was certainly a quick turnabout because she set sail for Melbourne just three days later on 19 March.[1]

Steerage passengers on board numbered 593 made up of 537 adults, 50 children under fourteen years of age and 6 infants under one year. In calculating the statute number of adult passengers, fifty children counted as twenty-five adults and the infants were disregarded! Following from this calculation the ship was only provisioned for 562 adults plus 15 further cabin passengers. The steerage accommodation would have been basic and while one would assume travel on a new ship would have had considerable benefits in respect of hygiene, the fact remains that the condition of food after several weeks including passing through the tropics and around the Cape of Good Hope[2] left much to be desired. Much of the meat and poultry was carried live between decks, a practice which could hardly enhance the hygiene and cleanliness of the ship.

In a way it comes as no surprise that James and many others fell victim to dysentery and upon arrival in Melbourne on 16 June 1854, after a voyage of thirteen weeks, James was immediately admitted to hospital. The fact that James had been taken ill was unknown to the family at Troon and neither had they any idea of the length of the voyage. So, on the assumption that all was well, John (3) composed a ten-verse poem to James which he called *An Epistle to My Brother*.

My long remember'd brother! ah, whither dost
 thou roam?
Why is it thou hast left so soon thy mother and
 thy home,
Kind brothers on the mountain-top that carol
 wild and free,
Sporting among the shelving crags they climb'd in
 infancy?

I wonder where thou travellest now, over the
 rolling seas,
Gazing upon the swelling wave, stirr'd by the
 passing breeze?
Or art thou rich as Croesus, boy, on Fortune's
 golden strand,
Shelter'd from want and pain and care in famed
 Australia-land?

I wonder where thy thoughts are now,
 wandering among our hills,
And gathering flowers that bathe themselves
 in Memory's sacred rills?
And art thou dreaming of thy sire, thy mother's
 kind caress,
I know these thoughts will call from thee fresh
 drops of tenderness.

Or art thou by the murmuring steam, lone
 musing on the past?
And does the tear-drop from thine eye rush o'er
 thy cheek at last?
And are thy playmates with thee there,
 bounding along the lake?

Thy brothers and thy sisters, too? Ah, no!
 young wanderer wake!
For we are on our mountain's head, watching
 the twilight grey,
And wondering why our brother thus so soon
 could haste away:
Ah, wondering why he thus could go from
 home's long-cherished bowers,
And leave us here alone to cull the Summer's
 brightest flowers!

I wonder what thine eyes behold, what now
 my brother sees?
O, does he walk at evening-hour beneath the
 forest-trees,
Gazing through tears with wild delight on the
 sweet-vesper star,
Flashing its beam of silvery light upon him
 from afar?

I wonder what thy feelings are, if they are aught
 like mine?
It may be so, and I will drop a tear or two with thine.
They fall upon our mountain's head within my
 heathy bower,
And hang, as doth the evening mist, upon the
 sleeping flower.

How sweet, on this delicious eve, my straw-thatch'd
 home appears!
Methinks, 'tis dearer now than erst, because
 enshrined in tears.
For every passing zephyr weeps, each flower-bud
 of the lea,
And all the little singing-birds sob forth a dirge
 for thee.

Thou canst not see my British home, with
 dusky twilight crown'd;
Thou canst not see old England's hills and valleys
 lie around;
Thou canst not see the rising moon peer o'er
 our mountain's brow,
How beautiful, how beautiful! But, brother,
 where art thou?

O, shall we never meet again? Perhaps on earth
 no more:
If not, farewell, until it be on heaven's
 unclouded shore.
But if below I felt for thee, and loved thee with
 such love,
O, how much greater will it be in that bright world
above!

The reader will note that verses five and nine are precisely the same as those quoted in the narrative on William B. Harris. There are, in fact, two versions of this poem. It seems that John (3) having written the original for William B, then adapted it for James.

John (3) was totally unaware of how prophetic the lines of the last verse were to be, for James died in the Melbourne hospital on 1 July 1854. It seems that William Carter and William Evans agreed that whereas the latter should proceed to the gold diggings, the former should stay with James. Imagine James dying alone except for his friend William Carter, after a voyage of 12,000 miles. James would have realised that it would not be possible for William Carter to write home and inform Christian and the family about the turn of events because William could neither read nor write.

James was buried in a common grave in Melbourne cemetery where they dug a grave each day for each denomination and buried the bodies en masse. Indeed, how reminiscent it is of his father's grave in Camborne churchyard:

'His grave is with the poor,
The rude unlettered clan.'

from The Death of My Father

By what means Christian and her family received the sad news is not definitely known, but possibly by the officiating Minister at the funeral. When the news arrived John (3) composed his third and last poem about James:

Down from the hills with a firm strong frame,
In the freshness of morning my brother came;
The morning of life when the world was fair,
And his heart unsoil'd with the dust of care;
When his hopes were high, as the land of gold,
Glitt'ring with gems, before him roll'd;
And as from rock to rock he stepp'd,
And his bending mother behind him wept
We heard him mid his sobbings say,
'I'll not forget you when far away.'
And had he lived, that loving boy
Would have gladden'd his parents' heart for joy.

A few months only had sped away,
When the tidings came of his decay.
On his ocean-journey affliction came,
And diseases fasten'd on his frame.
Thus he landed 'neath Australia's sky,
To breathe a fervent prayer and die.
Like a stately tree, with blossoms rife,
He quickly fell in the morn of life;

And his grave was dug by a stranger's hand,
Far, far away in a distant land.
Thus perish'd he in his youthful prime,
And pass'd away to the spirits' clime

Has it not been thus with many more,
Who left their own dear native shore?
Their friends have mourn'd when the letter said,
That the absent one was with the dead.
But he whose early dirge I write,
Who faded away in his morning's light,
Had a soul to love, and a heart to feel
For woes his kindness strove to heal;
And was early taught from that Book, the best,
The narrow way to the land of rest:
So when the last dread blow was given,
He surely flew to the bliss of heaven.

O, what a changeful world is ours!
Death's hands congeal the loveliest flowers;
He smites the shoot in the forest dim,
Where the lone one sobs her mournful hymn;
Uproots the tree with a pluck of ire,
Mows down the son with his grey-haired sire;
In the mother's side he drives the dart,
And drains the blood from the daughter's heart;
And friend from friend he severs wide,
In the flush of confidence and pride.
The fairest forms are soonest bow'd.
And pass away like the morning cloud.

from The Death of My Brother

How tragic is this short story of the short life of this son of John (2) and Christian, but he was only one of many unfortunate emigrants. Were not such deaths and suffering unnecessary, being solely due to the lack of common sense rules of hygiene on these emigrants' vessels?

8. Captain Samuel B. Harris

Early Life, Schooling, Training, Marriage and Emigration

Samuel, the seventh child and fifth son of John (2) and Christian, was born at Six Chimneys on 18 December 1834 and baptized at Camborne Parish Church on 22 February 1835.

It is possible that Samuel initially attended Mrs Percival's Endowed School at Treslothan, but it is certain that when he was seven years old he attended the National School at Camborne, which had been initiated circa 1820 by the Rector, Rev. Hugh Rogers. The school was originally held in the gallery, since demolished, of Camborne Parish Church and later moved to College Street.

The subsequent progress of Samuel's life suggests he showed such promise as a scholar that Rev. Hugh Rogers or another teacher at the National School, recognising his potential, convinced him that it was within his capability to attain a level of occupation beyond that of a working miner. It seems likely they helped him to obtain a position, when he left school at the age of eleven, as an assistant to a mine surveyor and assayer. He pursued this occupation for four years, eventually earning forty shillings a month.

If he was to emulate the mining captains of his day he also needed actual experience of mining practice underground, so he went into the mine to work for the next four years. This period of training does not suggest that Samuel would have mastered all the intricate calculations of mine surveying, or the wider aspects of metallurgy and mining practice, but he would have been well aware of the value of the measurement and assay of underground stopes and so on. This experience was to be of immense value to him later in the Copper Country of Upper Michigan.

At this point it appears that he had come to the conclusion that his prospects in Cornwall were limited. No doubt spurred on by reports from his elder brother William of the better prospects and quality of life in America, he decided to get married and set off with his wife for Wisconsin on 1 September 1854.

Samuel married Mary Bennett at Redruth Register Office on 31 August 1854. Mary was the daughter of Henry Bennett and Eleanor Jewell, who had been married at Illogan Parish Church on 8 March 1832. Henry was described as sojourner in Illogan and a miner. Shortly afterwards the family moved to Bolenowe where Mary's brother William Henry was born. Henry and Eleanor were not listed on the 1841 Camborne census, but Mary and William Henry were shown as living with the family of John and Jane Trezona at Carwynnen Carn, which suggests that the parents had passed away. By the 1851 census Mary was listed as a dressmaker and

Mary Bennett Harris

Samuel B. Harris

Photograph taken in their younger days but after they had taken the first steps up the social ladder

William Henry as a miner, but living as lodgers with the Trezona family.

The decision by this young couple to emigrate, although to some extent of necessity, was in due course proven to be the correct one and demonstrated their ability to think clearly and to readily adapt themselves to a completely different culture.

Samuel and Mary no doubt followed William, Ann (2), Matthew (2) and James by travelling from Camborne to Hayle by rail, by boat from Hayle to Bristol and from Bristol to Liverpool by rail. Arriving in Liverpool, Samuel and Mary secured passage on the vessel *Isaac Webb* bound for New York. The *Isaac Webb* was a vessel of 1,395 tons burthen with E.G. Tumber as Master.

Crossing the Atlantic they arrived in New York on 22 October.

Early Years in North America 1854–63

Samuel and Mary left New York by train on 23 October 1854, the journey taking them via Albany, Buffalo, Detroit and Chicago, reaching Galena nine days later. It appears they then made a diversion to south-east Wisconsin, possibly to visit acquaintances, finally arriving in Dodgeville on 13 November. Within a month of arrival their first child James was born.

After arrival in Dodgeville, Samuel possibly joined brother William and James Sims as a miner and then earned his first real money by contracting to sink and equip a one hundred-foot deep shaft. It seems that he did not see a future for himself in these lead mines and so in the spring of 1855 he sat a teachers' examination and obtained a certificate. He then taught school for about twelve months at a salary of $30 a month. The idea to become a teacher may well have been influenced by George Sims, an uncle of his brother-in-law James Sims. George Sims was himself a schoolteacher prior to emigration and had been resident in Dodgeville since 1843. During this time Samuel declared and filed his intention to become an American citizen to the Circuit Court of Iowa County.

Reports of the mining activity in Upper Michigan influenced him to leave his teaching post in Dodgeville and to go up to the Minesota Mine in Ontonagon County, where he arrived in March 1856. He spent the next two years here as a miner, enabling him to study and acquaint himself with the extraordinary ore bodies of the Copper Country. In February 1856 their second child was born in Dodgeville, who passed away in March 1858 while Samuel was still at Minesota Mine. Unfortunately we have no knowledge of the name or sex of this child as Samuel only referred to the child in his diary as 'H'.

Returning to Dodgeville in October 1858, it seems that he resumed lead mining but it is not known in what capacity. However, he is listed as a miner in the Iowa County census of June 1860, but in the summer of this year he paid a visit to Ontario, presumably to assess the mining opportunities there. At some point following this visit he was appointed School Superintendent in Dodgeville, WI, a position he held until August 1863. Samuel and Mary's daughter, Ellen Jane, was born in December 1860 at Dodgeville. In February 1860, Samuel joined the Methodist Episcopal Church and preached his first sermon in February 1861, being appointed a travelling preacher in September 1862.

Lured by the gold strike in Nova Scotia, he left Dodgeville on 31 August 1863 with two others, hoping to make a fortune. This proved a failure and so he returned to the Copper Country with only a dollar in his pocket. Here he quickly obtained a contract at the Isle Royale Mine and joined to the Houghton Grace Methodist Episcopal Church. Grace Church had only been in existence since 1854, when it had been formed with twelve members. The present university town of Houghton was then only a village. The Isle Royale Company had been incorporated to mine on the Isle Royale where it had been engaged for several years, but with limited success. In 1852 it opened the Isle Royale Mine on Portage Lake, thus becoming a pioneer mining company in this area. It can be appreciated that building up a mining enterprise in the midst of a wilderness was fraught with difficulty.[1]

On completion of this contract, Samuel secured another contract, this time with Mesnard and Pontiac Mines on the other side of the lake. At this point he brought his family up from Dodgeville and set up home in the Mesnard location, near Hancock. Upon arrival at their new home, Samuel was received into Hancock Methodist Episcopal Church by letter of transfer from Houghton Grace Church. At this time he was listed as a local preacher, and later as a trustee and local deacon. This was the first church of any denomination in Hancock.

The decision to move the family from Wisconsin to the Copper Country was not only brave but perceptive. Obviously Samuel was convinced that his future lay in the Copper Country and it was here that the greatest opportunities would present themselves. However, a further eight years would elapse before Samuel came into his own, but this can be interpreted as a period of apprenticeship in which he was able to study and absorb the peculiarities of the orebodies, mining and managerial practices.

Becoming Established in the Copper Country 1864–83

The Mesnard Mining Company was organised in 1862 immediately upon the discovery of a mass of copper of eighteen tons weight on the property. The mass had been moved a distance of forty-eight feet from its original bed by the ancient Indian miners, the evidence of whose work was plentifully apparent in the multitude of stone hammers and so on that were found surrounding the mass and in the place from where it had apparently been taken.[2]

Having completed his contract, Samuel was appointed mine captain of these mines in June 1864. However, this appointment only lasted for twelve months because, although great hopes had been entertained, the results were disappointing. In fact, only fifty tons of copper were obtained and work was suspended.

Despite the disappointment of Mesnard and Pontiac Mines, Samuel immediately obtained a position as mine captain at Phoenix Mine near Eagle River in Keweenaw County, where he commenced work on 11 June 1865. Phoenix Copper Company was the outgrowth of the old Lake Superior Copper Company, one of the pioneer enterprises in this region. The originators were among the first to take out permits from the War Department after the cessation of the Indian title in 1843.[3]

Shortly before relinquishing his appointment with the Phoenix Company, Samuel was elected a Justice of the Peace and while here had been connected with Clifton Methodist Church.

Having obtained some managerial experience, Samuel accepted a new position as agent in charge of Eagle Harbor Properties. It is not clear if the company actually operated mines or if it merely managed leases to small companies or tributers on the tract of land which it owned, which measured two miles by one and a half miles. One thing is certain, the secretary of the company was W. Hart Smith, of whom we shall read more later in relation to mines in Ontonagon County. Additionally, there is the suggestion that some of the mineral rights of the land managed by Eagle Harbor Properties may have been owned by the Calumet Mining Company of Houghton County where Samuel B.ecame mine captain in August 1868. During the time the family was living at Eagle Harbor their youngest child, John Luther, was born.

The Calumet Mine was first discovered in 1865. The development and prospects of the mine were discouraging in the first year, so much so that the shares originally worth $25 fell to $1 at the end of 1865. However, in 1866 the shares reached $30 in a short period and continued to rise and reached $75[4] a few months later. This rise was due to a new discovery. It is therefore not difficult to see why Samuel resigned from Eagle Harbor Properties to join the Calumet company.

While with the Calumet company Samuel B. became an American citizen, having made application for citizenship in Dodgeville in 1855. At this point he added the initial 'B' to his name, thus becoming Samuel B. Harris. During his association with Calumet Mine, Samuel B. was involved with Calumet Methodist Church. The Methodist Society had been holding services in the carpenters' shop of the Calumet and Hecla Mine but in 1869 a decision was taken to erect a church and Samuel B. was one of the original trustees as well as being Sunday School superintendent. He also continued duties as a local preacher.

Somewhat surprisingly, Captain John Uren, agent of the Franklin Mine and fellow Cornishman, induced Samuel B. to leave Calumet Mine to become mine captain at Franklin. This move was a mistake, however. Franklin Mine was organised and commenced operating in 1857. Six shafts had been sunk by 1861 and 250 men employed. By 1869 the indebtedness of the mine had been steadily increasing over a period of three years, the vein having pinched in and the product decreased. By November 1870 the company decided they could no longer make the mine pay and leased it to Pewabic Mine.[5] Left without employment, Samuel B. went back into teaching, taking a post in Franklin Township where he remained for another five months.

It is apparent that the progress and ability of Samuel B. had come to the notice of W. Hart Smith and the entrepreneur Thomas F. Mason, with whom Hart Smith was associated, for when a vacancy occurred for an agent of a group of mines in Ontonagon County, Samuel B. was asked to fill the position. On 1 May 1871 he became agent of the Ridge, Adventure, Hilton and Lake Superior Mines and moved with his family to the Ridge location. The Ridge Mine had been purchased by Thomas F. Mason in 1860 but only paid its first dividend, which amounted to $50,000, in 1872, that is, after Samuel B. had assumed management of the mines. Samuel B. made great efforts to modernise the mines but this was much restricted as he had to work to a limited budget due to the low price of copper. Indeed, because of this latter situation, Lake Superior Mine was put on tribute in 1873 and Adventure in 1877. This appointment was Samuel B.'s first significant step up the social ladder and his wife Mary was very much involved.

Mary continued to entertain and organise on a grand scale for the rest of her life. The question arises as to where and how she acquired this ability, as she had been a dressmaker prior to her marriage. It can only be concluded that Mary had been employed from time to time in the houses of local gentry in Cornwall making dresses for their servants and where she had the opportunity to observe preparations for big and festive occasions. The rise in social standing of Samuel B. and Mary is reflected by a request in June 1871 to Mark Smith Harris and his wife Jane for six yards of silk and a pair of gloves for Mary, which were duly despatched to her and the cost reimbursed. Samuel B. held this position under Thomas F. Mason for twelve years and for much of this period was Supervisor (Mayor) of Greenland Township.

Throughout his time in Ontonagon County, Samuel B. was associated with Maple Grove Methodist Church where he served as class leader, deacon, steward and local preacher. In 1883 he attended a Deacon's Conference at Flint, Michigan.

At this point in his career, Samuel B., by virtue of his ever-increasing knowledge of the metallurgy and mining practice of the Copper Country, was being commissioned by outside interests to report on other mines. This was parallel to his mentors, the Thomases of Dolcoath Mine at Camborne in his native Cornwall.

Reproduced with permission of First United Methodist Church, Hancock, from their Historic Church Calendar for 1988. Artist Frank Hawke, a member of the church and originally of St. Austell, Cornwall.

Eagle Harbor ME Church

Another church with which Samuel B. was associated
Subsequently remodelled as a private summer house

Phoenix M.E. Church

A Copper Country Methodist Church with which Samuel B. was associated.
Note the unusual construction of the roof of the bell tower. Church demoloshed 1929.

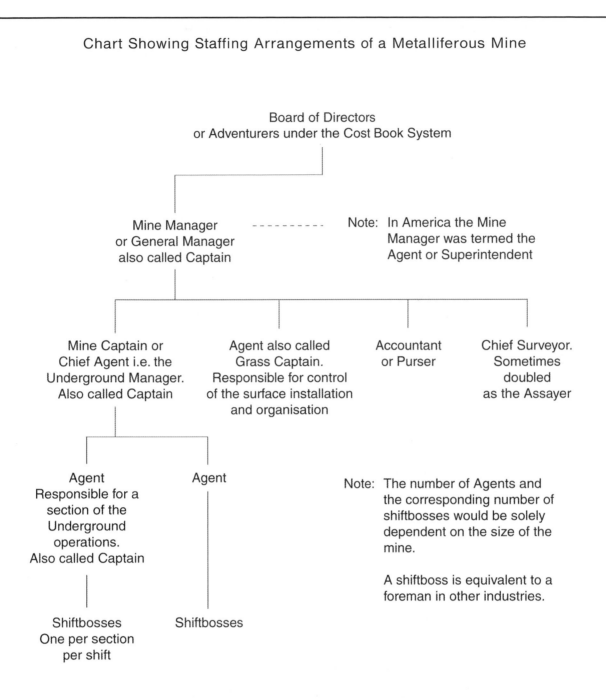

Chart Showing Staffing Arrangements of a Metalliferous Mine

Board of Directors
or Adventurers under the Cost Book System

Mine Manager
or General Manager
also called Captain

Note: In America the Mine
Manager was termed the
Agent or Superintendent

Mine Captain or
Chief Agent i.e. the
Underground Manager.
Also called Captain

Agent also called
Grass Captain.
Responsible for control
of the surface installation
and organisation

Accountant
or Purser

Chief Surveyor.
Sometimes
doubled
as the Assayer

Agent
Responsible for a
section of the
Underground
operations.
Also called Captain

Agent

Note: The number of Agents and
the corresponding number of
shiftbosses would be solely
dependent on the size of the
mine.

A shiftboss is equivalent to a
foreman in other industries.

Shiftbosses
One per section
per shift

Shiftbosses

The origin of the term 'Captain' in mining is probably due to the close association of the early Tinners with a seafaring life. In fact, the sixteenth-century tinners, who worked the elluvial deposit of tin in the moors and valleys of Cornwall, elected a spokesman or leader whom they called Captain.

The Quincy Years 1884–1902

When it became known in the Copper Country that Frank G. White was to relinquish his position as agent of the Quincy Mine in December 1883 after two years service, there was very considerable speculation as to who would be appointed in his place. However, there was no doubt in the mind of the Company President, Thomas F. Mason. For the past twelve years Samuel B. Harris had proved himself a loyal and competent manager of Mason's interests in Ontonagon County and so was appointed to succeed as agent at Quincy on 1 January 1884. Samuel B. was also appointed to the Board as the resident Director.

Although described in *Old Reliable* by Messrs Lankton and Hyde as 'The only Cornish miner to become Agent at Quincy' this is not strictly correct, as in Cornwall

The Agent's House photographed in 1985
now a private residence

The Quincy Smelter
Photograph by Richard Wilder of Madison, WI., great grandson of Samuel B. Harris and Mary.

Samuel B. had spent as many years working as a surveyor and assayer as he did as an underground miner. Furthermore, his experience in mine management and his accumulated knowledge of the orebodies and complexity of distribution of copper in its various forms was solely obtained in the Copper Country.

Samuel B. and his family took up residence on Quincy Hill in the spacious and imposing agent's house complete with tower. The company had provided and furnished this house in 1880–81 at a cost of $25,000.[6] It was in this house where Mary was to gain a considerable reputation for her generous and well-organised arrangements for the comfort and catering of the Company officials from New York when they visited the mine. On assuming his new post, Samuel B. was also appointed Supervisor of Quincy Township.

The Quincy Mining Company had been incorporated in 1848 and commenced operations on Quincy Hill in 1850. For the first twenty-two years the mine was operated manually with little mechanical equipment, although in 1872 steam drills were introduced, but these proved to be unsatisfactory. However, in 1879 compressed air equipment was installed which wrought considerable change, especially on the Pewabic Lode. We shall see that during the period of nineteen years in which Samuel B. was agent, very considerable progress was made in modernising the plant both underground and on surface, together with the acquisition of adjacent mines and property. This was only possible by comparable investment by the shareholders. Samuel B. clearly had the ability to accept and keep pace with the technological developments that were taking place in the mining industry. In addition, he possessed an innate desire and perception to carry out exploration and

**Samuel B. and Mary out for a drive
with their chauffeur**

development for additional orebodies whilst exploiting the existing lodes. Undoubtedly these progressions were the key to his success.

This particular policy of Samuel B. made it possible for the company to pay a dividend for *every year* of the long period of time in which he served the company. This gave rise to the company being known as 'Old Reliable'. Indeed, during the period the amount of copper produced per year rose from 2,802 tons to 10,270 tons, the labour force from 400 to 1,636, the dividends from $200,000 to $1,200,000 while the price of copper fluctuated only marginally from nine cents to seventeen cents per pound.[7]

During his first year of service, a man-engine was installed in one of the shafts to the twenty-seventh level and arrangements made to extend it to the deeper levels. The man-engine operated for eleven years when it was superseded by conventional winding gear.[8] In 1891 Quincy acquired the Pewabic Mine, followed by the Mesnard and Pontiac Mines in 1896.

For his care, energy and dogged persistence in exploiting the pockety character and tortuous course of the Pewabic lode which required a disproportionate amount of excavation in barren ground, Samuel B. was rewarded in 1892 by being given a sizeable plot of ground overlooking Portage Lake on which to build a retirement home. The transaction was legalised by Samuel B. paying the company the sum of $1.[9] By 1897 his salary had increased to $10,000.[10] Prior to owning a motor, car Samuel B. was reported to own the finest carriage and pair of greys in the Copper Country.[11]

Thomas F. Mason, the outstanding, astute and very experienced Company President and entrepreneur who had a considerable flair for selecting the most suitable persons for positions in his companies, passed away in 1899. Indeed, it was said that Quincy was the best officered company in the Copper Country.[12] However, Thomas F. Mason's act was a very difficult one to follow. His son, Thomas Henry Mason, who was appointed in his stead found it somewhat beyond his capability and left the onus of decision-making to the Company Secretary and Treasurer William Rogers Todd.

Immediately a personality clash resulted between Samuel B. and W.R. Todd. What brought this situation about? Samuel B. was by now of very considerable stature in the Copper Country, a wealthy man and greatly respected. He had been Township Supervisor of Hancock ever since his appointment to Quincy. He had been one of the originators of the Northern Michigan Building and Loan Association in 1889, being also a Director and Vice-President from that date. In the early 1890s he was General Manager of the Quincy and Torch Lake Railroad, a Quincy subsidiary, and by 1895 was Vice-President. In 1895 he was President of Hancock Sandstone Company and in the same year became a member of the Board of Supervisors and Bridge Committee for construction of the new bridge spanning Portage Lake between Hancock and Houghton. By 1897 he was President of the First National Bank of

An exhibit outside Houghton County Museum at Lake Linden which commemorates the construction of the second Portage Lake Bridge in 1895. Information on the plaque lists the involvement of Samuel B. Harris with the project.

Samuel B. Harris taking a stroll in contemplative mood at the height of his career with Quincy.

Hancock and by 1899 was a Director of the Peninsular Electric Light and Power Company. Did it therefore appear to W.R. Todd that Samuel B. was becoming too powerful?

In 1900, W.R. Todd initiated the demise of company paternalism which had so long been established, not only by Quincy but in most Copper Country companies. Indeed, it was no doubt originally instituted to attract labour and mine officials to the howling wilderness of the Copper Country. W.R. Todd argued that the time of paternalism was past.[13] Undoubtedly there were sound arguments for and against such a decision, but ultimately it was Samuel B. who was responsible for the loyalty and co-operation of those under him.

Outside of these considerations, the year 1900 had been traumatic for Samuel B. because his beloved wife Mary had passed away on 23 January. In March 1902, Thomas Henry Mason died and W.R. Todd officially assumed the position of Company President. Obviously the personality clash had not diminished and in June the same year Samuel B. tendered his resignation which was immediately accepted. However, there appears to have been a condition in Samuel B.'s contract by which he was entitled to be paid to the end of the year, but apparently a dispute arose as to the precise amount of salary and/or expenses. The authors of *Old Reliable* have stated that W.R. Todd was less than satisfied with some of the decisions made by Samuel B. but this statement does not agree with the history of his service and loyalty to the company since 1 January 1884, though admittedly he was now almost sixty-eight years of age.

It is possibly of significance that among the correspondence released by the company in recent years the letters leading up to and including the letter of resignation have not been released. Samuel B's title had been changed from agent to superintendent and although this should not have troubled a person of his stature, in the Copper Country it was of considerable significance and

The 1895 Bridge across Portage Lake between Houghton and Hancock
Photograph ex. Michigan Technological University Archives and Copper Country Historical Collections
Donor – Paul Hinzmann

would be interpreted as a reduction in status.

At the same time Samuel B. also resigned as Supervisor of Quincy Township, but historically this was a position invariably held in the Copper Country by the agent of the adjacent or nearby mine. The Copper Country press and inhabitants were surprised and stunned by the announcement of Samuel B.'s resignation. They were very much aware and acknowledged the huge contribution to the modernisation of the poorly equipped and developed mine which he had taken over in January 1884. The *Hancock Journal* eulogised that the fame attained by Quincy was largely due to Samuel B.'s able efforts: 'That no mine in the district was in a better condition in all that goes to financial success than the Quincy, and that the mines proud position would always remain as a lasting monument to his managerial ability'.

When the family took up residence in the agent's house on Quincy Hill, Samuel B. attached himself to the nearby Pewabic Methodist Episcopal Church. Both here and in the Franklin Circuit[14] he was very active. Originally the Pewabic and Hancock Methodist churches were served by the same minister but in 1880 they were divided with Pewabic having 135 members and Hancock 45, and so Samuel B. joined a thriving church.

In 1889 the Hancock Society decided to build a new and larger church on a more central site, and Samuel B. was instrumental in obtaining the site from the Quincy Company for the then low price of $2,500 and became involved in building the church. The old property was sold for $7,000 and the new church, which still stands on Quincy Street, was dedicated on 1 November 1903.[15] This church is still very active and has been partially remodelled and adapted to serve the modern age.

The Pewabic Church was demolished in 1961. There is a story within the Cornish branch of the family that Samuel B. preached to the Indians. This conjures up a picture of it taking place in some forest clearing but in reality it was doubtless in one of the Indian Missions in the Copper Country.

It has been stated by some American writers that Samuel B. insisted on being addressed as Captain, thereby implying that this was somewhat unusual and pretentious. However, in Cornwall all grades of agents and mine managers were and are known as captains as a matter of course. This usage and description has lasted for several centuries. Indeed, the tinners of the sixteenth century, who worked the elluvial deposits[16] of tin prior to major underground lode mining, appointed one of their number to allocate their work and to be their spokesman and called this person 'Captaine'.[17] The term 'captain' has maritime links and probably came into use as the Cornish tinners often combined this occupation with fishing.

The Eventide Years 1903-1927

When Samuel B. resigned from Quincy he continued and extended his business interests. Already Vice-President of Northern Michigan Building and Loan Association, he was elected President in 1906, a position which he retained until 1922. This association had been the brainchild, in 1889, of his son-in-law Charles D. Hanchette who, following his marriage, lived in a rented house but wished to own a home of his own. Charles had heard of building and loan associations and decided that this was what he and the Copper Country needed: a means by which folk could save money and finance homes.[18] One feels that it would not have been difficult for Charles to persuade Samuel B. to become involved in the scheme. It would have been in line with the latter's Christian beliefs and Methodist concepts. Indeed, it was the start of a very extensive business which would continue long after the originators had passed away.

In 1910 it extended south to Detroit and became one of the strongest financial institutions in the State of Michigan, changing its name to the Detroit and Northern Building and Loan Association. In 1949, its title was again changed, this time to Detroit and Northern Savings Loan Association. By 1980 it operated twenty-seven branches and twelve agencies and was still expanding.[19] On 5 January 1922, Samuel B. stepped down as President and Board Member having reached the great age of eighty-seven. He must have been very proud of the Association's success and of the part he had played in its creation and extraordinary progress.

In June 1906 the Hancock Consolidated Mining Company was formed under the Presidency of John D. Cuddihy with an authorised capital of $5 million.[20] The President was far and away the largest shareholder and among the Directors was Samuel B. Harris. The new company acquired the assets of the old Hancock Mining Company, whose eastern and northern boundaries adjoined Quincy Mine property and had been originally formed in 1859. The old company had had a somewhat chequered history and after using its capital of $500,000 was leased to tributers. In 1872 it was sold to a partnership and in 1879 was purchased by Ed Ryan of Hancock, who reorganised with a capital of $100,000.

The property now owned by the new company amounted to 936 acres of mineral-bearing ground. In reality this particular area was not as highly mineralised as its neighbours. Additionally, the mine had been served by an inadequate shaft, hoisting facility and surface plant. It now required expensive and extensive reorganisation and modernisation. No doubt the reason for inviting Samuel B. to join the Board was to benefit from his advice and experience. The low copper content of the orebody would necessitate arrangements to handle and treat large tonnages of rock in order to be in any way viable. In the event,Hancock Consolidated Mining Company did not attain the success achieved by other mines in the area. However, it did achieve in its time economic importance to the people of Hancock. The production costs did not get below twenty-two cents per pound of ingot copper; at this cost there was no market and so the mine ceased operation on 7 January 1919. It appears that Samuel B. held no great expectations for the project because as far as can be ascertained he did not hold any shares in the company.

There is no definitive written history of the First National Bank of Hancock. However, it is thought to have originated in 1874 and Samuel B. Harris was its President at least by 1894. It is not certain as to when Samuel B. stepped down as President but his obituary states that he was 'at one time' President. It is known that from 1914 to 1922 deposits at the bank increased by sixty-six percent. Apparently the bank went out of business around 1930, though whether this was a termination of business or a take-over is not clear. Certainly its premises in downtown Hancock was taken over and occupied by the Minerals Banking Group. Similarly, little is written about the Hancock Mortgage Loan and Surety Company of which, according to *Polk's Directory*, Samuel B. was Chairman from 1907 and President from 1916.

In respect of the Peninsular Electric Light and Power Company it appears that Samuel B. was a director at its inception and maintained an interest until his death. It was a forward-looking and expanding company. It built a generating plant at Lake Linden in 1899 and a dock was also built to facilitate the landing of coal supplies for the generator. Soon it supplied the Torch Lake area and then, as time progressed, to numerous communities, mines and so on.[21]

On the plaque commemorating the construction of the second bridge across Portage Lake in 1895, Samuel B. is designated as one of the members of the Board of Supervisors and one of the three members of the Bridge Committee. One is led to ask just what were the functions of these members? Were they supervisors of construction or operators of the bridge following completion? The construction of this steel bridge with a pivoted centre section to permit passage of vessels was a considerable engineering project somewhat removed from the practice of mining. That the project was vital to the communication system across the lake is beyond doubt as the wooden bridge, which replaced a ferry in 1872, itself needed replacing. The Portage River had been deepened and widened in 1860 and the Portage Ship Canal was cut in 1873.[22] All of these improvements were necessary as the production from and usage of materials for the mines increased. The wooden bridge had served as a vital link across the lake for twenty-three years. As it happened,

the second bridge was to have a life of sixty-four years until the third and present double-deck (road and rail) vertical lift bridge was opened in December 1959. This bridge is a marvel of civil, mechanical and structural engineering. Its towers rise 180 feet above the piers, the total length is 1,310 feet and the lift span weighs 2,000 tons.[23]

Unfortunately in 1922-23 Samuel B. became involved in a venture to acquire 360 acres of lead/zinc-bearing ground in Joplin, Jasper County, Missouri. His entry into the venture was based on very favourable reports from a consulting mining engineer, a forecast of likely earnings from a financial expert and promises of capital from major financiers in New York, Detroit and Chicago. The project was also backed by correspondence from prominent people in Joplin. Additionally, there was a syndicate of small investors from the Hancock area. Apparently some of the acreage was worked by lessees and sub-lessees. Although the intention is not absolutely clear, it appears that certain areas were to be mined on a more viable engineering basis and to construct a concentrator where the ore from all the various parties would be treated. To this end John Luther Harris, the younger son of Samuel B. was sent down to Joplin to take charge and an office was established in the Bartlett Building in Joplin, together with the necessary staff. An attorney was also employed to arrange the acquisition and new leases and to set up the agreements with the major financiers. On this basis and the firm belief of the integrity of the major investors, it seems that Samuel B. put up the initial monies for purchase and setting up the company, as did the small Hancock syndicate. However, delay followed delay after delay on the part of the major investors, resulting in Samuel B. having to bear the considerable initial outlay together with the running costs that continued month after month. The worry of this situation undermined his health and he wrote of those who reneged on their promises: 'There is no capital, no enterprise and nothing but selfishness by these people. Not one of them will put a dollar of their money into the enterprise. They write and talk so glibly and have ready excuses for not putting their money into the pool'. His one desire was to get out and cut his losses, but he remained as long as he could because of the loyalty he felt to the Hancock syndicate. Eventually, enough was enough and the syndicate accepted their losses, which permitted Samuel B. to withdraw after he suffered considerable financial loss. This latter situation evinced great concern from his immediate family who could see their inheritance being greatly reduced, but in characteristic fashion Samuel B. informed them that the onus was on his shoulders alone, that they had no say in the matter but he intended to provide for them.[24]

Despite the foregoing, Samuel B.'s investment portfolio was both impressive and extensive in its wide coverage and amounted to a total value of approximately $700,000. The spread of investment included the number one mining company of the Upper Peninsula, that is, the Calumet and Hecla, the Homestake Mining Company in South Dakota (still the largest gold-mining company in the US), the Mohawk Mining Company, Andes Copper Company and Anaconda Copper Mining Company. Bonds included American Liberty, Canadian Government, United States Treasury, United Kingdom Government, Commonwealth of Australia, Kingdom of Denmark and Kingdom of Belgium. Investment was also held in the Canadian Pacific Railway and Allis Chalmers, the American mining machinery manufacturers. There were also stakes in many other mining and industrial concerns.

Following his resignation from Quincy, Samuel B. continued to live in the agent's house with his younger son, John Luther, who had been appointed to succeed him. This arrangement continued until John Luther also resigned from the position in December 1905. Samuel B. then went to live with his daughter Nellie and her husband Charles D. Hanchette at 204 Center Street. At this point, Samuel B. set in motion the arrangements for the design and construction of his retirement home on the land he had received from Quincy in 1892.

He and his son John Luther took up residence around 1910, complete with indoor and outdoor staff. They lived there until their deaths in 1927. It was a great disappointment to Samuel B. that his wife Mary had not lived to share in the comfort of this new home. Possibly some of the delay in getting the house built was due to his anguish at her illness and death. She had died of abdominal cancer.

It certainly is an imposing brick house standing on the wooded slope of the north shore of Portage Lake. The strong room still contains a chest with the names of S.B. Harris and J.L. Harris in gold lettering on the mahogany doors. What a contrast this retirement home was to the thatched cottage with beaten earth floor at Six Chimneys and the tiny cottage at Laity Row, Troon where he had lived with his mother, brothers and sister before emigrating to America

Like most Cornish immigrants, Samuel B. was a Republican and remained so during his lifetime. He was also a Freemason, being a member of the Scottish Rite, an appendant body of the Grand Lodge of Free and Accepted Masons of the State of Michigan. To be a member it is necessary to be a Master Mason.[25] Additionally, Samuel B. was a member of the Hancock No. 381 Lodge of Elks. In the United Kingdom such an organisation would be known as a Friendly or Benevolent Society. According to Dr A.L. Rowse, the Order of Elks was formed in America by a Cornishman, C.A. Vivian.[26]

The cupboards in the strong-room of Samuel B.'s retirement home at Hancock, MI.

Photographed by Jay Harris with permission of the then owners, June 1985

The retirement home in Hancock of Samuel B. Harris. The house looks out over Portage Lake

Samuel B. was a member of the Onigaming Yacht Club but this was solely a social membership. He never owned a yacht although very much enjoyed sailing with his great friends, the Douglases of Houghton, who owned a yacht and a motor boat.[27] These friends were also much involved with the Northern Michigan Building and Loan Association. It seems likely that Samuel B. would also have attended the theatre in Hancock. The Kearedge Theatre in Quincy Street, Hancock, which seated an audience of 1,565, was equipped with 1,000 incandescent lights, presumably with power supplied by the Peninsular Electric Light and Power Company. The opening play on 5 September 1902 was *The Tempest*, the charge for box seats being $40. The theatre attracted famous performers including Sarah Bernhardt.[28]

Outside of the influence for good, which the large mining companies brought to the Copper Country in making available land for churches, they also brought considerable culture in the form of libraries and theatre.

After moving down the hill to live in Hancock, Samuel B. transferred his membership from Pewabic to the new First United Methodist Church in Quincy Street. Later in his will he left the latter church $1,000. When Samuel B. became established in the Copper Country he sent monetary gifts at regular intervals to his brother Mark in Cornwall and especially to his sister Kitty following the death of her husband in 1878. Samuel B. and his brother Mark maintained a continuous flow of correspondence while they were physically able.

Samuel B. had not enjoyed the best of health for a year or two and after a short illness passed away 18 October 1927. He was eight weeks and five days short of his ninety-third birthday. The funeral cortège assembled at his retirement home and the Rev. P.J. Clifford, the Pastor of Hancock Methodist Church, officiated and burial took place alongside his wife Mary at Forest Hill Cemetery, Houghton. The service was under Masonic auspices, Palestine Commandery. Knights Templar and Hancock Lodge of Elks provided an escort.[29] The obituary described Samuel B. as a highly-respected resident of Hancock and a pioneer mining man.[30] The proceedings of Lake Superior Mining Institute in their issue for 1929 reported as follows:

The death of Samuel B. Harris 18 October 1927 at the age of 93 years marked the passing of the last of the pioneer mining men who were responsible for the development of early mining projects in the Michigan Copper Country.

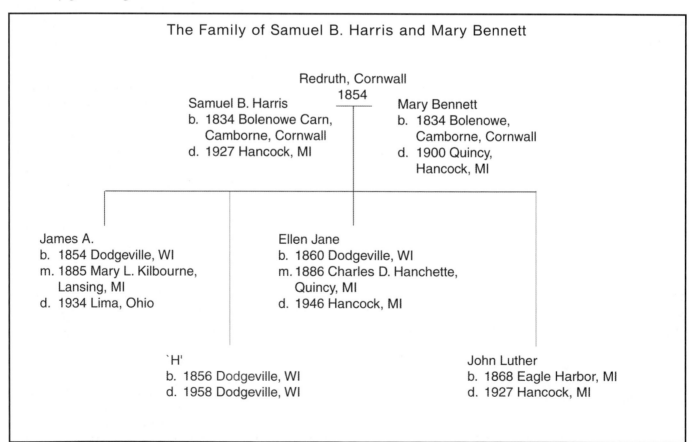

The Family of Samuel B. Harris and Mary Bennett

Redruth, Cornwall
1854

Samuel B. Harris
b. 1834 Bolenowe Carn,
 Camborne, Cornwall
d. 1927 Hancock, MI

Mary Bennett
b. 1834 Bolenowe,
 Camborne, Cornwall
d. 1900 Quincy,
 Hancock, MI

James A.
b. 1854 Dodgeville, WI
m. 1885 Mary L. Kilbourne,
 Lansing, MI
d. 1934 Lima, Ohio

Ellen Jane
b. 1860 Dodgeville, WI
m. 1886 Charles D. Hanchette,
 Quincy, MI
d. 1946 Hancock, MI

`H'
b. 1856 Dodgeville, WI
d. 1958 Dodgeville, WI

John Luther
b. 1868 Eagle Harbor, MI
d. 1927 Hancock, MI

Subsequently Harris Avenue, Hancock, was named after Samuel B.[31]

The final will of Samuel B., dated 22 September 1927, amounted to seventy-four pages and superseded a previous will dated 14 January 1927. The executors were First National Bank, Hancock and his surviving elder son James A. Harris, who were authorised to realise and dispose of the estate without an order from an appropriate Court of Law. Bequests included those to his staff: Hilda Seppanen, $1,000; Amanda Seppanen, $1,000; Norman Chegwidden, $300 and Oscar Ongie, $200, together with the bequest made to Hancock Methodist Church previously mentioned. In appreciation of the friendship and kindness shown to his deceased son John Luther Harris, he bequeathed to Joseph M. Turk and Barney Burritt $500 each. His son John Luther having died suddenly the previous January, a maximum sum of $35,000 was set aside to meet any debts outstanding to his late son's creditors. To his surviving son James and daughter Nellie he bequeathed $150,000 each, together with equal shares of the residue of the estate. In respect of his five grandchildren, Samuel B. made no specific bequest in the will but stipulated that should their parents predecease him, the proportions of the estate due to the parents was to be divided equally between them.

As a valediction to Samuel B. it should be said that he never forgot his humble origins or the family he left in Cornwall in 1854, despite his attainment of position and wealth. Neither did he discard the counsel proffered to him by John (3) in a poem entitled *Another Day of Work is O'er*.

> Goodbye, dear Samuel: ever show
> A heart to sympathise with woe.
> Revere the brave, admire the wise,
> And true neglected genius prize,
> No matter whether it be found
> In peasant - plots or courtly ground.

from The Land's End, Kynance Cove
and other Poems 1858.

The poem was published in 1858 almost four years after Samuel B. had emigrated and seventeen months prior to his joining the Methodist Episcopal Church in Dodgeville.

The Family of Samuel B. Harris and Mary Bennett

James A. Harris

James A., the elder son of Samuel B. and Mary, was born in Dodgeville, Wisconsin on 19 December 1854. He was listed in the 1860 Iowa County census and again in the 1870 Houghton County, Michigan census for the Township of Franklin when he was said to be fifteen years old but there was no occupation given and he was said to be 'at home'. Whether or not this implied that at this time he was at home from college is not known.

However, in the 1880 Ontonagon County census for Greenland Township he was listed as 'teaching school'. Shortly after, we find that he was teaching at Oxford, Oakland County, Michigan where he met his future bride, Mary L. Kilbourne of Lansing. Mary, born on 20 January 1863, was the daughter of Samuel L. Kilbourne, a very prominent attorney of that city who later, at the turn of the century, became the first President of the Ingham County Bar Association. James A. and Mary were married on 26 August 1885 at St Paul's Episcopal Church, Lansing where Mary's parents were very active members, the ceremony being performed by Rev. Ebenezer Thompson. The wedding was reported in the local newspapers as a most elegant social occasion. The reception was held at the bride's parents' home and the couple honeymooned in Detroit. One newspaper account, which included a list of presents, amounted to eighteen column inches! Apparently Samuel B. and Mary were unable to attend, but they and their daughter Nellie sent a hammered silver cake basket as their wedding present.

In a letter from James A. to his brother John Luther, we find that by May 1887 James A. was Principal of Schools at Oxford, but within a few years he was to move into the practice of law, probably at the suggestion of his father-in-law. Indeed, he was listed in Lansing City Directory from 1894 to 1934 as an attorney,[32] but it is recorded that he was admitted to the practice of law on 17 June 1892 with offices at the Holister Buildings. However, Mr Alison K. Thomas[33] in his research of the History of Ingham County Bar Association doubts that James A. was very active in actual legal practice but suspects that he was more involved financially as a man of considerable means. Just how this latter situation came about is not clear unless it was his wife's money, because he did not inherit from his father until 1927 when he was described in the obituary as an attorney. Nevertheless, when Ingham County Bar Association was formed in 1909, James A. was a signatory to its Articles of Association. Again in 1919 he was a signatory to their Schedule of Charges for legal services. James A. and Mary became very active at St Paul's Episcopal Church when they moved to Lansing from Oxford where their only child

Samuel Kilbourne Harris was born on 1 November 1886.

On 2 December 1934, James A. succumbed to coronary thrombosis at St Rita's Hospital, Lima, Ohio and was brought back for burial at Deepdale Cemetery, Lansing. He had been on a visit to his son Samuel K., then resident in Lima. Mary lived on at 710 Seymour Avenue, Lansing until her death on 6 May 1939 and was buried alongside James A. at Deepdale.

Samuel Kilbourne Harris

At the early age of six in 1894, Samuel K. became a member of the first Boys' Choir at St Paul's Episcopal Church, Lansing. A short time prior to his death he completed seventy-five years as a member of the Episcopal Church Choirs. After college he trained as a railroad draughtsman and was employed as such at the time of his father's death. He had an unfortunate first marriage, which ended in divorce, but his later marriage to Sally Estelle was a very happy one. Sometime after his father's death he set up home back in Lansing and presumably as a result of his inheritance became a member of the New York Stock Exchange, being elected 15 October 1942. He had purchased his membership from H Brevoort Seaman for $20,000.[34] For the next eight years or so Samuel K. did very well financially on the Stock Exchange. During this period he purchased a beautiful holiday home on the seacoast of New Jersey. Also in 1942 he gave $25,000 to St Paul's Episcopal Church, Lansing for construction of the Chapel of the Incarnation in memory of his parents and the families of his paternal and maternal grandparents.

Samuel K. Harris circa 1969 in his choir member's surplice.

The chapel replaced a small room with access direct from the church, which had been used on occasions as a chapel but mainly as a vestry room for choir and clergy. The new chapel formed an intimate place for smaller services and for private meditation.

Following his success on the Stock Market, Samuel K. then ventured into the commodity market and lost practically all his entire fortune. He resigned from New York Stock Exchange on 31 August 1950, having transferred his membership to George S. McNamee.[35] Following this catastrophe, Samuel K. associated himself with the Petroff Real Estate Company and sold real estate on commission for the rest of his life.[36]

Samuel K. was a most devoted and faithful communicant of St Paul's, serving many years as a Vestryman and from 1943 was Comptroller of the Parish. In civics he was a member of the Delta Planning Commission. After a very full life, Samuel K. passed away on 11 November 1972 and was buried in the family plot at Deepdale Cemetery. At the time of his death he had been living at 602 West, St Joseph's, Lansing. Sally Estelle lived on at Eton until 26 April 1975 and was laid to rest alongside Samuel K.

Ellen (Nellie) Jane Harris

Nellie was born in Dodgeville, Wisconsin, on 4 December 1860. For some inexplicable reason her marriage certificate says she was born in Platteville. The 1870 Michigan census for Houghton County, Franklin Township, lists her as nine years old and at school. On the 5 June 1880 census for Ontonagon County, Greenland Township, she is listed as nineteen years old but also at school! Whether this implies that she was home on vacation from school is not clear, but her granddaughter, J. Ellen Gilson Austin, has stated that Nellie was educated in Milwaukee. J. Ellen's childhood memory of her grandmother recalled that Nellie was very proper, difficult and feared.

Some time after Nellie and her parents moved to Quincy, Houghton County in December 1883, she met Charles D.avid Hanchette and they were married at Quincy on 14 December 1886. Charles D. had been born in Woodstock, Illinois on 13 December 1859 and grew up in Chicago where he graduated from High School in 1878. In 1880, as a young man full of enthusiasm and with a determination to work hard and make a name for himself, he came up to Hancock. Initially he entered the music business but soon gave up this career to study to become a lawyer, passing his Bar examination in 1886. He then joined a law partnership with Thomas B. Dunstan, a practising attorney who later from 1896 to 1898 was Lieut. Governor of Michigan. The law partnership was known as Dunstan and Hanchette, Charles D. being the junior partner.[37]

Charles D. was the third child and second son of Hiram Solon Hanchette and his wife Nancy Jane Griffiths. Hiram S. had been born 28 June 1825 in Warwick, Quebec Province, Canada and had married Nancy J. on 9 November 1852 in Sullivan County, Indiana. Following the outbreak of the American Civil War, Hiram S. enlisted on 4 November 1862 in the 16th Regiment Illinois Volunteer Cavalry and was commissioned with the rank of Captain 19 May 1863 to raise a further company of the Regiment. The company was in action in Tennessee in November 1864 and, according to a sworn statement by the Colonel of the Regiment, Robert H. Smith, Capt. Hanchette was taken prisoner by the Confederate Army on or about the 20th of the same month and held a prisoner of war in a jail at Cahamba, Alabama, since 9 January 1865.

On 11 May 1865, following the cessation of hostilities, Capt. Hanchette's wife, Nancy J., wrote to Union General A.J. Smith to the effect that she had not heard from her husband since 11 March 1865 when he had been permitted to write to her from his prison cell in Cahamba, at which time he was being held in shackles. She required the General to obtain information of her husband as she understood that all other prisoners from Cahamba had by this time been exchanged. Following receipt of her letter, General Smith ordered an investigation, which was carried out by a Capt. John Kennedy of 7th Minnesota Infantry. Capt. Kennedy's subsequent report makes very grim reading: he confirmed that Capt. Hanchette had been incarcerated at Cahamba on the order of a rebel Lt. Colonel Jones who was in command there. The jailer, town Mayor and other townsfolk of Cahamba had remonstrated with Jones about the cruel and inhuman treatment of Capt. Hanchette but Jones would have none of it and declared that Capt. Hanchette was a spy. The town of Selma was taken by Union forces on 2 April 1865 and when Confederate stragglers brought this news to Cahamba, Jones that night released all the prisoners except Capt. Hanchette and two others. Next morning, 3 April, Jones, his adjutant and two guards took Capt. Hanchette and left for Demopolis. When the party got about three miles from Cahamba, and in the woods, three men appeared who claimed to be from a unit of Independent Scouts and Jones turned Capt. Hanchette over to them. Capt. Kennedy swore under oath that Capt. Hanchette was then murdered on the instruction of the rebel Colonel Jones because Capt. Hanchette never arrived in Demopolis. When the charges were being prepared against Jones it was discovered that he had left the country! Small wonder that such infamous conduct by the rebel Colonel left Charles D. with such determination towards life.

Hiram S. Hanchette was promoted to the rank of Major during his captivity but the promotion was seemingly promulgated posthumously. Nancy J. eventually received a pension $25.00 per month for every child under sixteen years of age, backdated to 3 April 1865.[38]

A warranty deed dated 24 February 1890 shows that Charles D. purchased a fairly extensive plot of ground from Quincy Mining Company for the sum of $2,000. The plot was bounded on the north by Cooper Avenue, on the west by Dunstan Street and on the south by Front Street, that is, US 41. The residence when erected was known as 204 Front. The document was signed on behalf of Quincy Company by Thomas F. Mason and William R. Todd. The purchase was freehold but with a restriction, which was customary, to the effect that the Company retained the right to mine within fifteen feet of the surface.[39] We have already learned that Charles D. was essentially the founder of Northern Michigan Building and Loan Association in 1889, which was formed in order that Copper Country folk could save money and finance the building of homes. He and Nellie had been married for just over three years and by now had two children and had been living in rented accommodation at 506 Hancock.[40] Therefore, in buying the land and immediately starting the construction of their own house, Charles D. was seen to be putting into action what he had been preaching. The new house was in a very pleasant spot with views over Portage Lake. Curiously, the stable and barn appears to be of more substantial construction than their house. Presumably the former were built sometime after the house when they were more affluent. The adjacent plot of ground, of similar size, was where Samuel B. had his retirement home built and after 1892 the Hanchettes used it for grazing their horses.[41]

Five children were born to Nellie and Charles D.: Mary Estelle in 1887, Ellen Nanette in 1888 who died as an infant, Eleanor Anita in 1891, Darthea in 1896 and Alice in 1900. Eleanor recalled in her later years that she remembered the dressmaker coming twice a year for two to three weeks, four to five weeks if the weather was bad, and staying with her grandparents. Grandmother Mary would be in charge and she and Nellie would study books and catalogues to select patterns and fashions for the family. Obviously Mary was enacting the procedures she had experienced as a dressmaker with the local gentry in Cornwall.

Charles D. successfully built up a fair number of business interests and pursued them with vigour and acumen. Following the death in the early 1900s of Thomas B. Dunstan, Charles D. formed a law partnership with S.L. (Swaby) Lawton in 1902. The partnership, known as

Hanchette and Lawton, continued until 1920. At this point Charles D. established his legal address in Detroit. Charles D. also sold insurance during the time of his association with Swaby Lawton and was elected three times the Prosecuting Attorney for Keweenaw County.

The Northern Michigan Building and Loan Association remained from 1889, to the time of his death in 1923 as the organisation that gave him immense pleasure and satisfaction and of which he was justly proud. This was despite considerable differences and stormy encounters with other officials of the Association, together with his commitments to his law practices and numerous business interests. In 1910, Charles D. was the prime mover in opening a branch office in Detroit. Later, probably around 1950, the name was changed to Detroit and Northern Building and Loan Association. By 1895, Charles D. was Secretary of Hancock Brown Stone Company and by 1903 was its President. Also by 1895 he was Secretary and Treasurer of Hancock Sandstone and Land Company with which his father-in-law, Samuel B. Harris, was also associated. Charles D. also became a Director of First National Bank, Hancock, and Vice-President of Victoria Copper Mining Company. Other companies with which he was associated were Tremont-

Samuel B. Harris Family Group
Standing (L – R): Mary Bennett Harris, Wife of Samuel B. Harris; Charles D. Hanchette, Son-in-law of Samuel B. Harris; Samuel B. Harris; Ellen Jane (Nellie) Harris Hanchette, Daughter of Samuel B. Harris.
Seated (L – R): Mary Estelle Hanchette, Grand-daughter and Eleanor Anita Hanchette, Grand-daughter.
Photograph taken circa 1897/98 in the Agent's house on Quincy Hill, Hancock

Devon Mining where he was Secretary and Treasurer and Dakota Heights Real Estate Company where he held the same positions. In the public service domain he was Vice-President of Lakeside Cemetery Association, which had been incorporated in 1896. Upon his moving to Detroit to live in 1920, he became a partner in the law firm of Bell and Hanchette.[42] During his business visits to Detroit, Charles D. became acquainted with a Mrs MacMechan who had been the first woman attorney in that city. Their friendship deepened and Charles D. informed Nellie that he would be leaving her but he promised that he would stand by her until such time as their four daughters were in a position to be independent of her. At this point divorce proceedings were instituted and when declared absolute Charles D. married Mrs MacMechan.[43]

However, Charles D. died suddenly at his home in East Palmer Avenue, Detroit, on 8 March 1923. He had only returned a day or two previously from Boston where he had attended the annual board meeting of Victoria Copper Mining Company. The funeral took place from the chapel at Cass and Alexandrine Avenue and he was buried in Woodmere Cemetery. The service was conducted in accordance with Masonic ritual under the auspices of Damascus Commandery. There were nine honorary pall-bearers, one of whom was Judge Clyde I. Webster. The newspaper obituary stated that 'He was always known as a good host, storyteller, dreamer and worker'.

Following the death of Charles D., Nellie experienced considerable difficulty in respect of her alimony and for a time had to rely on the largesse of Samuel B.,[44] but eventually the problem was resolved. In 1928 upon the equal division of the residue of Samuel B.'s estate between Nellie and her surviving brother James A., then resident in Lansing, by mutual agreement she inherited her father's house at 108 Center Street, Hancock. So Nellie sold her house at 204 Front Street and moved into her father's house, together with her eldest daughter Mary Estelle.

In the spring of 1929 Nellie, Estelle and at least one other visited Cornwall and stayed at the imposing Queen's Hotel on the promenade at Penzance. They visited Land's End and St Ives but to the author's knowledge did not look up any relatives. This seems somewhat surprising as Nellie's uncle, Mark Smith Harris, was still alive as were her cousins Jacob (2) Harris, Edith Harris Langford and their families. However, it must be admitted that there is no evidence that the author's mother continued a correspondence with Samuel B. following the loss of sight by her father. This omission is not easily understood as she did correspond with several other emigrant members of the family. Following their visit to Cornwall, Nellie and her party also spent some time in London, Cambridge, Oxford and Stratford-upon-Avon. It is also understood that prior to their visit to Cornwall they spent some time in Europe.

In 1941 Nellie was taken ill and for the next four and a half years was paralysed on one side. On 17 January 1946 Nellie passed away at 108 Center Street and was buried in the Samuel B. Harris family grave at Forest Hill Cemetery, Houghton. She had been an active member in the First Congregational Church and a pioneer member of Hancock Home Study Club. She had also been an early and active member of St Cecillia Club.

The Hanchette family home in Hancock on the adjacent plot to the Samuel B. Harris Home. Charles D. Hanchette built this house in the early 1890s. The building to the left of the tree was the stable and garage

Another view of the Hanchette home
Photographed and graciously presented in 1988 by the then owners Daryl and William Laitila who were restoring it to its original state

In 1915 Eleanor married Wesley John Gilson who had been born on 29 May 1890 at Idaho Springs, Colorado. Wesley was the son of Robert Wesley Gilson and Jane Ross. Wesley took himself through college, graduating from Worcester Polytechnic Institute. Following graduation he joined the Stone and Webster Management Association in Boston. Later he held an appointment with Adirondack Power and Light Corporation and, afterwards, with its successor the New York Power and Light Corporation, becoming operating Vice-President and Director. In 1944 when this latter corporation became part of Niagara/Mowhawk he became in 1950 its Vice-President and Director. Wesley was also a Director of Niagara Commercial Bank and Trust Company.

Eleanor and Wesley had five children: Wesley John Junior, born 12 July 1916 at Houghton, MI; Robert Charles, born 27 March 1918 at Laurium, MI; Eleanor Anita, born 1922; James Allyn, born 1923 and J. Ellen, born 1 July 1925 at Schenectady, NY. From first living in Houghton and Laurium, MI, they were living in Schenectady from at least 1925 and by 1946 at Ballston Spa, NY. Retiring to California, Wesley died on 10 November 1979 at Guina Hills, Los Angeles, and Eleanor passed away on 20 May 1984 at Santa Ana, CA.

Darthea Hanchette

Darthea, the fourth daughter of Nellie and Charles D., was born at Hancock, MI, on 16 November 1896. In *Polk's Directory* for 1916/17, Darthea was listed as a student living with her parents. One supposes that this was after she had graduated from Vassar College, Poughkeepsie,

Wedding group at marriage of Eleanor A. Hanchette and Wesley J. Gilson. L – R as author believed: Estelle; Bride; Bridegroom; Nellie; ? and Alice

NY, but prior to taking a teaching appointment. She had gained a Masters in history in 1917 and then did some training as a nurse. Presumably she underwent nursing training as the United States had entered the First World War in 1916. With the end of the war in 1918 she taught history at High School level.

On 9 July 1921, Darthea married Perry Wilder at Hancock. Perry had been born in Beloit, Wisconsin on 27 November 1891 and became a consulting engineer in Public Utilities. By the nature of his employment the family moved their home fairly frequently. Initially they lived in Houghton, MI, but by 1925 were in Melrose, MA. By 1928 they lived in Madison, WI, and by 1946 were in Winnette and Glencoe, Illinois.

Darthea and Perry had five children: Perry Wadsworth, born Hancock, MI, 30 May 1923; Richard Hanchette, born Melrose, MA, 13 April 1925; Ann Louise, born Melrose 16 July 1926; Nancy Jane born, Madison, WI, 2 February 1928 and Daniel Adams, born Madison 3 July 1935.

In 1986 Richard H. Wilder and his wife Jean made their third visit to the Copper Country of Upper Michigan from their home in Madison, WI. The reason for this visit was to take photographs and to gather historical information in respect of their Harris and Hanchette forebears and relatives. Richard and Jean had thought it would be fun to present the result of their peregrination to their brothers and sisters when they all met in Arizona on 16 November that same year. The occasion of the get-together was to celebrate their mother's ninetieth birthday. During their quest they visited the Samuel B. Harris retirement home at 108 Center Street, Hancock and were surprised to learn that relatives from Cornwall and Detroit had visited the house in 1985! Unfortunately, the then occupants could not remember the names of the visitors. However, when Richard and Jean later visited the MTU Library at Houghton they were asked to sign the visitors' book. Hope sprang eternal so they thought to check the visitor entries for 1985 to find the names and addresses of the relatives who had visited that year. But all in vain, for the library does not maintain visitor records for more than one calendar year. It was not until March 1992 that the author succeeded in locating Richard and Jean.

Perry passed away on 23 October 1980 aged eighty-nine and was buried at Evansville, WI. Darthea lived on for another ten years until she passed away on 27 July 1990 at Tempe, Arizona, and was brought back to Evansville for burial. She was just four months short of her ninety-third birthday.

The Family of Eleanor A. Hanchette and Wesley J. Gilson

Eleanor A. Hanchette
b. 1891 Hancock, MI
d. 1984 Santa Ana, CA

1915

Wesley J. Gilson
b. 1890 Idaho Springs,
   Colorado
d. 1979 Guina Hills,
   Los Angeles

Robert Charles
b. 1918 Laurium, MI.
d. 1952 Ashland, Kentucky
m. Dorothy Speers
Dorothy born 1919
Philadelphia.

Their son, Robert Wesley,
was born in 1943 at
Albany, New York, and
lives with his wife Mary
at San Jose, California.

Eleanor Anita
b. 1922
Assume died
as an infant

James Allyn
b. 1923
Was a fighter pilot in the
Second World War and
flew P51 Mustangs. During
the Battle of the Bulge
1944 - 45, he landed behind
enemy lines to rescue a
friend who had been shot
down. After the war he was
much involved in the
aeronautics industry.

Wesley John
b. 1916 Houghton, MI.
Graduated from Cornell University
in 1937 with a degree in Electrical
Engineering and joined General
Electric the same year; held
several appointments in Erie,
Pennsylvania and Fort Wayne.

Served in United States
Army Signal Corps in the
Second World War.

Joined the large Steam-Turbine
Generator Dept. in 1947.
Received a General
Electric Managers' Award in 1954.

He was the author of several
technical papers, and became
unit manager of General
Electric Turbines.

J. Ellen
b. 1925 Schenectady, NY
EDUCATION:
St Agnes School, Albany, New York
The Baldwin School, Bryn Mawr, Pennsylvania
Bradford College, Bradford, Massachusetts. AA
University of North Carolina, Chapel Hill, North Carolina. BA
Fairfield University, Fairfield, Connecticut, MA
Western University Graduate School of Theology. D.Min
USC Lenard Andrus School of Gerontology, Los Angeles
UNDERGRADUATE AND GRADUATE SCHOOLS:
University of Nice, Nice, France
Silvermine College of Arts, Silvermine, Connecticut
University of Connecticut, New Haven, Connecticut
Pratt Institute, Brooklyn, New York
Laguna College of Art, Laguna Beach, California
DAMA Art Foundry, Norwalk, Connecticut (Apprentice
 Craftsperson, bronze casting, chasing, welding, etc)
Studied with Vincenzio Loggario and Anthony Amato,
Master Stone Carvers
JURIED SHOWS:
Silvermine College of Art, Silvermine, Connecticut
University of Connecticut, New Haven, Connecticut
Waveny Art Barn, New Canaan, Connecticut
New Canaan Society of the Arts, New Canaan, Connecticut
Laguna College of Art, Laguna Beach, California
Lighthouse Art Center, Crescent City, California
Hanson Howard Gallery, Ashland, Oregon
Sun River, Sun River, Oregon
Laura Knott Gallery, Bradford, Massachusetts

Alice Hanchette

Alice, the fifth and last child of Nellie and Charles D., was born at Hancock on 3 December 1900. Alice received the usual education of this family and then trained as a nurse at Harper Hospital, Detroit. It was in Detroit that she met Dunbar Dene MacMechan, the son of Mrs MacMechan whom her father subsequently married after his divorce from Alice's mother.

During a visit to Europe Alice informed her mother that she intended marrying Dunbar. The announcement caused her mother great distress as Nellie could not contemplate such a union. This resulted in Alice running away from her mother and returning to New York where she married Dunbar at the Church around the Corner.

Dunbar was born on 26 June 1893 and had been a pilot in the First World War. They had one son, Michael David. Dunbar passed away at Grosse Pointe, MI, 14 February 1979 aged eighty-five years. Alice passed away on 21 August 1980 in her eightieth year.

The above drawing of the JEGA Gallery and Sculpture Garden in the Historic Railroad District at Ashland, Oregon was built by J. Ellen G. Austin herself a sculptor, who was also responsible for the design concept.

At the official opening, J. Ellen declared, 'I built this Art Co-operative out of a concern that there wasn't a place for people to express themselves and learn through art. Both live-in and guest artists will be operating open workshops that focus on various modes of art such as music, poetry, painting, photography and sculpture.'

In a letter to the author in January 1995, J. Ellen wrote, 'I hope my mission of educating the many ways of seeing, perspective, and absorbing diverse culture through the arts will show the greed, environmental destruction and violence of our era.'

One of J. Ellen's sculptures The Ghost of Valdez depicts seals made of white Italian translucent alabaster on lava rock splashed with black oil, to symbolise the environmental disaster of the Exxon Valdez oil tanker spillage.

Grandchildren of Samuel B. Harris and Mary Bennett. February 1950. Left to right: Alice Hanchette MacMechan; Darthea Hanchette Wilder; Eleanor Anita Hanchette Gilson and Mary Estelle Hanchette Seeber

Great-grandchildren of Samuel B. Harris and Mary Bennett
Daniel A. Wilder, b. 1935 and Richard Hanchette Wilder, b. 1925. Photograph taken February 1950

The Wilder Family

John Luther Harris

John Luther Harris circa 1890

John L. , the fourth and last child of Samuel B. and Mary, was born at Eagle Harbor, MI, on 21 June 1868 at the time his father was employed by Eagle Harbor Properties. The family moved to Ontonagon County in 1871.

We have no detailed knowledge of the initial education of John L. but the 1880 census for Greenland Township records him as being at school. The Michigan Mining School at Houghton was set up in 1885 and commenced its first classes in 1886. It grew to be internationally famous, and is now Michigan Technological University. John L. enrolled in the first classes. The education requirements for entry were very exacting. Additionally, no student under the age of eighteen was admitted to a course years, except upon ample evidence of exceptional ability.[51] John L. would not have been eighteen until 21 June of the year of his entry, and so the foregoing indicates that he had probably graduated from High School with distinction.

John L. graduated from the Mining School in 1888 with a Bachelor of Science degree. The graduate was then required to undertake practical work in some capacity in the mining industry during the following two years. To this end John L. was employed as a surveyor on the Quincy Mine Railroad. Following this practical work he did a post-graduate course at the Massachusetts Institute of Technology in Boston. In a letter dated 26 October 1890 from R.H. Richards of the Institute to

Dr Wadsworth of the Michigan Mining School, he wrote: 'We have two of your boys, John L. Harris and Joseph Daniel, with us. The former is doing well, the latter is not with me so cannot judge.

Sometime after his return from Boston to continue his career with Quincy Mining Company, John L. became President of the Alumni Association of Michigan College of Mines, a position he held for a number of years. A letter dated 28 July 1894 still exists, from John L. to Dr Wadsworth, then in Marquette, agreeing the date of the Alumni Meeting and annual dinner to be held at the Douglas House, Houghton.

John L. continued to serve the Quincy Mining Company in various capacities and became known and respected for his marked ability in his chosen career. He was appointed Assistant Mining Engineer in 1895 and Chief Mining Engineer in 1897 to both the Quincy Company and Quincy and Torch Lake Railroad. In fact, he was being groomed both practically and technically to succeed his father as the mine agent. There can be no doubt that this was with the acquiescence and support of the Company President, Thomas F. Mason. In December 1897, work commenced on the excavation and equipping of a new shaft at Quincy which was designated as No. 7. John L. planned and superintended the work in connection with this project. Because of the fact that the lodes at some point had a varied angle of dip he elected to sink the shaft in the form of a catenary rather than a straightforward incline. This was indeed unique and at the time the only shaft in the world to be formed in this manner. Unusually work on this shaft was commenced in the lower levels after extending the main drifts and driving cross-cuts to intersect the proposed line of the shaft. By this latter means it was possible to sink and raise simultaneously. In fact, the press described the construction of the shaft in this form and manner as being classed among the most successful accomplishments in the history of the district.[52] Special mention should also be made of the very accurate mining survey control required in a project of this nature.

According to the authors of *Old Reliable*, John L. was appointed Assistant Superintendent to his father in June 1899 at a salary $3,500 per year. This suggests that he had been acting in this capacity for some time with the agreement of Thomas F. Mason but the appointment was not promulgated until after Mason's death on 2 January 1899. Obviously the Company was honouring the predetermined wishes of the late President, despite W.R. Todd's personal dislike of the Harrises. From this point onwards the mutual trust and confidence between the Board of Quincy Mining Company and the Harrises disappeared, never to be reinstated. As previously mentioned, Samuel B. resigned in 1902 after nineteen years' service.

The Wilder Family

Hancock, MI
9 July 1921

Darthea Hanchette ——————— Perry Wilder
b. 1896 Hancock, MI   b. 1891 Beloit, WI
d. 1990 Tempe, AZ   d. 1980

Buried Evansville, WI   Buried Evansville, WI

Perry Wadsworth
b. 1923 Hancock, MI
m. Mary Price

Perry was an Industrial
Manager.

Perry and Mary had
two sons and a
daughter.

Ann Louise
d. 1936 Melrose, MA
m. Stanley Paull Dittmar

Stanley was a Regional
Manufacturing Manager,
(Shipping Containers).
Stanley died 1988.

Ann and Stanley had a
daughter and three sons.

Daniel Adams
b. 1935 Madison, WI
m. Donna Miller

Daniel owns a corporate
Relocation Company.

Richard Hanchette
b. 1925 Madison, WI
m. Jean Williams

Richard was a Director of
Recruitment for a Tech.
Electronic School.

Richard and Jean have a
son and a daughter.

Nancy Jane
b. Madison, WI
m. Daniel Zahzrko

Daniel was a Pharmacologist,
Ph.D.

Nancy and Daniel had two
sons and a daughter.

It was generally assumed by the outside world that John L, with his proven technical and practical ability and in-depth knowledge of Quincy, would be immediately promoted to succeed his father. This was not to be. W.R. Todd wished to find someone else of equal or superior ability and decided to give himself time to find another person. According to newspaper reports, John L. was granted a temporary position as acting superintendent. Obviously W.R. Todd's initial quest for some other person was not successful, so after several months John L. was appointed Superintendent at a salary of $7,500, which was very much lower than that paid to his father. However, it must be admitted that it was back-dated to his appointment as acting superintendent.

Outside of his personal anti-Harris stance, it appears that W.R. Todd and his Board could not understand or accept the quite dramatic change which had taken place in the character of the Quincy orebody. Whereas masses of native copper weighing anywhere from 100 to 300 tons had been relatively commonplace and constituted about one-third of the total product, it now only averaged one-tenth. The native copper could be sent direct to the smelter, thus saving the cost of milling. Endeavouring to overcome these problems, John L. continued development of the mine to locate additional orebodies, a procedure vital to prolonging the life of any mine. In other ways he sought to reduce production costs. Some of the measures that he put in motion included the introduction of electric haulage underground, which was highly successful. Also, he had five 100-ton rock-bins secured to the hanging wall of the shafts which served the main production levels. In addition, the skips for hauling the broken rock to surface were increased in capacity from five and three-quarter to eight tons. All these and other improvements reduced production costs, enabling the company to pay dividends in excess of half a million dollars for each year in which he was superintendent. Despite all John L's efforts, W.R. Todd and his Board displayed no enthusiasm or appreciation. In fact, it seems that they were unable to understand that any mine is a wasting asset.

In July 1905, W.R. Todd engaged Charles L. Lawton to assume the post of assistant superintendent. Then, in the following November, he notified John L. that Charles L. Lawton was to take over as superintendent with effect 1 December.[53] Not surprisingly, John L. resigned. Apparently, W.R. Todd did not tell John L. face to face but sent the communication from his New York office. From the company's point of view, it was essential that there was continuity of management at the mine but the appointment of Charles L.Lawton for three months as assistant to John L. with the intention to replace the latter, cannot be described as top of the class in ethics. Charles L. Lawton was a brother to Swaby Lawton, the partner of Charles D. Hanchette in a law practice in Hancock. In fact, the Lawtons, Hanchettes and Harrises were friends.

The entirely unexpected resignation of John L. caused the various Copper Country newspapers to reminisce about the performance of both John L. and Samuel B. Harris. They censured the company for what, in fact, amounted to the constructive dismissal of John L. Abstracts from the newspapers are as follows:

The retirement of John L. Harris means the end of the Harris regime in local management of Quincy. Samuel B. Harris his father was the man of all men who deserve the credit for placing Quincy in the (Old Reliable) dividend paying class and keeping it there. John Luther Harris his son continued the policies successfully. The Quincy was of high standing in local mining circles as an economically managed, conservatively managed corporation. Samuel B. Harris and John L. Harris have had much to do with making it such and keeping it in such condition. John L. Harris followed mining all his life and has been more than successful. In whatever path his future may be directed we bespeak success for him and wish him well. A wish that is fathered as much by his excellent mining capabilities as by his pleasant and agreeable personality. Mr Todd of Quincy Mining Company and John L. Harris, Superintendent, could not agree on certain things and Mr Todd has chosen Charles L. Lawton to succeed him. This will be a surprise to many people as Mr John L. Harris was looked upon as a fixture. He is a capable man thoroughly schooled in the copper mining business, and knew every inch of the Quincy. We used to meet him there when we were officially inspecting the property and always found him a courteous and obliging gentleman who knew what he was talking about. It was always a pleasure to visit the property because of his association and that of his esteemed father Samuel B. Harris. Of course John L. Harris could not put more copper in the rock than had been provided by nature. He made a fine record in saving what there was and in getting the rock cheaply to surface. The Quincy copper content of the rock has steadily decreased. This could only be offset by high rock production and greater tonnage of the lode treated as the mass work lessened perceptively. The shafts were rigged to draw the masses into special pockets. Now about only one-eleventh of the output is mass and barrel work, and this makes a great difference in the cost of making a pound of refined metal. The Company has its own furnaces and nothing is lacking to take advantage of the slightest opportunity for saving. The Quincy has been well run by the Harris people. There have been no senseless frills or fads or costly experiments that failed, nothing but straight mining, milling and smelting. We know nothing of the differences between John L. Harris and his company. There will be plenty who will want his services.

We admire Mr Harris's very frank manner in quitting the company. He doesn't quibble about the facts and doesn't attempt to make anyone believe that he quit the position because he wanted to, or because he felt a call somewhere else.

It would please a great many Lake people to see Mr Todd's eastern management of the Quincy hoisted instead of the Harris local management.

The circumstances leading to the change which was not unexpected and partially known to the writer, are not particularly creditable to the gentlemen in the east. In the writer's opinion the best interest of the mine as well as the best interests of the shareholders demands the retention of Superintendent Harris, and time will but emphasis that opinion. The Quincy is a mine that wants to be thoroughly understood, to be worked with great success, but of course if gentlemen in the east know all about running the mine, as some claim, it possibly may not matter who is designated superintendent at this end.

Under the Harrises, mining at Quincy has been developed from the crude methods to the most elaborate and perfect of modern systems. The Quincy is one of the largest, best known and most presentative in the Lake Superior copper mining district. Under Capt. Samuel B. Harris and his son John L. Harris the mine has seen many changes. It is only eight years since the miners went to work underground on a man-engine, the old inclines which were as crooked as a ram's horn have been replaced with straight shafts and winding engines of modern design. The changes and straightening of the working shafts, putting double skip-roads and systemizing matters generally have been made with such efficiency that there is a distinguished reputation attached to the name of Harris in the mining world. New shafts have been sunk, the surface plant remodelled on modern lines, a railway has been built, new mills erected, smelters completed and dock construction, and the mine's operating power has been changed from steam to electricity, the operations involving the expenditure of millions of dollars. Notwithstanding this, so conservative has been the management that dividends have been paid regularly since 1862, with the exception of the years 1866 and 1867. John L. Harris brought with

him to Quincy Mine an inherited loyalty and ambition worthy of his large opportunities.

The press of Michigan seems to be united in its opinion of Mr Todd and the retirement of Superintendent Harris, and the expressions agree with those originally given publicly in these columns. Both displeasure and regret have been manifested and action of the company two months ago dispensing with the services of Superintendent John L. Harris who with his father for over twenty years directed the organisation that made Quincy what it is today. The best and most effectively equipped amyglamoid[54] producer in the district. There is but one opinion in the district and that is that the best interests of the company have been badly sacrificed to personal feelings.

When the *Financial News* says the Copper Country people including a large number of shareholders did not like the way the Quincy treated John L. Harris, it doesn't get away from the truth for one solitary moment.

In spite of the fact that the Quincy cost for mining a ton of rock is less today than ever before in the history of the mine, and is among the lowest on the Lake being about one dollar fifty cents per ton inclusive of smelting and construction. Last year as will be shown from an inspection of the annual report of the company, adding mining costs and taxes and dividing the sum by the number of tons handled it was one dollar fifty-three cents and in 1903 one dollar sixty-one cents whilst in 1900 it was one dollar ninety-six cents. It cost no more to mine a ton of rock containing fifty pounds of copper than a ton containing only ten pounds, but the cost per pound of copper would be five times in the latter instance than in the former. These are probably factors that led to this difference of opinion between the eastern officers and the local management of Quincy operations.

Extracts are generally from *The Daily Mining Gazette*, *Evening Journal*, *The Times* and so on.

Although Charles L. Lawton served the company for a very long period before his death in 1946, he never had an easy ride. According to the authors of *Old Reliable* he had many battles with W.R. Todd and his successor. Initially W.R. Todd gave him a one-year contract followed by a three-year extension. The members of the Board were apparently more or less pleased with his performance but in 1913 gave W.R. Todd absolute authority to sack him if the former thought it was in the best interest

CERTIFIED COPY OF RECORD OF DEATH.　　　　　　2161

STATE OF MICHIGAN,
COUNTY OF ......Houghton......... } ss.

I,............Nancy Fenili...........................Clerk of the County of......Houghton.................., and of the Circuit Court thereof,

the same being a Court of Record having a seal, do hereby certify that the following is a copy of the record of death of......John Luther Harris.................

now remaining in my office, and of the whole thereof, viz:

RECORD NUMBER	DATE OF DEATH			FULL NAME OF THE DECEASED	MALE OR FEMALE	WHITE, BLACK, MULATTO, ETC.	MARRIED, SINGLE, WIDOW OR WIDOWER	AGE			PLACE OF DEATH
	MONTH	DAY	YEAR					YEARS	MONTHS	DAYS	
1	Jan.	1	1927	Harris, John Luther	Male	White	Single	58	6	11	City of Hancock

DISEASE OR CAUSE OF DEATH	BIRTHPLACE	OCCUPATION	PARENTS		DATE OF RECORD
			NAMES	BIRTHPLACE	
Acetanilid Bromine Poisining	Michigan	Mining Engineer	Samuel B. Harris	England	April 6, 1927
			Mary Bennett	England	

In Testimony Whereof, I have hereunto set my hand and affixed the seal of the Circuit Court, the......25th......day of......October......A. D. 19.93.

Nancy Fneili　　　　　　　　　　CLERK.

By......................................DEPUTY CLERK.

Death certificate of John L.

of the company. It is reported that in 1924 at a Board Meeting, W.R. Todd 'delivered a blistering attack on Lawton's overall performance, citing a disastrous effort to import Mexicans as one example of his incompetence.' So the discord as between W.R. Todd and the Harrises continued with Charles L. Lawton. The real reason for the discord is not difficult to discern. Obviously from the time of Thomas F. Mason's death, W.R. Todd started and continued to burn his boats behind him, as far as superintendents were concerned. In fact, he made approaches to several other people before engaging C.L. Lawton and they bluntly refused. (Indeed, there had been other resignations in Ontonagon County of mine officials of a company controlled by W.R. Todd and his associates. It is obvious that there were no better people clamouring to serve under W.R. Todd. It seems that W.R. Todd felt very insecure at the head of this huge enterprise and tried to imply by shouting and domineering that he knew best) A summary of the history of Quincy Mine is aptly detailed in certain chapter headings in *Old Reliable*:

Disappointing Decade　　1846 – 1856
Pioneer Profits　　　　　1856 – 1870
Greatest Growth　　　　 1870 – 1905
Boom to Bust　　　　　　1905 – 1931

Whether the availability of John L. prompted the setting up of Hancock Consolidated Mining Company is not known, but certainly John D. Cuddihy and his associates had the company set up and ready to commence operations by the 11 June 1906 with John L. as superintendent. One is not sure if John L. entertained great expectations for the ultimate financial success of the company but he was nevertheless prepared to contribute the best of his engineering and managerial ability. He took a modest holding of ten shares at $15 each, but possibly these were qualifying shares.

After eleven years of considerable effort in bringing the mine to its maximum potential, John L. decided to retire and tendered his resignation 1 June 1917. He was succeeded by Mr C.E. Wood, who had previously managed the Lake Copper Company.[55] However, the mine closed only eighteen months later in January 1919.

John L. had been one of the original organisers of Northern Michigan Building and Loan Association and in retirement occupied a prominent position in civil and political affairs and in the mining industry. In 1916 he had been granted the degree of Engineer of Mines in recognition of his valuable contribution to mining. He was a member of the County Board of Supervisors and later became Chairman of Hancock Republican Committee of which he had always been a staunch member. He also enjoyed golf and yachting, being a member of the Portage Lake Golf Club and the Onigaming Yacht Club. He was also a member of the Masonic Blue Lodge, Gate of Temple Chapter, Palestine Commandery, Scottish Rite Masons and Hancock Lodge of Elks.

Following this very full life, John L. died in tragic circumstances on 1 January 1927. In discussing this distressing event with his great-niece Ellen in 1995, she vouchsafed the opinion that he became ill with an incurable disease. This raises the question if it was cancer, the disease from which his mother had died. If so, he would have been only too aware of the agony she had suffered. The *Daily Mining Gazette* of 3 January 1927 described John L. as a highly respected resident, adding that his prominence caused the news of his death to spread rapidly to every section of the Copper Country. Also that he had been popular with those in his employ, and that his passing removed from the district one of its highly respected residents and the regard which the news of his death was received was attested by numerous expressions of sorrow. Interment was in Forest Hill Cemetery, Houghton, alongside his mother.

The Samuel B. Harris Family Grave in Forest Hill Cemetery, Houghton, Michigan
Interred here are:
Samuel B. Harris and his wife Mary Bennett Harris
His daughter Ellen Jane (Nellie) Harris Hanchette
His younger son John Luther Harris
His granddaughter Mary Estelle Hanchette Seeber and her husband Professor Rex Seeber

9. Christiania (Kitty) Harris

Christiania (Harris) Trevithick
Photograph taken by her nephew John Alfred (1) Harris

Kitty, the third daughter and eighth child of John (2) and Christian, was born at Six Chimneys on 18 August 1836 and was baptized at Camborne Parish Church on 10 September the same year.

Just as James had escorted Samuel to the National School at Camborne, so in turn Samuel escorted Kitty, probably commencing when Kitty was about eight years old. On the 1851 Camborne census, when she would have been only four months short of her fifteenth birthday, Kitty was recorded as a scholar which means that her period at school was the longest of any member of this family, seemingly not less than seven years.

With little choice in respect of her employment, despite her lengthy period at school, it was almost inevitable that she should 'work to mine' which was the description of her occupation in the Camborne 1861 census. She was doubtless employed on the dressing floors carrying out manual work in the open air with little or no protection from the elements. The effects of this exposure caused her great suffering in later years. The 1871 and 1881 census returns describe Kitty as a milliner, showing that she had managed to escape the drudgery of the mine dressing floors for a more congenial form of employment.

On 23 January 1877, when forty years of age, Kitty was married at Camborne Wesleyan Church to a widower, William Henry Trevithick. William Henry, who was in business in Troon, had originally been a miner and had spent some time in the mines in Mexico.[1] He had been born at Sithney, near Helston in Cornwall, the son of Richard Trevithick, a mine steam-engine operator. William had lost his first wife, Mary Rule Webster, nine months previously. He had been left with several children, four of whom were under fourteen years of age, including a baby.

Unfortunately, Kitty and William Henry's life together was cruelly terminated when, after a relatively short illness, William Henry died on 30 November, 1878, just twenty-two months after their marriage. A prominent Freemason and Founder Member of Mount Edgcumbe Lodge at Camborne, William was buried at Treslothan in accordance with Masonic Ceremony by his express wish and by reason of a dispensation granted by the Provincial Grand Master, the Earl of Mount Edgcumbe. It was the first Masonic funeral to be held in the Troon area[2] and it is recorded that about a thousand people assembled at the graveside.

In his Will, which he made only five days before he died, William Henry bequeathed to Kitty the sum of £7 to be paid to her as soon as convenient after his death. Additionally, Kitty was to occupy, if she wished, a house in New Row, Troon, which William Henry let at that time to a William Barnes; alternatively, she was to receive the rent from this house as long as she remained William Henry's widow and did not marry again. On Kitty's death the property was to form part of William Henry's residuary estate.

William Henry's eldest daughter, Elizabeth Mary, aged twenty-two or thereabouts, was required under the will to take over and run the grocery and drapery business, and also to take over the attached house. Interestingly she was also required to provide a home for her brothers and sisters who were under twenty-one years old, and to provide proper clothing and education for such children so long as they were under twenty-one.

Apparently the children could not accept Kitty as a mother, a situation which was obviously known to William Henry when he made his will. Beyond doubt this situation became an even greater problem to the children after their father's death. There is, however, no doubt that it was William Henry's wish that Kitty and his children should have a home together despite the fact that he had stipulated that Kitty was to pay for her own maintenance! In the event, by the time of the 1881 census, three of the children, Lucretia, Phillip R. (Fred) and Annie R. were living with Elizabeth and her husband Mark Trebilcock. The fourth child, Olivia, was living with her maternal grandmother, Mary Rule Webster. Kitty had returned to live with her mother and the family of her brother, Mark Smith Harris.

Kitty continued in her occupation as a milliner and subsequently as a grocery assistant, but after a time had to give it up because of her rheumatism. In this situation, despite having the rent of the house in New Row, money was scarce but the position was somewhat relieved by her brothers overseas who, from time to time, sent her gifts of money. Sending money to relatives back home by emigrants was quite commonplace and indeed the facilities for doing so seem to have been established at an early date.

In 1895-96 Kitty entered, as it were, the legal arena in that she, on her own initiative, submitted a case for a claim to the ownership of Roswarne House, Camborne. At this time a dispute had arisen as to the rightful ownership of the property, resulting in a lawsuit at Bodmin Assizes in June 1895 and the Queen's Bench, London, in August the same year.[3] At the time, ownership was claimed by L.S.L. van Grute, a half-blood relative of William Harris Hartley, the latter being a grandson of William Harris who at one time owned and lived at Roswarne and died there in 1815. This William Harris had been Sheriff of Cornwall. Van Gruten won his case. Roswarne was subsequently sold to James M. Holman in 1911. The Holman family, mining machinery manufacturers, lived there until the house became the Head Office of Holman Bros. Limited in 1951. Currently the house is a residential and nursing home. Apparently the issue of its historical ownership was complicated in that it was far from clear if certain descriptions referred to the estate, the adjacent land or the house. Although Kitty's submission was unsuccessful, it was said by some people to have been as good a case as any other!

Kitty died at Pendarves Street, Troon, at the home of her brother Mark, on 16 March 1901, at sixty-five years of age. She was buried in Troon Cemetery. Her obituary records that there were many signs of respect for her, the house blinds being drawn throughout the village on the day of the funeral. Among family mourners was the poet's wife, Jane, then aged eighty, who had travelled up from Porthleven. Charitably, several of Kitty's stepchildren also attended.

A deeply religious person, Kitty had attended Troon Wesleyan Chapel all her life and had been a church member for fifty years. Additionally, she had taught in the Sunday School for over thirty years. Her obituary states that she had been one of the first people to distribute religious tracts in Troon. One wonders if these tracts those written by John (3).

Kitty had been very attached to her next younger brother, Benjamin (4), who had emigrated to the Copper Country of Upper Michigan in 1865 and who by the time of her death had risen to a very responsible position with the great Calumet and Hecla Mining Company in Lake Linden. When Benjamin (4) received news of Kitty's death, he composed four verses of farewell, the first and last verse reading as follows:

> My sister is gone,
> She is gone to her rest.
> She has laid her burden down.
> She will weep no more, nor tire with pain,
> For the goal is reached she sought to gain,
> And the cross exchanged for a crown.
>
> My sister is gone,
> And we bid her good-bye.
> Till we meet on the other shore,
> And mingle anew, amid scenes of delight,
> With tireless fingers, and days without night,
> And joys that will last evermore.

10. Benjamin (4) Harris

Benjamin (4) Harris 1838-1915
Photograph taken 1911

Early Life and Marriage

Benjamin (4), the ninth child and sixth son of John (2) and Christian, was born at Six Chimneys, Bolenowe Carn on 6 July 1838 and baptized at Camborne Parish Church on 15 September the same year.

There is every indication that Benjamin also attended the National School at Camborne, undoubtedly being led there initially by his sister Kitty. Throughout his life Benjamin (4) held Kitty in high esteem. There was an affinity between these two which no doubt developed from the time when she escorted him to school, and in this and other ways became a second mother to him. He never forgot her, and following the early death of her husband he frequently sent her monetary gifts to help ease the burden of her life. It was at the little National School that Benjamin developed an interest in books which remained with him throughout his life; in fact, his obituary stated that 'good books had a charm for him', and as far as he was concerned he possessed an enquiring and inventive mind.

By the 1851 Camborne census, just prior to his thirteenth birthday, Benjamin (4) was underground mining copper, undoubtedly at Dolcoath, and by the 1861 census, when the mine had entered the tin zone, he was listed as a tin miner. It is quite probable that before going underground, Benjamin, like John (3), spent some time working on the dressing floors on surface; this being the case, it would have provided for him an insight, however brief, of the intricate process of ore refinement which he would turn to his advantage and that of the mining company for whom he later worked in the Keweenaw Peninsula of Michigan.

Benjamin (4) had, of course, moved to Troon[1] to live with his mother and remaining brothers and Kitty when he was eleven years old, and along with the other members of the family attended Troon Wesleyan Sunday School which possessed a fair library. Beyond this, despite his hard life as a miner, he continued a self-imposed regime of private study, not least to become a fully accredited local preacher. He was admitted 'On Trial' by the Camborne Wesleyan Circuit on 25 February 1858 and within a couple of years was accepted on 'Full Plan'. It could be said that in this context he was following in John's (3) footsteps, but there were other influences at work in Methodism and in the mining field. Indeed, in Camborne at this time these two sources of influence went hand in hand in the daily lives of such people as Dr George Smith and Capt. Charles Thomas, together with the latter's son Capt. Josiah Thomas. Whilst not suggesting that they took a personal interest in Benjamin (4), it has to be accepted that their example was there for all to see and Benjamin (4) was observant. Dr Smith (1800-1868) and Capt. Charles Thomas (1794-1868) had both risen from humble beginnings but never lost the common touch. They were local preachers and their names were to be found, along with those of Capt. Josiah Thomas and Benjamin (4), on the Camborne Circuit Wesleyan Preachers' Plan. Dr Smith, a scholar and industrialist, was a person of remarkable talent and Capt. Charles Thomas, by his close study of the Dolcoath orebody, coupled with his tenacity of purpose and ability to convince the mine owners of the efficacy of his arguments, prolonged the life of the mine for another fifty years and made it extremely profitable. It was under the overall management of Capt. Charles Thomas that Benjamin (4) laboured as a miner in Dolcoath. Capt. Josiah Thomas (1834-1901) was trained by his father to become manager of the mine. Benjamin would have been aware that Josiah was working underground when only thirteen, that by seventeen he was employed as a clerk in the office and sometime later became an agent. As a matter of record, Josiah was appointed manager in 1866. This progression would not have been unnoticed by Benjamin; indeed, he followed the fortunes of Dolcoath and Capt. Josiah for the whole of his life, requesting his younger brother Mark to forward to him in American the company's Annual Reports. There was yet another member of the Thomas family: Capt. James

Thomas (1778-1867) of Bolenowe, mine agent, local preacher and great-uncle of Capt. Josiah Thomas. It seems reasonable to assume that Capt. James Thomas was also a mentor to Benjamin (4), not least because they would have associated in Methodist circles and Capt. James had helped John (3) and permitted the latter to use his library, but most importantly because Benjamin (4) was courting his granddaughter Jane Florence Allen. Jane and her mother, Mary Thomas Allen (c.1818-1879), lived at Bolenowe with Capt. James Thomas. In the 1841 census Mary was described as a schoolmistress and by the 1851 census as housekeeper to her parents. Actually, Jane's maternal grandmother died just a few weeks after the 1851 census. Mary had married John Allen, a sojourner and tailor, in 1837. In 1839, John Allen went to America leaving his wife and baby daughter Jane at home. After keeping in contact for a few years, John was subsequently never heard of again.[2]

Benjamin (4) and Jane were married at Camborne Wesleyan Church on 28 May 1863 and set up house at Troon Moor, most probably in the same house as the poet had lived and in fact still owned. Here their first child James Hugh (1) Harris was born on 20 December 1864 and baptized at Troon Wesleyan Church on 27 February 1865.

Benjamin (4) was obviously building up a library of his own as we find that he became a pre-publication subscriber for three of his brother's books:

Land's End, Kynance Cove and Other Poems	1858
The Mountain Prophet, The Mine and other Poems	1860
The Story of Carn Brea, Essays and Poems	1863

The Decision to Emigrate and the Journey to the Keweenaw Peninsula

The decision to emigrate was jointly taken by Benjamin (4) and his younger brother Jacob (1) but is in a way not easy to understand. As far as their employment at Dolcoath was concerned, the prospects for the mine looked good. It had paid its first dividend on tin in 1853 when the price of a share was £90, and by 1857 the same share was worth £210! By 1863 it was declared the largest tin mine in Cornwall.[3] Admittedly it was to have its ups and downs due to fluctuations in the price of tin and the quality of the orebody, but it was well managed and must have appeared likely to continue for a long period. It did not finally close until 1923, but obviously Benjamin (4) and Jacob (1) were not to know that it would have such a long life. Maybe, despite the prosperity of the mine, they did not feel that there was any prospect of advancement for themselves. They would, of course, have been fully aware of the progress of their brothers already in

America. William B. was now farming eighty acres in south-west Wisconsin. Matthew (2), despite his accident in 1861, was apparently settled and contented in the mining field in Ontonagon County, Michigan, whilst Samuel B. was now a mine captain of Mesnard and Pontiac Mine in Houghton County, Michigan. Also their brother-in-law, James Sims, had entered the Methodist Episcopal Ministry in Wisconsin. The ultimate success of the Copper Country of Michigan was not yet manifest and it was not generally realised that in due course it would produce more wealth than all the gold mined in California![4] Samuel B. could not have foreseen this but it seems likely that he had conveyed to them his opinion of the possibilities and prospects of this embryo mining field.

Finally the decision was taken, and as far as Benjamin (4) was concerned this was a whole new phase of his life so he took Jane and their young son James Hugh (1) with him. James Hugh (1) was only five months old. On the assumption that they had been living in the poet's house at Troon Moor, the time was fast approaching when they would have to move for reasons over which they had no control. Building of the row of houses on the north side of the present Pendarves Street had commenced from the Treslothan or western end in the late 1850s and as the building works continued eastward it would have been apparent to them that their house would have to be demolished. In fact, John (3) relinquished the lease in 1869.

The whole of their journey was to be less complicated and much more comfortable than that previously experienced by other members of the family. They set out on 20 May 1865. It was now possible to travel direct by rail from Camborne to Liverpool, although there was the inconvenience of having to change trains because of the difference in gauge of certain sections. Brunel's great masterpiece, the Royal Albert Bridge, now spanned the River Tamar between Cornwall and Devon, having been opened in 1859. Arriving in Liverpool, the little party including Jacob (1) took second class passage on the steamship *City of Washington* of 2,386 tons burthen. According to Jacob's (1) son, the 'pare' in which his father and Benjamin (4) had worked in Dolcoath had, by Jacob's (1) astute observation of the orebody, led them to a very rich mass of ore and this in turn enabled them to put by a fair sum of money for their journey. They arrived in New York on 6 June.

The third and final stage of their journey was now to begin, but unlike Matthew (2) and Nanny in 1855 and Samuel B. and Mary in 1854, they did not detour to Wisconsin but, as recorded in Benjamin's (4) biographical sketch,[5] 'Went first to Lake Superior'. In this context they would have known that for the past twelve months Samuel B. had been mine captain at Mesnard and Pontiac Mine at Portage Lake and was most likely to be in a position to offer them employment; but they probably did not know until they arrived at Portage Lake that Samuel B. was relinquishing his position at Mesnard and Pontiac Mine in order to accept a similar position at Phoenix Mine in Keweenaw County on 16 June. Possibly this surprised them and may have been something of a disappointment or setback. However, they decided to go to Phoenix and chance their lot with Samuel B. It should not be assumed they entertained any thoughts to the effect that by right Samuel B. had to find them employment. This approach would not have been in line with their upbringing or nature.

It will be seen that the arrival of Benjamin (4) and his little party, as well as the whole journey from Troon, had been a quite civilised arrangement compared with that of William B. Harris and James Sims in 1845. How thrilled and delighted they would have been to be greeted by Samuel B. and his family. Although thousands of miles lay between them and Troon it must have seemed as if they had come 'home'.

Benjamin (4) and Family in the Copper Country

While, for the first year at least, Benjamin (4) was employed at Phoenix Mine, some time during the next six years he worked at Delaware, Central and Schoolcraft Mines. According to his biographical sketch, all of these employments were in a labouring capacity as a 'copper washer'. However, it appears that he may have returned to Phoenix Mine for a second spell because he and his family are recorded on the 22 June 1870 census for Houghton Township, Keweenaw County, where he was listed as an engine driver, their Post Office being Phoenix, but a month or so later on 18 July census for Calumet he is shown as a boarder in the home of Mary Paul, which suggests that he was then employed at Schoolcraft Mine just east of Calumet Mine. Initially the family lived at Eagle River immediately north of Phoenix. Prior to 9 March 1866 they had moved into a log cabin at Phoenix where their second child James Hugh (2) was born. There they remained until 1872 when they all moved to Lake Linden. Their third child, Mary J. (Mamie) was also born in the cabin in 1869. Obviously during his employments at Central and Delaware Mines, Benjamin (4) lodged in these localities while Jane and the children remained at Phoenix. These must have been lonely times for Jane.

The reason for Benjamin's (4) changes of employment during his first seven years in the Upper Peninsula should not be looked upon as his seeing greener fields at every move, but as necessary and prudent due to the state of the mining industry. That these were relatively early years in the growth of the Copper Country. There were continual changes in ownership and organisation of the mines, coupled with inadequate procedures for treating the broken rock and extracting the copper. Some of the treatment plants had been designed by inexperienced and unqualified people. All this, combined with poor management skills of the promoters, resulted in undermining the confidence of the workforce. Take the Phoenix Mine, for example, which was a good producer of copper. There were several years when production amounted to over a million pounds but for some reason it never paid a dividend. One can only infer that this latter situation was due to poor management. Benjamin (4) was interested in companies who paid dividends, as witnessed in later years when he requested the author's grandfather to send him copies of the Annual Reports of Dolcoath Mine. Nevertheless, out of this early and somewhat chaotic stage of economic development of the Copper Country would emerge the great mines with methods and machinery, some of the latter on a mammoth scale, all of which would become renowned throughout the world. Such a mine was the great Calumet and Hecla combine. The Calumet Mining Company was first organised in 1864 with a part of their holdings named Hecla Mining Company.[6] The conglomerate lode had been discovered by E.J. Hulbert in 1855. In 1869 Hecla paid its first dividend of $100,000 and Calumet followed in 1870 by declaring a dividend of the same amount. The dividends continued for many, many years and in 1899 the dividend for that year was $10 million.[7]

In 1867 the companies built two stamp mills at Torch Lake and in 1871 the two companies amalgamated to become Calumet and Hecla Mining Company. In fact,

The log cabin at Phoenix, Michigan, Benjamin and Jane's home for almost seven years prior to moving to Lake Linden. James Hugh (2) and Mamie were born in this cabin

these mills were the largest of their type in America and between 1870 and 1880 produced more than half of all copper mined in the US. To Benjamin (4) much of the foregoing was in the future but as far as he was concerned the die was cast and he commenced work at Hecla Mills as a copper washer in April 1872, his works number being 798. The family moved to Lake Linden to live in company house numbered 5426. This move indicates that Benjamin (4) felt very confident of the prospects for Calumet and Hecla and his own future with the company. There were other considerations in the decision to work for Calumet and Hecla and to take up residence at Lake Linden. Firstly, the foreman at Hecla Mills was Henry Krause, an outstanding Methodist who with other well-known figures was responsible for organising the Methodist Society at Lake Linden. Secondly, by the late 1870s there were more Cornishmen working at Calumet and Hecla than any other copper mine in the world.[8] And so in more ways than one, Benjamin (4) had come into his own. In 1879 he was appointed foreman of the Calumet stamp mill and, in 1894, he took over the same position at Hecla stamp mill.

Now responsible for the day-to-day management of both mills, his salary was $130 and in 1898 this was increased to $150 per month. This amount was approximately double that which he had received as a labourer. Considering he only paid $1 per month rent to the company for his house of four to six rooms located on a plot measuring fifty by one hundred feet, he was now in a better financial position than he had ever been. Medical, educational and other facilities were provided under the paternalistic stance of Calumet and Hecla management, a far cry from the conditions of employment to which he had been accustomed in Cornwall. It is obvious that Benjamin (4) enjoyed his employment with Calumet and Hecla, for he remained with them for the rest of his working life, a total of thirty-four years. Here again we witness the solid, reliable and upright character of the children of John (2) and Christian Smith Harris. In an eventual obituary[9] of Benjamin (4) it stated that 'He had an aggressive and inventive mind which made him a leader in his business', and according to his grandson, Benjamin Harris Wells, he invented a vibrator for screening the copper ore but in his unassuming attitude and loyalty to the company the patent rights were vested in his employer's name. Indeed, it is also mentioned in his obituary that 'he was respected by those who worked over him and by those who worked under him, and by those who lived by him.' Benjamin (4) held a position of considerable responsibility; the massive plant which he controlled was capable of crushing and treating 9,000 tons of rock every 24 hours. Precisely what his official title was is difficult to say as he is variously described as superintendent, overseer and foreman, and possibly he

wasn't too concerned.

There is no doubt that Benjamin (4) was well known to the company President. Alexander Agassiz, when making his six-monthly visits to the mine, usually sought out Benjamin (4) for a conversation. The company showed their appreciation of his service by presenting to him at his retirement in 1906 a memorial in recognition of his long and valuable service.[10] Additionally, it was reported that the memorial included $1,000 as an appreciation of his fidelity and profitableness to the company. His grandson also states that the retirement gifts included a gold watch and gold-headed walking cane, the whole constituting something of an accolade for Benjamin (4) as he held President Agassiz in high esteem. Agassiz, the son of a Swiss father and German mother, had come to America when thirteen years old and was trained as an engineer and naturalist. First impressions suggest this as an unusual combination but, in the event, it was no doubt a considerable advantage when he assumed management of mines in the wild and undeveloped Keweenaw Peninsula. Quincy A Shaw of Boston, brother-in-law of Agassiz and the largest stockholder in the company at that time, asked Agassiz to take over control of Calumet and Hecla, which the latter did in March 1867. He worked indefatigably to

James Hugh (2) Harris 1866–1942.
A first-generation American. Superintendent of Schools

Photographed circa 1937

bring the mines to maximum production and was not afraid to pour stockholders' money into numerous projects he thought necessary for the success of the enterprise. The original investment was $1,200,000. The company reinvested millions and between 1869 and 1946 paid dividends amounting to a total of $200 million.[11]

That Benjamin (4) would have been associated with whatever Methodist groups met in Eagle River, Central, Delaware and Phoenix there can be no doubt. In these early days, before they had their own churches, these groups met in folks' houses, schoolhouses or any suitable location. The groups consisted not only of Cornish Methodists but European Protestants as well. However, we have details of Benjamin's (4) involvement with Lake Linden Methodist Church when he arrived in 1872 and where he held important positions in the organisation and early growth of this particular church, which was started in 1868 by Alfred Johns and Henry Krause, the foreman at Calumet and Hecla mills who also held services in his house. A year younger than Benjamin (4), Henry Krause was born in Saxony, Germany and came to America with his parents when a boy.

In 1868 about twenty families joined together for worship, being roughly the total population of Lake Linden at this time, when the Society was a branch of Calumet Church. In 1873, the number of worshippers, Benjamin (4) and his family amongst them, had increased to such an extent that it was decided to build a church, which was dedicated on 10 November 1874. The church property was at that time valued at $3,000. In 1878 the church was made a separate charge to Calumet. By 1885 the congregation had grown to such an extent that it was found necessary to build a larger church. The building committee for the new church was headed by Capt. William Harris of legislature fame and included, amongst others, Henry Krause and Benjamin (4). With concentrated effort the new church was dedicated in November 1886 and cost $18,000. In 1898 a pipe organ was installed at a cost of $2,500. Benjamin (4) was involved as a local preacher, class leader and Sunday School superintendent, which latter post he held from 1879-82 and again from 1893-98. At these times the school consisted of over 200 scholars, officers and teachers. Here again the paternalism of the Calumet and Hecla Company was manifested when they made one of the company houses available as the Methodist Parsonage.[12]

The Family of Benjamin (4) and Jane

James Hugh (1) Harris

James Hugh (1) was born in the cottage at Troon Moor on 20 December 1864 and baptized at Troon Wesleyan Chapel on 27 February 1865. He crossed to America with his parents three months after his baptism but did not survive his first winter in the harsh climate of Lake Superior. Although it is not proven, he probably passed away at Eagle River before March 1866. There is the possibility that his death prompted the move to their own cabin at Phoenix.

James Hugh (2) Harris

James Hugh (2), who was destined to be a great educationist, was born in the log cabin at Phoenix on 9 March 1866. He attended grade school at Lake Linden where the family had taken up residence in April 1872. He also took part in high school work at Lake Linden and went on to complete his high school education at Ann Arbor, MI, where he graduated in 1886. He then proceeded to the University of Michigan, obtaining his BA degree in 1891. For one year he became a graduate student at the University of Chicago and then proceeded to do post-graduate work in education at the University of Minnesota.

His teaching career began at Saginaw, MI, High School, after which he taught Latin and Greek at Michigan Military Academy at Orchard Lake. In 1897 he became High School Principal for Bay City, MI, until 1901 when he was appointed Principal of Michigan Military Academy. He moved on in 1903 to become superintendent of Schools at Pontiac, MI. In 1906 he was appointed Assistant Superintendent of Schools at Minneapolis and in 1910 became Superintendent of Schools at Dubuque, Iowa until 1921 when he returned as Superintendent at Pontiac, where he remained until he resigned in June 1939. So it will be seen that James Hugh (2) gained a very wide experience in teaching and executive office in the education system, and there is much more for which he was responsible.

James Hugh (2) established the Junior High School system at Pontiac, which became considerably extended and resulted in the fulfilment of his long-cherished dream. He modernised the school systems and saw the number of pupils increase from 5,000 to 14,000. He backed and obtained for the schools an auto-mechanical course in February 1922, a printing department in September 1922 and a dental clinic in conjunction with the Board of Health in January of the same year. Additionally, he introduced a household mechanics course in October

1923 and a free textbook system in September 1926. School buildings were enlarged and new ones built. A School for Crippled Children was established in July 1928 and a Prevocational School in November 1927. A new Industrial Arts building was occupied in May 1929.

When James Hugh (2) retired in 1939, Harold L. Blackwood, Head of the Board of Education, had this to say:

We owe him an especial debt of gratitude for throughout his administration he has commanded the complete respect of his pupils, the teaching staff, the successive Boards of Education and the citizens at large. Mr Harris has been a tireless worker and has been steadfastly on the job twelve months in the year. The Board almost had to compel him to take a vaca-

tion. I am certain that the schools can continue to make use of Mr Harris's experience, information and training in some capacity in the years ahead. He is still essentially young in spirit and the younger children interest him. The schools have had the advantage of a progressive attitude, coupled with wide experience, and there was always a note of optimism in his general outlook on life and educational problems. During the past several years we have been faced with unusual financial problems and during this period he has been ready and willing to co-operate with the Board. In addition to his educational abilities he has been sufficiently shrewd in his purely business outlook, to help reduce expenses drastically and yet preserve a valuable measure of harmony. Throughout his long service here and regardless of the material aspects of the schools' expansion in building, enrollment and faculty, Superintendent Harris always remained the educator with his greatest interest centred in making certain that the finest facilities were provided for the children of the city. He always made certain that Pontiac High School retained its rating with higher institutions of learning so that graduates here would have access to colleges and universities.

The Family of James Hugh (2) Harris and Grace Galbraith

James Hugh (2) Harris
b. 1866, Phoenix, MI

Educationist

d. 1942, Pontiac, MI

1901

Grace Galbraith
b. Pontiac, MI

Daughter of Dr Franklin B. Galbraith and Mary Smith

d. 1943, Pontiac, MI

Katherine Galbraith Harris
b. 20 July 1902 Pontiac, MI.
Grew up in Dubuque, Iowa. Graduated from Vassar College in 1925 and in 1927 received her degree in Library Science from University of Michigan where she also obtained her Masters degree in 1939. From 1927 to 1942 she held library positions in several Michigan cities. In 1942 she joined Detroit Public Library and eventually held a top administrative post there. She was an executive in State and National Professional Associations until she retired in 1947.

In 1968 she married a widower, Ronald J. Preston, who prior to retirement was Chief Forester for Ohio Edison Co., with whom he served for 42 years. Ronald served in the American Army during the Second World War as a captain. He was born in Shelby Township, MI, in 1901 and was a graduate of Michigan State University with a B.Sc. degree in Forestry. He died aged 92 on 15 December 1983 at Akron, Ohio.

In his student days at University of Michigan, James Hugh (2) was editor of the Journal of the *Student Christian Association*. He was author of a *Manual for the Teaching of English* and wrote many articles for leading educational journals of the US. Indeed, he was widely known as an author in the educational field and up to his retirement had spent forty-eight years in educational activities.

In the public field James Hugh (2) had been a Director of Pontiac Community Chest. He was a member of the Board of Commerce and a past President of the Rotary Club, a member of the Masonic Fraternity, and in politics an Independent Republican. He was a member of the Episcopal Church, which he served as a Vestryman. He was a Life Member of the National Education Association, of Michigan Schoolmasters' Club, the North-eastern Iowa Teachers' Association, and past President of his

Chapter of Delta Upsilon. He also belonged to Phi Beta Kappa. Altogether the foregoing presents an impressive picture of this first-generation American.

On 7 August 1901, James Hugh (2) married Grace G. Galbraith, who had been born in Pontiac. Grace was the daughter of Dr Franklin B. Galbraith and Mary Smith. To this happy union was born a daughter, Katherine Galbraith Harris.

In June 1929, James Hugh (2) made, on his part, a quite unexpected and very brief visit to Cornwall. A friend of his was going on a business trip to London and Paris and invited James Hugh (2) to accompany him at very short notice, so he decided to take the opportunity. In London his friend had business to attend to for a couple of days and it occurred to James Hugh (2) that he could pay a quick visit to Cornwall to see something of the area where his parents had been born. He did not personally have any real interest in genealogy and was totally unaware of any relatives in the Camborne area.

Deciding that Truro seemed to be a reasonable centre for his foray, he immediately travelled down by train and booked himself into that grand old Elizabethan town house known as the Red Lion Hotel. Unfortunately, the Red Lion no longer exists, having been demolished in 1967. After settling himself into the hotel, James Hugh (2) went out and struck a bargain with a taxi driver to take him on a brief tour of west Cornwall the following day. The visitor very much enjoyed his brief tour and appreciated the scenery. He arrived in Camborne mid-afternoon. Camborne surprised him as he had expected to find a drab mining town, instead of which he found it attractive. It then occurred to him that he should get some picture postcards of Camborne to take home, but alas it was early closing in Camborne that afternoon. However, the taxi driver, fortunately for his American passenger, knew of a card shop where the owner lived over. Arriving at the shop, a lady answered the door and quickly confirmed that she would be happy to supply the picture postcards.

In the manner of the Cornish, and realising her customer was an American, she asked him his name and he told her it was Harris. One question led to another and she soon found out that his mother was connected to the Thomas family of Dolcoath fame. Indeed, James Hugh (2) had heard his mother speak of Capt. Josiah Thomas.

'Well,' the shop lady said, 'the Thomas family are a very prominent family here, now and are direct descendants of Capt. Josiah.'

On that basis James Hugh (2) thought that it might be interesting to meet them and so the lady directed the taxi driver to the Thomas residence, Lowenac. On arrival, James Hugh (2) first met Donald W. Thomas and a little later the latter's father, C.V. Thomas, both being practising solicitors in Camborne. CV, as he was always known, was a noted Methodist lay preacher. James Hugh (2) had a very cordial and enjoyable conversation and subsequently carried on a brief correspondence with CV but strangely, from his own record of the visit and subsequent correspondence,[13] James Hugh (2) never quite understood the genealogical details of the connection between the Thomases and himself, least of all that CV was his third cousin. Returning to Truro, he caught the train next morning to return to London.

James Hugh (2) passed away on 12 February 1942 at Pontiac after a full life and one spent in the service of education in which he left his indelible imprint. He was buried in the Galbraith family plot at Cole Hill Cemetery, Pontiac. Grace did not long survive him, passing away on 23 April 1943.[14]

Mary J. (Mamie) Harris

Mamie was also born in the log cabin at Phoenix, MI. The happy event took place in December 1869. Like James Hugh (2), she received her education at Lake Linden where she had come with her parents when she was three years old. Unfortunately, we have no

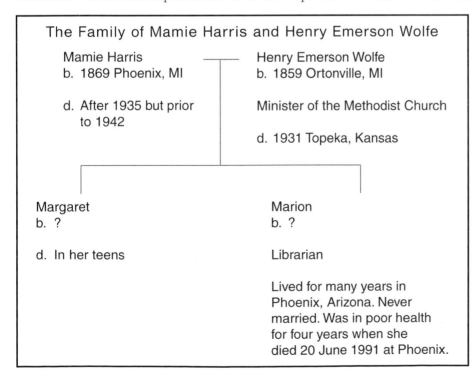

The Family of Mamie Harris and Henry Emerson Wolfe

Mamie Harris
b. 1869 Phoenix, MI

d. After 1935 but prior to 1942

Henry Emerson Wolfe
b. 1859 Ortonville, MI

Minister of the Methodist Church

d. 1931 Topeka, Kansas

Margaret
b. ?

d. In her teens

Marion
b. ?

Librarian

Lived for many years in Phoenix, Arizona. Never married. Was in poor health for four years when she died 20 June 1991 at Phoenix.

great detail available about her early life and eventual death. As will be seen later, she must have met her future husband when he was Methodist Pastor at Calumet from 1889 to 1892, and seemingly their marriage was between these dates or soon after.

Her husband was Rev. Henry Emerson Wolfe, who had been born on a farm at Ortonville, MI, on 5 August 1859. Following completion of his early education he taught school for two years. Henry graduated from Albion College and the Boston School of Theology with an MA degree and later received the honorary degree of Doctor of Divinity. He joined Detroit Methodist Conference on trial in 1886 and his first charges were Sagina, Calumet and Flint. In 1902 he transferred to Kansas Conference and served in Atchinson and Hutchinson. Then in 1909 he was transferred yet again to Southwest Kansas Conference, serving in Lawrence and Topeka. In 1918 he became Executive Secretary, Centenary, then to Manhattan District and from 1926 to 1927 was Executive Secretary for Homes for the Aged. A pastor for twenty-nine years and an executive for thirteen years, he gave a total of forty-two years service to the Methodist Connection.

Following his retirement in 1927, he was only to enjoy a further four years of life, passing away at Topeka in 1931. Funeral services were held both in Topeka and Ortonville, where he was buried. Henry's Conference obituary stated that he had given his heart to Christ at the young age of fourteen and emphasised that he was a leader and one of God's noblemen. It was also said the efforts of his long life of Christian service were impossible to measure.[15]

Mamie, who had faithfully discharged her duties as the wife and helpmeet of a pastor, lived on for a few years and then passed away and was buried at Ortonville with Henry.

John Mortimer Harris

Benjamin (4) and Jane's fourth child, John Mortimer, was born at Lake Linden 10 December 1873. He attended grade and high school at Lake Linden and obtained the customary certificates of education.

Having completed high school he seemed destined to follow in the footsteps of his father when, in July 1889, he commenced working in Hecla mill as a copper washer. This was probably considered the correct initiation for a career in ore dressing, as at the end of two years he enrolled in September 1891 as a student for the full course at Michigan Mining School at Houghton. However, it seems that John M. decided that a career in mining, in whatever particular subject, was not the profession in which he wished to spend the rest of his life, and so he left the mining school in 1895 before graduating.

In 1896, John M. moved to Detroit and as he was still residing there in 1915 when he attended his father's funeral at Evart it is reasonable to assume that he was employed in the automotive industry, especially so because his niece understood that he was an engineer. Unfortunately, this is yet another instance where it has not been possible to trace full details of the subject's life.

He was reputed to be charming person, attractive and popular but apparently never married. It is believed that he died somewhere in one of the eastern States.

Florence Harris Wells, c.1878–1935
Youngest daughter of Benjamin (4) and Jane Allen
Author
Photograph taken around 1932

Florence Harris

Benjamin (4) and Jane's last child, Florence, was born at Lake Linden in 1878. After attending grade school at Lake Linden, and because she was sensitive to the rigours of Lake Superior winters, she was sent to the Arthur Hill High School at Sagina, MI, where for a time she lived with her sister Mamie and the latter's husband, Rev. Henry E. Wolfe. Following her course at high school she graduated from the University of Michigan and it was here at Ann Arbor that she met her future husband Benjamin Warren Wells.

Dr Benjamin W Wells graduated from the School of Dentistry in 1901 and he and Florence were married on 14 August the same year. Benjamin immediately opened a dental practice in Evart, MI, where they lived until 1923 when they moved to Grand Rapids, MI. To this union was born an only child, Benjamin Harris Wells, on 11 June 1906.

Florence became well known as an author of children's and Christmas stories. She was a member of Michigan Authors' Association and Michigan Academy of Literature, Science and Art. She was an active member of the Ladies' Literary Club, Scribblers and Michigan Federation of Women's Clubs and had been Chairman of the two former and also Vice-President of Shakespearia.

Florence died at her home, 215 Prospect Avenue, Grand Rapids, in 1935 and was brought back to Evart for burial in the same plot as her father and mother. The services both at Grand Rapids and Evart were Methodist. It is not known where or when her husband passed away, but presumably his death and burial took place at Grand Rapids some little time after her own.

It seems that Florence returned to her sister's home at Sagina for the birth of her son Benjamin Harris Wells. He became a student at Indiana University in 1922 and graduated from there in 1925 with a Bachelors' degree. In 1926 he attended the University of Michigan at Ann Arbor and was awarded a Masters degree in English Language and Literature in 1931.

Between 1929 and 1938 Benjamin taught English for two periods, each of two and five years, at John Burroughs School at Ladue, St Louis County, and later served as a Trustee of the school for a period of seven years. Because he was appalled by the poor spelling of some students, he co-authored a spelling book used by the school for many years.

On 17 June 1938, Benjamin married Katherine Gladney of St Louis, Missouri. Katherine was the daughter of one of the co-founders of the Seven Up Beverage Company. From an early age she was interested in piano music and did a small amount of composition. Later she became a very accomplished musician and prolific composer, and the author of *Symphony and Song*, which is an account of the first hundred years of St Louis Symphony Orchestra. This book went into a second edition. Additionally, Katherine wrote poetry.

Benjamin and Katherine had two children, Katherine Wheeler, a Member of the New Hampshire Legislature, and Ben, a lawyer in Houston, Texas.

Benjamin Harris Wells was engaged on a freelance basis in 1938 to write advertising copy and slogans for the infant Seven Up Company. At this time the total number of employees was just ten. Two years later, Benjamin Harris Wells joined the company full time in charge of sales promotion. He remained with the company until his retirement in 1978. He became Vice-President of Sales and Advertising in 1943, President and Chief Executive in 1965 and Chairman of the Board in 1974, by which time Seven Up was the third largest soft drinks company in the world. He held this latter position until his retirement.

He was instrumental in developing a number of marketing strategies which, in due course, were considered classics. In 1974 he was named Marketing Man of the Year by St Louis Chapter of the American Marketing Association and Distinguished Executive of the Year by the Sales and Marketing Executives of St Louis. He also became a Member of the Beverage Industry Hall of Fame.[16]

The drive, initiative, foresight and entrepreneurial flair of this second-generation American was more than demonstrated when, under his chairmanship, Seven Up was sold for $520 million in 1978.

In 1977 Benjamin H. Wells was honoured by the University of Michigan and received honorary degrees from the University of Missouri and Westminster College, Fulton.

However, all of his flair and energies were not confined to Seven Up, for he and Katherine devoted much of their time to cultural and civil organisations and are known for their active involvement as artists, advisers and philanthropists in these spheres.[17] Their list of service was most impressive. Benjamin participated on the executive bodies of at least the following organisations:

St Louis Conservatory and Schools for the Arts
Laumeier International Sculpture Park
Opera Theatre of St Louis
St Louis Arts and Education Council
Missouri Citizens for the Arts
St Louis Community Foundation
First Street Forum
St Louis Council of Boy Scouts of America
United Way of Greater St Louis
St Louis Arts and Humanities Committee
St Louis Art Museum
Music Association of Aspen (Colorado)
Winston Churchill Memorial Library, Fulton, Missouri

He was also associated with the American Symphony Orchestra League. Even this formidable list is not exhaustive, and in an article by Gayle R. McIntosh in *Symphony Sound* in 1988, Winter Edition, Benjamin Harris Wells is described as the 'crown jewel' of St Louis Symphony Orchestra, and in 1984 he was the first person to receive the Missouri Arts Award.

In 1970, he and Katherine won an opportunity, through a fund-raiser, to conduct the St Louis Symphony Orchestra. Katherine took an anthem that her Presbyterian Church Choir had rendered on a few occasions and scored it for a full orchestra. At this first attempt in conducting the orchestra, Katherine amazed the musicians and captivated the audience, since which time she conducted a concert almost every year. Katherine Gladney Wells' character is summed up in a statement she made to Gayle R. McIntosh in which she said, 'I find every time an orchestral piece of mine is played that it is a miracle. I write a thank-you note after every concert I conduct, thanking them for letting me play ball with the professionals.'

As a result of this couple's tireless devotion and largesse to the arts, they received the annual St Louis Arts and Education Council's Lifetime Achievement Award on 23 January 1994.

Mr. and Mrs. Ben H. Wells

invite you to a

Very Special Concert

by the

Saint Louis Symphony Orchestra

in Powell Symphony Hall

Thursday Night,

April 23, 1987

8:00 p.m.

This concert has been made possible by
the Radio Music Marathon for the benefit
of the Saint Louis Symphony Orchestra.
Primarily, it has been made possible by
the generosity of Maestro Leonard Slatkin
and the musicians
of the Saint Louis Symphony Orchestra,
who will allow Mrs. Ben H. Wells
to participate briefly.

The concert will start promptly at 8:00 p.m.

Refreshments afterwards in the foyer.

Please reply on enclosed card.

Benjamin Harris Wells and Katherine accompanied the orchestra on a Far East tour in 1989. Travelling on a bus in India, it overturned on the road between Delhi and Jaipur and both suffered injuries; Benjamin H. a compressed disc and Katherine a crushed right arm. Not surprisingly, she wondered if she would be able to play the piano again. Her arm was in plaster for three months but when the plaster was taken off she immediately commenced short spells on the piano, initially playing simple pieces and gradually building up to more complicated scores until she regained full use of her arm, at least as far as the piano was concerned.

Sadly, Benjamin Harris Wells never fully recovered from the accident, and after a very full and gracious life passed away 18 July, 1995.

Retirement and Death

When Benjamin (4) retired in 1906, he and Jane decided to move from Lake Linden to Evart in Lower Michigan where they would be near their younger daughter Florence and her husband Dr Benjamin Warren Wells. To this end they had a house built at Evart and moved there in 1908.

Florence's young son, Benjamin Harris Wells, who had been born in 1906, was therefore privileged to spend his young years in close contact with his grandparents Harris. His memory of them paints a picture of two outstanding Christians. Of his grandfather he wrote, 'I remember my grandfather for his courtliness, his love of family, writing poetry and knowledge of copper and its ramifications, including copper stocks,' and he went on to say, 'My grandmother Harris was a strong personality, with an undeviating sense of Methodist righteousness. We never played cards on Sunday. We didn't swim on Sunday. We were the pillars of temperance and the WCTU. We also believed in tithing for the Church and helping the poor.'

What a vivid and accurate description and portrayal of this God-fearing couple who had been born at Bolenowe over a century and a half ago. What a contrast to those people of today who claim that Methodism must move with the times, with the result that worship is reduced to entertainment with hand-clapping dancing antics and potted music, all of which they claim is of the Spirit. Benjamin (4) and Jane would never have blamed the Spirit for such raucous and undignified behaviour in worship! Theirs was a steadfast and deep faith which was encapsulated in the following poem written by Benjamin (4) and based on Romans, Chapter 8, Verse 28:

'And we know that all things work together for good to them that love God, to them who are called according to His purpose.'

How weary and how worthless this life at times appears.
What days of heavy musing, what hours of bitter
tears.
How dark the storm clouds gather along the winter
skies.
How desolate and cheerless the path before us lies.

And yet those days of dreariness are sent as from
above,
They do not come in anger, but in tenderness and love,
They come to teach us lessons which bright days
could not yield.
And to leave us blest and thankful when their purpose
is fulfilled.

They come to draw us nearer to our Father and
our Lord.
More earnestly to seek His face, to listen to His word,
And to feel, if now around us a desert land we see,
Without the stars of promise, what would its
darkness be.

They come to lay us lowly, and humbled in the dust.
All self-deception swept away, all creatures hope
and trust:
Our helplessness, our vileness, our guiltiness to own.
And flee for hope and refuge to Christ and Christ
alone.

They come to break the fetters which here detain
us fast,
And cause our long reluctant hearts to rise to
heaven at last.
And brighten every prospect of that eternal home.
Where grief and disappointment and fear can
never come.

Then turn not in despondence, poor weary heart
away.
But meekly journey onward through the dark and
cloudy day:
Even now the bow of promise is above thee painted
bright.
And soon a joyful morning shall dissipate the night.

Thy God hath not forgotten thee, and when he sees
it best,
Will lead thee into sunshine, will give thee bowers
of rest:
And all thy pain and sorrow, when the pilgrimage
is o'er.
Shall end in Heavenly blessedness and joys for
ever more.

Little wonder that in 1923 the church at Lake Linden
erected, among others, a memorial window to Benjamin
(4) and Jane.

Although the descendants of Benjamin (4) assume
that he became an American citizen, strangely the relevant documents cannot be located. One supposes that
there is a possibility that his loyalty to the land of this
birth prevented him as a matter of conscience from taking such a step, but one cannot be certain. Nevertheless,
in politics he was a Republican and one cannot equate his
character with a person who wanted the best of both
worlds. On 7 February 1884 he joined the Duncan Lodge
of the Grand Lodge of Michigan. Upon his removal to
Evart he transferred to that Lodge on 10 March 1908.

Benjamin (4) and Jane celebrated their Golden Wedding
at Evart on 28 May 1913, but the earthly pilgrimage of
Benjamin (4) was drawing to a close. In September 1915
he and Jane left Evart in the best of health to visit their
daughter Mamie Wolfe in Topeka, Kansas, where they
hoped to spend the next three to four months. They had
been in Topeka only two days when Benjamin (4) was
taken with an illness which terminated fatally a few days
later on 23 September. His remains were taken back to
Evart accompanied by Jane, her daughter Mamie and
son James Hugh (2), who had hastened up from Dubuque, Iowa.

The burial took place at Forest Hill Cemetery, Evart,
amongst the pines and hillocks, where the casket was
placed in a steel vault. Then years later, in 1925, Jane's remains were also interred there, to be followed by those of
their daughter Florence Harris Wells in 1935.

Before leaving this account of the life of Benjamin (4)
Harris, it seems necessary to correct a story related some
years ago by a member of Falmouth Old Cornwall Society and which the author's own family accepted at the
time as being correct. The statement revolved around the
history of a chased silver jug in the possession of Earle's
Retreat Home at Falmouth, of which John (3) Harris was
a member of the governing body. The statement was as
follows: 'Fifty years ago a family named Harris resided

> Mr. and Mrs. Benjamin Harris
>
> announce their
>
> Golden Wedding
>
> May 20th, 1863   May 20th, 1913
> Camborne, Cornwall, England   Evart, Michigan

Golden Wedding Announcement
Note: the marriage certificate states 28th May!

in Falmouth. One of them had a reputation as a poet, and wrote a number of hymns in the Earle's Retreat book. Another member of the family went to the United States of America, and when he left there the people gave him a parting gift of a large number of silver dollars. These he made into the jug which he sent to the Retreat, and has been used ever since for the collections.' The large number of silver dollars obviously refer to the $1,000 presented to Benjamin (4) on his retirement from Calumet and Hecla Mining Company, but as will be seen, the jug was made and inscribed eight years prior to Benjamin's (4) retirement and eleven years before the Retreat was opened in 1869. The inscription on the jug reads:

Theodore Shaef Harris, Boston, 3 April 1858

T.S. Harris was not connected in any way to the Harrises of Bolenowe, but may have been a friend of George Earle, founder of the Retreat.

The graves at Forest Hill Cemetery, Evart, Michigan of Benjamin (4), his wife Jane and daughter Florence Harris Wells. Photograph taken 1985

The Family of Benjamin (4) Harris and Jane Florence Allen

Benjamin (4) Harris — 1863 — Jane Florence Allen
b. 1838 Bolenowe Carn   b. 1838 Bolenowe

Miner - Superintendent of Copper Mill. Methodist Lay Preacher.   Granddaughter of Capt. Jimmy Thomas

d. 1915 Topeka, Kansas Buried Evart, Michigan   d. 1925 Evart

James Hugh (1)
b. 1864 Troon, Cornwall
d. Prior to March 1866, Keweenaw Peninsula

Mamie
b. 1869 Phoenix, MI
d. After 1925
m. Rev. H.E. Wolfe, Methodist Episcopal Minister. Both buried Ortonville, MI

Florence
b. 1878 Lake Linden, MI

Author

d. 1935 Grand Rapids, MI
m. 1901 Dr B.W. Wells

Buried Evart

James Hugh (2)
b. 1866 Phoenix, MI

Educationist, Author

d. 1942, Pontiac, MI
m. 1901 Grace Galbraith

Grace died 1943

John Mortimer
b. 1873 Lake Linden, MI

Student at Michigan Mining School 1891 to 1894

11. Mark Smith Harris

His Boyhood

Mark Smith, the seventh son and tenth child of John (2) and Christian, was born at Six Chimneys on Bolenowe Carn on 11 January 1841 and was baptized at Camborne Parish Church the following March. Curiously, he was registered at birth as Mark but baptized Mark Smith Harris.

Mark's boyhood was spent in happy company with eight brothers and sisters, whose ages at his birth ranged from three to twenty-one years. A short poem he wrote about Hangman Barrow[1] in 1892 gives a brief glimpse of their playing around this ancient barrow and his boyhood impressions of it.

Hangman

Hoary Hangman wild and rugged, on
  the lonely Carn,
Dark the tales we've heard about thee, still
  there's more to learn.
Tradition tells strange stories, how thou didst get
  thy name,
And how those granite stones were piled,
  and how the title came.
It says a noble chieftain, a Briton bold and brave,
Here fought and bled, and died at last, that
  here he has his grave.
How then from hill and valley, and from
  the country round,
These stones were carried one by one,
  which form this granite mound.
It also says that on this spot once stood an iron cage,
And in it was confined a man, none knew his
  name or age.
And here from day to day he pined, no food, no
  drink, no rest,
Until his spirit passed away, to the home among
  the blest.

One story, if around it nine times we ran as for
  some prize,
Up from its very centre, a spirit would arise.
And well do we remember as we ran with
  bated breath,
We fancied ghosts arising, we looked as pale as death.
We remember stories told us in childhood's
  early years,
About the lonely Hangman, its shrieks, its cries,
  its tears.

Yet somehow we believed them, and looked with
  fear and dread,
And now when wild storms gather and lightnings
  flash at night,
We hear strange echoes ringing around this
  heathy height.
O, Hangman, Hoary Hangman, thy history who
  can tell,
The rocks around are silent, the hills can't break
  the spell.

Likewise, Mark's poem *Bolenowe Hill* featured at the beginning of this book portrays his love of his birthplace, and brings back memories of his happy childhood there. It is interesting to note that in John's (3) poem The Burial Mark, at the age of five, was seemingly the leader among the younger members of the family. Interesting because, although he grew up fearless in the cause of his Master, he never pushed himself and always adopted a humble stance.

Education

Mark attended Mrs Percival's Endowed School at Treslothan, commencing when about six years old and remaining until he was twelve. His future wife, Jane Rule, also attended this school. Jane was seven years Mark's senior, and so it would seem their period there together could only have been in the later years of her time at school. But together they were, and apparently at this early age young Mark was attracted to the older girl, and an amusing story of their association has been handed down through the family. It seems that each pupil was required to sweep the schoolroom on a rota, and on the occasions when it was Mark's turn he made especially certain that the area around Jane's desk was cleaned to the best possible standard.[2] John Leslie Harris possessed one of Jane's exercise books from the Endowed School at Treslothan. Jane and the other pupils were each only permitted to write sparingly, in fact just six lines per day. This demonstrates the level of economy required in the use of scholastic materials in those days.

Mark strived after self-improvement and was always a great listener and avid reader until his sight failed. Statements, sentences and whole paragraphs or pages which Mark considered significant were duly marked with a vertical wrinkled line in the book margin

An interesting reminder of old-world courtesy and respect which children were expected to accord their elders is contained in the actions of the pupils attending the Endowed School: when they passed the vicarage and met or saw the incumbent, Parson Bull, the boys were required to raise their caps and the girls to curtsy.[3]

Working Life

At twelve years of age, Mark left school and commenced working at Bolenowe Mine. This small copper mine had been re-opened by Capt. Jimmy Thomas in 1823, and in 1853 when Mark started work it was about 50 fathoms or 300 feet deep. One of Mark's duties, for the little group of miners to whom he had been assigned, was to climb down into the mine alone on Sunday nights, his only form of illumination being a tallow candle, to wheel the broken ore from the stope or end out to the shaft 'platt' ready for hoisting to surface on Monday morning. It must have been a somewhat daunting task for a twelve-year-old, especially without any company. The levels, driven on the strike and dip of the lode, were so narrow that secondary metal handles were fitted inside the wheelbarrow handles to prevent Mark's knuckles being grazed by the rock in the sides of the level. It has been said that it was easy to distinguish a person who had worked in narrow underground drives because he invariably held a normal wheelbarrow with his thumbs to the rear, which was another method of protecting the knuckles. How long Mark remained at Bolenowe Mine is not known. He probably left when the mine closed down yet again, and at that point obtained work at Dolcoath. It is certain that on 30 May 1857, when sixteen years old, he began operating the Dolcoath man-engine, which had commenced working in October 1854.[4] Imagine being given such huge responsibility at such a young age. Here was a lad who was being put through the mill of responsibility and individual manual endeavour at a very early age, but beyond doubt this early training was instrumental in moulding the reliable, conscientious and caring person that was Mark Smith Harris.

At this time, the single-rod man-engine was powered by a nineteen-inch steam engine of five-foot stroke, the engine itself being sited some twenty-seven fathoms from the man-engine shaft. The connection between the engine gearing and shaft being effected by horizontal wooden rods on rollers. The rods in the shaft, on which the miners rode, had platforms every ten feet corresponding to stages fixed in the shaft and the stroke of the engine. The rods at this time extended 220 fathoms or 1,320 feet below surface. By the time the first miner reached the bottom level, when going on shift, there could have been around 100 miners on the rods and stages, all depending on the skill and reliability of a sixteen-year old boy!

After operating the man-engine for just over two years, Mark left Dolcoath and went to work the Cornish pumping engine at West Frances Mine on 1 November 1859. The reason for leaving Dolcoath and the man-engine was probably to obtain an increase in wages for, despite his reliability, he was most probably still considered by the management as a boy, a trait that was all too common in industry and families. West Francis was a tin and copper mine situated on the south-western extension of the subsequent Basset Group of Mines. The pumping engine had a fifty-eight inch cylinder,[5] which was just over three times the size of Dolcoath man-engine, and was drawing water from a depth of almost 600 feet. Mark operated this engine for almost fourteen years, during which time he married his childhood sweetheart, Jane Rule, and their first child Edith, the author's mother, was born to them.

It seems that on 12 May 1873, Mark was probably seconded to South Wheal Crofty. This copper mine was now running into larger quantities of tin and instead of continuing to sell the broken tin ore to neighbouring mines for the latter to process,[6] South Wheal Crofty decided to erect a tin-processing plant to treat their own ores. As part of this scheme, they installed eighty-four heads of Cornish gravity stamps powered by a steam engine having a cylinder of forty inches diameter. This engine, which Mark was now to operate, was situated on approximately the same site as the present South Crofty concentrator. Mark's change of location meant that his travel to work distance was more than doubled but only from three quarters of a mile to about two miles each way, and this was always accomplished on foot. However, the price of tin slumped, a not uncommon and always recurring event, even to the present day. South Wheal Crofty had to effect savings and so we find on 11 June 1873 Mark had returned, not to West Francis but to the adjacent mine South Wheal Francis. Here at South Francis one assumes that Mark must have operated the seventy-five inch Cornish pumping engine on Marriott's shaft. Mark remained here for precisely five years, leaving on 15 June 1878.

Apparently the opportunity presented itself to go back to Dolcoath man-engine because he started there again on 17 June 1878. Beyond doubt, as far as beam-engines were concerned, the man-engine was his great love for in a prayer of thankfulness recorded in his diary on the day of his return he said, 'May I get through my work, and may I devote my time and attention more than ever to the service of my God.'

In 1876, the man-engine had been extended from 212 to the 240-fathom level and a larger engine installed to work at almost double the previous speed.[7] Mark drove this engine continuously until 9 June 1896, when he was taken off to operate the engine driving the air compressor at the new Williams' shaft being sunk near the southern boundary of the mine; this particular shaft was vertical and eventually reached a depth of 3,000 feet from surface.[8] However, on 25 March 1897, Mark returned again to the man-engine and remained there until the day it ran for the last time on 28 September 1897.

Mark must have had mixed feelings when he brought the man-engine in for the last time; it was the end of an era for him, but what he probably did not realise was that this great mine which had been worked, with some breaks, for over one and a half centuries was entering its final quarter century of operation.

In all, Mark operated the man-engine for almost twenty-one years. Of his second spell of eighteen years, 1878-96, his daughter Edith recorded that on numerous occasions, especially on pay day, the Dolcoath miners who lived in Troon would come and knock on Mark's door to ask him to come in and lower them into the mine because the operator who should have been on shift had imbibed too freely and they were afraid to go down with him at the controls. Mark never failed them and these miners used to make the claim that 'When Mark was driving they could ride the man-engine asleep'. A testimony indeed to Mark's sense of duty and reliability. Two verses from the poem *Dolcoath Man-engine*[9] written by John (3) seem appropriate as a valedictory to this invention:

> Help of the miner brave,
> Man-engine, hail to thee!
> Lifting him up from Plutus' cave,
> Light as the air and free!
> Lifting him up! up! up!
> Light as the Zephyr's wing,
> So that dull Lassitude's lean form
> Is now evanishing.
>
> Hurrah for those below,
> Who're digging in the ground!
> Hurrah for thinking minds above,
> Who such a help have found!
> Hurrah, Man-engine, come,
> Ye miners sing with me:
> Lift up your voices like a trump, -
> 'Eternal strength to thee!'

On 29 September 1897, Mark was transferred to operate the pumping engine on Harriet shaft. The masonry of this engine house still stands, one of the last remaining on the Dolcoath site, and is situated near the main-line railway crossing at Pengegon. At this time new pitwork was being installed to drain the lower levels of the mine. Mark remained here for six years until 31 October 1903, when within two months of his sixty-third birthday he decided to retire and to devote his time and energy to the service of God. Considering that he had only been earning fifteen shillings a week or thirty-nine pounds a year, and therefore had had no opportunity to accumulate savings, this commitment to the service of his Master demonstrated the depth of his faith and belief.

Miners riding the Dolcoath man-engine. Mark Smith Harris operated this engine intermittently for a total of almost twenty-one years from the age of sixteen in 1857.
Photograph reproduced by courtesy of the
Trounson-Bullen Collection

The remains of Wheal Harriet engine house at Dolcoath where Mark Smith Harris operated the Cornish Pumping Engine until he retired in 1903.
When the photograph was taken in 1989 this engine house was the only one of conventional type still remaining our of a total of ten on this once great copper and tin mine.

Additionally, the Old Age Pension Act was not passed until 1909 and Mark received his first pension of five shillings per week on 20 January 1911 when he became seventy years of age and eight years after he retired.

Mark joined the Local Preachers' Aid Association on 17 April 1874, paying a ten-shilling entrance fee in instalments over a period of nine months, together with subscriptions of three shillings per quarter. Following his application to become an annuitant, he was granted five shillings per week from 7 June 1913. This was increased to eight shillings from October 1919 and to ten shillings from April 1921, the latter continuing until his death in 1931.

Despite becoming an annuitant, his quarterly payments to the fund continued until May 1926. Mark recorded receiving additional payments at Christmas from the LPMA: 1914 ten shillings, 1915 five shillings, 1917 twelve shillings and sixpence, 1918 fourteen shillings and sixpence, 1919 ten shillings, 1920 twelve shillings and sixpence, and 1921 one pound.

Marriage and Homes

Mark married Jane Rule at Camborne Wesleyan Church on 7 July 1869. The witnesses to the marriage were Mary Sally Thomas and Alice Jane Hall, neither of whom could write but appended their marks. Jane was the second child of Henry and Elizabeth Rule. Henry was a husbandman and a crack shot with a sporting gun. His cottage was situated on the south side of the lane from Killivose to the Ramsgate Lodge of Pendarves House, and lay 140 yards east of the lodge.

A story of interest in connection with Jane's family concerns her cousin Samuel James Rule, one of the younger sons of her uncle Capt. Richard Rule, a Master Mariner of Clifton Terrace, Hayle, Cornwall. Samuel first went to sea with his older brother, Capt. Richard Thomas Rule at twelve years of age.[10] At one time Jane's uncle had been the Master and then sixty-fourth owner of the *Betsy James*,[11] a schooner engaged in coastal trade between South Devon and various intermediate ports up to Bristol and Liverpool, and this was the type of trade in which young Samuel was originally employed. Later Samuel joined the White Star Line with whom he served for forty years. He was transferred to the ill-fated *Titanic* as soon as she arrived at Southampton and was the Chief Bathroom Steward. As it transpired, he was the last person to be taken off the liner. Apparently in the final moments another oarsman was required for No. 15 lifeboat and he was detailed for this duty. Samuel in due course gave evidence at the *Titanic* enquiry.[12]

A brother of Jane, William Henry Rule, who had been the senior gardener in charge of flowering shrubs on the Pendarves Estate, emigrated to South Island, New Zealand in 1862 and successfully farmed about 3,000 acres about 20 kilometres north of Ashburton and named the spread Pendarves, by which name it is still known. Additionally, he designed, patented and set up a factory to manufacture a portable water filter which was most effective and was sold in two continents.

A crack shot, like his father, William Henry was an ardent member of the Volunteer Forces in this country and in New Zealand and won many outstanding trophies for his marksmanship.

Jane's youngest sister, Julia Hannah, married William Dunstan at Treslothan in 1870 and emigrated to New Zealand in 1876 with her husband and three small children aged five years, three years and nine months.

Henry Rule (1805–1878) with two of his daughters sitting in the garden of his cottage in Killivose Lane.

Samuel James Rule – The *Titanic* Survivor

Jane was about twenty years old when her mother died in 1853 and was housekeeper for her father for a further sixteen years until her marriage.

It was to his mother's home that Mark took his bride, and it was here that their three children, Edith, John (4), who died of croup as a young boy, and Jacob (2) were born. From the date of his marriage Mark assumed responsibility for the rent of the cottage at 48 Laity Row, Troon, which at that time was fixed at ten shillings per quarter. Jane must have been a very patient, understanding and equitable person because during her married life of thirty-nine years there was only one year in which she did not share the cottage with relatives. Her mother-in-law Christian was with her for twelve years, her sister-in-law Kitty for thirty years and her sisters Catherine Rule and Elizabeth (Rule) Crook for six years. Sometime after Christian's death in 1881, the family moved from Laity Row to Pendarves Street, Troon.

Mark and Jane's married life, though tinged with sadness at the death of their young son John (4) in 1878, and again when Jane became seriously ill towards the end of 1891, also despite the meagre wages of the time, was loving, happy and endearing, and coupled with absolute regard and respect for each other. These feelings are portrayed in some verses which Mark wrote to Jane following her recovery from a serious illness and grim operation. Dr Gardiner of Camborne, who had been

attending Jane, finally decided that there was no option but to operate. The lack of surgical facilities in the area at the time is illustrated by the fact that the operation was carried out in Jane's cottage, the operating table being none other than her kitchen table. The author often heard his mother speak of this event.

After a slow convalescence Jane was able once again to attend to her household duties, and Mark's pleasure and gratitude is recorded in the following verses written in May 1892:

Dearest wife how pleased to see you,
After weeks and months of pain.
Seated by the cheerful fireside
In the old armchair again.

O how sad the days and weeks were,
As you lay confined to bed,
Racked with pain, laid low with weakness
Scarcely strength to lift your head.

In the mine my thoughts were with you,
Wondering how you got along;
Picturing things so dark and dreary,
Heart so sad, the days seemed long.

Then when evening came, how anxious
Did I feel to hear your voice.
And to find that you were better,
How my troubled heart rejoiced.

Now to see you at the table,
Filling your accustomed place,
Serving out the well cooked supper,
Pleased to see your smiling face.

Pleased to see you looking better,
Gathering strength from day to day.
Walking out among the flowers,
In this welcome month of May.

Home is sweeter, brighter, better,
Anxious fears, in part all gone.
Hearts aglow with joy and sunshine,
Music, melody and song.

Dearest wife, may we be thankful.
Thankful to the Lord above.
He heard our cries, He raised you up,
He used the rod, yet all through love.

And now if spared a little longer,
May life's best acts show forth His praise,
And journeying down life's changing pathway,
May song and sunshine fill our days.

Jane Rule Harris with her brother and two sisters
Standing: Jane; William Henry Rule. Seated: Catherine Rule; Julia Hannah Rule who married William Dunstan

Then when life's fierce conflicts over,
And we have passed from earth away,
And reached that home, where change can't enter,
O happy thought, eternal day.

Mark and Jane's idea of a day's outing would be to walk from Troon to Falmouth to visit the poet's family. While at Falmouth, Mark would carry out shoe repairs for the poet and his family. During the poet's lifetime Mark would also accompany him on his visits to the sick, and also attend, if held on that particular day, one of the poet's cottage meetings. Then Mark and Jane would walk back home to Troon, the distance being about ten miles each way.

Methodist Lay Preacher – Church Official – Troon Missionary – Authority on the History of Local Methodism

From the early age of eight years, Mark spent many hours in the company of Capt. Jimmy Thomas of Bolenowe, listening to the latter's exposition of the scriptures and accounts of the early days of Methodism in the area. Capt. Jimmy permitted Mark to copy his notes of these early stages in establishing Methodism in Troon. Mark's copy was subsequently passed to his nephew, James Howard Harris, who edited and published it in the *Camborne Wesleyan Circuit Magazine* and *Monthly Greeting* of June 1889.

Becoming a lay preacher, Mark preached his first sermon at Pengegon Wesleyan Chapel on 7 June 1868. Mark's self-effacement on this occasion is recorded in his notebook, when noting the date and place he wrote: 'Mark Harris *tried* to preach for the first time'. His text was taken from the Book of Esther, chapter four and verse sixteen: 'Go, gather together all the Jews that are present in Shushan, and fast for me, and neither eat or drink for three days, night or day. I also and my maids will fast as you do. Then I will go to the king, although it is against the law, and if I perish, I perish.' It was the message of Esther the queen to Mordecai the Jew, not the easiest of texts on which to base a sermon.

Whilst it is not difficult to visualise Mark's probable treatment of Ester being prepared to give her life for her people, the Jews, the rationale for hanging Haman, the king's adviser and enemy of the Jews, on the gallows intended by Haman for Mordecai would not be easy for anyone to expound in Christian terms, much less a fledgling lay preacher. One would like to have seen Mark's notes for this particular sermon.

Mark often quoted excerpts from scholars in his sermons, together with analogies of events and incidents of which he had intimate knowledge. The author remembers his older brothers and sisters recalling instances when stories of their deeds, sometimes good and sometimes not so good, were related from the pulpit without mention of names, but easily recognised by certain listeners! Mark was well acquainted with the works of Wordsworth, Cowper, Ruskin and Tennyson, and used quotations from C.H. Spurgeon, F.R. Havergill, Abraham Lincoln, Pollack and Gladstone. In Mark's obituary, Rev. H. Strawson wrote, 'His poetic fancy and love of nature added charm to his discourses', and J.F. Odgers in

Photograph of a group taken when Mark Smith Harris performed the opening ceremony for the new main entrance doors at Troon Wesleyan Chapel in 1928.
Back row, L–R: Mr P.W. Cowlin, Mr E.A. Shaw – Circuit Stewards. Front row, L–R: Rev. A. Brockbank, Mr John Dennis, Mrs Edith Langford, Mark Smith Harris, Mr Jim Carter.
The clock held by MSH was presented to him on this occasion by the Trustees of the Church.

The procession of Troon Wesleyan Sunday School Tea Treat passing up New Road in 1910. In the centre of the three men at the front is Mark Smith Harris, then 69 years of age.

his *Early Methodism in Camborne* spoke of 'Mark Harris with his natural flow of lyrical speaking'.

Mark was a local preacher for sixty-three years and at the time of his death in 1931 was the oldest local preacher in Camborne Wesleyan Circuit. On his ninetieth birthday he received a congratulatory letter from Albert M. Bray, junior circuit steward of Camborne Wesleyan Circuit. A portion of the letter contained this tribute:

I cannot undertake to express the esteem and affection with which you are personally held in our circuit, or to tell you how much your Christian example and faithful service have been valued. The influence of your personality and preaching will be remembered for a great many years, even after your active service with us has ended.

Mark, at one time or another, held all offices open to a layman at Troon Wesleyan Chapel, now called Troon Methodist Church. He was a Society Class Leader for fifty years and Sunday School Superintendent for forty-two years (6 July 1879 to 18 December 1921). He was also a teacher in the Sunday School, Treasurer of the school, Society Steward and Trustee.

Following Mark's retirement from Dolcoath, he daily walked many miles to comfort the sick, the poor, the old and the infirm. He set a consistent Christian example and devoted his life to the service of others. He officiated by special request at 349 funerals in Troon Cemetery between 1903 and 1924. It is small wonder that in his life of service to others he became known at the 'Troon Missionary'. He carried out these duties without fuss or payment and in humility. Mark summed up in his notebook a guide to the manner in which he should conduct himself. Headed 'A Good Man's Character' he recorded: 'He makes no noise about his good deeds, and blows no trumpet to tell of his visits to the sick and dying, but quietly works in the great vineyard of the Master'. He obviously wrote it down for his own private instruction and as a reminder of how he should conduct himself, never thinking that it would sometime be made public. Mark wrote numerous letters for the wives of Troon men who had emigrated. These wives could not read or write, were not very articulate and could think of little to say. On one occasion when he enquired what this particular person wished him to write she replied in the vernacular, 'I doan knaw, tell 'un there's bags of flays [fleas] here.' He also kept up a prodigious correspondence with his emigrant brothers and sister and their families, recording the date of every letter sent and received.

With a keen sense of history Mark spoke with authority of the early days of Methodism in the area, a result of his association with Capt. Jimmy Thomas. In a talk which he gave to the Society at Troon there is, however, a shade of mystery. The latter portion of this talk refers to a person from the area who, in Mark's own words, 'I knew well and was intimately acquainted with'. He goes on to describe how this person, a pale-faced boy and miner at Dolcoath, later went out to the Copper Country of Upper Michigan, and although initially reluctant, began to preach and subsequently joined the Methodist Ministry.

Within the family this person has been assumed to be Mark's younger brother, who became Rev. Jacob Harris of the Methodist Episcopal Church, serving mainly in Missouri and Arkansas. Research has however shown that either the family are incorrect in their assumptions or the records of the talk has been subjected to incorrect editing. The main sticking point – and there are others – is contained in a statement by the minister which says, 'I am down on the boundary lines between the Northern and Southern Armies, but thank God peace is proclaimed and last night I preached to the liberated slaves of the Sunny South. Talk about tears that we shed on that memorable night 9 May.' As Jacob did not arrive in America until 6 June 1865 and was not licensed to preach until 1869 and not ordained until 1870, it follows that he could not have been present when the War for Southern Independence ended on 9 May 1865.

Mark presented a stained-glass window to the chapel at Troon in 1929. The simple inscription 'Given by MH' being consistent with his unobtrusive character.

The stained-glass window which MSH gave to Troon Wesleyan Chapel.

Poetic Utterances

Mark, like his brother John (3), loved walking in the countryside and communing with nature, so it was almost inevitable that he should commit his feelings to verse and the following lines illustrate his perception and love of nature:

A May Morning Ramble

What a quiet ramble,
I have had today.
Down through a lovely valley,
On this bright morn in May.

The trees arrayed in grandeur,
The fields in living green.
On right and left, on hill and vale,
New beauties to be seen.

At first I saw the cromlech,
Down in Pendarves Park,
I thought about its history,
But all was void and dark.

I fancied ancient Druid,
Performing cruel rite,
Bowed down with superstition,
And mind as dark as night.

Then adown the valley,
I lingered by a stream
The place was full of gladness,
Heaven's glories seemed to gleam.

Sweet music seemed to echo
From brooks and vales and flowers
It was indeed a pleasure,
To linger here for hours.

May nature's beauties teach me,
To love my Father God;
To read his word, and pray to Him:
As on my way I plod.

And then what joy and gladness,
Above what earth can give:
In our Father's house for ever,
With the bright and blest to live.

To the Cuckoo

Welcome pretty cuckoo, singing in the glen;
Long have we been waiting to hear thy note again.
Other forest songsters have been heard
  among us long,
But notes of thrush and linnet, are not like thy
  sweet song.

Thy note tells all of summer, of flowers and
  fields and lanes,
Of quiet long walks, and pleasant talks,
  through woods and dells and plains.
It tells of coming harvest, and autumn's pleasant time,
When songs of merry reapers, like Church
  going bells chime.

The children hail thy coming, with gladness
  and delight,
And all are cheered to hear thee, both morning
  noon and night.
O cuckoo pretty cuckoo, come linger with us long,
And may our lives be brighter, while listing to
  thy song.

And when alone with nature, communing with
  her hills,
And hearing sweetest music from brooks and
  vales and rills,
May thy note remind us of the songs of heaven above,
Where all is light and gladness, and peace and joy
  and love.

The Reens

O lovely spot, sequestered place
The quiet secluded Reens,
Here's music for the troubled soul,
And grand and glorious scenes.

The trees arrayed in living green,
Their leafy branches spread,
And at my feet the ivy climb
As if by instinct led.

The scented May, the Cuckoo blue,[13]
The primrose pale and fair,
And wild flowers of every hue
Breath fragrance on the air.

Just at my right a lovely stream
Is tumbling o'er the rocks.,
And down the vale it leaps and runs,
And at pursuers mocks.

On right and left, from tree and brake
The birds are singing sweet,
I feel its pleasant to be here
In such a quiet retreat.

O may I learn from nature's book,
From brooks and trees and flowers,
To love, and live for God alone,
Give Him my life, my hours.

June 1892

The Reens was a lovely woodland walk along a stream from the western side of Troon, down through the valley to a point on the road below Treslothan Church. The author remembers Mark's sorrow when the trees were felled and the beauty of the walk destroyed.

Spring

Cheering springtime O how welcome
After snow and frost and rain,
Winters storms and midnight tempest,
Pleased to see thy face again.

Rich and poor all hail thy coming,
Young and old alike rejoice.
King and subject, prince and pauper,
All are glad to hear thy voice.

Hills with furze and heath all covered,
Lift their voice and gladly sing,
Winter's past its storms are over,
Welcome, welcome lovely spring.

Lovely valleys clothed in beauty,
Echo forth their songs of praise.
Spring is come, the gentle springtime,
How we love these warm bright days.

Shady wood with buds and blossom,
And its coat of living green,
All aglow with life and beauty
In the springtime now are seen.

Then the notes of feathered songsters,
Make the hills and valleys ring,
As they fill the grove with music.
O how sweet to hear them sing.

We hear too the welcome cuckoo,
Singing sweetly in the glen,
Chasing grief and care and sadness,
From the troubled hearts of men.

Everything is bright with beauty;
Nature smiles on every hand.
Lovely springtime, fragrant flowers,
Gladden hearts throughout the land.

Passing seasons all remind us
Earthly scenes will soon be o'er,
And we hope to join the ransomed,
On the bright celestial shore.

23 April 1894

His Children

Edith Harris

Mark and Jane's eldest child, and mother of the author, was born in the cottage at Troon on 26 August 1871.

Edith's education commenced at Troon Board School, which was opened in 1875. The first Headmaster at Troon was William Jago, from Gosport in Hampshire, who remained at the school until 13 August 1886 when he left to assume the headship of Pool Board school, a village between Redruth and Camborne.[14] William Jago encouraged Edith, who made good progress in her studies. Prior to her fourteenth birthday she was appointed a monitor, remaining in this position until she was engaged as a pupil-teacher on 1 January 1889,[15] eight months before her eighteenth birthday. During her period as monitor she pursued a special course of studies as laid down by HM Inspector of Schools.

The family still have her original contract of employment as a pupil-teacher. It shows that she was to be paid seven pounds ten shillings per annum for the first year, increasing by thirty shillings in each subsequent year. Her father Mark, as surety, had to agree with Camborne School Board and their successors to clothe, feed, lodge and watch over her in a proper manner for the duration of the agreement, and the document was signed and sealed.

Edith's first pay as a pupil-teacher prompted Mark to write these verses:

To My Daughter Edith on receiving her First Pay

Up through the garden, my daughter she ran,
To tell the good news as good children can.
Her eyes sparkled brightly, and shone with delight,
And well I remember that heart cheering sight.

She shouted with gladness, and cried, 'Father see,
The bright silver coin they have given to me.
Yes its my own, how delighted I feel,
That I can do something in earning a meal.'

If riches and honours were laid at her feet,
No joy could be greater, no bliss so complete.
Than that of the maiden, on this sunny day,
So thinks her loved parent, in this his first lay.

Her joyous expression, her actions and looks,
They can't be forgotten, or written in books.
They live with me still amid conflict and strife,
And will follow me down through the
  journey of life.

Edith my darling, may thy pathway be bright,
And onward thy motto, to the mansions of Light.
And Jesus the Saviour, be thy refuge and rest,
Then heaven for ever, with the bright and the blest.

Again, on her twentieth birthday, Mark wrote further verses to Edith:

To My Daughter on her Twentieth Birthday

On this your birthday dearest daughter,
Pleased we are to see you well,
Pleased to see you hale and hearty,
Glad beyond what words can tell.

God has spared you, blessed you, led you,
Onward through another year;
Crowned your life with loving kindness,
Love Him, serve Him, without fear.

Spared to see your twentieth birthday,
At this welcome harvest time.
Emblem of your youth and brightness,
In your native sunny clime.

As the years roll by dear Edith,
May each birthday happier be,
Crowned with joy and peace and plenty,
Years of gladness may you see.

Father, Mother, brother wish you,
Birthdays many bright and sweet,
Then when time and years are ended,
In our Father's house to meet.

Edith avidly pursued her chosen profession and course of studies to become a Certificated Teacher. She was periodically examined in her subjects by HM Inspector of Schools, the examinations taking place at Trewirgie School, Redruth. At this time when a pupil teacher reached the stage when it was necessary to take the qualifying examination, it was taken at the nearest Teachers' Training College, presumably at Truro Diocesan Training College.

Edith had a love and inclination for history and in later years never ceased to try to interest the author in the subject.

Unfortunately Edith had to leave her studies and school at the end of 1891 when her mother became ill, in order to nurse her and to look after her father and younger brother Jacob. But typical of her upbringing and faith she never complained or talked about relinquishing her career. As far as she was concerned her duty to her parents came first, but she must have been very disappointed.

According to her contract, by leaving her employment without being able to give the School Board six months notice she would have been liable to pay liquidated damages of four pounds for her first year and one pound for each succeeding year. This meant that her total liability would have been six pounds. Her total pay for three years had been ten pounds ten shillings, which left her with four pounds ten shillings for three years work. Whether the liquidated damages clause was actually enforced is not known.

Edith Harris on right of picture with her class at Troon Board School, about 1891. The person on the left is probably Miss E.J. Gundry who was appointed Assistant Mistress on 18 January 1889.

On 1 June 1895, Edith was married at Camborne Wesleyan Methodist Church to Walter Harold Langford, then living at Bolenowe, but who had been born on 23 January 1871 at Polgooth in St Mewan Parish. Walter Harold was the only son and fourth child of Walter Hicks Langford and Elizabeth Bunney. Walter Hicks, Elizabeth and their family had moved from Polgooth to the St Day area in 1883, when Walter Hicks found work in the mines of that area. The family subsequently moved to Bolenowe arond 1887.

At their marriage, Edith and Walter moved into a new rented house at New Road, Troon. By 1902 they moved into their own house at Laity Road, Troon, which they had had built, Walter having been appointed Chief Agent of the Basset Mines twelve months previously.

Edith lost her first and another child in infancy, but nine others grew to adulthood, the author being the youngest of the family.

On 28 December 1917, Edith and Walter together with their family moved from Troon to the village of Lanner where Walter was employed at Tresavean Mine erecting a new stamp battery. The mine was situated just south of the village two miles south-east of Redruth.

After an illness lasting for six years, Edith passed away at Lanner on 1 August 1946, just twenty-five days before her seventy-fifth birthday, closing a life of self-sacrifice and duty to her God and her family.

As an anecdotal finale to Edith's life, it appears that as a child she apparently exhibited a somewhat out-of-character trait by seeking vengeance on the torturers of the Christians in *The Book of Martyrs* by John Foxe (1517-87). Apparently, she and her younger brother would turn the pages of the book and when they came to the pictures they proceeded to stick pins through the eyes of the torturers. How bizarre!

John (4) Harris

John (4), the second child of Mark and Jane, was born at Troon on 7 August 1873 and died there from croup on 23 September 1878, just five years, one month and nineteen days old.

He had been attending Troon Board School and the school Log Book[16] recorded his death: 'John Harris died on Monday morning from bronchitis'. One can but imagine the heartache his death caused this devoted couple, and for that matter his seven-year-old sister Edith.

He was buried at Treslothan where his young cousin Lucretia had been buried twenty-three years previously, but there is no record in respect of the grave's location.

Jacob (2) Harris

Jacob (2) was the third and last child of Mark and Jane, born at 48 Laity Row, Troon, on 25 May 1875.

Jacob attended Troon Board School and after leaving school commenced work as an apprentice in the blacksmith shop at Dolcoath Mine. There was no signed apprenticeship and in this context no responsibility on the part of the mine management; an apprentice relied solely on the goodwill of the craftsmen in the shop and by observation to gain knowledge of his trade. Despite these conditions, he became in due course a master of his trade.

Having served his apprenticeship, young Jacob decided to explore other possibilities and on 11 December 1895 began driving the man-engine at Dolcoath, no doubt after having the rudiments and requirements explained in detail by his father. After driving the man-engine for seven months, Jacob decided to carry out a reconnaissance of the Copper Country of Upper Michigan, following which he returned to this country and went into the blacksmith shop at South Frances Mine.

For the next twenty-seven years he worked at various mines in the area, the changes in employment being decreed by the fluctuations in the fortunes of the mines. On 25 August 1924, Jacob found employment at Holman Bros. Engineering Works at Camborne, where he remained until overtaken by ill health in 1934.

Jacob became a fully accredited Methodist Local Preacher in 1908. Like his father before him, he was a great walker and sick-visitor. Indeed, when his father ceased in 1924 to officiate at funerals in the area, Jacob took over for the next ten years until his health prevented him. Additionally, he was a teacher and secretary of the Sunday School and a trustee of the Wesleyan Chapel.

Jacob was a raconteur of no mean ability, and always had a great fund of stories to tell, many of which were extremely humorous. He also wrote a certain amount of verse, and below are some lines he composed for his twin grand-daughters on their second birthday:

Anniversary of the Birth of Twins
18 February 1936

Two years have run their cycles o'er,
Since the twinlets did arrive;
They were so weak and fragile then,
'Twas doubtful they'd survive.

But now they are two robust girls,
Can run, and romp, and play.
Their mother has a busy time,
And granny too - they say.

They laugh, and cry, with roguish pranks,
As other children do:
Just pay a visit to their home,
They'll grin and welcome you.

A chocolate they won't refuse,
A toffee's price - a kiss;
The pleasure flashing from their eyes
Is what I would not miss.

The future's hid from human ken,
Its pathway none can see;
May you dear children all your lives,
By heaven prompted be.

Then others will be blessed through you,
There's satisfaction here,
More than heaping piles of wealth,
For selfishness is dear.

Jesus himself – He taught that truth,
Whilst here upon this earth;
Compared the world with all its wealth,
The soul was of more worth.

Put first things in their place my dears,
Life will be a song,
Cheering some other troubled soul,
Just as you move along.

Farewell for the time dear children,
May smooth your future be;
For usefulness in life my dears,
Lives through eternity.

On 9 April 1899, Jacob was married at Centenary Wesleyan Methodist Church at Camborne to Myra Alice Pascoe, daughter of Thomas Pascoe and Alice Thomas Sims.[17] To them were born three children, John Leslie, Hazel Rebecca and Mark Thornton, but had more than their fair share of sorrow and tragedy. Their second child, Hazel, born on 14 June 1902, contracted meningitis and died on 1 May 1905. Their third child, Mark Thornton, was born 9 April 1909. He attended Troon Board School and Camborne School of Art and on leaving school obtained employment at Holman Bros. Engineering Works where, on 2 May 1924, he received multiple injuries during the course of his work. Admitted to Redruth Miners and Women's Hospital, it was deemed necessary to amputate both legs, but despite surgery Mark passed away on 10 May following. He was fifteen years and one month old. At the subsequent inquest, Mark's foreman described him as a very ambitious and industrious lad.

Mark's funeral at Troon was described as one of the largest and most impressive seen in the village for many years.[18] The choirs of the Anglican and both Methodist Churches assembled at the house and, as part of the huge procession, led the singing all the way to the Wesleyan Church. At the service conducted by Rev. E.E. Hall, who gave the eulogy emphasising Mark's association with the Church and Sunday School, Mark's favourite hymns *Thou Great Redeemer*, *Give me the Wings of Faith*, and *Safely Safely Gathered In* were sung.

Jacob and Myra's eldest child, John Leslie, was born on 21 May 1899. Leslie attended Troon Board School from the age of five until he was fourteen. The day following his fourteenth birthday, Leslie started work at Wheal Grenville Mine on the tin dressing floors and a few months later transferred to the blacksmith shop to learn the trade of blacksmith. By 1915 his parents moved from Troon to live near Carn Brea railway station, and he then took a job at Tincroft Mine blacksmith shop where he earned an additional four shillings per month.

Mark Thornton Harris, who was fatally injured at Holman's Engineering Works on 10 May 1924. He was only fifteen years old.

The Twins
Elizabeth and Marguerite Harris
Photographed June 1939

Mark Smith Harris, Myra Alice Pascoe Harris, wife of Jacob (2) Harris and Jacob (2) Harris.

During the early years of the First Word War, Leslie joined the Camborne Division of St John Ambulance Brigade. One of his duties to attend war wounded at Tregenna House, Camborne, which was then a sanctuary for service personnel.

Whilst at Tincroft Mine, his foreman advised him to register as a 'munitions engineer' so that he could gain experience living away from home prior to call-up to the armed forces. Leslie accepted the advice and in due course found himself in Lancashire at the works of Nasesmith and Wilson in a huge workshop containing thirty forges and upwards of six steam hammers.

Soon after his eighteenth birthday, Leslie received his calling-up papers and, at his own request, was drafted into the Royal Engineers. After taking a trade test at Woolwich he was sent to Gillingham and finally to Chatham to undergo his basic training in the 2nd Reserve Battalion. On completion of his initial training he was sent with a Field Company RE to Christchurch, Hampshire, for intensive training in bridge building. The training being completed, he was at home on embarkation leave when the Armistice was declared on 11 November 1918.

Following his military service, Leslie attended evening classes at Redruth School of Mines where he studied mining, ore dressing, chemistry, sampling panning and vanning, together with mathematics and in 1919 found employment in his trade at Wheal Agar Mine. There he 1,530 feet underground in the blacksmith shop which serviced the drive that became known as Tolgus tunnel. Later he worked on surface in the blacksmith shop until operations ceased in 1921.

In 1922, Leslie obtained an appointment with Messrs John Godden and Company in Curacao, Dutch West Indies, where the company operated phosphate quarries. Going out as foreman blacksmith, he soon found himself in charge of most of the technical support services of the quarries.

In 1923 Leslie accepted employment with Bolivar Venezuela Gold Mines Limited at Cuidad Bolivar. At this time the company was opening a new mine. Sometime afterwards the company was taken over by New Consolidated Gold fields and Leslie was asked to become a shift boss in the mill, which he accepted, and put to use the training he had received at Redruth School of Mines. He completed his first three-year contract with the company and commenced a second term in 1926. Upon completion of the second term he decided to return home for good.

After working for building contractors, latterly on the construction of a new tool-room at Holman's No. 3 Works at Camborne, Leslie became an employee of Holmans and was engaged on the installation and maintenance of plant and machinery. Demonstrating his skill,

pride and conscientious attitude to his work, he was given semi-skilled status in the tool-room and soon was put to operate a universal mill, where he remained until his retirement in 1964.

As a boy Leslie voluntarily attended Methodist Class Meetings with his father, and resulting from a 'Tent Mission' at Tregajoran in 1920, he became a church member. Like his father and paternal grandfather before him, Leslie was always a devoted visitor of the sick in Troon. He held the following offices at Troon St John's Methodist Church (Wesleyan): Trustee, Secretary of the Trust, Treasurer of the Trust, Chapel Steward, Poor Steward and Society Steward.

On 10 September 1929, Leslie married Ethel J. Crocker, a highly respected and well-known Troon resident. To this union twins, Elizabeth H. and Marguerite A.G., were born in 1934. But in 1939 this little family was destined to bear the ultimate bereavement when Ethel passed away. With two infant daughters to care for, Leslie married Christiana Jane Watters in 1940 and to this second union was born a daughter, Gwendoline Eleanor, in 1941. Although the three daughters subsequently married, the unity, loyalty and Christian charity of this family will always be an example to all.

Passed and raised in Igauldad Lodge No. 653 in Curacao in 1922, Leslie joined Mount Edgcumbe Lodge No. 1544 at Camborne in 1920, and in 1947 became Master of his mother lodge. In 1988 he was awarded the Provincial Grand Master's Certificate of Service to Freemasonry. At the presentation it was said that Leslie's charge after initiation was always 'A masterly demonstration of Masonic meaning and sincerity.'

On 6 April 1991, just six weeks before his ninety-second birthday and as the most senior church member, Leslie opened the new vestibule and unlocked the new main entrance doors of Troon Methodist Church, repeating a similar ceremony which his grandfather, Mark Smith Harris, had carried out in 1928. Prior to unlocking the door, Leslie quoted the following dedication: 'O God, make the door of this house wide enough to receive all who need human love and fellowship, narrow enough to shut out all envy, pride and strife. Make its threshold smooth enough to be no stumbling block to children, nor to straying feet, but rugged and strong enough to turn back the tempter's power. God, make the door of this house the gateway to thine eternal kingdom. Amen.'

Following the ceremony, a photograph of Leslie and his wife Chrissie was taken of them standing in front of the stained glass memorial window which Leslie had presented to the church in February 1927 in memory of his sister Hazel and brother Mark. A measure of Leslie's Christian charity can be appreciated by the many deeds of kindness to numerous people in an unobtrusive way. For instance, in March 1928 he purchased for his parents their home at 23 Pendarves Street, Troon. Also, when he returned from South America in 1929, he paid a weekly visit to Lanner and, whilst there, carried out various duties for his grandfather, Mark S. Harris.

Leslie passed away peacefully at his home on 12 February 1996, aged ninety-six. Prior to interment in Troon cemetery, a Service of Thanksgiving for his life was held in St John's Methodist Church. The service was conducted by Rev. Andrew Sowden, who had come down from Okehampton to honour the memory of this long-time servant of God and His church. Leslie's death witnessed the termination of the work and association with Methodism in Troon of a male line of four generations of Harrises, from his great-grandfather John (2), to his grandfather Mark S., to his father Jacob (2) and, finally, to himself.

Jacob (2) was buried in Troon cemetery following a funeral service in Troon St John's Methodist Church, conducted by Revs. Bone and Inwood. There was a large attendance of Methodist Local Preachers from Camborne Circuit.

His wife, Myra, lived on for another twenty-two years and died at Leslie's home, 3 Laity Road, Troon, on 26 October 1958 aged eighty-nine.

John Leslie Harris 1899–1996
Photographed 1989

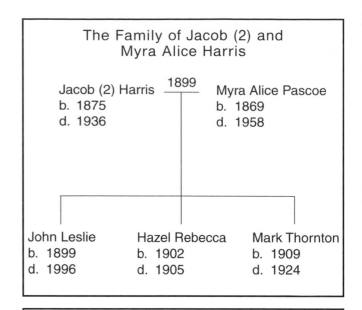

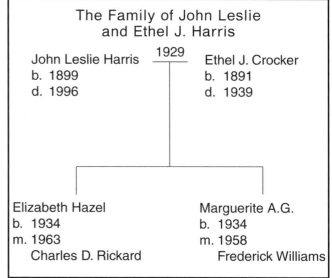

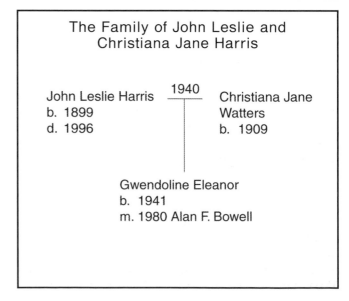

Mark and Jane's Later Years and Deaths

Mention has already been made of Jane and Mark sharing their home with other relatives. Mark's sister Kitty (Harris) Trevithick had lived with them since the death of her husband in 1878 and she passed away in early spring 1901. In the autumn of 1902, Jane's two sisters, Elizabeth (Rule) Crook and Catherine Rule, came down from Lancashire and made their home with Jane and Mark. It must have been something of an Old Folks Home; Jane was sixty-eight, Elizabeth seventy, Catherine sixty-seven and Mark sixty-one.

Elizabeth Crook, who had spent several years in New Zealand, had later, after her marriage to John Crook, been in business in Burnley, Lancashire. Following the death of her husband, and not being in good health, her doctor advised her to return to Cornwall to seek the benefit of the pure Cornish air. Catherine Rule had been a teacher in the Industrial School at Kirkdale, Liverpool.

Jane's health had been failing for some time and she passed away on 8 September 1908, aged seventy-four, and so this devoted and loving partnership between Mark and Jane ended. Following a service in Troon Wesleyan Chapel, the burial took place in Troon cemetery amid many signs of respect from the villagers. Mark was left to carry on his visitation of the poor and sick in the service of his Master.

Elizabeth Crook passed away in the summer of 1911 and like Jane was buried in Troon cemetery. Catherine Rule lived on until the spring of 1919 and was buried in the same grave as Elizabeth.

Mark was now left in somewhat lonely circumstances and now in his seventies was also losing his eyesight, and so in November 1921 his son Jacob (2) and his wife Myra, together with their two sons, John Leslie and Mark Thornton, came to live with him and to look after him.

Mark remained in his beloved Troon until January 1928. He then moved to Lanner to the home of his daughter Edith Langford and later that year returned by special request to Troon Wesleyan Church to perform the opening ceremony when new main entrance doors had been installed; he regaled the gathering with a brief history of Methodism in the village.

Mark passed away at Lanner 26 August 1931, aged ninety. He was taken back to Troon for burial. At the funeral service Mr George Willoughby, a senior local preacher of the circuit, paid tribute and Rev. H.S. Strawson drew attention to 'The wonderful influence for God which Mark had exerted in Troon and through Camborne Methodist Circuit.'

> He walked with God and he was not,
>   for God took him.
>
> Genesis 5, verse 24.

It is of interest that the book *Mark Harvey the Engine Driver and other Stories* by W. Kago, published by C.H. Kelly, London, in 1896 is based on the life of Mark Smith Harris.

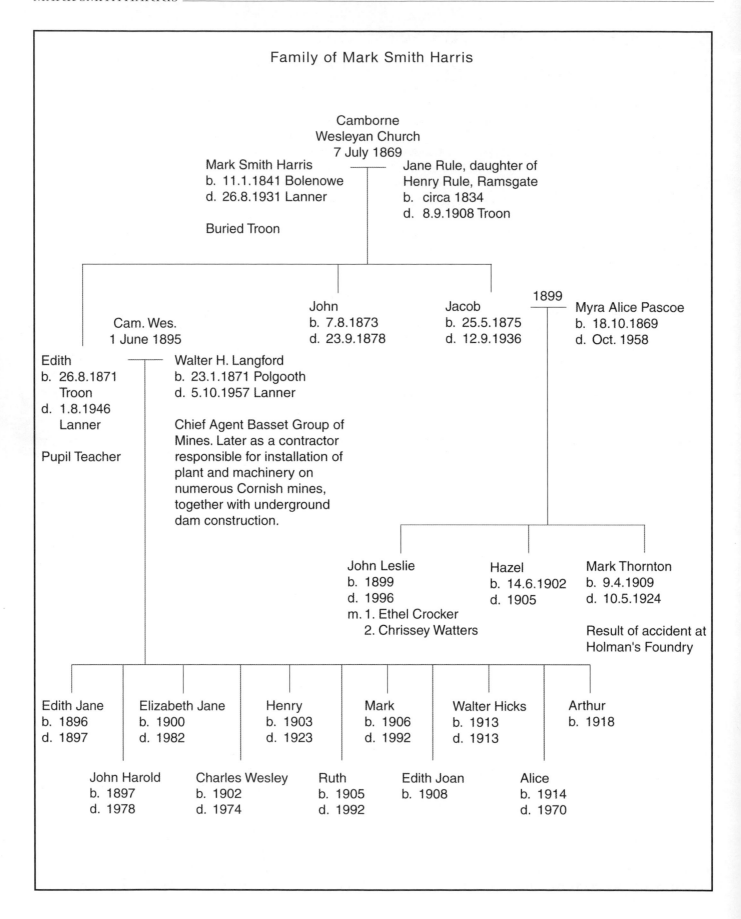

Family of Mark Smith Harris

Camborne
Wesleyan Church
7 July 1869

Mark Smith Harris
b. 11.1.1841 Bolenowe
d. 26.8.1931 Lanner

Buried Troon

Jane Rule, daughter of
Henry Rule, Ramsgate
b. circa 1834
d. 8.9.1908 Troon

Cam. Wes.
1 June 1895

John
b. 7.8.1873
d. 23.9.1878

Jacob
b. 25.5.1875
d. 12.9.1936

1899

Myra Alice Pascoe
b. 18.10.1869
d. Oct. 1958

Edith
b. 26.8.1871
Troon
d. 1.8.1946
Lanner

Pupil Teacher

Walter H. Langford
b. 23.1.1871 Polgooth
d. 5.10.1957 Lanner

Chief Agent Basset Group of
Mines. Later as a contractor
responsible for installation of
plant and machinery on
numerous Cornish mines,
together with underground
dam construction.

John Leslie
b. 1899
d. 1996
m. 1. Ethel Crocker
2. Chrissey Watters

Hazel
b. 14.6.1902
d. 1905

Mark Thornton
b. 9.4.1909
d. 10.5.1924

Result of accident at
Holman's Foundry

Edith Jane
b. 1896
d. 1897

Elizabeth Jane
b. 1900
d. 1982

Henry
b. 1903
d. 1923

Mark
b. 1906
d. 1992

Walter Hicks
b. 1913
d. 1913

Arthur
b. 1918

John Harold
b. 1897
d. 1978

Charles Wesley
b. 1902
d. 1974

Ruth
b. 1905
d. 1992

Edith Joan
b. 1908

Alice
b. 1914
d. 1970

12. Rev. Jacob Smith Harris

Early Life 1843–65

Jacob, the eleventh and last child of John (2) and Christian, was born at Six Chimneys, Bolenowe Carn, on 25 May 1843 and was baptized at Camborne Parish Church on 9 August the same year. In Chapter 10 on Benjamin (4), Jacob S. was designated Jacob (1) but it has been necessary to change this as later, following his arrival in America in 1865, he added a middle name of Smith. Presumably this was to differentiate between himself and another of the same name. As in the case of his next older brother, Mark Smith Harris, 'Smith' was derived from his mother's maiden name. Beyond eventually sharing the additional initial, there was a very close bond between these two brothers, for from the time that Jacob S. left for America until his death in 1914 they exchanged over 250 letters.

John (2) had passed away just a month before to his youngest son's fifth birthday and John (3) was compelled to compose a few verses for his youngest brother. It told of the youngster's carefree life despite the death of his father, and postulated as to where Jacob S. would be on his fiftieth birthday:

Five springs have come and gone;
Five summers thou hast seen,
With mirth and music tripping on,
And mantled o'er with green;
Five autumns sad and still,
Withering the forest-leaf,
When Robin, on our dear old hill,
Sings by the oaten-sheaf.

Five winters, with their storm,
Have smote thee on thy way;
And thou, poor little orphan one,
Art five years old to-day.
This birthday on our hill
Is spent in childish glee;
But change is written everywhere;
Where will thy fiftieth be?

Toss'd on the ocean-wave,
Or roaming the green sod,
Or falling ere thou art so old,
Thy spirit with its God.
Or, far from England's isle,
The land we so admire,
Thou mayst sit down alone, alone,
Beside the stranger's fire.

Sweet is the month of song,
But, brother, we are sad;
Thy Father to the grave is gone,
Thou art an orphan-lad.
But O, thou leapest round,
With laughing, loving joy,
As if, indeed, thou never wert
A little orphan-boy.[1]

It is assumed that Jacob S. attended the National School at Camborne from the age of seven, which instilled in him a desire for self-improvement. Indeed. he developed an interest, no doubt inspired by the teachers at the school, in geology and mineralogy. Then when at almost eleven years of age he commenced working at the famous Dolcoath Mine, initially on surface and later underground with his brother Benjamin (4), he was able to develop this interest by close observation of the mineralisation of this extraordinary mine, which in 1853 had paid its first dividend on tin although still producing a certain amount of copper. Jacob S. laboured on, increasing his knowledge of practical mining, together with the vagaries of the lodes. He and Benjamin (4) were eventually to benefit from his increasing ability to detect the indication of richer masses of ore; so much so that they were able to put by a reasonable sum of money which, in turn, gave them the idea that they could take the opportunity of going out to the Copper Country of Upper Michigan. The decision was taken and Jacob S. set out from Troon just prior to his twenty-second birthday, together with Benjamin (4) and his wife and young son.

Surprisingly, when John (5) wrote a short *John Harris Family History* in 1972, he recorded some very mistaken details about Dolcoath Mine. He claimed that 'Dolcoath was the deepest mine in the world, and that it had been worked since 55BC when Julius Caesar had tin brought from the mine to Rome.' In fact, underground mining in Cornwall only commenced during the sixteenth century. That Dolcoath became the deepest and most extensive mine in Cornwall is not disputed. Although the actual start date of Dolcoath is not positively known, a conclusion can be made from the following details:

(a) The first recorded mention of the name Dolcoath appears in a document concerning dues paid to the owner of the mineral rights in 1731.[2]

(b) The mine was only 792 feet deep in 1789.[3]

From this it can be seen that the depth of the mine only increased by just over thirteen and a half feet per year over a period of fifty-eight years and therefore it is unlikely that the mine operated prior to 1731. It is accepted that in the early twentieth century the Williams' shaft of the mine was sunk to 3,000 feet. Even this does not compare with the eventual depths of mines in South Africa, the Kolar goldfields in South India or those in the Copper Country of Upper Michigan to name but a few. As a matter of interest, T.A. Morrison in his *Cornwall's Central Mines - The Southern District* states that in February 1863 and Easter 1866 the bottom of Dolcoath was 1,830 and 1,902 feet respectively. By interpolation we can see that when Jacob S. left the mine in May 1865, the probable depth was only 1,884 feet.

Concerning the statement in respect of the Romans, it is true that there was a Cornish tin trade in antiquity. No doubt the Romans were aware of the trade between Cornwall and the Phoenicians of the eastern Mediterranean; although they may have been on the fringe of this trade, there is no positive evidence that the Romans settled in Cornwall or that any Legions were stationed here. Indeed, their most westerly city in Britain was Exeter[4] in Devon. An important consideration in respect of the Cornish tin works in antiquity is that the tin was recovered from the elluvial deposits in the valleys, low-lying ground and the disintegrated rock on the lode outcrops. Subsequent to this period, and after underground mining was developed on a big scale, the alluvial[5] deposits were also worked.

Emigration and Mining in America 1865-69

The little party arrived in New York on 6 June 1865. They probably did not know until they landed that Confederate General Lee had surrendered at Appomatox Courthouse, Virginia, eight weeks and two days previously. They went straight to the Copper Country and obtained employment with the Phoenix Copper Company in Keweenaw County, where their brother, Samuel B., had been appointed Mine Captain five weeks after their arrival in New York. It is of interest to note that one of the originators of the company, Col. Charles Gratiot, had previously been engaged in lead mining in Missouri. The Phoenix Company was first registered in 1843 but ran out of money, prompting a reorganisation in 1849.[6] At the time of Samuel B.'s appointment, the company had undergone a further reorganisation with still more capital, so it would have seemed to Jacob S. to be a fair prospect. However, within a few months, the Lake Superior winter was upon them and Jacob S. did not relish the harsh climate.

A story has been handed down which claims that on coming up from underground on a particular occasion, Jacob S. went to the mine office to speak to Samuel B. and, among other things, complained very strongly about the weather. With Samuel B. at the time was a representative from St Joseph Lead Company who owned tracts of mineral land in Missouri. The representative was probably in the Copper Country to note the latest mining practice and to recruit labour for the Missouri mines. He apparently enquired of Jacob S. if he would like to go down to the warmer climate of Missouri to help develop the lead mines, a proposal to which Jacob S. readily agreed. Having engaged a small number of Cornish miners from the Copper Country, the story goes that Jacob S. agreed to take charge of them. This would have been a reasonable request, considering that Jacob S. was the brother to an up-and-coming mine captain and also had an interest in mineralogy. Thus the party went down to the St Joseph Lead Mines in St Francois County.

The protracted development of the lead mines in Missouri is somewhat surprising, not least because of their eventual vast production. In 1723 a Mr D. Renault, accompanied by a mineralogist and a labour force, went to Missouri under the authority of a permit from the French Government issued to a company owned by John Law. They discovered and mined lead in the area now known as the Lead Belt. The St Joseph Lead Company was organised in New York on 26 March 1864 with a capital of a million dollars, *all* of which was paid for the ownership of a tract of land containing 946 acres. In order to develop the property, a mortgage of $75,000 was obtained, but in reality they were trying to operate without working capital. This was an encumbrance which resulted in only working the outcrops and then not in an organised manner. At the Annual Meeting of the company on 13 June 1865, work was reported to be progressing very slowly and not very satisfactorily, resulting in a new Board of Directors being elected. It was admitted that many setbacks had been experienced at the mines, namely a drought in July 1864 and a raid by Confederate Forces in the autumn which prevented a return to work for almost two months, followed by a bad winter. This led to operating costs being double the value of sales. In view of the situation, the majority of directors decided to visit the site.

Following the visit, a Resident Superintendent, Mr J.C. Winslow, was appointed on 17 July 1865 and on 28 September 1865 Mr J. Wyman-Jones was elected President. Soon after, it was decided to recruit some Cornish miners to exploit the operation. Enter Jacob S. Harris. In May 1867 Mr C.D. Parsons replaced Mr Winslow as Resident Superintendent at the mines, a post which he held for the next twenty-four years.[7]

But what of Jacob S. Harris? Although it has been reported that he became Superintendent for St Joseph Lead Company, the foregoing information on this particular staff position suggests the report is incorrect. However, it does appear that Jacob S. was given a roving commission by the company to inspect and report on the possibilities of certain locations in Missouri, together with some developments in North Carolina. Certainly on 16

September 1867, his brother Mark S. in Cornwall recorded: 'Received Jacob's first letter from North Carolina', the address being Jamestown, Guilford County, NC. Then, in July and September 1868, Jacob S. was back in Missouri on St Joseph Lead Company locations. Just what duties Jacob S. was carrying out for the company in North Carolina is not definitely known.

North Carolina's mineral resources included iron, copper, silver, lead, zinc and gold. Very few business concerns survived the Civil War, but as soon as the war ceased, speculators from the northern States arrived to buy out failing concerns and start new ones.[8] This indicates that St Joseph Lead Company or some of its shareholders may well have had holdings in these post-Civil War enterprises. Both the Gardiner Hill and North State mines were three and two and a half miles respectively from Jamestown. Both mines were working in 1867 and produced copper, some lead and some gold.[9] It is on record that Cornish miners were brought in to work the gold mines in Guilford County after 1853 but the mines were in decline by 1861 and never recovered.[10]

Jacob S. was back in North Carolina following another spell in Missouri in 1868 but, in 1869, he was granted a Licence to Preach by the North Carolina Methodist Conference[11] and resigned his employment with St Joseph Lead Company.

In concluding this section, it is necessary to say that, unfortunately, there is nothing in the records of St Joseph Lead Company in their Clayton, Missouri, office or Viburnum in the Lead Belt in respect of Jacob S. Harris.[12]

Service to Methodism in America 1869-96

Having obtained his Licence to Preach, Jacob S. returned to Missouri to attend a course at what subsequently became known as Carleton College. In his own words, the reason for attending college was 'to improve his mind'. Whether this had been suggested to him by the Methodist Church or if he personally felt it was necessary is not known but, on balance, it would seem to have been suggested by the Church. Actually, at this time he had decided to become a full-time travelling preacher and therefore this course of action was both wise and desirable. His decision to preach was not sudden, for he had become a member of Troon Wesleyan Church in 1862, three years prior to going to America. It is also clear that he attached himself to whatever Methodist Church there was in his various previous locations in America.

Carleton College at Farmington was originally known as Carleton Institute and had been founded by a Miss Eliza Ann Carleton in 1854. The building was a log cabin located in the vicinity of French Village, a pioneer settlement in Missouri. It attracted many young people.

In 1859 Miss Carleton obtained a charter from the General Assembly of Missouri, which granted the Institute the rights and privileges common to universities. By 1879, owing to its growing reputation, it relocated to a larger and more accessible site in Farmington, occupying a large four-storey building on a campus of sixteen acres. This thirty-room building was extended in 1884 by a large addition.

Up to this time, the Institution and College had been affiliated to the Methodist Church but was then officially deeded to the Church.[13] One may conclude that this was the log cabin Institute that Jacob S. attended.

Jacob S. was determined to succeed in his new vocation. He would have been able to earn much more money in mining than as a travelling preacher; indeed, in his autobiography *Pioneer Life in the West* 1853, Rev. James B. Finley quoted General Harrison as saying in respect of travelling preachers: 'Their condition is just the same as though they had taken the vow of poverty.' Possibly the position of Jacob S. was somewhat better. He would have been well aware of the doctrines and disciplines of the Methodist Episcopal Church, which were being formulated at the time and finally published in 1876. To start with, there were the regulations regarding 'Receiving Travelling Preachers on Trial':

144 (1) A preacher is to be received on trial by the Annual Conference.

(2) In the interval of Conference by a Bishop or Presiding Elder of the District, until the sitting of the Conference.

145 No one should be received unless he first produces a recommendation from the Quarterly Conference of the Circuit or Station. We may then, if he gives us satisfaction receive him on trial. But before any such candidate is received on trial, or into full connection, or is ordained Deacon or Elder, he shall give satisfactory evidence respecting his knowledge of those particular subjects which have been recommended to his consideration.

146 When a preacher's name is not printed in the minutes he must receive a written Licence from a Bishop or Presiding Elder, but while he is on trial the Annual Conference alone has jurisdiction over the question of his authority to preach, and his continuance on trial shall be equivalent to the renewal of his Licence to Preach.

147 Observe! Taking on trial is entirely different from admitting a preacher into full connection.

One on trial may be either admitted or rejected without doing him any wrong: otherwise it would be no trial at all.

148   At each Annual Conference, those who are received on trial, or are admitted into full connection shall be asked whether they are willing to devote themselves to the missionary work, and a list of the names of all those who are willing to do so shall be taken and reported to the Corresponding Secretaries of the Missionary Society; and all such shall be considered as ready willing to be employed as missionaries whenever called for by either of the Bishops.[14]

Having taken steps to improve his mind and fully understand the doctrines and disciplines of the Church, Jacob S. had now to present himself to be received On Trial by the Missouri Annual conference. In this he was successful in 1870. Immediately following his being accepted On Trial, Jacob S. began his full-time work in Bloomfield Church in south-east Missouri, the town itself being about forty-five miles from the Mississippi River and the Kentucky border. Then, after twelve months, he was moved, presumably as a supply, to the Arkansas Conference Circuit of Murfressboro near the western border of the state with Oklahoma. The area around Murfressboro is noted for its Ancient Indian graves, and one wonders if he also became interested in archaeology.

Then, in 1872, Jacob S. returned to the St Louis, Missouri Conference. He had now completed his two-year trial period and on acceptance by the Annual Conferences of Missouri and Arkansas he was received into full connection[15] and appointed to the Marshfield Circuit in south-west Missouri. The manner of receiving travelling preachers into full connection demanded absolute commitment, which can be appreciated from the following:

149   In receiving a preacher at the Conference into full connection, after solemn fasting and prayer, every person proposed shall be asked, before the Conference, the following questions, (with any others which may be thought necessary,) namely:

1.   Have you faith in Christ?

2.   Are you going on to perfection?

3.   Do you expect to be made perfect in love in this life?

4.   Are you groaning after it?

5.   Are you resolved to devote yourself wholly to God and his work?

6.   Do you know the rules of Society?

7.   Do you keep them?

8.   Do you constantly attend the Sacrament?

9.   Have you read the Form of Discipline?

10.   Are you willing to conform to it?

11.   Have you considered the Rules of a Preacher, especially the first, tenth, and twelfth?

12.   Will you keep them for conscience' sake?

13.   Are you determined to employ all your time to the work of God?

14.   Will you endeavour not to speak too long or too loud?

15.   Will you diligently instruct the children in every place?

16.   Will you visit from house to house?

17.   Will you recommend fasting or abstinence, both by precept and example?

18.   Are you in debt?

150   Then if he gives us satisfaction, after he has been employed two successive years in the regular itinerant work on Circuit, in Stations, or in our institutions of learning, which is to commence from his being received on trial at the Annual Conference, and being approved by the Annual Conference, and examined by the President of the Conference, he may be received into full connection.[16]

With his appointment to Marshfield, Jacob S. was certainly living up to his job description of travelling preacher. But Jacob S. enjoyed the countryside and was very interested in observing the flora and fauna and to indulge in his study of geology.

It was at Marshfield that Jacob S. met and married Sarah Charlotte Wharton. Sarah (Sallie) had been born on 14 February 1847 in Saline County, Missouri, and was the daughter of John Green Wharton and his wife Margaret. Following a short courtship they were married on 2 March 1873 and immediately left for Cuba in the St James Circuit, Missouri, where Jacob S. had been appointed Pastor of the small Methodist Episcopal Society which had been first organised in 1872 with twelve members.[17] Jacob S. remained with this Society for two years and it was here that their only child John (5) was born. The family came to love this particular area of the Ozarks. Curiously for the period 1873–74 inclusive, no Cuba address is recorded in his brother Mark's notebook.

In 1875 he was transferred to Iberia Church, also in St James Circuit. Here they were much nearer the Lake of the Ozarks and it was here that they were able, on occasions, to indulge in the relaxing pastime of fishing.

In 1876 he moved to Ironton Church in the east of the State, in the St Louis district, where he remained for two years. This appointment was followed by another year at De Sota Church, also in St Louis district.

In 1879 he moved to Sedalia District in charge of Schell City and Walker Churches. The following two years, 1880 and 1881, were spent at Lebeck Church, still in Sedalia District.

In 1882 Jacob S. was transferred to the Arkansas Conference where he initially served Dayton church in Fort Smith District for two years. Then he served another two years at Charleston Church, also in Fort Smith District. At the end of his final year at Charleston he was granted the singular honour of being selected for duty as a Conference member of Triers of Appeals.

When the author discussed this honour with an American Methodist couple, unrelated to the family, they immediately responded by saying, 'He must have been held in high esteem for this to happen.'

The selection of Triers of Appeals is described in the Discipline of the United Methodist Episcopal Church 1896 and is as follows:

The Judicial Conference

262   The several Annual Conferences shall at each session, select seven Elders, men of experience and sound judgement, in the affairs of the Church, who shall be known as Triers of Appeals.

The duties of this judicial committee of seven were to hear and to submit judgement, whenever required, on Ministers, Local Preachers and members who had previously been disciplined.

In 1886, Jacob S. was appointed to Russelville Church and, in 1887, to Waldron, where he remained for two years and then in 1889 to Magazine Church. These three appointments were in Fort Smith District.

In 1890 he became responsible for Marble City Church in Eureka Springs District. Marble City was his last appointment under the Arkansas Conference and at this point he was seconded to the Kansas Conference for twelve months, where be became Pastor of Wellsford Church in Kiowa County.

Initially he seems to have visited Anthony, near the southern border of Kansas with Oklahoma, before taking up residence in Wellsford; at least he wrote to his brother Mark from Anthony Wellsford, on the Kiowa-Pratt County border, lies west of Wichita. It is now a ghost town of Kansas with only a few citizens. In 1969 it was reported to have only eight citizens, the Mayor

Marriage Certificate of Jacob S. Harris and Sarah C. Wharton

having been elected with just six votes! It was first established as a rural post office in 1886 and was a stop on the Cannon Ball Stage prior to the arrival of the railroad in 1887, after which it became a railroad boomtown.

The Methodist Society in Wellsford was initiated mainly by three brothers, Isaiah, George and Aaron Starkey, their families and sister Louis. These folk had come from Ohio in April 1884, travelling first by railroad and finally by wagon. Their first home was a four-roomed dugout. It was wonderful land for growing crops, with plenty of quail and wild chicken.

The Starkeys were said to have been 'dyed in the wool Methodists'. They and other families felt the need for religious services and started holding meetings and Sunday Schools in their dugouts. Their first regular established meeting place was in the upstairs hall of a building that was shared with other denominations.

The first Methodist Class Meeting in Wellsford was organised by a Circuit Rider in 1885, and the first regular Pastor to the Circuit was appointed in 1887. As soon as a school was built, Methodist services were held there.

The early 1890s saw a drought and hot winds scorched the area, causing many families to leave. It was during this drought that Jacob S. commenced his Pastorate. Surprisingly in these conditions, he received $356, including housing for twelve months. However, as a result of the work of preceding Pastors and that of Jacob S., by the end of his term of office the Methodist Church was chartered and at this time numbered ninety-four members.

Twenty years later a new church was built and consecrated. In 1960 the Society celebrated the seventy-fifth anniversary of its founding. Five years later, due to the fast-diminishing population, the church was declared abandoned at the Annual Conference in Dodge City in May 1965, and placed in the hands of the Conference Trustees for disposal.[18]

At the end of his term in Wellsford Jacob S. returned to St Louis, Missouri Conference to serve Vichy Springs Church, where he remained for two years. In 1894 he became responsible for Newburg and Dixon Churches, both in Lebanon District, and in 1895 was appointed Pastor to Lebanon Church. This was the last active pastorate of Jacob S., for he was superannuated in 1896.

Last Years and Death 1896-1914

Following twenty-six years of continuous service in the travelling ministry by Jacob S., it is unfortunate that there is no written record of his day-by-day experiences. There must have been hard and complex decisions for him to make, oft-times in difficult and frustrating situations when his faith must have been tested to the limit.

He had served in places where it is known that outlaws operated. Indeed, his third church appointment in

Marshfield was near the homes of the James brothers, the Younger brothers and Sam Hilderbrand.[19] In fact, during a pastoral visit to one of the families of his congregation he met Sam Hilderbrand and shook hands with him. Jacob S. asked Hilderbrand to become a Christian and gave him a religious tract. Was it possibly one of the tracts written by his eldest brother John (3)?

The Civil War had ended just five years prior to his entering the full-time ministry. One can only conjecture as to the wounds that had been left in human relations and how far the harsh feelings between people, which had been caused by the war, had abated. The numerous letters Jacob S. wrote to his brother Mark may well have told the story and answered these questions. Mark kept these letters for up to sixty years but in the late 1920s they were foolishly destroyed.

However, Jacob S. did in another way endeavour to inform Mark in 1893 of the problems and conditions appertaining to the daily routine of a travelling preacher in America during the first half of the nineteenth century. He sent Mark a copy of *Pioneer Life in the West* by the Rev. James B. Finley. The book is currently in the possession of the author's family. It is understood that his period as a travelling preacher left Jacob S. in poor health.

It is not certain how soon after superannuation Jacob S. moved from Lebanon District, but he and Sarah were residing in Cuba, Missouri by January 1899 and the 1900 census for Crawford County shows Jacob S. and Sarah living in Washington Street, Cuba. Their son John (5) was already living in Cuba. Then, in 1905, John (5) decided to move to St George, Georgia and was followed by Jacob S. and Sarah in 1907.

On the 1910 Charlton County census for St George, the two families were next-door neighbours in Gordon Street. But the state of health of Jacob S. was deteriorating and from 1906 he was unable to continue his correspondence with Mark, and from that date Sarah took on the responsibility of letter writing. Additionally, there is no record of Jacob S. being involved in the Methodist Church in Georgia.[20]

In 1912 the scholastic duties of John (5) caused him to rent lodgings in Folkston, some twenty miles north of St George, but he maintained his new St George home, which he had named Bolleno Lodge. This was the address from which Sarah wrote to inform the family in Cornwall that Jacob S. had passed away on 17 January 1914 and was laid to rest in Pineview Cemetery, Folkston. It is surprising that for a Minister who had given such loyal and faithful service a Conference obituary cannot be traced, despite enquiries to Conference Archival Institutions across the United States. Neither does an obituary appear in the *Charlton County Herald* and no copies of a St George newspaper of the time can be found.

Sarah, the faithful and devoted wife of Jacob S., lived on for another fourteen years, making her home with John (5) and Cora. She was known to her friends as 'Mother Harris'[21] and was greatly loved and respected. Jacob S. and Sarah had had the pleasure of bringing up their only child and of seeing him mature as a person of absolute integrity and ethical values. Her particular influence on his life had surely been of paramount importance.

Sarah had intimated earlier in the year that she would like to pass away when the flowers in the garden were in full bloom,[22] and so it was, when a gorgeous display of autumn blooms filled the garden of John (5) at Bolleno Lodge, St George on 17 October 1928. Her illness was of only short duration, just a few days in fact, and she was laid to rest alongside Jacob S. in Pineview Cemetery.

John (5) Harris 1874-1979

John (5), the only child of Rev. Jacob S. and Sarah Charlotte Harris, was born in Cuba, Missouri on 20 January 1874. They became a close-knit little family and due to the itinerant nature of the ministry of Jacob S., they moved to six different locations by the time John (5) was nine years old. In these times, school attendance was not compulsory so, because of the ever-changing locations, Jacob S. and Sarah educated John (5) at home.

Their instruction must have been of a high order, because when he commenced school in 1883, he was placed in the fourth grade. Obviously he was a very adept pupil, for he points out in an autobiographical sketch that the fourth grade included literary selections that were equivalent to Upper High School level in 1974. But let it not be thought that he was a goody-goody. He was never behind in school pranks, even to chewing tobacco. However, the result of this latter experience made him vow never to have anything further to do with tobacco, and he never did.

At the young age of eight, John (5) passed examinations in the catechism and portions of scripture and became a member of the Methodist Church. He and his father enjoyed a very close companionship. The two went on frequent excursions into the hills and woods to study the rock formations and bird and plant life.

At thirteen years of age, in 1887, John (5) enrolled in the preparatory department of Carleton College, Farmington, Missouri, to prepare for the college entrance examination the following year. Carleton College was the educational establishment that had developed from Carleton Institute, which his father had attended in 1869. Having passed the entrance examination, John (5) had intended to study for a degree in mining engineering, but when one of his friends was killed by a premature explosion in a local lead mine he decided to change to a degree in literature. The only subject that caused him difficulty was Latin, but much working late into the night

enabled him to master this subject. This did not prevent him from participating in student capers. Nevertheless, at the age of sixteen, he graduated from Carleton College with a B.Litt. Degree, majoring in Greek and Latin.

Leaving college in 1890, John (5) returned for a short while to live with his parents in Eureka Springs, Arkansas. Here, at his father's suggestion, he set up a small printing business which soon thrived.

In 1891 his father was appointed to Wellsford, Kansas, so John (5) decided to move to Marshfield, Webster County, Missouri, the town where his parents had met. Here he lodged with his aunt and uncle and their family of seven children. Not surprisingly, living with a family of this size gave John (5) a whole new perspective of family life and one which he greatly enjoyed with substitute brothers and sisters. Here at Marshfield he became involved in setting up a newspaper in Webster County, the *Marshfield Mail*. Then, in November 1894, he moved to Cuba, Missouri, the town of his birth.

In Cuba he revived the publication of the *Crawford County Telephone* newspaper and changed its name to *Cuba Telephone*. According to his own account, editing and printing the newspapers occupied his time by day and by night. The newspaper office and printing plant occupied a new stone-built structure on North Sixth Street, Cuba.[23]

John (5) Harris 1874 – 1979
At age seventeen in Marshfield, Missouri

On 21 January 1895, John (5) married Cora Lewis at a civil ceremony in Cuba and on the following day his father came from Lebanon City, Missouri to perform the religious ceremony. It is interesting to note that the civil ceremony took place the day following John's (5) twenty-first birthday. Under the State law, the man was required to be twenty-one prior to marriage.

Like his father's courtship, that of John (5) was equally brief. Cora was the daughter of Laurence Harrison Lewis (1840-1921) and his wife Elizabeth C Evans, who had married on 4 March 1874. L.H. Lewis had been born in Amboy, New York, and as a young man attended the State Law College in Cleveland, Ohio. Here he obtained a Diploma of Bachelor of Law and was admitted to the Bar and the Courts of the United States. For health reasons he was advised to move to the West and arrived in Cuba, Missouri in 1871. Here he became involved in the development of Cuba. He represented Crawford County for three terms on the State Legislature. A keen Republican, he was very proud of the fact that his first presidential vote was for Abraham Lincoln.[24]

Pursuing his Methodist tradition, John (5) was elected Superintendent of Cuba Methodist Sunday School in the same year as his marriage.

His unflagging efforts for his newspaper were displayed when, on 8 July 1898, a flash-flood washed away much of the town of Steelville, the Crawford County seat, situated eight miles from Cuba. He boarded a train for Steelville, the last to cross the bridge over the Meramec River before it was washed away. For the next two nights and three days, John (5) reported on the scene of death and destruction for a special edition of his own newspaper and for the *St Louis Republic* and *St Louis Post & Despatch* newspapers.

In 1899 John (5) was elected President of Crawford County Sunday School Association and visited various Sunday Schools in the county to institute ways of improving their efficiency.

In 1901, a proposal to hold a Crawford County Fair was made with John (5) as temporary secretary. As soon as the officials were all elected John (5) became secretary. The first Fair was held a year later in October, and John (5) reported in his newspaper that it was a great success and healed many differences between communities. No doubt the experience gained in organising this event was later valuable to John (5) for similar events in Georgia.

On 16 August 1902, John (5) joined the Freemasons, becoming a Master Mason of Cuba Lodge. Also in this year he made his first annual visit to Jefferson City during the session of the State Legislature as Clerk to the Committee on Private Corporations. This brought him into contact with leading lawyers and gave him an insight into the procedures of legislation.

When the telephone came to Cuba in 1903, John (5) changed the name of his newspaper from *Cuba Telephone* to *Cuba Review*. Then, in 1904, perhaps unknowingly, he served his last term as Clerk at the State Legislature.

In January 1905, leaving the *Cuba Review* in charge of a trusted employee, T.L. Baxter, John (5) and Cora left Cuba and moved to the colony town of St George, Charlton County, Georgia.

During his period with *Cuba Review*, John (5) campaigned for many causes aimed at improving conditions and prospects for the communities of Crawford County, and also in exposing certain political misdemeanours. Notably he fought hard to get a brick schoolhouse, one of the first in south-east Missouri. The paper was also instrumental in promoting the Crawford County Fair. When a new railroad cut the wheat-growing area in the north by thirty miles, destroying the trade in wheat, the paper spent time and effort in arousing interest in chicken and egg production, in raising and shipping strawberries by the railcar load and in growing big red apples that for years made the county famous. In the first season that Cuba shipped over a hundred railcar loads of these apples to eastern and northern markets, it was considered a banner achievement; the loss of the wheat trade had been overcome. John (5), in the *Cuba Review*, declared Cuba the Crown City of the Ozarks, and every subsequent issue listed the same accolade. Indeed, in 1972 James Ira Breuer recorded: 'If John Harris should be here at Christmas time he would see his slogan in brilliant colors on the water tower, a crown of honor to his name. The brilliant colors on the water tower are designed as a symbolic crown of stars. These stars, many in number, some of them dim in the distance because it was long ago. The lights of these pioneers are our heritage, they laid the foundations and others built.'[25]

In respect of the *Cuba Review*, Lois B. Mays also records that under the title of each issue of the paper there was a motto which appropriately described John's (5) philosophy:

It is not wealth nor fame, nor fate,
but **Git Up and Go** that makes men great.[26]

The Move to St George, Georgia

After spending eleven, apparently successful, years in Cuba, it does seem surprising that John (5) and Cora decided to move to a somewhat distant State. Curiously, John (5) gives no reason in his book *How to Live to be a Hundred* or in his autobiographical sketch in *Charlton County Historical Notes*. However, it has been mooted that a number of people in this particular area of Missouri began to idolise the notorious bands of outlaws. This would obviously have been totally contrary to John's (5) upbringing and way of life. One can therefore assume that he made his feelings known in the columns of his newspaper.

Apparently this stance did not meet with universal approval and one of the gangs paid him a visit; and so it appears that John (5), not wishing to put one section of the community against the other, decided it would be in the best interest of everyone for him to move out. In this context he moved from the town and State of his birth and from his beloved Ozarks to the State of Georgia and the new colony town of St George. There could have been several reasons for his choice of this location, not least perhaps its distance from Cuba and Crawford County. Possibly he wished to experience the kind of life near the Atlantic Ocean. It is much more likely that the idea of joining a new and embryonic community was the focus of his attention.

The colony of Georgia was founded in 1732 and was named after King George II. It became one of the original thirteen States of the USA and the largest east of the Mississippi River. It was the fifth Confederate State to secede from the Union at the time of the War for Southern Independence. Those who remember the film *Gone with the Wind* will be aware it depicted plantation life in Central Georgia.[27]

St George, to the south of the State, is situated on the east of a finger of land which juts into the neighbouring State of Florida. It lies on the coastal plain, the latter being punctuated by the massive Okefenokee Swamp that covers an approximate area of 412,000 acres and extends into Florida. Both the St Mary's and Swanne Rivers flow from the swamp. The name derives from a Seminole Indian word meaning 'trembling earth'. *Charlton County Historical Notes* describe the swamp with its flowers, foliage and moss-draped cypress trees as a strange, mysterious and beautiful place, always changing, always fascinating. It can be appreciated that the scenery down in this latitude was very different to that which John (5) had been accustomed in his native Ozark mountains.

The subsequent conurbation which became known as St George was originally called Battenville by the Dyal-Upchurch Lumber Company at the time they extended their tram-road from Moniac to this location. Later the tram-road was acquired by A.B. & W. Railroad and they changed the name to Cutler; a small village sprang up around this flag-stop. The name Cutler was retained until 1904.[28]

In 1904, P H Fitzgerald of Minneapolis, Indiana, publisher of the *American Tribune* newspaper, set up the 1904 Colony Company. Its aims were to populate the flatland of the southern tip of Georgia. It strikes one that the use of the noun 'Colony' in the company name appears surprising for an American, but thus it was. Fitzgerald made great effort in advertising the aims of the company and offered stock to interested investors. This arrangement would mean that stockholders would receive parcels of land equivalent in value to their stock. No doubt the concept and the idea of being in at the start appealed to John (5) and indeed Fitzgerald had already successfully completed a similar scheme at Fitzgerald in Georgia. The scheme aimed to attract people from the northern States, especially ex-service Union soldiers.[29] The concept of attracting ex-Union Army soldiers as settlers into what had been a Confederate State would seem a very brave, possibly controversial but praiseworthy idea.

Initially the stock sold well and on 31 December 1904 John P. Fitzgerald, a son of P.H. Fitzgerald, purchased about 9,000 acres of land at Cutler from the then owners, Georgia Southern and Florida Railroad. P.H. Fitzgerald decided to call the new conurbation St George in memory of his son George who had died shortly before the 1904 Colony Company was floated.[30]

Of the arrival of John (5) and Cora in St George, Jack Mays recorded: 'As the small well-dressed man and his immaculately dressed wife stepped from the train's dusty passenger coach at the tiny St George railroad depot, three burly unshaven settlers sniggered. The three men had no way of knowing that this small man standing there was destined to be the town's first Mayor, editor of its first newspaper and a political influence in Charlton County for many years.[31]

Life in Georgia

On 24 February 1905, John (5), in a determined and uncompromising mood, walked into the real estate office of John P. Fitzgerald and in a public allocation received nine of the town of St George's nearly two thousand residential lots in exchange for his stock holding in the 1904 Colony Company.[32] In the following June, John (5) produced the first issue of his newspaper, the *St George Gazette*.

Sometime in 1906, John (5) sold his interest in the Cuba Review to M Godwin[33] and, at the same time, he demitted from Cuba Masonic Lodge and became an affiliated member of Moniac Lodge No. 432 at St George. He remained with this lodge until it was disbanded in 1917.[34] At about this time John (5) commenced cultivating and planting a beautiful garden at his home in Gordon Street, St George. It was the first of three such tasks during his lifetime, each succeeding one being larger than the former. He advocated mental and physical exercise involving creative work linked to an appreciation of the beauty of nature as some of the essentials for long life. How well designing and cultivating gardens fall into this category.[35]

Following the official allocation for plots of land in 1905, buildings were erected at a rapid rate to accommodate a thousand settlers and fifty-four businesses of varying types. However, the 1904 Colony Company failed to carry out their promised public service improvements. As a result, despite the initial rapid influx of settlers, St George failed to grow. Without industry to generate employment and without cultivation and resultant production from the surrounding countryside, population growth ceased with many settlers returning to their native northern homes. Added to this situation, P.H. Fitzgerald was indicted by a Federal Court for illegally selling some of the stock of the 1904 Colony Company, for which he subsequently pleaded guilty and was fined. A receiver was appointed to wind up the affairs of the company. Of interest also is the fact that the original purchase of land was in the name of Fitzgerald and not in the name of the 1904 Colony Company. However, most of the settlers who remained made a determined effort to develop a successful St George community.[36] On 24 August 1906 the General Assembly passed an Act incorporating the city of St George. This came about particularly because of the campaign waged by John (5) in his *St George Gazette*. An election was held for the new town's first Mayor and Alderman. John (5) was elected Mayor, Tom Wrench who worked with John (5) on the Gazette was chosen as Clerk, together with a full Board of Alderman, Marshal, Treasurer and Assessor. Armed with his town's brand-new city charter, handsome, hard-driving John (5) Harris started town workmen grading streets, digging drainage ditches, building bridges and planting trees.[37]

Together with his newspaper publishing and pressing civic duties, John (5) was chosen as Superintendent of the Southern Methodist Sunday School at St George and soon had a well-planned and organised school operating in a vacant store building.

The year 1907 was also to prove a very busy time for John (5). His parents moved down from Cuba, Missouri, and he settled them into a property adjacent to his own in Gordon Street. The St George school had grown and was settled in a three-classroom unit in the Union Hall. In a way, the latter event was something of a precursor to a new and different era in John's (5) life. When the principal of St George school failed to arrive to open the school after a spree in Jacksonville, Florida, which resulted in his spending time in police custody there, the School Trustees came to the *Gazette* office and asked John (5) to come and open the school. John (5), in his inimitable way, readily consented on the understanding that he would only do it for one day. The Trustees failed to get an immediate replacement and so John (5) continued and began to like teaching so much that he hoped a replacement would not be found! It was later discovered that the Trustees had made no real attempt in this respect and so John (5), at thirty-three years of age, commenced a new vocation which lasted for thirty-seven years. Perhaps it is not surprising to learn that, with John (5) as School Prin-

cipal, St George School had its own press and the pupils printed all school stationery.[38]

Sometime after the 1910 census for Charlton County and prior to early 1914, it appears that John (5) moved from his original home in St George to another house situated on the banks of St Mary's River. There he started planning and planting his second beautiful garden; and this new home he called Bolleno Lodge. The reason for John (5) calling his home by this name was possibly in deference to his father and to perpetuate the name of the native village of the Harrises. Although the spelling differs considerably from the modern usage it is very similar to that of the eighteenth century 'Bolenno'.

In 1912, John (5) left St George School to become Principal at Folkston High School, a position he held for twelve years. Folkston was about twenty miles north of St George, so he and Cora rented accommodation there but maintained their St George home which, by this time, his parents were sharing with them. Additionally, he gave up publication of the *St George Gazette*, and the printing plant was removed to Greenville, Florida.

His father, Rev. Jacob S. Harris, passed away on 17 January 1914 at Bolleno Lodge and it was from this address that his mother Sarah wrote to inform the family in Cornwall of the news.

On 2 June 1917, John (5) affiliated to Georgia's Folkston Lodge No. 196.[39] One assumes that soon after John (5) became Principal at the High School, his wife Cora also commenced teaching there, but certainly by 1917 she was teaching the first and primary grades.[40]

The first issue of *Folkston High School Annual* was published in 1918, perusal of which shows that Mayme Askew,

A glimpse of Bolleno Lodge from the entrance in Main Street, Folkston. The house stood on a plot of ground the size of a whole city block.

destined to become John's (5) second wife, was then a student in the senior class. In this year John (5) became Worshipful Master of Folkston Lodge of Free and Accepted Masons.[41]

In 1921 Folkston High School, under Principal John (5) Harris, became accredited as Charlton County High School. Inspirationally, John (5) initiated the building of a dormitory for the benefit of pupils who lived outside the immediate vicinity of Folkston. The dormitory soon became known as the Teacherage, as both teachers and pupils lived there. Indeed, John (5) and Cora lived there for a couple of years during the school week. The dormitory arrangement engendered a family atmosphere and each evening everybody gathered in the living room when John (5) read a couple of chapters from the classics.[42]

In September 1923, John (5), by virtue of his excellent performance as Principal of the High School, was nominated for the position of County Superintendent of Schools and immediately became Acting Superintendent. He then began formulating plans for the organisation and administration of the schools for the following year.

The State Department made a survey of the schools in Charlton County in March 1924. This showed a total of 17 schools with 1,114 pupils. Beginning that year, a new plan for overall supervision of the schools was introduced, whereby every school was visited weekly by the Superintendent and graded under the following headings:

Teacher's qualifications; Pupil attendance; Bus operation: Upkeep of buildings and grounds; Scholarship progress of Pupils, Janitorial services; Physical education; Lunch room operation; Extra-curricular activities.

Each heading was divided into ten sub-headings and marked accordingly. Monthly performance figures were then displayed at each school.[43]

From being Acting superintendent, John (5) commenced his duties as Superintendent on 1 January 1925.[44]

During the late 1920s the teachers, in drafting their 'Plan Book', designated a period in mid-afternoon to relax pupils in the lower grade. There were periods of singing, puzzle making, parlour games and the Superintendent, in his

---

Folkston High School

Nineteen Seventeen-Eighteen Enrollment

FACULTY:

JOHN HARRIS, PRINCIPAL
MRS. J. D. RODDENBERRY, 7TH AND 6TH GRADES
MISS JULIA BELLE DeGRAFFENRIED, 5TH AND 4TH GRADES
MRS. H. C. PAGE, 3RD AND 2ND GRADES
MRS. JOHN HARRIS, 1ST AND PRIMARY GRADES

HIGH SCHOOL	34
7TH AND 6TH GRADES	31
5TH AND 4TH GRADES	25
3RD AND 2ND GRADES	25
1ST AND PRIMARY GRADES	44
TOTAL	159

HIGH SCHOOL PUPILS:

SENIOR CLASS

Closs Pickren	Jennie Smith
Domingo Stewart	Everett Mizell
Mamie Askew	

SOPHOMORE CLASS

Earl M. Garrison	Cleo Mizell
Margaret Robinson	Eva Rodgers
Albert Stewart	Jewell Walker
Floy Wilson	Hiram Huling

FRESHMAN CLASS

Leola Dalton	Friedolin Farvour

Herbert Huling	Rudolph Mills
Irene Robinson	Waudelle Vickery
Jewelle Wilson	Hoke Askew
Clifford Kennison	Nina Vickery
Crystal Wainwright	Lucile Mills
Nellie Pickren	Verne Pickren
Bernice Rogers	Fannie Rodgers

SUB-FRESHMAN CLASS

Sallie Lou Walker	Emily Allen
Eva Mae Allen	Elma Moore
Garland Stephens	

GRAMMAR SCHOOL PUPILS:

SEVENTH GRADE		SIXTH GRADE	
Tector Bauman	Marguerite Collins	Johnnie Allen	Pearl Allen
Paul Dalton	Erma Hinds	Beryl Bauman	Cleo Dalton
Seab Mills	Archie McQueen	Gaston Davis	Clyde Donahoo
Tillman Rodgers	Bernice Vickery	Jodie Donahoo	Gussie Drury
Roscoe Wainwright	Donald Wilson	Joanna Mizell	Marion Pearce
		Eva May Petty	Verona Phillips

— 15 —

Folkston High School 1917 - 18 Enrollment listing
John Harris as Principal, Mrs John Harris as 1st & Primary Grades and Mamie Askew as Senior Class High School Pupil.

turn, told stories. For a time he related stories from the classics, but one day pressure of work had prevented him from making any preparation. As he came down the stairs wondering what story he could tell the children, he espied a squirrel perched on the saddle of a boy's bicycle. Immediately an idea sprang to his mind. Why not tell an imaginary tale about a swamp squirrel? From this incident the 'Bobby Squirrel' stories were born. They became extremely popular with the children who, whenever they saw John (5), implored him to tell them more about Bobby Squirrel. Indeed, when he reached the age of 100, a number of his former pupils gathered in his living room to hear some of the stories yet again.[45]

Alex S. McQueen published his *History of Charlton County* in 1932, in which he recorded the following: 'Hon. John Harris, County Superintendent of Schools, has a beautiful country home on the banks of St Mary's River near St George.'

In October 1933, Georgia was celebrating its bi-centenary and asked each county to make a contribution. Mayme Askew and another teacher of the seventh grade at Folkston School came up with the idea of publishing a commemorative booklet printed on paper made from Charlton County splash pine. The wood was given and transported free of charge to Savannah where it was pulped and made into paper, these latter operations also being free of charge. The booklet was entitled *Charlton County Gets a Chance to Tell Her Story*. Twelve seventh-grade pupils contributed articles featuring the history and customs of the county. This was the first use of Charlton County splash pine for paper making. The effort was highly praised by the State press.[46]

During his service as County Superintendent of Schools, John (5) was responsible for many innovations, some of the outstanding ones being:

Hot school lunches; All year payments for teachers; Establishing libraries; County finance for textbooks; Construction of new school buildings.

These innovations and their success focussed the attention of State educationists and became accepted all over the State. John (5) also arranged the amalgamation of certain schools when it was in everyone's interest, but only when the parents were in full agreement.[47]
It seems likely that John (5) and his cousin James Hugh (2) Harris (1866-1942) maintained a correspondence, not least because their fathers had come out to America together in 1865. James Hugh (2) had also been a Superintendent of Schools and an outstanding educationist, and in this context it would be surprising if they did not compare notes.

On 10 November 1943, John (5) became one of the original members of Folkston Lions Club[48] and in the following year, within a month of his seventy-first birthday, retired as Superintendent of Schools. The following comment and tribute to John (5) by Jack Mays appeared in the *Charlton County Herald* on 21 September 1988 is quoted verbatim:

Harris was criticized by some for his seemingly autocratic approach to school management. He meticulously outlined every small detail of his school programs and then vigorously pushed them to completion. Those who stood in his way learned of the resolution of purpose of the small man from Missouri... He was respected by the teachers and loved by his students. The County's school system under Harris became a model for other counties of the State to follow. National and state schools named Harris to high level study groups as his renown spread throughout the South.

Following his retirement from scholastic duties John (5) became City Clerk of Folkston in 1945 and, soon after, Clerk to the County Commissioners. He held this latter post for twenty-four years, after which he became Deputy Clerk. Also in 1945 John (5) moved from the Methodist to the Baptist Church in Folkston when a close friend, Rev. R.W. Waterman, came there as pastor. John (5) was ordained Deacon and also became the church treasurer. Sometimes he deputised for the Pastor in conducting services and for five years taught a large and enthusiastic men's Bible class.

In September 1947, John (5) became an emeritus member of Folkston Masonic Lodge[49] and two years later, at seventy-five, commenced writing a column for *Charlton County Herald*, which he continued until the end of his life.

After fifty-five years of happy married life, Cora passed away in 1950. There were no children of the marriage but at some point Cora and John (5) had adopted a retarded boy who died when still young.

Cora was laid to rest in Pineview Cemetery, Folkston alongside John's (5) parents. Also in this year, John (5) was requested to take on the men's Bible class at Folkston Methodist Church and, after due consideration and prayer, he acceded to their request because their leader had died and there was no other person willing to take on the task.

On 19 December 1952, John (5) and Mayme Askew were married in the home that was to be theirs - Bolleno Lodge, Folkston - when he was within a month of his seventy-ninth birthday, and Mayme devoted the whole of their time together to his welfare and well-being. Indeed, twenty-four years later he was quoted as saying, 'I am spoiled by the tender loving care of Mayme.[50] Even after their marriage Mayme was always affectionately known as 'Miss Mayme'.

Mayme was born circa 1908 and was the seventh of ten children of Albert Wallace Askew and his wife Fannie Bell Davis. A .W. Askew was a planter, merchant and timberman who also farmed extensively in Harris County, Georgia. The family had moved to Folkston in 1912.

Mayme attended high school in Folkston and, on leaving, her Diploma was signed by her father as Chairman of the School Board. She then went to the University of Georgia and graduated from Appalachian State University with a BSc in Education (Magna cum Laude) and MA degree. She taught in Charlton County schools, being Building Principal and teacher for thirty-seven years. A member of Delta Kappa Gamma Tau Chapter, she was also a member of John Floyd Chapter, Daughters of the American Revolution.[51]

Charlton County had come into being in 1854, and Col. A.S. McQueen had suggested some years earlier that a county centennial celebration ought to be held in 1954. This was very much in line with the thoughts of John (5) and so he convinced the county and local authority leaders, together with the people of Charlton County, to embark on an ambitious celebration. As a result, the Charlton County Centennial Commission was formed with John (5) as General Chairman. No doubt John (5) drew on his experience of the Crawford County Fair in Missouri in 1902.

During the week commencing 18 February 1954, a week-long spectacular celebration took place with some 21,000 people attending. Each night a huge historical drama entitled *CHARLORAMA* was presented on a stage 300 feet long and with a cast of 300 local people. It portrayed scenes from the history of Charlton County and began with the days of the Seminole Indians. The script was written by John (5), who received praise from all quarters on the success of the celebration.[52]

In 1968, at ninety-four years of age, John (5) resigned as Clerk to the County Commissioners but remained as Deputy Clerk.[53] In 1970, the General Assembly created Charlton County Historical Commission following a local bill enacted by Robert W. Harrison Jnr. John (5) became Chairman of the fourteen members of the Commission, which included his wife Mayme.[54]

At age ninety-seven in 1971, John (5) broke his hip. People assumed that, due to his age, he would not recover, but he did and in 1972, two years after the Historical Commission had been set up and under his hard-driving enthusiasm, the *Charlton County, Georgia - Historical Notes* was published. It was a volume of 538 pages. When a reporter from a Jacksonville, Florida, newspaper interviewed John (5) in 1971 he informed the reporter that at ninety-seven he was much too busy to consider retirement! From 1938 to 1972, John (5) was the recipient of ten awards from various organisations in the county.

John (5) celebrated his ninety-ninth birthday on 20 January 1973 when he was treated by the Commissioners to a surprise party at the County Courthouse. There were flowers, a birthday cake and coffee. The table had been decorated by his successor as Clerk, Mrs Glynn Brooks.

In reply to the good wishes proffered by the gathering, John (5) said: 'I've had many things in life but have found through the years that friends are the best things that anyone can have. You can disagree with people but you must do it in a friendly way. It doesn't pay to argue. If I have an enemy, I don't know who it is as I consider everyone my friend.' In conclusion he maintained that a person's attitude to life had most to do with a long life.[55]

Having passed his ninety-ninth birthday and upon entering his hundredth year, John (5) reflected on his longevity and this resulted in a thesis on the possible reasons for having lived to such a great age. He published a limited edition book, solely for distribution to his close friends, just prior to his hundredth birthday, its title being *How to Live to be a Hundred By One Who Did*. The title originated from a joke with these particular friends. It was dedicated to his second wife: 'Mayme Askew Harris who had devoted her life to the service of others and by her loving devotion has added years to my life.'

John (5) as Chairman of Charlton County Historical Commission 1970 – 1979
Photograph reproduced by kind permission of Charlton County Historical Society

Initially under the heading 'Philosophy of Life' John (5) recorded: 'Christian parents imparted an early and firm belief in God as the giver of life in His image; in the Bible as His Word and our guide for living; in Christ as His Son and our Risen Redeemer; and in God's promises of long life to those who sought to do His will... Also a deep-seated belief was early fixed that creative work is an essential factor in determining one's spiritual, intellectual and physical well-being and leads toward a long and happy life.'

The principles enumerated in the thesis were generally as follows:

1. Belief in God and His promises.

2. Work - A major factor, both mental and physical.

3. Good Habits make for Good Health.
    Avoid intoxicating liquors and tobacco. Eat fresh vegetables and fruit. Eat little meat. Exercise.

4. Mental Attitudes - Creative Thinking.

    Among the mental attitudes propounded were:

    Think love, not hate.

    Think success, not failure.

    Think health, not disease.

    Think good, not evil.

    Think prosperity, not poverty.

    Think safety, not danger.

    Think life, not death.

    Think friendship, not hostility.

    Think joy, not sorrow.

    Think hope, not despair.

    Think tranquillity, not tension.

    Look forward, not backward.

5. Attitude toward Reading - A progression from childhood to youth to maturity of the right material.

6. Love of the Beautiful - In the natural world and in cultural pursuits.

7. Associates and Environment.

8. An appreciation of humour - Laughter a good medicine.

It is apparent that John (5) kept pace with modern developments, for in a chapter headed 'A Hundred Years of Progress' he dealt with transportation from railroads to automobiles, from the airplanes to jumbo jets exceeding the speed of sound. In technology from telephone to radio to television to putting man on the moon. Also modern appliances in the home. He compared the imaginative Jules Verne story *Twenty Thousand Leagues Under the Sea* to the ultra-modern submarine. He pointed out the debit side, but accepted all the innovations and developments for the greater good.

Under the heading 'Ancestry' in his Autobiographical Sketch at the end of the book, John (5) was somewhat misinformed in regard to the ownership of Six Chimneys, the old family home and smallholding on Bolenowe Carn near Troon; it was not owned by the Crown but by Pendarves Estate, that is, the local squire. Additionally, the great grandfather of John (5) was Benjamin (2) Harris, and it was he who obtained the first Harris lease of Six Chimneys from Pendarves Estate. The idea that the successors to the lease had to bear the first name of John is also erroneous. It was the general custom that a lease was held on three lives but at the will of the particular owner; also unless a new lease had been negotiated, the property eventually reverted to the owners. In Chapters 1 and 2 of this book, it will be seen that the lease of 1779 was on the lives of Benjamin (2), his wife Joan and their son Benjamin (3). This lease of 1779 was renewed in 1817 by John (2), the father of Jacob S. There were only two lives on the latter lease, that of John (2) and his brother Matthew (1). John (2) died in 1848 but Pendarves Estate permitted Kitty, the widow of John (2), to continue living on the property but she became too poor to continue payment of the rent; additionally, the house was falling down. Pendarves Estate dealt with this situation by writing off the debt, and Kitty moved down to a small cottage in Troon. It will therefore be seen that there were only two Harris leases of Six Chimneys.

On 20 January 1974 John (5) celebrated his 100th birthday. Four days prior to this event the *Charlton County Herald* carried a banner headline: JOHN HARRIS TO BE HONORED HERE ON SUNDAY AS CENTENARIAN. Some brief extracts follow: 'Charlton County's No. 1 citizen, John Harris, will celebrate his hundredth birthday on January 20. The life of this man has been an inspiration to all who have known him, not only for his longevity but for his record of selfless service to his fellow man. On the occasion of his hundredth birthday it is only fitting that those who have been served by him set aside a portion of their day to pay their respects to this great man. In conjunction with their plans both the City of Folkston and the Charlton County Commissioners have issued proclamations designating 20 January as John Harris's Appreciation Day. Citizens throughout the county are making plans to attend activities honoring his dedication to public service. Throughout his life Mr Harris has been an inspiration and example to those of us around him'.

Two days after the celebration the same paper, among other things, had this to say: 'This issue is dedicated to Mr John Harris. There was standing room only as crowds of appreciative people lined the walls of Folkston Elementary School auditorium to pay tribute to Mr John Harris on his hundredth birthday last Sunday. 'Mr John' was honored with a reception and program attended by hundreds of City and County officials and townspeople and many out of town guests. The surprise of the day came when Mrs John Kopp, Chairman of the John Harris birthday committee, presented Mr Harris with a bound copy of a Book of Letters written by close friends of the man. The book had been compiled in secret by the committee as a gift to him on his hundredth birthday. We at the *Herald* hope that we speak for the entire county in saying that selflessness such as Mr Harris has displayed is deserving of more than we can offer in thanks'. The foreword to the Book of Letters was written by Mrs Lois B Mays and appeared under the heading A Master Artist. It is indeed an outstanding tribute to an outstanding man. A copy is included in this chapter.

In 1975 John (5) commenced researching for another book on the Indians of the Okefenokee. It was subsequently published in serial form in a Charlton County newspaper. A complete series of cuttings of the work is held in Folkston Public Library.

On 20 January 1976, John (5) celebrated his one hundred and second birthday. From the start of the month he relinquished all public duties, including teaching Folkston Methodist Men's Bible Class.

It was announced in a Masonic magazine that John (5) was the oldest Freemason in Georgia, by virtue of age and years of continuous service. In view of this the editor said it was fitting that John (5) should be the central theme of an article. In a résumé of his life the article went on to say that one of John's (5) special hobbies was in cultivating beautiful camellias and azaleas in his huge garden at Bolleno Lodge, Folkston, and that he and Miss Mayme spent their time industriously looking after the flowers and fruit trees which grew so profusely. Brother C. Pearce Stapleton, secretary of the Folkston Lodge for thirty-one years, contributed to the article a note of admiration which said: 'To meet this man is an inspiration, for he will always greet you with his famous response, "I'm well and happy". Couples like Brother and Mrs Harris are the kind of folk that make our county and small town what it is today, and all the members of Folkston Lodge and the community are proud of them'. To this comment the article concluded: 'So is Georgia and Freemasonry proud of them'.[56]

As a matter of interest, the splendid garden of John (5) and Mayme at Bolleno Lodge, Folkston, was the third he had planned and cultivated,

---

A MASTER ARTIST

There are many artists among us. Musicians compose and play unforgettable melodies, a piece of stone is transformed by loving hands into a beautiful sculpture, a song is sung with such sweet clarity it raises the spirits, or a picture is painted that will be a tribute to the artist for years to come. These are the artists well known by most everyone. But there are others also ... those who unaffectedly and most of the time unknowingly accomplish in their own way, by their genuine feeling of good will to all persons, a masterpiece of life.

There is one such artist living in Charlton County that through his life has painted a portrait of the old-fashioned, yet ever new, values of integrity, honesty and honor -- John Harris.

His life has been a living paintbrush designing a trail of education through swamp, ridge and village, teaching as his foremost subject the moral values by which man should live, knowing that on the education of the young depends the strength of this country.

He has painted with firm strokes the figures he knows best - the leaders of city and county government. His influence has molded many of them into unselfish persons who are not afraid to take a stand for the good of the county. Impossible tasks of building new schools or hospitals become possible when leaders know he will stand with them in their decisions. He set the moral tone for Charlton County government many years ago and it stands strong today because of it.

His palette of colors was chosen from the rainbow and they were splashed in any bare spot of his garden, making a feast for those who came to admire, and producing some of the most beautiful flowers grown in the county from tulips to camellias.

With an artist's inborn perspective he has based the paints of his life on the Old and New Testaments. Studying the scriptures and applying them to his style of living has made him a master. In his actions through the years have been woven the virtues all men seek but few find -- matchless integrity and ethics.

John Harris has taken invisible canvas and paints and produced a masterpiece of life strengthening one's faith, bolstering another's confidence, soothing another's hurts, and made him a true artist.

The foreward to the Book of Letters presented to John (5) on his 100th birthday. It was written by Mrs Lois B. Mays and is reproduced here by her kind permission.

as detailed in his book *How to Live to be a Hundred*.

On 5 April 1978, Grand Master William L. Barrineau Jnr and Grand Secretary Carl F. Lester Jnr travelled to Georgia to make a very special presentation to John (5), that of the Grand Lodge Award for completing seventy-five years of Masonic membership. He had joined the Masons in Cuba, Missouri on 16 August 1902. It was a great day for Freemasonry in Georgia. Several members of Folkston Lodge also attended the ceremony at the home of John (5) and Mayme, and all extended their very best wishes to this 104-year-old patriarch and his wife.[57]

John (5) passed away peacefully on 12 August 1979 in Charlton Memorial Hospital, Folkston, following a long illness. The funeral service took place at Folkston Methodist Church on 14 August, and was followed by interment

---

Awards to John (5) and 'Miss Mayme' from the people of Folkston and Charlton County.

1. 16 February 1938: At a public dinner and county-wide meeting in Folkston a trophy was presented bearing the following inscription: 'Presented to Mr John Harris by the citizens of Charlton County for the high ideals of scholarship he has inculcated in their children during his many years of faithful service.

2. 1939: At a banquet given by the Charlton County High School Alumni Association another trophy was given, inscribed: 'Presented to John Harris by Charlton County High School Alumni in appreciation of his nobility of character and life of service.'

3. 1944: At the Commencement Exercise of the County High School he was given a trophy which said, 'You the Victor, our friend and teacher Superintendent John Harris, from the Folkston teachers.'

4. February 1954: During the Charlton County Centennial Celebration, another trophy was presented to John (5) who had served as Chairman of the organisation responsible for the celebration. The inscription on the trophy read, 'Presented to Hon. John Harris - Charlton County Centennial 1854-1954 a leader culminating in his untiring efforts for a successful celebration. By the people of Charlton County.' [The use of the appellation 'Honourable' was solely an instinctive tribute to John (5) by the people and of the people, on account of his unstinted service to Charlton County. It should not be confused with an hereditary title or political award.]

5. 17 February 1969: A plaque was awarded with the inscription: 'To John Harris, in appreciation for outstanding service to Folkston and Charlton County by Folkston-Charlton County Chamber of Commerce.

6. 10 September 1971: A similar plaque with the same inscription was presented to John (5).

7. 20 June 1972: Folkston Exchange Club awarded a page in its 'Book of Golden Deeds' inscribed on a golden plaque: 'Presented to Mr John Harris in recognition of outstanding community service by the Exchange Club of Folkston.

8. 19 September 1972: The Folkston-Charlton County Chamber of Commerce held its annual Award Meeting in the High School lunch room. Some 300 people were seated at the tables. Mrs John Kopp, President of the Chamber, called on Mr Stanley Golaszewski, Chairman of the Award Committee, who made the Citizen of the Year award. It read 'To Mr and Mrs John Harris, Citizens of the Year 1971. Gratefully presented for outstanding civic contributions to Folkston and Charlton County. Folkston-Charlton County Chamber of Commerce.' This award was made on recommendation of every civic organisation in the county. At this same meeting the following Citation was awarded. 'Folkston-Charlton County Chamber of Commerce presents this Citation for Excellence to Mr and Mrs John Harris in appreciation for extraordinary effort in compiling the History of Charlton County. September 19, 1972. (Signed) Mrs Jewell M Kopp, President Folkston-Charlton County Chamber of Commerce.' A Life Membership in the Chamber of Commerce was also presented to the recipients of the Award at this meeting.

in Pineview Cemetery alongside his first wife Cora and his parents. The inscription on the granite slab simply says: 'John Harris, January 20th 1874, August 12th 1979'.[58] Jack Mays later wrote: 'The Cuba, Missouri man who arrived in St George, Georgia in 1905, became one of he county's outstanding educational, community, church and civic leaders, and one of the South's foremost authorities on education. He found time for his church, time to grow exquisite flowers and time for others.'[59] Indeed, when Jay Harris of Michigan, a first cousin twice removed to John (5), visited Folkston in February 1987, he said: 'Folk spoke of "Mr John" as they affectionately called him, as if he had brought them into the twentieth century.'

'Miss Mayme' passed away 17 April 1989. She had been unwell for a number of years and Bolleno Lodge had been sold around 1986 to help pay for her care. This shows that John (5) in his extremely active life did not pursue wealth but worked for the greater good of the folk whom he served.

Memorabilia of John (5).
The list of honours and awards is detailed on the previous page and was taken from How to Live to be a Hundred by one who did.

Life Membership of Georgia Women's Christian Temperance Union. 3 March 1975

John (5) viewing his One Hundredth Birthday Cake.
20 January 1974

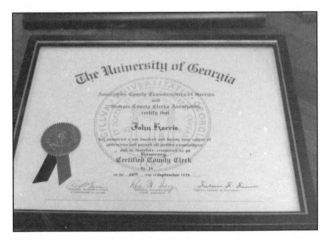

Certificate as Honorary Certified County Clerk.
20 September 1974

13. Reflections

The Harrises of Bolenowe, like many other Cornish folk, did not sit around bewailing the circumstances into which they had been born, but did something about it. They did not know they would eventually be seen as following the motto of a later Harris, John (5), a phrase of which read 'Git Up and Go'. What then was the driving force that compelled these folk to make the effort? It has been suggested in a general sense that it was Methodism. More positively it was their unswerving faith in the goodness of God, closely coupled with absolute adherence to the discipline of Methodism. This applied not only to those of the family who emigrated but also to those who remained in their native Cornwall. Unfortunately, much of the discipline in Methodism has been eroded and lost, especially since the Second World War, although not necessarily because of the War.

The definition of discipline in *Collins Dictionary of the English Language* is given as: 'Powers of self-control, training to obedience, regulations and authority and a system of rules for behaviour.' Rev. Thomas Shaw has stated: 'The members of the Society (Methodist) were under discipline which governed not only their ecclesiastical, but also their civil conduct.'[1] The effect of this discipline can also be appreciated in a statement by W H Pascoe in a reference to the Cornish Copper Company which says: 'Growth was greatly sustained in the early years of the Partnership by the effect which an ever strengthening Methodist influence had on the workforce.'[2]

Yet another aspect is quoted by Arthur Bryant: 'Nothing did more than Methodism to unite Britain in the face of the revolutionary peril.'[3]

In a similar vein, but in a broader sense, Christine and Lauri Leskinen,[4] in reference to the immigrants said: 'The ethnic groups that congregated in the Copper Country seemed to be dedicated to the proposition that honesty and hard work would win out.'

A summary of the lives of the children of John (2) Harris and Christian Smith will show that faith and discipline were paramount and influenced them throughout their lives.

Firstly, consider John (3) who, from early in life, and against all odds, produced an astonishing amount of verse. He spent over twenty years working in hard, unhealthy and dangerous conditions underground in order to support his family, whilst at the same time taught Sunday School classes and qualified as a local preacher. Subsequently, he became Bible reader at Falmouth which involved conducting services and trudging around the town bringing solace to people living in harrowing and unhealthy conditions. Yet he never complained, saying 'I've toiled in my humble way, without the least regret.'

William B. also attended the one-legged miner's school at Forest Gate, practised self-improvement while working as a copper miner at Dolcoath, and was the first member of the family to emigrate. Without complaining he withstood the harsh conditions of those early emigrants crossing the Atlantic and the hard pioneering life of lead mining in Wisconsin. He remained steadfast after his wife passed away, leaving him with several young children. Leaving the lead mines, he built up a farm of 240 acres but found time to serve his church and the community, and never forgot his mother and the rest of his family in Cornwall. His obituary in 1892 stated: 'He was an exceptionally upright, honest and industrious citizen, and was held in the highest esteem among all his neighbours and friends.'

Ann (2), who as a child received no formal education, experienced the drudgery of working manually on the surface of a mine but through all developed a deep faith and learned in the hard school of life. Consider her single purpose of mind in making the hazardous, several-thousand mile journey to Wisconsin and, among strangers, to marry James Sims. She faithfully assisted James in his duties in the Pastorate and brought up a large family who subsequently distinguished themselves in their various callings. Ann's Methodist Conference obituary stated: 'Very early in life Mrs Sims gladly recognised the voice of the Master calling her to a life of communion and service, and in this fellowship she walked until her journey's end.'

Matthew (2), like Ann, had no formal education yet travelled to mining camps across the world to find his Shangri La before returning after five years to marry Nanny Sims and take her out to Ontonagon. After falling over 300 underground, Matthew was assumed to be dead but was 'rescued' by Nanny who nursed him back to health. They struggled to make ends meet at this period. During his convalescence Matthew learned to read and write and, although permanently disabled, moved to South Dakota to homestead 160 acres of prairie. As members of the Methodist Episcopal Church, their faith and discipline can plainly be seen.

James, after attending the National School at Camborne, developed an interest in reading poetry and became a miner at Dolcoath. Then, with two other lads from Troon, he opted to go out to the Victorian goldfields. The shocking conditions on the thirteen-week voyage proved too much for James and on arrival at Melbourne he was immediately admitted to hospital where he died a week later, aged twenty-two. His body lies in an unmarked grave in a Melbourne cemetery. His family were unaware of this tragedy until some considerable time later, but drew solace from the knowledge that he died in the faith after breathing a fervent prayer.

Samuel B., from his period at the National School and with the help of the teachers there, made an effort to plan a career and thereby, in due course, attained high positions in mining and business in the Copper Country of Upper Michigan. He possessed the determination to gain experience and to succeed. Alongside these efforts he became a Methodist lay preacher and class leader, held offices in community affairs and amassed considerable wealth, but never forgot the family in Cornwall.

Christiania (Kitty), devout and hard working, taught a Sunday School class at Troon for over thirty years. After leaving the National School, she worked manually on the surface of a mine but later obtained more congenial employment as a milliner. However, the exposure to the manual work left its mark in later life when she suffered greatly from rheumatism. At forty she married a widower with a young family, but twenty-two months later her husband passed away and his children would not accept her as mother. Despite this trauma and deep distress, she retained her faith and returned to live with her mother.

Benjamin (4) became a Methodist lay preacher in Camborne Circuit at twenty-two years of age and, after emigrating to the Copper Country, was very much involved in building two Methodist Churches in Lake Linden, one in 1874 and the other in 1886. He was also superintendent of the Sunday School there for eight

years which had over 200 scholars, officers and teachers. Taking his wife and infant son to America in 1865, the child passed away soon after their arrival. Spending thirty-four years with the great Calumet and Hecla Mining Company, he worked his way up from labourer to superintendent of their huge mills at Lake Linden, during which time he invented certain machinery for processing copper ore. On his retirement he was given a testimonial for his integrity and contribution to company profits.

Mark S. attended Mrs Percival's School at Treslothan for just a few years, but developed into an avid reader of good books. Influenced in early life by Capt. Jimmy Thomas, he became interested in local Methodist history. He joined the Methodist Society, becoming a lay preacher in 1868 and remained so until his death sixty-three years later. He held every office open to a layman at Troon Wesleyan Church, being superintendent of the Sunday School for over forty years. He had never earned more than fifteen shillings a week, but retired in 1903 to devote the remainder of his life to pastoral work, entirely without remuneration. In this capacity he daily walked many miles to comfort the sick and to write letters for wives who could not read or write and whose husbands were working overseas. He officiated by special request at 349 funerals in Troon Cemetery alone and was always humble

The author, his wife Glencoe, their sons Roger and Tony together with Ann Dittmar (see Chapter 8).
Photograph taken June 1993 when Ann visited the author and his family at Redruth, Cornwall.

and self-effacing. He commenced working underground at twelve years of age, drove the man-engine at Dolcoath for twenty-one years and never failed to work a double shift when the miners themselves requested it because the operator who should have been on shift had imbibed too freely. Consider his notes on a good man's character: 'He makes no noise about his good deeds, and blows no trumpet to tell of his visits to the sick and the dying, but quietly works in the vineyard of the Master.'

Jacob S., as a young miner at Dolcoath, developed an interest in geology and mineralogy. Then after going to America, his interest in these sciences and his ability to lead was noticed by certain mining officials there, so he was sent to Missouri in charge of a group of miners to prospect for mineral. Although he was much involved in the church, he was at first reluctant to preach but he eventually left mining and took himself through college to prepare for the Methodist Episcopal Ministry. Subsequently he served the Conferences of three States. Because of his steadfast character and sense of justice and sound judgement he was elected a Trier of Appeals of the Judicial Conference to administer discipline where necessary within the church.

It is obvious that their deep faith and practice of Methodist disciplines guided and governed this family in their varying spheres throughout their lives.

In conclusion, the author wishes to place on record the great joy and pleasure he and his immediate family have derived in tracing, corresponding and meeting previously unknown cousins in the United States, together with members of Harris-related families, both in England and New Zealand. Also, of being able to welcome some of them into our home and to show them Bolenowe, Troon, Treslothan and the surrounding countryside, not forgetting other delectable places in Cornwall. Indeed, our lives are the richer for knowing these folk and without their aid this book would not have been written.

Acknowledgements

Grateful acknowledgement for their help is extended to the following people and institutions:

Mrs C.R. North, County Archivist and Staff, County Record Office, Truro, Cornwall

Mr T. Knight, Principal Librarian and Staff, Cornish Studies Library, Redruth, Cornwall

Ms A. Broome, Librarian, Royal Institution of Cornwall, Truro, Cornwall

Mrs M.M. Rowe, County Archivist, Devon Record Office, Exeter, Devon

Mr Peter Gilson, Historian, Royal Cornwall Polytechnic Society, Falmouth, Cornwall

Mr D. Kitto, Town Clerk, Town Hall, Penryn, Cornwall

Dr Stephen Dennis, Perth, Western Australia

Shakespeare Birthplace Trust, Stratford-upon-Avon, Warwickshire

The Matron, Earle's Retreat, Falmouth, Cornwall

Mr G.J. Oatey, Headmaster, Porthleven Junior School, Cornwall

Mr Richie Thomas, Bolenowe, Camborne, Cornwall

Mr and Mrs Ivor Vincent, Illogan Downs, Redruth, Cornwall

Mr Rod L. Lyon, Nancegollan, Helston, Cornwall

Mr J.A.S. and the late *Mrs Pascoe*, Porthleven, Cornwall

Mr Douglas George, Helston, Cornwall

Mr J.C.C. Probert, Redruth, Cornwall

Royal Historical Society, University College, London

Mr Ken Babbage, Breage, Helston, Cornwall

Mr H.D. Poole, Le Muy, France

Mr L.G. Matthews Jnr, Strasbourg, France

The late *Mr Lavin Matthews*, Porthleven, Cornwall

Mrs Joseph Williams, Porthleven, Cornwall

Dr A.R. Yates, Kemptville, Ontario, Canada

Ms Aruelia Pucinski, The Clerk, Circuit Court, Cook County, Chicago, Illinois

Mr Robert Thomas, Stockton, Illinois

Office of the Secretary of State, Robert Williams Library, North-eastern Illinois University, Chicago

Ms Barbara Heflin, Office of the Secretary of State, Springfield, Illinois

Dr Donald W. Jackanicz, Archivist, National Archives, Great Lakes Region, Chicago, Illinois.

Centre for Oxfordshire Studies, Oxfordshire County Council, Central Library, Westgate, Oxford

Mr J.L. Hansen, Reference Librarian, State Historical Society, Madison, Wisconsin

Ms Helen Volkmann, Archives Librarian, Iowa Wesleyan College, Mount Pleasant, Iowa

Iowa County Historical Society, Dodgeville, Wisconsin

General Commission on Archives and History, United Methodist Church, Madison, New Jersey

Rev. Richard A. O'Neil, Pastor of the Methodist Church, Mineral Point, Wisconsin

Ms Pamela Tucci, Research Correspondent, National Geographic Society, Washington, DC

Dr A.C. Todd, Leamington Spa, Warwickshire

Mr Peter W. Bunce, Director National Archive, Chicago Branch, Chicago, Illinois

Mr Stanley Kusper, County Clerk, Chicago, Illinois

Mrs A. Olschefski, Orange, Texas

Miss Gladys M White, Quinnesec, Michigan

Mr Alva Spargo, Mineral Point, Wisconsin

Mr A.L. Johnson, Free Public Library, Council Bluffs, Iowa

Mr J. Arthur Harris, Plymouth, Michigan (formerly of Carthage, South Dakota)

Mr Tom Williams, Eaglewood, Colorado

Mrs Lucie Stewart, Deming, New Mexico

The late *Mr and Mrs John M. Harris*, Scotland, South Dakota

Ms Della M. Calhoon, County Clerk and Recorder, Kit Carson County, Burlington, Colorado

Ms Marvene Riis, Archivist, South Dakota Historical Society, Pierre, South Dakota

Mr Steven E. Neil, Reference Assistant, Minnesota Historical Society, St Paul, Minnesota

Ms Judy Rokusek, Recorder of Deeds, Hutchinson County, Oliver, South Dakota

National Archives, Central Plains Region, Kansas City, Missouri

Mr Douglas Williams, Journalist, Penzance, Cornwall

Mr Jim Piper, Clifton Springs, New York

Mr and Mrs Richard Wilder, Madison, Wisconsin

Mr and Mrs Peter Hampton, Khandalla, Wellington, New Zealand

Mrs Katharine Preston, Akron, Ohio

Canadian Institute of Mining, Metallurgy and Petroleum, Montreal, Canada

The late *Mr Charles Willman*, The Historical Museum, Ontonagon, Michigan

Nebraska State Historical Society, Lincoln, Nebraska

Lt. Col. (Retd) R.M. Ripley, Houghton, Michigan

Mr James Kurtii, Houghton, Michigan

Rev. Donald J. Emmert, United Methodist Church, Ontonagon, Michigan

Rev. T. Bradley, First United Methodist Church, Hancock, Michigan

Professor Larry D. Lankton, Michigan Technological University, Houghton, Michigan

D. & N. Savings Bank, Hancock, Michigan

The Secretary, Minnesota Annual Conference, United Methodist Church, Minneapolis, Minnesota

Mr Thomas J. Keast, Ignatius, Montana

Mrs Doris Rule-Bable, Saline, Michigan

Mr William J. Foster, Calumet, Michigan

Mr Richard R. Amon, Business Manager, The Grand Lodge of F. & A.M. Masons, Grand Rapids, Michigan

Raymond J. Hosking, County Clerk, Houghton, Michigan

Mr and Mrs S. Hawke, Hancock, Michigan

Ms Joanne Adams, Chief Clerk Probate Sub-Registry, Bodmin, Cornwall

National Archives of Canada, Ottawa, Canada

Mr Eddie Neil, Recorder of Deeds Jasper County, Carthage, Missouri

The late *Benjamin H. Wells*, St Louis, Missouri

Mrs Winifred Carleton Watkins, Farmington, Missouri

Mr and Mrs C.B. Gibson, Folkston, Georgia

Ms Joy Dodson, Archivist Technician, United Methodist Archives, Fayette, Missouri

Ms Karen McPeters, Clerk of the County Court, Steelville, Missouri

Mr Bob Crump, Webster County Commission, Marshfield, Missouri

Mr William F. Erwin, Senior Research Librarian, Duke University, Durham, North Carolina

Mauzel Beal, United Methodist Archives, Bailey Library, Conway, Arkansas

Rev. Ned and Mrs Ellie Adams, Columbus, Ohio

Ms Nancy Spaine, Assistant Archivist, Commission on Archives and History, Conference Historical Society, United Methodist Church, Charlotte, North Carolina

Mrs Mary A. Browning, Guilford County Genealogical Society, Greensboro, North Carolina

Ms Maxine Kreutziger, Kansas East Commission on Archives & History, Baker University, Baldwin City, Kansas

Dr John Rowe, Par, Cornwall

Ms Marcia J. Hodges, Reference Librarian, Brunswick, Glynn County Library, Georgia

Mr Jack Watters, Marshfield, Missouri

Mrs G. Eleanor Bowell, Beacon, Camborne, Cornwall
Mrs Elizabeth H. Rickard, Troon, Camborne, Cornwall
Mrs Marguerite A. G. Williams, Beacon, Camborne, Cornwall
The late *Miss Kathleen Evans,* Feock, Cornwall
Mr A. Anthony Langford, Redruth, Cornwall
Mr Roger J. Langford, Redruth, Cornwall
Mr Brian Harding, Falmouth, Cornwall
Mr Stephen Crossman, Penzance, Cornwall
Mrs B. Mambly, Falmouth, Cornwall
Mrs J. Eddy, Falmouth, Cornwall
The late *Mrs C. Wesley Langford,* Lanner, Redruth, Cornwall.

Special mention and thanks for the following for their unstinted help:

The late *Miss E. Jane Langford,* Lanner, Redruth, Cornwall, for initially providing two diaries of Mark Smith Harris.
The late *Mr J. Leslie Harris, Troon,* Camborne, Cornwall for supplying in the early days of research the precise dates of birth of the children of John (2) and Christian Harris.
The late *Dr F.L. Harris, OBE,* of Redruth, Cornwall, for his consistent help and encouragement.
Professor Charles Thomas, CBE, DL, Truro, Cornwall, for generously sharing his research on the Harrises and associated families.
Mr Richard S. Sims, Borehamwood, Hertfordshire for reproducing many photographs.
Mr and Mrs Jay Harris, Plymouth, Michigan for encouragement and escorting the author and his wife around the Midwest during 1985, and for taking numerous photographs.
Mr Jack Harris, Alexandria, Virginia for painstakingly searching the Ships' Passenger lists at National Archives, Washington, DC.
Mrs Lois B. Mays, Folkston, Georgia for considerable help and correspondence in respect of John (5) Harris.
The Wilder family, per *Mrs Ann Dittmar,* Seattle, Washington, for a financial contribution to the cost of research.
Mrs J Ellen G. Austin, Ashland, Oregon for voluminous photocopies of information on the Capt. Samuel B. Harris family, and for a financial contribution.
Mrs Alice L. Davis, Steelville, Missouri for generously loaning her copy of James Ira Breuer's Crawford County and Cuba Missouri.
Mrs R. Jungbluth, Mineral Point, Wisconsin, the late Gerald Harris and Mrs Delva Anderson, Dodgeville, Wisconsin for very detailed information of the William B. Harris family.
Mr and Mrs Robert Gilson, San Jose, California for a complete file on the capture and so on by the Confederate Army of Major Hiram S. Hanchette.
Mr and Mrs Richard Buechler, Scotland, South Dakota, who took the author and his wife across the State to see the remarkable Badlands and the haunting Black Hills.
Mr Norman Bunney, Ludgvan, Penzance, Cornwall for carrying out the initial editing of this book.
Mrs Jean Hathaway, Florida for making available the Peking diaries of her grandmother Mary Sims McCarger Bainbridge.

References

References consulted other than those quoted in the text and footnotes:

Readers' Guide List, British Museum Library.
Camborne Feast Magazine, 1982.
Kelly's Directories.
Come-to-Good and the Early Quakers in Cornwall by Harry Pallett, 1968.
The Worship and Devotion of Cornish Methodism by J.C.C. Probert, 1978.
Coventry Herald, March 1870.
Lake's Falmouth Packet and Cornwall Advertiser, from 1874.
Lake's Falmouth Almanac, 1882.
Shakespere's Shrine, An Indian Story, Essays and Poems by John Harris, 1866.
Luda: A Lay of the Druids. Hymns, Tales, Essays and Legends by John Harris, 1868.
Bulo; Reuben Ross; A Tale of the Manacles; Hymn, Song and Story by John Harris, 1871.
The Cruise of the Cutter and other Peace Poems by John Harris, 1872.
Wayside Pictures, Hymns and Poems by John Harris, 1874.
Walks with Wild Flowers by John Harris, 1875.
Tales and Poems by John Harris, 1877.
Last Lays by John Harris, 1884.
The Cornishman newspaper, Penzance, Cornwall.
Camborne-Redruth Leader, 1984-91.
Western Morning News, Plymouth, Devon.
Camborne-Redruth Packet, 1971-95.
Fennimore Times, Wisconsin, 1897-1910.
The Mining Ventures of this Ontonagon Country by James K. Jamison, 1950.
The Adventure Story by Jack Neph, Ontonagon, Michigan, 1950.
The World's Great Copper Mines by B. Webster Smith, FGS.
History of Methodism in the Upper Peninsula of Michigan, published by the Historical Society of Detroit Annual Conference.
Phoenix, Michigan's History by C.J. Monette, 1989.
History of Eagle Harbor, Michigan by C.J. Monette, 1977.
Biographical Record of Leading Figures of Houghton, Baraga and Marquette Counties - Michigan, published Chicago, 1903.
Lansing State Journal, Michigan, 1939.
Who's Who in America, 1968-69.
The Symphony Review, St Louis, Missouri, Winter 1988.
St Louis Post and Despatch, Missouri, 19 July 1995.
History of Charlton County - Georgia by Alex S. McQueen, 1932.
Guilford County, published by High Point Public Library, North Carolina.
Lake Superior Miner, 13 April 1861.
History Around the Fal, 1986.
Mills & the Manor Mills of Mylor by Thomas H. Bradly.
Dictionary of National Biography, 1887.
Bibliotheca Cornubiensis by Boase & Courtney, 1874.
Collectanea by Boase, 1890.
Life in Cornwall in the Early Nineteenth Century edited by R.M. Barton, 1970.
Life in Cornwall in the Mid Nineteenth Century edited by R.M. Barton, 1971.
Life in Cornwall in the Late Nineteenth Century edited by R.M. Barton, 1972.
Life in Cornwall at the End of the Nineteenth Century edited by R.M. Barton, 1974.
The Industrial Archaeology of Cornwall by A.C. Todd and Peter Laws, 1972.

Notes to Chapters

Chapter 1
1   Cornwall Record Office (CRO) Ref. PD/27.

Chapter 2
1   The Cornish Miner by A.K. Hamilton Jenkin, 1948.
2   History of Copper Mining in Cornwall and Devon by D.B. Barton, 1968.
3   Cornwall Record Office Ref. PD/27.
4   Edward William Wynne Pendarves was born a Stackhouse but changed his name after succeeding in 1815 - ex. Mrs Percival's Endowed School at Penponds and Treslothan Camborne 1761-1876 by Charles Thomas. Institute of Cornish Studies 1982.
5   Constituents of blackpowder: sulphur, charcoal and sodium or potassium nitrate. The nature of the fumes produced by exploding blackpowder is such that adequate ventilation is imperative.
6   Historical Relationship of Mining, Silicosis and Rock Removal by Treve Holman, August 1946.
7   Life in Cornwall in the Mid-nineteenth Century by R.M. Barton, 1971.
8   Manor of Treslothan Rentals, CRO Ref. PD58/14.

Chapter 3
1   Aunt Meg, sister to John (2), who lived with her mother Granny Joan in the cottage next door to John's (2) family at Six Chimneys.
2   Probably packed earth or limeash.
3   The Sunday School was enlarged 1886-87 and opened by Mrs Josiah Thomas on 2 June 1887 - ex. late Mrs Edith Langford - the memorial stones of the extension having been laid 18 October 1886 - ex. Troon Board School Log Book, CRO SR/CAMB/6/1.
4   Mrs Percival's Endowed School at Penponds and Treslothan, Camborne 1761-1876 by Charles Thomas, Institute of Cornish Studies, 1982.
5   Ex. Mr David H. Thomas.
6   Transcribed and edited by J.A. Buckley, 1994.
7   The process of separating the gangue of worthless mineral from the valuable mineral of the ore.
8   Life in Cornwall in the Early Nineteenth Century by R.M. Barton, 1970.
9   q.v. History of Copper Mining in Cornwall and Devon by D.B. Barton, 1968.
10 Sabine Baring-Gould 1834-1924, squire/parson of Lew Trenchard, Devon; antiquarian, writer and folklorist; wrote the hymns Onward Christian Soldiers, Through the Night of Doubt and Sorrow and Now the Day is Over.
11 The Cornish Beam Engine by D.B. Barton, 1966.
12 q.v. The Cornish Miner by A.K. Hamilton Jenkin, 1948.
13 Capt. James Thomas of Bolenowe 1778-1867, Dolcoath Agent, 1806, walked as a boy of 13 years from Bolenowe to Gwennap Pit to hear John Wesley preach; Methodist local preacher 1808; reopened Bolenowe mine 1823. Buried Treslothan.
14 Possibly Rev. Hugh Rogers became aware of John's efforts in self-improvement and poetry writing through John's younger brother James, when the latter attended the National School at Camborne Church.
15 q.v. The Search for Silver - Cornish Miners in Mexico 1824-1947 by Dr A.C. Todd, 1977.
16 Monro by John Harris: 'Two aged sires were all that gathered there.'
17 The Metalliferous Mining Region of South West England by H.G. Dines, HMSO, 1956.
18 West Briton 13 May 1864.
19 As William left for America just before the marriage of John (3) and Jane Rule, it follows that the raising of stone must have been started some time previously.

20 CRO Ref. PD62/1.
21 Mr David H. Thomas, Archivist, Cornwall Record Office.
22 William Catcott of Wells, Somerset - Baker/Poet.
23 John Gill 1811-1905; bookbinder, printer, Quaker, pacifist and vegetarian; born St Ives, died Penryn; buried St Gluvias.
24 John Gill of Penryn by Wendy Monk.
25 Linto and Laneer by John Harris.
26 Death of the Prince Consort, Queen Victoria at the Royal Marriage, Marriage of HRH the Prince of Wales, Cornubia to the Prince and Princess of Wales, HRH the Prince of Wales, Cornwallia's Welcome to their Royal Highnesses.
27 Druggist, grocer and Quaker. Edward Bastin's wife, together with Mesdames Jenkin and Cornish, established the Ragged Sunday School at Redruth in 1854.
28 In 1860, the scripture reader at Redruth was paid double this amount - ex. Annals of an Ancient Cornish Town - Redruth by Frank Michell, 1978.
29 Founded in 1862 to provide training for 'deserving respectable girls as domestic servants' and to give them the advantage of obtaining additional training in the families of subscribers in the neighbourhood - q.v. Home Along Falmouth and Penryn by David Mudd, 1980.
30 Foundation stone of Falmouth Docks laid 26 February 1860 and first vessel in dock 10 July 1861 - ex. Life in Cornwall in the Mid-nineteenth Century by R.M. Barton, 1971.
31 First engine ran over the line from Truro to Falmouth 30 July 1863. Opened to public 21 August 1863 - ex. Do You Know Cornwall by Edith Martin, 1937, RCI, Truro.
32 George Smith 1800-1868, Hon. LL.D, New York; Chairman of Cornwall Railway; Fellow of the Society of Arts; Vice-President Camborne Trustee Savings Bank; industrialist; county magistrate; Member of Royal Society of Literature; Member of Royal Asiatic Society; Wesleyan Methodist historian; Fellow of Genealogical Society - ex. Views and Likenesses by Charles Thomas, 1988 Royal Institution of Cornwall.
33 Born 1788 at Greenbank, Falmouth of a Scottish father and American mother; was chairman of Eagle Star Insurance Co., and City of London Gas Co; died 1877 at Camberwell - ex Dictionary of National Biography.
34 Baroness Burdett-Coutts 1814-1908; philanthropist, her benevolence embracing, among others, the welfare of the Church of England, housing the poor, elementary, scientific and technical education, care of neglected children, protection of dumb animals, care of the wounded in war, and so on; leader of RSPCA and helped set up NSPCC as Miss Angela Coutts.
35 Thomas George Baring became second Baron Northbrook in 1866; created Viscount Baring and Earl Northbrook in 1875; MP for Penryn and Falmouth Parliamentary seat March 1857 to September 1866 - ex Dictionary of National Biography.
36 A Cornishman at Oxford by Dr A.L. Rowse, 1965.
37 CRO Ref. SF 146.
38 Do You Know Cornwall by Edith Martin, 1937, RCI.
39 CRO Ref. MR/F/1
40 George Earle 1807-1876; born Falmouth. Responsible for laying out three towns in Indiana, USA, namely Lake, Liverpool and Hobart. Superintended the erection and donated the Retreat to the aged poor of his native town; buried Hobart, Indiana - ex. Earle's Retreat, Falmouth 1869-1969 by Frank Lean.
41 William Catcott the Baker/Poet of Wells, Somerset.
42 q.v. A Chapter in Cornish Banking History by R.M. Fitzmaurice, Royal Institution of Cornwall, Journal Part I, 1991.
43 It is understood that Mrs Rapson was a niece to Mr F. Chegwidden, foreman to John Gill and who eventually took over the Penryn business.
44 Professor Charles Thomas, CBE, MA, FBA, FSA, four times great-nephew of Capt. James Thomas of Bolenowe who threw open his library door to John (3).

45 In Oxfordshire since the county boundary changes of 1974.

46 Now forms part of the Killigrew Inn.

47 Per courtesy of Mrs Elizabeth Rickard, Troon, Camborne.

48 The Classical School had originated as early as 1824/25 - ex. Tercentenary of Falmouth 1661-1961 by Ms Beckett, Head Librarian, Falmouth Public Library.

49 Penryn Advertiser, 28 December 1872.

50 Sithney School Board Members: W. Bickford Smith, Chairman; Rev. H.H. DuBoulay, Vice-Chairman: Mr John Williams, Mr William Tyack and Mr William Rowe.

51 All school information - ex. CRO Ref. SRB/S1T/1 and SR/S1T/1/1.

53 Programme of the opening of the new Porthleven Infants' School, 2 May 1980, per courtesy of Mrs V.E. Gilbert, Head Teacher.

53 Poems of Cornwall by Thirty Cornish authors, W. Herbert Thomas, 1892.

54 Dr J.A. Langford, Member of Birmingham School Board and campaigner against the employment of children in industry.

55 Camborne Feast pie, containing meat and dried fruit. It has probably ceased to be made. Certainly Mark Smith Harris enjoyed them up to the time of the Camborne Feast prior to his death in 1931.

Chapter 4

1 A round trip of about fourteen miles.

2 The small rural Methodist chapel which the Sims family attended.

3 Dating from the 1820s.

4 The Cornish Miner in America by Dr A.C. Todd, 1967.

5 Redruth and Hayle Railway opened 1835, becoming a passenger line in 1843.

6 The Ship Registers of the Port of Hayle, National Maritime Museum, by G. Farr.

7 A touch of exaggeration, but Harveys of Hayle and others had in fact started a steam packet service between Hayle and Bristol in 1831 - ex. The Industrial Archaeology of Cornwall by Dr A.C. Todd and Peter Laws, 1972.

8 Ships Passenger Lists - National Archives, Washington, DC.

9 The Great Migration by Basil Greenhill.

10 History of the Post Office Packet Service by A.H. Norway.

11 History of Travel in America by Seymour Dunbar.

12 For further information on travel to and in America consult: A History of Travel in America by Seymour Dunbar; The National Geographic Society, their Historical Atlas, Atlantic Gateways Map, Great Lakes Map, Ohio Valley Map, and Tidewater and Environs Map; and Reader's Digest Family Encyclopaedia of American History, Trails to Rails by C.J. Corliss and their World Book Encyclopaedia.

13 Wisconsin - A Pictorial Memory by Bill Harris, New York, 1991.

14 Perhaps incredibly, the first public holidays of Easter Monday, Whit Monday and Christmas Day were only created by parliament in their Bank Holiday Act of 25 May 1871.

15 History of Mining in Iowa County by Stanley T. Holland, 1983.

16 The Hard-Rock Men by Dr John Rowe, 1974.

17 Laxey in the New World article on Frederick Jewel by Jim Jewel, 1982.

18 Seen on a visit in 1985.

19 Ms Lynn T. Martin, Recorder of Deeds, Iowa county, Dodgeville, Wisconsin.

20 The Mineral Point Room per Mrs R. Jungbluth.

21 Register of Deeds, Dodgeville, Wisconsin.

22 Idem.

23 Per courtesy of Mr Jim Jewell, Mineral Point, Wisconsin.

24 Cumbria since the county boundary changes of 1974

25 Cumbria Record Office, Barrow-in-Furness.

26 The Mineral Point Room per Mrs R. Jungbluth.

27 Wisconsin Room, Karrman Library, University of Wisconsin, Platteville.

28 Mrs R Jungbluth, Mineral Point, Wisconsin.

29 Ibid.

30 Manx Museum, Douglas, Isle of Man.

31 Register of Deeds, Dodgeville, Wisconsin.

32 Ibid.

33 Sioux Valley Genealogical Society per Mrs J. Allard-Fiskum, Sioux Falls, South Dakota

34 National Archives, Rocky Mountains Region, Denver, Colorado.

35 The Mineral Point Room per Mrs R. Jungbluth.

36 Laxey in the New World, article on The Harris Family of Bloomfield by Kenneth Harris, 1982.

37 Rev. Ronald Brunger, Adrian College, Michigan.

38 History of Iowa County, Butterworth, 1881.

39 Dodgeville Chronicle 29 April 1892.

40 Dodgeville Chronicle 28 August 1903.

Chapter 5

1 Register of Deeds, Iowa County, WI.

2 Mrs Jean (McCarger) Hathaway, Florida.

3 Ships Passenger Lists - National Archives, Washington, DC.

4 Register of Deeds, Dodgeville, and National Archives, Washington, DC.

5 University of Wisconsin - Platteville.

6 The Hard-Rock Men by Dr John Rowe, 1974.

7 1909 Conference Minutes, West Wisconsin Conference, M.E. Church.

8 Report Council Bluffs Nonpareil, 23 June 1907.

9 List of Charges were supplied by Ms M. Schroeder, Archivist, Wisconsin Conference Commission on Archives and History, the United Methodist Church, Sun Prairie, WI.

10 Council Bluffs Nonpareil. 23 January 1931.

11 Council Bluffs Nonpareil.

12 Pottawattamie County Recorder, Iowa.

13 Council Bluffs Nonpareil.

14 Much of the information on Thomas William McCarger was provided from the Nonpareil, courtesy of Thomas W.'s granddaughter Mrs Jean Hathaway.

15 All information, reference WEB's appointment, is quoted per courtesy of the Herbert Hoover Library, West Branch, Iowa.

16 This was on 11 May 1900 when Mary Ann nursed Lou Hoover during the latter's illness. Herbert Hoover, US President 1929-33, and his wife Lou were great friends with the Bainbridges.

17 Author's note: Assume this should read British - see entry in paragraph 3 of this date.

18 The diary of Mary Bainbridge has been included with the permission of the State Historical Society of Iowa, together with that of Jean McCarger Hathaway who also supplied the typescript., Jean being the granddaughter of the diarist. The State Historical Society hold the original diary which was written in a notebook and was presented to them by the diarist's son, James F. McCarger and his daughter Mary.

19 Mary Ann's elder son.

20 Information from this section of the diary is included with the permission of the Herbert Hoover Library, West Branch, Iowa.

21 United States Department of State, Washington, DC.

22 Mrs Jean Hathaway, Holdredge, Nebraska.

23 Council Bluffs Nonpareil.

24 Copy of Lou Hoover's telegram per Mrs Jean Hathaway.

25 Council Bluffs Nonpareil.

26 Mrs Fern M. Brown, historian of Epworth Church, Council Bluffs, Iowa.

27 Ms Ona McNay, historian, Silver City Methodist Episcopal Church; her brother had been baptised by Rev. James Sims.

28 Billy Sunday by Jim Holston, Iowa magazine, 1985.

29 Minutes of 1909 West Wisconsin Conference M. E. Church

30 Cornish Post and Mining News, 29 June 1894 and 6 July 1894

31 Ms M. Schroeder, Archivist, Commission on Archives and History, U. M. Church, Sun Prairie, WI.

2 Report of the Royal Commission on the Mineral Resources of Ontario, 1890.
3 Copper Country History by Christine and Lauri Leskinen, 1980.
4 Royal Commission, ibid.
5 Purchased by the US for $5,000,000, The National Encyclopaedia.
6 The railway across the isthmus was not opened until 1853.
7 Fortunes Children by Arthur Vanderbilt (2). All information on the New York-Nicaragua-San Francisco route emanates from this book.
8 The Cornish Miner in America by Dr A.C. Todd, 1967.
9 The Cornish Miner in Australia by Philip J. Payton, 1984.
10 Ibid.
11 Ibid.
12 Ibid.
13 Recollections from the notebook and letters of James Skewis, 1826-1911, compiled by his granddaughter Mrs Anita (Skewis) Rosendahl.
14 Brunel's remarkable railway suspension bridge over the River Tamar was not completed until 1859.
15 Sextons appear very frequently in church registers as marriage witnesses! Obviously they were readily available if at the time they were in the churchyard carrying out their normal duties.
16 Copper Country History by Christine and Lauri Leskinen, 1980.
17 The Hard-Rock Men by Dr John Rowe, 1974
18 Copper Country History by Christine and Lauri Leskinen, 1980.
19 Ibid.
20 Per Ms R. Ristola, Ontonagon County Historical Society.
21 South Dakota - History and Heritage, 1987.
22 Homestead Act, 1862, per County Clerk, Minnehaha County, South Dakota.
23 Dakota Panorama - Dakota Territory Centennial Commission, 1961.
24 Buffalo - The Critters Meant for This Land by Charles Laurence, Daily Telegraph Magazine.
25 South Dakota - History and Heritage, 1987.
26 County Clerk, Minnehaha, South Dakota.
27 Information from the personal Homestead Files in respect of Matthew (2) and Matthew (3) was obtained per courtesy of National Archives, Washington, DC.
28 The Cornish in America by Dr A.L. Rowse, 1969.
29 Laxey in the New World published by the Laxey Committee in 1982.
30 The Mill on the Floss by George Eliot.

Chapter 7
1 Information on the Saldanha - ex. Mrs L.V. Harvey, Blackburn, Victoria.
2 Suez Canal not opened until 1869.

Chapter 8
1 History of the Upper Peninsula of Michigan by Andreas, 1883.
2 Ibid.
3 Ibid.
4 Ibid.
5 Ibid.
6 Old Reliable by L.D. Lankton and C.K. Hyde, 1982, Quincy Mine Hoist Association.
7 Ibid.
8 Agents Annual Reports pp MTU Archives and Copper Country Collections.
9 Documents - ex. Register of Deeds, Houghton County, Michigan.
10 Old Reliable, ibid.
11 Ex. John Leslie Harris, Troon, Camborne, Cornwall.
12 Ibid.

17 Bailiff of Blackmoor by Thomas Beare, 1586.
18 From the Peninsula South by Sandra Seaton Michel, 1980, D. & N. Press.
19 Ibid.
20 Booklet by Wilbert Maki.
21 The History of Lake Linden by C.J. Monette, 1975.
22 Calumet Copper and People by Arthur W. Thurner, 1974.
23 Postcard by Penrod/Hiawatha Co., Berrian Centre, Michigan.
24 Ex. letters of Samuel B. Harris.
25 Letter from Grand Lodge of Michigan A. & F.M. dated 2 November 1993.
26 The Cornish in America by Dr A.L. Rowse, 1969
27 Ex. J. Ellen G Austin, great-granddaughter of Samuel B. and Mary.
28 East Hancock Revisited by E.A. Alexander, 1984.
29 Daily Mining Gazette, 22 October 1927.
30 Daily Mining Gazette, 19 October 1927.
31 East Hancock Revisited by E.A. Alexander, 1984.
32 Michigan Department of State letter, 17 March 1989.
33 Of husband, Fox, Thomas, White and Bengtson, PC, Law Offices, Lansing.
34 S. Wheeler, Archivist, New York Stock Exchange.
35 Ibid.
36 Alison K. Thomas, Lansing.
37 East Hancock Revisited by E.A. Alexander, 1984.
38 All information regarding Hiram S. Hanchette has been collated from documents provided by Robert and Mary Gilson of San Jose, California, great-great grandchildren of both Hiram S. Hanchette and Samuel B. Harris.
39 Register of Deeds, Houghton County, Michigan.
40 Polk's Directory.
41 East Hancock Revisited by E.A. Alexander, 1984.
42 All information of Charles D. Hanchette's business interests has been obtained collectively from: Polk's Directories, From the Peninsula South by Sandra Seaton Michel, 1980, East Hancock Revisited by Eleanor A Alexander, 1984.
43 Information supplied by Nellie's granddaughter, J. Ellen Gilson Austin.
44 Letter from Samuel B. Harris to his elder son James A. in July 1923.
45 J. Ellen G. Austin, Oregon State, niece of Estelle.
46 Ibid.
47 Alumni News, MTU, Houghton, Michigan.
48 Ann L. Dittmar, Seattle, niece of Estelle.
49 J. Ellen G. Austin, Ashland, Oregon, niece of Estelle.
50 Daily Mining Gazette.
51 Ms T.S. Spence, archivist, Michigan Technological University.
52 Hancock Journal.
53 Old Reliable by L.D. Lankton and C.K. Hyde, 1982.
54 Amyglamoid - volcanic rock containing almond-shaped pockets of copper.
55 Further information on the Hancock Mine may be obtained from John L. Harris's Annual Reports, per courtesy of MTU Archives.

Chapter 9
1 Per Mrs J.F. McDiarmid, Yorba Linda, California, granddaughter of William Henry Trevithick.
2 Per John Leslie Harris, great-nephew of Kitty.
3 The Roswarne District of Camborne by T.R. Harris.

Chapter 10
1 48 Laity Row.

2   Ex. Professor Charles Thomas, CBE.
3   Dolcoath – Queen of Cornish Mines by T.R. Harris, The Trevithick Society, 1974.
4   Copper Country History by Christine and Lauri Leskinen, 1980.
5   History of the Upper Peninsula of Michigan by A.T. Andreas.
6   Copper Country History by Christine and Lauri Leskinen, 1980.
7   Calumet Copper and People by Arthur W. Thurner, 1974.
8   The Cornish in America by Dr A.L. Rowse, 1969.
9   The Evart Review, 1 October 1915.
10 Ibid.
11 Calumet Copper and People by Arthur W. Thurner, 1974.
12 All information regarding the Methodist Church was obtained from the History of Lake Linden Church by the courtesy of Rev. Wm Peter Bartlett.
13 I am indebted for copies of the correspondence about the visit, to his daughter Katherine G. Preston and Professor Charles Thomas.
14 Considerable information on James Hugh (2) Harris has been obtained from Michigan - A Centennial History of the State and its People, Vol. 5, C. Lewis Publishing, 1939, by courtesy of his daughter Katherine G. (Harris) Preston, Akron, Ohio.
15 Kansas Conference Minutes, 1931.
16 Ex. Seven Up Leader, Spring 1994.
17 St Louis Educator TV Magazine, 1994.

Chapter 11
1   q.v. Royal Institution of Cornwall Journal XIV, Thurstan Peter.
2   Ex. John Leslie Harris, Troon, Camborne, Cornwall.
3   Ibid.
4   The Cornish Beam Engine by D.B. Barton, 1966.
5   Observation of the West of England Mining Region by J.H. Collins, 1912.
6   A History of South Crofty by J.A. Buckley.
7   The Cornish Beam Engine by D.B. Barton, 1966.
8   Dolcoath – Queen of Cornish Mines by T.R. Harris, The Trevithick Society, 1974.
9   Lays from the Mine the Moor and the Mountain, second edition, 1856.
10 Cornwall County Record Office, Ref. MRS Hayle 733.
11 The Ship Registers of the Port of Hayle, Maritime Monographs and Reports No. 20 of 1975, National Maritime Museum.
12 Mr Douglas Williams, Penzance, journalist.
13 The bluebell or wild hyacinth.
14 William Jago, who is also credited with having introduced the game of cricket to Troon.
15 CRO Ref. SR/CAMB/6/1.
16 Cornwall County Record Office, Ref. SR/CAMB/6/1.
17 Alice Thomas Sims was a first cousin to Rev. James Sims who married Jacob's aunt, Ann Harris, and to Nanny Toy Sims who married Jacob's uncle, Matthew Harris; she was also a first cousin to Capt. Josiah Thomas of Dolcoath.
18 West Briton, 22 May 1924.

Chapter 12
1   The Land's End, Kynance Cove and Other Poems by John Harris, 1858.
2   Dolcoath – Queen of Cornish Mines by T.R. Harris, 1974.
3   The Cornish Miner by A.K. Hamilton Jenkin - 1948.
4   A History of Cornwall by F.E. Halliday, 1959.
5   The detritus resulting from man's mining operations.
6   History of the Upper Peninsula of Michigan by Andreas, 1883.
7   A History of St Joseph Lead Company by J. Wyman-Jones, 1892.
8   North Carolina and its Mineral Resources, 1890.
9   Ibid.
10 Gold Mining A Forgotten Industry by Brent D. Glass.
11 Smiley Memorial Library, Central Methodist College, Fayette, MO.

12 Letter of April 1986 from Marvin E. Lane, Vice-President Mining, St Joe Minerals Corporation.
13 The Methodist Church in Missouri by Frank Tucker.
14 Ex. the Commission on Archives and History and Conference Historical Society - Western North Carolina Annual Conference - The United Methodist Church.
15 Ex. General Minutes of the United Methodist Church per Maxine Kreutziger, Kansas East Commission of Archives & History.
16 Ex. the Commission on Archives and History and Conference Historical Society - Western North Carolina Annual Conference - The United Methodist Church.
17 Crawford County and Cuba, Missouri by James Ira Breuer, 1972.
18 All information in reference to Wellsford and the Methodist Society, together with extracts from the Wichita Eagle and The Beacon, was supplied by Leda Bechiel, Archivist, Kansas West Conference, Wichita, Kansas.
19 How to live to be a Hundred by One who Did, John (5) Harris, 1974.
20 Ex. Ms Mary MaCook, archivist, The Methodist Museum, Epworth by the Sea, St Simon Island, Georgia.
21 Ibid.
22 Charlton County Herald, 19 October 1928.
23 Crawford County and Cuba, Missouri by James Ira Breuer, 1972.
24 Ibid.
25 Crawford County and County Missouri.
26 Settlers of Okefenokee, 1975.
27 History of Charlton County by Alex S. McQueen, 1932.
28 The National Encyclopaedia.
29 History of Charlton County by Alex S. McQueen, 1932.
30 Charlton County Georgia - Historical Notes, 1972.
31 Charlton County Herald, 21 September 1986.
32 Ibid.
33 Charlton County Georgia - Historical Notes, 1972.
34 Masonic Messenger, October 1986.
35 Charlton County Georgia - Historical Notes, 1972.
36 Ibid.
37 Charlton County Herald, 21 September 1986.
38 Mrs Lois B. Mays.
39 Masonic Messenger, October 1976.
40 Folkston High School Annual, 1917-18.
41 Masonic Messenger, October 1976.
42 Settlers of Okefenokee, Lois B. Mays, 1975.
43 Charlton County Georgia - Historical Notes, 1972.
44 Charlton County Herald, 21 September 1988.
45 Charlton County Georgia - Historical Notes, 1972.
46 Ibid.
47 Settlers of Okefenokee, Lois B. Mays, 1975.
48 Charlton County Georgia - Historical Notes, 1972.
49 Masonic Messenger, October 1976.
50 Masonic Messenger, October 1976.
51 Charlton County Georgia - Historical Notes, 1972.
52 Ibid.
53 Charlton County Herald, 21 January 1974.
54 Charlton County Georgia - Historical Notes, 1972.
55 Charlton County Herald, 24 January 1973.
56 Masonic Messenger, October 1976.
57 Masonic Messenger, April 1978.
58 Charlton County Herald, 19 August 1979.
59 Charlton County Herald, 21 September 1988.

Chapter 13
1   A History of Cornish Methodism by Thomas Shaw, 1967.
2   The History of the Cornish Copper Company by W.H. Pascoe.
3   The Age of Elegance 1812-1822, by Arthur Bryant, 1954.
4   Copper Country History by Christine and Lauri Leskinen, 1980.